Content

AIRFIELDS UNDER ATTACK:
A DIARY, 19 AUGUST 1940–6 SEPTEMBER 1940

Author's Note and Glossary

The aviation-minded reader will notice that I have referred to German *Messerschmitt* fighters by the abbreviation 'Me' (not 'Bf', which is more technically correct), or simply by their numeric designation, such as '109' or '110'. This not only reads better but is authentic: during the Battle of Britain, Keith Lawrence, a New Zealander, flew Spitfires and once said to me 'To us they were just "Me's", "109s" or "110s", simple, never "Bf".'

In another attempt to preserve accuracy, I have also used the original German, wherever possible, regarding terms associated with the Luftwaffe, such as:

Adlerangriff: 'Attack of the Eagles'
Adlertag: 'Eagle Day'
Eichenlaub: The Oak Leaves, essentially being a bar to the *Ritterkreuz*.
Erprobungsgruppe: Experimental group, in the case of *Erprobungsgruppe* 210, a skilled precision bombing unit.
Experte: A fighter 'ace'. Ace status, on both sides, was achieved by destroying five enemy aircraft.
Fallschirmjäger: Paratroopers.
Freie hunt: A fighter sweep.
Gefechstand: Operations headquarters.
General der Jagdflieger: General of Fighter Pilots.
Geschwader: The whole group, usually of three *gruppen*.
Geschwaderkommodore: The group leader.
Gruppe: A wing, usually of three squadrons.
Gruppenkeil: A wedge formation of bombers, usually made up of vics of three.
Gruppenkommandeur: The wing commander.
Jagdbomber ('*Jabo*'): Fighter-bomber.
Jagdflieger: Fighter pilot.
Jagdgeschwader: Fighter group, abbreviated JG.
Jagdwaffe: The fighter force.
Jäger: Hunter, in this context a fighter pilot or aircraft.
Kampfflieger: Bomber aircrew.
Kampfgeschwader: Bomber group, abbreviated KG.
Kanal: English Channel.
Katchmarek: Wingman.

BATTLE *of* BRITAIN

AIRFIELDS
UNDER
ATTACK

BATTLE *of* BRITAIN

AIRFIELDS
UNDER
ATTACK

19 AUGUST 1940–6 SEPTEMBER 1940

DILIP SARKAR
MBE, FRHistS, FRAeS, BA (Hons)

AIR WORLD

First published in Great Britain in 2024 by
Pen & Sword Airworld
An imprint of Pen & Sword Books Limited
Yorkshire – Philadelphia

Copyright © Dilip Sarkar, 2024

ISBN 978 1 39905 796 7

The right of Dilip Sarkar to be identified as
Author of this Work has been asserted by him in accordance
with the Copyright, Designs and Patents Act 1988.

A CIP catalogue record for this book is
available from the British Library

All rights reserved. No part of this book may be reproduced or
transmitted in any form or by any means, electronic or mechanical
including photocopying, recording or by any information storage and
retrieval system, without permission from the Publisher in writing.

Typeset by Mac Style
Printed in the UK by CPI Group (UK) Ltd, Croydon, CR0 4YY.

Pen & Sword Books Limited incorporates the imprints of After
the Battle, Atlas, Archaeology, Aviation, Discovery, Family History,
Fiction, History, Maritime, Military, Military Classics, Politics,
Select, Transport, True Crime, Air World, Frontline Publishing, Leo
Cooper, Remember When, Seaforth Publishing, The Praetorian Press,
Wharncliffe Local History, Wharncliffe Transport, Wharncliffe True
Crime and White Owl.

For a complete list of Pen & Sword titles please contact:

PEN & SWORD BOOKS LIMITED
47 Church Street, Barnsley, South Yorkshire, S70 2AS, England
E-mail: enquiries@pen-and-sword.co.uk
Website: www.pen-and-sword.co.uk
or
PEN AND SWORD BOOKS
1950 Lawrence Road, Havertown, PA 19083, USA
E-mail: uspen-and-sword@casematepublishers.com
Website: www.penandswordbooks.com

Kriegsmarine: German war navy.

Lehrgeschwader: Literally a training group, but actually a precision bombing unit, abbreviated LG.

Luftflotte: Air Fleet.

Oberkannone: Literally the 'Top Gun', or leading fighter ace.

Oberkommando der Marine (OKM): German naval high command.

Oberkommando der Heer (OKH): German army high command.

Oberkommando der Luftwaffe (OKL): German air force high command.

Oberkommando der Wehrmacht (OKW): German armed forces high command.

Ritterkreuz: The Knight's Cross of the Iron Cross.

Rotte: A pair of fighters, comprising leader and wingman, into which the *Schwarm* broke once battle was joined.

Rottenführer: Corporal.

Rottenflieger: Wingman.

Schwarm: A section of four fighters.

Schwarmführer: Section leader.

Seelöwe: Sealion, the codename for Hitler's proposed seaborne invasion of England.

Seenotflugkommando: Luftwaffe air sea rescue organisation.

Stab: Staff.

Staffel: A squadron.

Staffelkapitän: The squadron leader.

Störflug: Harassing attacks, usually by lone Ju 88s.

Stuka: The Ju 87 dive-bomber.

Sturkampfgeschwader: Dive-bomber group, abbreviated StG.

Vermisst: Missing.

Wehrmacht: Armed forces.

Zerstörer: Literally 'destroyer', the term used for the Me 110.

Zerstörergeschwader: Destroyer group, abbreviated ZG.

Each *geschwader* generally comprised three *gruppen*, each of three *staffeln*. Each *gruppe* is designated by Roman numerals, i.e. III/JG 26 refers to the third *gruppe* of Fighter Group (abbreviated 'JG') 26. *Staffeln* are identified by numbers, so 7/JG 26 is the 7th *staffel* and belongs to III/JG 26.

Rank comparisons may also be useful:

Gefreiter:	Private 1st Class
Unteroffizier:	Corporal, no aircrew equivalent in Fighter Command.
Feldwebel:	Sergeant
Oberfeldwebel:	Flight Sergeant
Leutnant:	Pilot Officer
Oberleutnant:	Flight Lieutenant

Hauptmann:	Squadron Leader
Major:	Wing Commander
Oberst:	Group Captain

RAF Abbreviations:

AAF:	Auxiliary Air Force
AASF:	Advance Air Striking Force
A&AEE	Aeroplane and Armament Experimental Establishment
AC1:	Aircraftman 1st Class
AC2:	Aircraftman 2nd Class
ACW1:	Aircraftwoman 1st Class
ACW2:	Aircraftwoman 2nd Class
AFC:	Air Force Cross
AFDU:	Air Fighting Development Unit
AHB:	Air Historical Branch
AI:	Airborne Interception radar
AOC:	Air Officer Commanding
AOC-in-C:	Air Officer Commanding-in-Chief
ASR:	Air Sea Rescue
ATA:	Air Transport Auxiliary
ATS:	Armament Training School
BEF:	British Expeditionary Force
CAS:	Chief of the Air Staff
CFS:	Central Flying School
CGS:	Central Gunnery School
CO:	Commanding Officer
DAF:	Desert Air Force
DES:	Direct Entry Scheme
DFC:	Distinguished Flying Cross
DFM:	Distinguished Flying Medal
DSO:	Distinguished Service Order
E/A:	Enemy Aircraft
EFTS:	Elementary Flying Training School
ENSA:	Entertainments National Service Association
FAA:	Fleet Air Arm
FIU:	Fighter Interception Unit
FTS:	Flying Training School
GPC:	Guinea Pig Club
HE:	High Explosive
HF:	High Frequency
HQ:	Headquarters
ITW:	Initial Training Wing

LAC:	Leading Aircraftman
MC:	Military Cross
MO:	Medical Officer
MOD:	Ministry of Defence
MRAF:	Marshal of the Royal Air Force
MSFU:	Merchant Ship Fighter Unit
MT:	Motor Transport
MTB:	Motor Torpedo Boat
NCO:	Non-Commissioned Officer
OR:	Other Ranks
ORB:	Operations Record Book
OTC:	Officer Training Corps
OTU:	Operational Training Unit
PDC:	Personnel Distribution Centre
RAFVR:	Royal Air Force Volunteer Reserve
RFS:	Reserve Flying School
RN:	Royal Navy
RNAS:	Royal Navy Air Service
R/T:	Radio Telephone
SASO:	Senior Air Staff Officer
SHAEF:	Supreme Headquarters Allied Expeditionary Force
SMO:	Station Medical Officer
SOO:	Senior Operations Officer
SSC:	Short Service Commission
SSQ:	Station Sick Quarters
TAF:	Tactical Air Force
VHF:	Very High Frequency
UAS:	University Air Squadron
U/S:	Unserviceable
WDAF:	Western Desert Air Force

Also:

'Angels' refers to height measured in thousands of feet, hence 'Angels 15' means 15,000ft. A 'vector' is a compass course, measured in degrees, a 'Bandit' is a confirmed enemy aircraft while a 'Bogey' and an 'X-Raid' are as yet unidentified but potentially hostile radar plots. 'Tally Ho!' was shouted when the enemy were sighted and the leader was ordering an attack. To the Germans, hostile aircraft were 'Indians' and the German fighter pilot's victory cry was 'Horrido'.

Foreword

In this fourth volume of an eight-volume series, Dilip Sarkar moves into the phase of the Battle where German tactics changed, with the Luftwaffe conducting a series of attacks on coastal airfields used as forward landing grounds for RAF fighters. Later, the airfield attacks moved further inland.

The 15th of August was 'The Greatest Day', when the Luftwaffe mounted the largest number of sorties of the campaign.

The 18th of August, which had the greatest number of casualties on both sides, has been dubbed 'The Hardest Day'.

This volume takes the reader through these trying times using unique memories. These sometimes reveal new interpretations of what was happening as the German air offensive faltered and German leaders altered their tactics. It reveals the great efforts of 'the many' to ensure that RAF airfields remained available to rebut the attacks on infrastructure that the Germans had switched to from their previous approach to try to exhaust the RAF in the air.

The Battle of Britain Memorial Trust maintains the National Memorial to The Few, but also exists to provide education and resources to ensure a full understanding of the importance of the Battle of Britain. It is pleased to be associated with Dilip Sarkar's series, which assists greatly in this task.

Air Chief Marshal Sir Richard Knighton KCB ADC FREng
Chief of the Air Staff

Introduction

In *The Gathering Storm* (Volume I) the background and wider context of the Battle of Britain was explored, in which it became clear that the fighting between the opposing air forces had begun on 2 July 1940 – on which date the *Oberkommando der Wehrmacht* (OKW) informed the German armed forces that an invasion of southern England was planned, providing the necessary conditions could be met.

Our narrative history *The Breaking Storm* (Volume II) began on 10 July 1940, the date which, when writing his Despatch soon after the Second World War, Lord Dowding, Fighter Command's chief during the pivotal summer and autumn of 1940, 'somewhat arbitrarily' chose as the Battle of Britain's start-date.

As our investigation proceeded, we learned how Hitler played 'Air Fleet Diplomacy' in July 1940, with increasingly large formations being committed to battle over the Channel and, as the clock ticked towards his 'Last appeal to reason' speech on 19 July 1940, coastal targets, such as the port of Dover, came under attack. Indeed, on 16 July 1940, Hitler issued his infamous *Führer* Directive 16, expressing a clear intention to invade Britain should peace terms be rejected. Hitler knew full-well, however, that his *Kriegsmarine* was inferior to the Royal Navy (RN), his service chiefs were in dispute regarding invasion plans, and was reluctant to enter a prolonged struggle with Britain. Hitler's strategy, therefore, already focused on an invasion of the Soviet Union, relied firmly upon a quick and successful war against Britain, best achieved, in the dictator's mind, through blockade and diplomacy – not a high-risk and extremely hazardous seaborne invasion. Even after his 'last appeal' was firmly rejected by Britain, Hitler remained indecisive, still hoping that British Prime Minister Winston Churchill and his War Cabinet would agree terms. Churchill, however, knew his history, and believed that states which meekly capitulate are forgotten – whereas those that go down fighting rise again (which, given the situation in Ukraine, certainly has modern-day connotations). Hitler's commitment, therefore, to a peaceful solution, with Britain accepting his peace terms, was delusional.

By the end of July 1940, having dallied further still following rejection of his 'appeal' by British Foreign Minister and former Appeaser Lord Halifax, Hitler knew that he had no choice but to proceed with the proposed invasion, codenamed Operation *Seelöwe* (sealion). The reality, however, was that Hitler's service chiefs had no experience of such a grandiose combined operation; the army was used to assault river crossings but not the English Channel. Differences of opinion between the German service chiefs, therefore, over virtually every aspect of the undertaking, was inevitable. By 31 July 1940 though, German plans were clearer – and crystal was the fact that Churchill would not back down.

On that day, Hitler conferred with his warlords at the Berghof, his mountain retreat, and decided that aerial supremacy over Britain was pre-requisite to a sea crossing:

> The air war will start now … If the results of the air war are not satisfactory, [invasion] preparations will be stopped. But if we gain the impression that the English are being crushed and that the air war is, after a certain time, taking effect, then we shall attack … An attempt must be made to prepare the operation for 15 September [1940].

If we understand the Battle of Britain as being fought to prevent German air superiority over southern England, thus paving the way for the launch of a seaborne invasion, then arguably, from this point onwards and until the invasion was postponed indefinitely, the Battle of Britain, actually began on this day, 31 July 1940. Not only was there a directive from the OKW or a bluff by the *Führer* (16 July 1940 refers), but a very definite order from Hitler himself to begin an aerial campaign against Britain – the objective of which being to achieve aerial superiority over southern England prior to launching *Seelöwe*. From that particular day, therefore, the die was cast.

Reichsmarschall Hermann Göring, Hitler's political deputy and Luftwaffe chief, consequently ordered his *Luftflotte* (Air Fleet) commanders to prepare an unprecedented aerial assault on Britain, initially targeting radar sites and Fighter Command's airfields. The intention was to destroy Britain's fighter force, and the first phase of this new plan, already the second phase of the Battle of Britain, was investigated in *Attack of the Eagles* (Volume III). However, bad weather and miscommunication somewhat blunted the talons of the *Reichsmarschall*'s much-vaunted 'Adler Tag' (Eagle Day) on 13 August 1940; two days later, 12 and 13 Groups of Fighter Command dealt such a body-blow to *Luftflotte* 5's attack on north-east England that *Generaloberst* Stumpff's command saw no further part in the daylight campaign against Britain. Then, on 18 August 1940, having already suffered heavy losses, after a further beating the 220 remaining *Stuka* dive-bombers of Fliegerkorps VIII were withdrawn from the battle. Losses were also being incurred by the Me 110 heavy-fighter units, and casualties among the Luftwaffe bomber force were disconcerting. Looking for a scapegoat, so the story goes, Göring blamed his single-engine Me 109 fighter pilots for failing to sufficiently closely protect the bombers – completely forgetting, charged the German ace General Adolf Galland, the First World War's lessons in which fighters were more successful when free to roam, rather than tied to slow-moving bomber formations. At this stage of the Battle of Britain, however, that is a moot point – as we will shortly see from the actual evidence available.

Setting aside that the Luftwaffe was ill-equipped for such a strategic aerial campaign, with medium bombers and no long-range single-engine offensive fighter, by now the failure of Luftwaffe air intelligence was apparent. In simple terms, the Luftwaffe intelligence chief, *Oberst* Hans 'Beppo' Schmid, and his department failed to grasp the true significance of radar (RDF), or how Fighter Command was deployed or controlled. Air Chief Marshal Dowding, however, knew that the whole of the British Isles was within range of German bombers and that consequently he had to maintain an effective defence nationwide – rather than fall into the trap of concentrating his fighters exclusively in southern England. Certainly, the best-equipped units were largely in 11 and 10 Groups, while the more northerly groups, 12 and 13, being away from the main combat zone, were perfectly located for depleted squadrons in the South to rest and rebuild, their place in the frontline being taken by fresh squadrons from the North. According to Churchill, Dowding's 'generalship' in this regard, leading to the defeat of *Luftflotte* 5 in a single day, was 'genius'.

With this broad defensive strategy and the advance warning provided to the RAF by RDF – although Schmid assured his chief that Fighter Command was being seriously depleted – the Luftwaffe was being met wherever it appeared by, it seemed, increasingly more fighters. When the battle began, Air Vice-Marshal Keith Park, commander of 11 Group, covering London and the south-east, very cautiously responded using sections of three, or flights of six, rather than whole squadrons, which were the formations around which pre-war training had revolved and in order to preserve limited resources. Now, with larger enemy formations incoming, whole squadrons, and plenty of them, were being scrambled to intercept the enemy. And at the Ministry for Aircraft Production (MAP) Lord Beaverbrook had supercharged the factories with a sense of urgency, leading to there never being a shortage of replacement fighters. Pilots too, were replaced, although new pilots fresh from operational training units were often woefully under-trained and lacked combat experience – which was the vital thing. Nonetheless, it was clear that Fighter Command, like Churchill himself, was proving a most obstinate adversary.

For Göring, given Schmid's interpretation of the battle's progress, it was impossible for him to comprehend why his Luftwaffe had not simply swept the RAF from the skies in just a matter of days. There had been successful raids on British airfields – but because Luftwaffe intelligence failed to understand Dowding's System of Fighter Control, target selection was invariably faulty. Far too much effort had been expended on airfields unconnected with Fighter Command, the crucial importance of sector stations' operations rooms not being appreciated, although Kenley had been badly hurt on 18 August 1940, on which day Biggin Hill, another sector station forming an important link in London's defences, was also damaged. Although the RDF stations at Poling and Ventnor had been dive-bombed and taken off air, adjacent inter-locking stations provided cover, and no further attacks were made – when RDF stations should have been an absolute priority. Things would not improve, however, with Schmid simply telling the 'Iron One' what he wanted to hear. Inevitably, therefore, Luftwaffe strategy and target selection was consistently misinformed.

Sunday, 11 August 1940 had seen the most Spitfire and Hurricane pilots lost in a single day – twenty-five – and 15 August 1940 went down in history as the 'Greatest Day', both sides having flown more sorties than on any other day throughout the Battle; 18 August 1940 was 'The Hardest Day', according to my old friend and mentor (the sadly now late) Dr Alfred Price, with both sides losing the most aircraft in a single day. Then, on 19 August 1940, the Battle of Britain entered a new and even more violent phase, which might collectively be called the 'Crucial Days' – because 11 Group's essential airfields, in spite of poor Luftwaffe intelligence, were to be targeted.

On this day, Göring issued new orders from Karinhall, his opulent country estate, aimed at ensuring that Luftwaffe losses, going forward, were minimal, and 'the enemy air force swiftly and irrevocably destroyed … Until further notice the main task of *Luftflotten* 2 and 3 will be to inflict the utmost damage possible on the enemy fighter forces.' Attacks on Bomber Command's 'ground organisation' were also ordered, but were of secondary importance.

At the time, promotion in the RAF revolved around seniority on the Air Force List – meaning that at this stage of the war squadron commanders either killed, missing, wounded, being rested or promoted to other roles, were largely replaced by officers next in line for promotion, most of which had little experience of modern fighters and had never seen combat. For a short time these men may have flown as 'supernumerary' with an operational squadron to gain current experience before taking command of their own units – but such a spell did not necessarily equip them for the job. The sensible among them, like Squadron Leaders Philip Pinkham of 19 Squadron, and Graeme 'Minnie' Manton of 56, would allow their senior flight commanders to lead in the air, until they themselves felt sufficiently confident to take the helm. Across the Channel at Karinhall, *Reichsmarschall* Göring, however, recognised that waging such an aggressive aerial campaign was a young man's war – and only possible if 'unit commanders at all levels are of the best type. I have therefore ordered that in future, unit commanders are to be appointed regardless of rank and exclusively from among the most suitable and capable officers … appointed from their own unit'. Moreover, at every level, the suitability of existing unit commanders was to be assessed and 'removals effected where necessary. Not only unsuitable, but also highly inexperienced officers whose lack of experience may lead to unnecessary losses, must be replaced'.

It was now that the purging of the *Jagdwaffe* began, with the more elderly *Kommodoren* replaced by younger men. Already, *Major* Werner Mölders had taken over JG51, and soon, on 22 August 1940, the 28-year-old *Major* Adolf Galland replaced 31-year-old *Major* Gotthard Handrick as JG 26's *Kommodore*. Immediately, Galland installed his preferred, young and combat-experienced, officers in command positions: *Hauptmann* Gerhard Schopfel succeeded 'Dolfo' Galland as *Kommandeur* of III/JG26; Rolf Pingel, from JG 53, took over I/JG 26; 21-year-old *Oberleutnant* Joachim Müncheberg became *Staffelkapitän* of 7/ JG 26, and *Oberleutnant* Eberhard Henrici took over 1/JG26. It would be the same story as experience replaced aged seniority throughout the fighter arm. This was forward-thinking of the *Reichsmarschall* – and would take the socially segregated RAF much longer to replicate.

Significantly, considering criticisms levelled at the Luftwaffe chief regarding his insistence for fighters to rigidly provide close protection for his bombers, Göring now ordered the following concerning fighter deployment and operations:

> Commanders of fighter units must be given as free a hand as possible. Only part of the fighters are to be employed as direct escorts to our bombers. The aim must be to employ the strongest possible fighter forces on free-lance operations, in which they can indirectly protect the bombers, and at the same time come to grips, under favourable conditions, with the enemy fighters. No rigid plan can be laid down for such operations, as their conduct must depend on the changing nature of enemy tactics, and on weather conditions.

The foregoing is illuminating, because clearly at this stage of the Battle, Göring had not yet forgotten his own experiences as a First World War fighter ace. Splitting his fighters between free-hunting sweeps and close escort was perfectly sensible – whether or not this would work in practice, given the fighters' limited rage and numbers available, remained to be seen. Göring also ordered that the withdrawal of bomber formations back across the Channel must be undertaken by designated fighter units, and that this role was a suitable one for young pilots not yet sufficiently experienced for operations over England to contribute to, under supervision.

Ground-attack by fighters was also envisaged, when practical:

> fighters are also to attack the enemy on the ground. They must, however, be protected on such missions by succeeding waves of other fighters. Twin-engine fighters are to be employed when the range of single-engine aircraft is insufficient, or when they can facilitate the breaking off from combat of single-engine formations.

It has often been claimed that early on in the Battle of Britain the Me 110 was so vulnerable to attack by single-engine RAF fighters, owing to its wider turning circle and slower speed, that it required escorting by single-engine fighters. Again, this is clearly not case; the *Reichsmarschall* – a great supporter of the Me 110 heavy-fighter – had yet to give up on his *Zerstörer* units and fully intended their continued use as both fighters and fighter-bombers.

Göring continued:

As long as the enemy fighter defences retain their present strength, attacks on aircraft factories must be carried out under cover of weather conditions permitting surprise raids by solitary aircraft. Such operations demand the most meticulous preparation, but can achieve very satisfactory results. The cloudy conditions likely to prevail over England in the next few days must be exploited for such attacks. We must succeed in seriously disrupting the material supplies of the enemy air force, by the destruction of the relatively small number of aircraft engine and aluminium plants.

Had the *Reichsmarschall* been aware of Fighter Command's actual 'present strength', instead of that perceived by his incompetent intelligence chief, he may well have considered aircraft factories targets suitable for heavy attacks – rather than nuisance raids by single aircraft when weather conditions permitted (or at night, when bombing accuracy was likely to be reduced). That such lone daylight raiders could sufficiently disrupt the flow of replacement aircraft to Fighter Command also underlines the failure of Luftwaffe air intelligence to appreciate the effect of Lord Beaverbrook's dynamism on aircraft production. Furthermore, although previously attacked by KGr 100's *Pfadfinders* (Pathfinders) the considerable importance of the new Spitfire factory at Castle Bromwich, and Supermarine's vulnerable Spitfire-producing premises at Woolston, Southampton, was clearly unappreciated. Both locations should have been priority targets from the outset.

The *Reichsmarschall's* frustration with the Luftwaffe's lack of progress is clear: 'There can no longer be any restriction on the choice of targets. To myself I reserve only the right to order attacks on London and Liverpool.'

In this, Göring overstepped the mark; Hitler, as *Führer* and supreme Nazi warlord, had already reserved for himself any decision to bomb London.

Bomber and fighter commanders were to achieve maximum cooperation by means of conferences before each attack, and in summary, Göring concluded:

We have reached the decisive period of the air war against England. The vital task is to turn all means at our disposal to the defeat of the enemy air force. Our first aim is the destruction of the enemy fighters. If they no longer take the air, we shall attack them on the ground, or force them into battle by directing bomber attacks against targets within the range of our fighters … Once the enemy air force has been annihilated, our attacks will be directed as ordered against other vital targets.

Much of what Göring said made sense, although this new plan saw the German assault deflecting away from attacking radar stations – an important feature of the previous phase. Moreover, this represented the third change of direction since the battle began.

At the time, Air Vice-Marshal James 'Johnnie' Johnson was a young pilot officer still in training; ultimately the official top-scoring RAF fighter pilot of the Second World War, he would later consider that:

The great thing in war is to devise a plan and stick to it, no matter what. A perfect example of this in action was the American daylight bombing offensive from 1942 onwards: at first their losses were horrendous, due to a lack of long-range fighter support, but they kept at it and eventually, really once the Mustang, Thunderbolt and Lightning fighters appeared, all of which were designed as long-range escorts, produced some terrific results: accurate precision bombing from high altitude. During the Battle of Britain, Göring kept changing his mind, first switching this way but then soon afterwards changing tack. This is exactly what you must not do. After the war I got to know the German ace 'Dolfo' Galland pretty well and he agreed that Göring was wrong to do this.

Instead of changing tack so soon, and abandoning attacks on RDF stations, the *Führer* and his *Reichsmarschall* may have done well to look to the writings of Prussian Carl von Clausewitz – the 'spiritual father of the German army' – and his essay, 'The Most Important Principles for the Conduct of War', written 200 years earlier. In sum, in terms of the 'General Principles' influencing strategy, Clausewitz advised that the first and main object of warfare was 'To conquer and destroy the armed power of the enemy,' and to accomplish this, 'we should always direct our principal operation against the main body of the enemy army or at least against an important portion of his forces.' Further, 'in order to seize the enemy's material forces we should direct our operations against the places where most of these resources are concentrated'. Military strength should be concentrated 'as much as possible against that section where the chief blows are to be incurred [and the] third rule is never to waste time'. 'Finally', Clausewitz opined, successes must be followed up 'with the utmost energy'. The 'great difficulty', he cautioned was 'To remain faithful throughout to the principles we have laid down for ourselves', but already, with the Battle of Britain just six weeks old, it was now entering its third phase – which did not bode well for Germany and contravened Clausewitz's sound advice.

On the same day that Göring issued his latest orders from Karinhall, Air Vice-Marshal Park, working in the somewhat less luxurious surroundings of his underground 11 Group Operations Room and adjacent Uxbridge office, issued a memorandum to his controllers:

- Despatch fighters to engage large enemy formations over land or within gliding distance of the coast. During the next two or three weeks, we cannot afford to lose pilots through forced landings in the sea;
- Avoid sending fighters out over the sea to intercept reconnaissance aircraft or small formations of enemy fighters;
- Despatch a pair of fighters to intercept single reconnaissance aircraft that come inland. If clouds are favourable, put a patrol of one or two fighters over an aerodrome which the enemy are approaching in clouds;

- Against mass attacks coming inland, dispatch a minimum number of squadrons to engage enemy fighters. Our main objective is to engage enemy bombers, particularly those approaching under the lowest cloud layer;
- If all our squadrons around London are off the ground engaging mass attacks, ask No 12 Group or Command Controller to provide squadrons to patrol aerodromes Debden, North Weald, Hornchurch;
- If heavy attacks have crossed the coast and are proceeding towards aerodromes, put a squadron, or even the Sector Training Flight, to patrol under clouds over every sector aerodrome;
- No 303 (Polish) Squadron can provide two sections for patrol of inland aerodromes, especially while the older squadrons are on the ground refuelling when enemy formations are flying overland;
- No 1 (Canadian) Squadron can be used in the same manner by day as other fighter squadrons.

As ever, the astute Air Vice-Marshal Park was carefully preserving his resources, these instructions being sensibly directed at preventing wastage through pilots being lost in the sea, or the use of large formations which might be wiped out en masse. Also, and as per his Commander-in-Chief's specified System of Air Defence, 12 Group was to be called upon to patrol his airfields north of the Thames when their fighter squadrons were engaged further forward. It is also often lamented, in certain circles, that the Polish 303 Squadron was kept out of the Battle for too long (more of which later), not having being made operational until 30 August 1940 (as we will see). This memorandum, however, clarifies the actual position: which is that Air Vice-Marshal Park was prepared to use elements of 303 Squadron, when necessary, even though the unit was not yet officially operational. This, therefore, suggests, again contrary to popular myth, that the Poles were actually seen, certainly by their Air Officer Commanding (AOC) 11 Group, as a resource to be used unhesitatingly.

   With both sides thus reappraised and briefed, the new phase began – the Battle of the Airfields.

MBE FRHistS FRAeS BA (Hons), 2024

Airfields Under Attack:
A Diary, 19 August 1940–6 September 1940

Monday, 19 August 1940

Between 11 and 18 August 1940 inclusive, the Luftwaffe had launched some significant aerial assaults on convoys and southern England. Such determined activity, however, was unsustainable indefinitely – not least given the unpredictable weather. After these exertions, there followed a lull, partly because cloudy weather conditions were unsuited to large-scale operations, but equally because the Luftwaffe in north-west France was incapable of mounting intensive operations for more than a week at a stretch. Nonetheless, 19 August 1940 would not pass without drama and derring-do.

The reduction in enemy air activity on 19 August 1940, however, provided an opportunity to rest Squadron Leader Don MacDonell's 64 Squadron, which, since the Battle began and while based at recently hard-hit Kenley, had suffered the loss of three pilots killed and five wounded (two of which later succumbed to their injuries), and one captured; eight of the squadron's Spitfires had been destroyed in combat, and three damaged. With Kenley having been badly battered the previous day, along with Biggin Hill, it was obvious that the enemy was now looking to attack vitally important sector stations – which must be defended by squadrons at full-strength. Prime Minister Winston Churchill had described Air Chief Marshal Dowding's 'generalship' as 'genius' by deploying his squadrons throughout the land, thereby being able to defeat *Luftflotte* 5's major raids on north-east England on 15 August 1940; another facet of Dowding's far-sighted strategy was that depleted squadrons from the South could be withdrawn to the more northerly 12 and 13 Groups, providing an opportunity to rebuild to strength in quieter sectors, receiving and training replacement pilots before returning to the main combat zone. The place of these squadrons in the frontline was taken by those at full-strength in 12 and 13 Groups. So it was that on this day, 64 Squadron was relieved by Squadron Leader Marcus Robinson's 616 Squadron, whose place at Leconfield in Yorkshire was taken by Squadron Leader MacDonell's men. Upon receiving the news, MacDonell was 'very upset' but 'saw the wisdom of the decision'. His squadron had fought hard over Dunkirk and during the Battle of Britain to date, and although recommended for the DSO, which 11 Group HQ felt was 'premature', a DFC was forthcoming for 64 Squadron's CO; it was well-deserved.

Pilot Officer Richard Jones, 64 Squadron:

On 19 August 1940, we were relieved at Kenley, operating thereafter from Leconfield, in 12 Group, with one flight deployed there and the other at Ringway, Manchester.

I had been posted to 64 Squadron at Kenley straight from OTU in June 1940, meaning that I was fortunately able to gain more Spitfire experience before the Battle of Britain really got going. Squadron Leader MacDonell tried to give us battle practice whenever time allowed. We were paired off with a battle-experienced pilot to practice dog-fighting and yet more dog-fighting, to give us both experience in battle conditions and confidence in the Spitfire. I was lucky. Had I been posted to 64 Squadron later in the summer of 1940, there would just not have been the time for this extra-curricular training.

I well remember my first operational engagement with the enemy. We were about nine Spitfires against thirty–forty enemy fighters. Before meeting them I had butterflies in my stomach, wondering what to expect. When they were spotted we waded into them and once engaged all fear disappeared – we immediately realised it was them or us – all hell appeared to be let loose with aircraft everywhere. The next moment, as so often happened, we were alone and the sky was empty. In fact, in the panic of my first engagement I don't think I even fired a shot, as it appeared to take all of my concentration just to avoid a collision. I felt that it was the most valuable experience that I had ever received in my life. I returned to base a more mature individual and felt extremely lucky to have survived to tell the tale.

Pilot Officer Lionel 'Buck' Casson, 616 Squadron:

We were a confident lot. Up North we had chased about after reconnaissance jobs and enjoyed great success during the 'Junkers Party' off Flamborough Head on 15 August 1940. We thought air fighting was pretty straight-forward, I suppose. When we were posted to Kenley the Squadron went off from Leconfield, and I just said 'Cheerio, see you later', as I was to follow on 24 August 1940 with a replacement Spitfire.

Pilot Officer William Walker, 616 Squadron:

I was among the fifteen pilots of 616 Squadron who flew South to Kenley, which we found to be in quite a state. The Mess there was quite a sombre building, far removed from the modern, light and cheerful Mess at Leconfield. Kenley had been bombed on several occasions prior to our arrival and many scars bore witness to the damage and loss of life. An atmosphere of purpose prevailed and the Squadron had to respond to a life of far greater activity than at Leconfield, where only a few raids had disrupted our lives.

No.616 Squadron would find the tempo of battle over the 11 Group area incomparable to its experience to date; for those who survived, the next few days would be unforgettable. Fortunately, having landed at 14.10 hrs, 616 Squadron would not be troubled by the enemy that day, so at least was able to settle into its new, war-ravaged, surroundings.

Another rotation in the line was 17 Squadron flying south from Debden in Essex to relieve 601 Squadron at Tangmere on the West Sussex coast.

Being somewhat quieter than the previous day, 19 August 1940 provided Air Vice-Marshal Keith Park, AOC 11 Group, to review the fighting to date and issue a memorandum to his sector controllers. These instructions made clear how they were to fight the battle, going forward:

a) Despatch fighters to engage large enemy formations over land or within gliding distance of the coast. During the next two or three weeks, we cannot afford to lose pilots through forced landings in the sea;

b) Avoid sending fighters out over the sea to intercept reconnaissance aircraft or small formations of enemy fighters;

c) Despatch a pair of fighters to intercept single reconnaissance aircraft that come inland. If clouds are favourable, put a patrol one or two fighters over an aerodrome which the enemy are approaching in clouds;

d) Against mass attacks coming inland, dispatch a minimum number of squadrons to engage enemy fighters. Our main objective is to engage enemy bombers, particularly those approaching under the lowest cloud layer;

e) If all our squadrons around London are off the ground engaging mass attacks, ask No 12 Group or Command Controller to provide squadrons to patrol aerodromes Debden, North Weald, Hornchurch;

f) If heavy attacks have crossed the coast and are proceeding towards aerodromes, put a squadron or even the Sector Training Flight, to patrol under clouds over every sector aerodrome;

g) No 303 (Polish) Squadron can provide two sections for patrol of inland aerodromes, especially while the older squadrons are on the ground refuelling when enemy formations are flying overland;

h) No 1 (Canadian) Squadron can be used in the same manner by day as other fighter squadrons.

These new instructions made clear to 11 Group's controllers how the battle was to be fought. They also provide clarity that 11 Group was not hogging the battle deliberately, as 12 Group had charged. Park was, in fact, complying perfectly with the Dowding System and clearly receptive to requesting reinforcements from 12 Group – which was always an important part of the overall plan. Another oft-quoted myth is that the Polish 303 Squadron was deliberately kept out of the fighting for too long owing to a lack of confidence by the RAF High Command – again, these instructions confirm that was not the case: the Northolt-based Poles were given clearance to provide a flight to protect inland aerodromes while squadrons were refuelling at times of enemy air activity. The only reason 303 Squadron was not made fully operational at this point was nothing to do with any kind of prejudice, but simply because the language barrier had yet to be fully overcome – which did not apply, obviously, to the Canadians, also based at Northolt, and hence why 1 (RCAF) Squadron could from now on 'be used in the same manner by day as other fighter squadrons'. Without doubt, both the Poles and Canadians were much-needed reinforcements.

Sergeant Bill Green, 501 Squadron:

I joined 501 Squadron on 14 August 1940, by which time I had had flown seven hours on Hurricanes, most of which was ferrying aircraft to the various airfields around Biggin Hill: Hawkinge, Croydon, Northolt etc. On 19 August 1940, I took a Hurricane to Gravesend, and bumped into our CO, Squadron Leader Hogan, who asked me what I'd done. I told him, and he said 'Oh, that's fine, they're too slow over there, you come back here and we'll train you quicker than that. Come back here, to Gravesend, tonight.' Unbeknown to me, the squadron had lost five aircraft the previous day, hence the sudden need for my return. When I duly returned to Gravesend, I was shown into a room with several beds in it and given the one next to 'Ginger' Lacey. Supper was a mug of cocoa and a cheese sandwich, and away I went to bed.

About 0300 hours, I was awakened by someone shaking me in the dark, an airman waving a torch in my face. I said 'No, not me, I'm new here, I'm Green.' He said 'Yes, you're Green 3!' I can't recall having any breakfast but on the way down to our aeroplanes I asked Ginger Lacey 'What's all this "Green 3" business?' Not very reassuringly, he said 'Well, we're the "Arse-end Charlie Section". When we get in the air, we're the last section behind the other three, and when we get up there you'll see me do a turn to the right. The idea is to have a good look round and make sure the squadron isn't bounced by any fighters. When I turn to the right, you do a turn to the left.' Well, he turned to the right, so I thought 'Right, here goes', and did what I thought was a very gentle, very short duration, turn to the left, because I didn't want to lose the squadron, so soon turned back, but in the split-second I'd flown at a right angle, they'd disappeared. They had just forged ahead, doing 300 mph plus. I knew that we were going to Hawkinge, so I made my own way there. That was the pattern of each day: get up early, fly down to Hawkinge at dawn, and sit around at dispersal tents, waiting for the telephone to go, scrambling us into the air. I recall being quite on edge, wondering whether the telephone would ring, and if it did when, and if it meant us scrambling and climbing up into what was clearly a dangerous activity.

At midday on 19 August 1940, RAF Coltishall in 12 Group was attacked on this quieter day, as recorded by that Station's ORB: 'Fair day but cloudy. A bombing raid was carried out by an enemy raider who suddenly came through the clouds and dropped six bombs, doing little damage to an unfinished hangar but killing and injuring several workmen.'

Two of the bombs crashed through the roof of No.2 Hangar, exploding within, damaging the huge hangar doors. Such was the damage to Hangar 5, which remained under construction, that it was never completed. The three dead civilian contractors were all local men, and a direct hit on a Bofors site caused casualties among the soldiers there. RAF Coltishall was a Fighter Command Sector Station, but no Luftwaffe record exists regarding which unit was responsible, and RAF records unhelpfully do not identify the enemy aircraft type involved. Nonetheless, this cloudy day, while unsuitable for mass raids, did lend itself to raids by lone, fast, Ju 88s on airfields and aircraft factories. Heavily engaged in these operations further west was KG 51, the crews of which were not sufficiently trained for night operations so carefully selected 'destruction crews' for these daylight harassing attacks. For these dangerous operations, often requiring long, unescorted, flights over enemy territory in broad daylight, these aircrews received a bounty, over and above usual flying pay, of 400 *Reichsmarks*. 'Destruction crews' were drawn from the most experienced men of each *Gruppe*, and although given target briefings, tactics were a matter for each crew to decide. When provided a target brief, crew commanders carefully monitored the weather and air operations, deciding for himself when and how the raid would be made.

From surviving Luftwaffe air intelligence records, we know that on 19 August 1940 KG 51 went ahead with attacks on various targets, as *Hauptmann* Genst (see Volume III) reported (times are continental):

I/KG51, one Ju 88. Take off 2.15 pm. Attack on Abingdon airfield. Target not recognised due to cloud. During the attack, bombs were dropped on another airfield (recognisable through cloud hole). Attack of 30–40 enemy fighters [*sic*]. Right engine failed, left engine damaged, forced-landing Carpiquet. One Spitfire shot down.

III/KG51, one Ju 88, take off 2.10 pm. Attack on Little Rissington carried out 4 pm, all of bombs hit line of planes in front of the hangars. About ten single-engine aircraft destroyed or badly damaged. Personnel were caught pushing out the planes. Likely significant staff losses. Amount of bombs dropped: four SC250, drop-height 500m.

III/KG51, take off 2.40 pm, one Ju 88, attack on Little Rissington airfield. Plane missing.

III/KG51, one Ju 88, take off 3.05 pm. Attack on Brize Norton airfield. Order not carried out owing to overlying cloud and anti-fighter defences. At 5.10 pm railway station facilities on western edge of Weymouth were attacked as an alternative target. Hits observed in the middle of station building, on rails and on a fuel dump near the station. Amount of bombs dropped: four SC250.

Fighters at Little Rissington, Abingdon and Portsmouth. Medium, poorly positioned anti-aircraft defences at Little Rissington and Weymouth.

One Spitfire shot down by I/KG51 in air combat.

Two Ju 88 III/KG51 – attacked by fighters over coast 3 pm, emergency jettison onto railway facilities on southern edge of town at Bognor. Results not observed.

1 Ju 88 II/KG51, start 1.25 pm, Yeovil. Three SC250 and 1 Flambo 250.

Airfields at Odiham and Harwell also bombed.

As was so often the case, given the clear failure of Luftwaffe air intelligence, not one of the target airfields selected was connected with Fighter Command, at the Westland Aircraft Factory at Yeovil, although producing the ill-fated Westland Whirlwind heavy fighter, was not manufacturing Spitfires or Hurricanes. The first of these raiders to be intercepted was at 13.17 hrs, over Exeter and out to sea, by Sergeant Reginald Llewellyn of 213 Squadron. At 12.41 hrs, Flight Lieutenant Jackie Sing had led Red Section, comprising Sergeants Michael Crosskell and Llewelyn up on patrol, encountering a Ju 88 which disappeared into cloud. Sing ordered Llewellyn below cloud, but there was no sign of the bomber until the Hurricane pilot sighted an aircraft a mile away, flying south-east. Assuming it to be his leader, Llewellyn approached – identifying the machine as twin-engine and, at 13.17 hrs, immediately informed Control:

> When I was approximately 800 yards astern E/A opened fire upon me with a cannon [*sic*]. When I was 600 yards astern I gave one very short burst. The E/A then flew just within the base of cloud in a SE direction. It climbed into a cloud as I began to close with it, and I turned and flew East through the same cloud. Shortly afterwards it appeared above the cloud and I carried out a beam attack. The enemy did not appear to have noticed me, and I opened fire at 250 yards, closing to 150 yards with a burst of two–three seconds. The aircraft emitted a considerable amount of smoke, black in colour, from the fuselage, followed by a glow of fire. Then it fell through the cloud but no one was seen to abandon the aircraft.

This Ju 88 was credited as destroyed.

The four Spitfires of 602 Squadron's 'B' Flight made the next interception, at 14.49 hrs, at 3,000ft over Tangmere. Pilot Officer Thomas Ritchie sighted a Ju 88 flying west, slightly north of Tangmere:

> [I] called Tally Ho. E/A turned South and Blue 2 attacked, adopting ¼ astern attack from above, opening fire 300 yards, closing 100 yards, four second burst. Blue 2's aircraft was hit by machine-gun fire from top stern gunner and caught fire; pilot baled out.
>
> I saw, from dead astern and below, E/A jettison bombs. I then attacked, adopting ¼ attack at same altitude, opening at 100 yards and closing to 10/20 yards with a two-second burst. I saw my bullets rake fuselage from nose to tail. I did not experience any return fire and surmise that rear-gunner was killed by Blue 2's fire.

'Blue 2' was Pilot Officer Henry Moody, who baled out over Arundel with burns to both hands. Bognor Police reported a Ju 88 down in the sea south of Bognor, so this Ju 88 was credited as destroyed and shared between the four Spitfire pilots of 602 Squadron. Pilot Officer Moody, however, had been shot down by the gunner of 1/KG 51's *Leutnant* Dr Stahl, who returned safely to base. A Ju 88, though, had crashed into the sea – and therein lies a tale…

The Spitfires of 10 Group's 92 Squadron were based at Pembrey, in South Wales, from where the fighters provided some protection to the ports of Cardiff, Swansea, Bristol and the West Country aircraft factories. Across the Bristol Channel on the South Devonian coast lay RAF Exeter, at which the Hurricanes of 87 Squadron were stationed, and on 7 August 1940 Flight Lieutenant Ian 'Widge' Gleed had led his 'A' Flight to temporarily operate from 'Bibury Farm' – or more precisely RAF Bibury, located at Ablington, near Cirencester, in Gloucestershire's Cotswolds – for night-flying duties. Built in 1939 as a relief landing ground for 3 Service Flying Training School (SFTS) at nearby South Cerney, Bibury – a Cotswold beauty spot – was an unlikely scene for the violence of war. When Gleed's Hurricanes arrived at Bibury, facilities were scant: a dispersal hut and several Nissen huts had been erected on the north-eastern side of the airfield, which became 87 Squadron's dispersal area. Groundcrews were accommodated in bell tents, while the more fortunate pilots found officers billeted at Walton House in Northleach and sergeant-pilots at the 'Red Lion'. Despite the tranquil setting 87 Squadron soon had action when, on 'A' Flight's first night at Bibury, Pilot Officer Peter Comely claimed a He 111 destroyed. After eleven days 'on point', it was now the turn of 92 Squadron's 'A' Flight, commanded by Flight Lieutenant Brian 'Kingpin' Kingcome, to relieve 87 Squadron and take their turn in providing a nocturnal defence.

Flight Lieutenant Brian Kingcome, 92 Squadron: 'Our landing field in Bibury did little to inspire confidence. It was a small meadow commandeered from a local farmer, and it really did look like a pocket handkerchief as you made an approach from the air.'

Nonetheless, Kingcome had until 15.00 hrs on 19 August 1940 to get organised at Bibury and ensure that 'A' Flight was operational. At exactly that time, however, 'A' Flight's new base was attacked by a Ju 88 from low-level, machine-gunning and lofting bombs, aiming for the dispersal area. Spitfire L1080 was seriously damaged, and three more 92 Squadron aircraft slightly so. While everyone ran for cover, AC2 Arfon Jones of 92 Squadron's Defence Section, ran for a machine-gun site and opened fire on the raider – which made the 19-year-old Welshman the focus of its venom. The Ju 88 nose-gunner returned fire, hitting the brave young airman twice, in the arm and heart, killing him instantly. AC2 Jones was the only personnel casualty arising from the attack; originally from Anglesey, the Jones family home was now in Garden City, Neath, and it was in the cemetery there, at Dylais Higher (Brynbedd) that Arfon Jones was buried.

The attack on Bibury was not actually planned, however. In *Hauptmann* Genst's report of 'Erfolgsmeldungen' (literally translated as 'success stories') from Fliegerkorps V to Luftwaffe high command – the *Oberkommando der Luftwaffe* (OKL) – we know that the actual target of the Ju 88 (which belonged to III/KG 51 'Edelweiss', based at Etampes-Mondésir, south of Paris) was not Bibury airfield, but the established aerodrome and RAF station at Little Rissington, ten miles to the north-east. Having mistaken Bibury for their intended target, this enemy crew got lucky, given that RAF fighters were operating from this minor airfield – unlike Little Rissington, which was unconnected with Fighter Command. That 'luck', however, would be their downfall.

As the Ju 88 attacked, 92 Squadron's Flying Officer James Paterson, a New Zealander, Yellow 1, and Pilot Officer Trevor 'Wimpy' Wade, Yellow 2, scrambled and gave chase. Paterson later reported that:

> Yellow 1 and 2 went in a southerly direction following enemy aircraft (E/A) until lost in cloud. Sometime later when near Southampton they got a vector from Filton which took them towards Anti-Aircraft fire from Southampton Docks. Ju 88 was first sighted flying south-east, down the Solent. Yellow 1 did a beam attack on the starboard from underneath from 200 yards. Coming round to a stern attack firing short bursts at various angles of deflection. Thick smoke poured from port engine and top two guns could be seen hanging down the sides of the E/A. As I pulled away having expended all my ammunition I noticed the port engine had stopped and was on fire, and E/A was losing height rapidly. I saw Yellow 2 take up the attack from astern and expend all his ammunition. E/A now flew low over the sea in SE direction for a few minutes and then turned and flew parallel with the coast, and then was seen to turn inland. Immediately it turned I saw E/A dive into the sea and disappear.

*Feldwebel*s Moser, Haak and Schachtner, and *Unteroffizier* Bachauer, were all killed.

Pilot Officer Wade's Spitfire, R6703, though, had been hit by return fire from the Ju 88 and so badly damaged that he struggled to regain the coast. Fortunately he did, and having crash-landed wheels-up, in a field near Selsey Bill, even luckier was that fact that Wade got clear of the aircraft just before it exploded.

The next Ju 88 intercepted was approaching St Catherine's Point when sighted by Squadron Leader Sandy Johnstone, patrolling at 6,000ft with 'A' Flight of 602 Squadron:

> I led Flight to attack and E/A dived to sea-level, turning South and making out to sea, jettisoning bombs at 50ft. I attempted to overtake and adopt head-on attacks, but E/A was going so fast I just had to abandon this, so took ¾ beam attack: saw bullets rake machine from nose to stern and machine rocked violently.

Further attacks were carried out by other members of 'A' Flight, until Red 2 climbed and saw the Ju 88 'hit the water'.

According to German records, a Ju 88 of I/KG 51, probably that of *Leutnant* Dr Stahl, was damaged in action with RAF fighters and crash-landed at Caen, but otherwise only the III/KG 51 aircraft which had attacked Bibury is recorded as destroyed – and yet 602 Squadron's report specifically states that this Ju 88 crashed into the sea. Although German loss returns are often lauded for their Teutonic accuracy, incidents such as this do bring into question just how comprehensive they are in reality.

The next action was fought by Red Section of 66 Squadron's 'A' Flight, up from Coltishall at 16.10 hrs and ordered to intercept a 'bogey'. At 17.25 hrs, the section, comprising Pilot Officers Hugh Kennard and Crelin 'Bogle' Bodie, and Sergeant Matthew Cameron, sighted a He 111 flying east, twenty miles east of Sherringham, over the North Sea. The Spitfires attacked, Bodie reporting black smoke pouring from the bomber's engine, which stopped, the port engine also damaged and the raider lost height 'steadily'. The bomber, however, disappeared into cloud and was claimed by Red Section as probably destroyed.

At 18.05 hrs, 66 Squadron's Blue Section, Pilot Officers John Studd and Arthur Watkinson, and Sergeant Donald Campbell, took off from Coltishall on an interception patrol, and five minutes later Squadron Leader Phillip Pinkham AFC, the CO of 19 Squadron, another 12 Group unit and based at Fowlmere, the Duxford satellite airfield, led 'B' Flight, comprising Flying Officer Leonard Haines, Pilot Officers Walter 'Jack' Lawson and Raymond Aeberhardt, Flight Sergeant Harry Steere and Sergeant David Cox on patrol.

Sergeant David Cox:

Green Section comprised Haines, Steere and myself. We were given a vector of 90°, which was in the direction of the East coast. We flew at about 2,000ft under 10/10ths cloud. As we approached the coast near Aldeburgh, the cloud started to break up and I, who was flying on the left and looking out to sea, saw a twin-engine aircraft. As was the rule, being the pilot who had the enemy in sight, I took over the lead. At about 300 yards I opened fire with my cannons in a quick burst of about three seconds. I then broke away, allowing Haines and Steere to attack. On making my second attack I saw the port engine catch fire, which rapidly enveloped the whole aircraft. Three of the crew baled out. Haines said it was an Me 110 fighter-bomber. I had my doubts as I thought they only had two crew, but as Leonard Haines was a senior flying officer I entered it in my log book as a 110.

Cox was right. The Luftwaffe lost no Me 110s that day but did lose a 7/KG 2 Do 17Z engaged by Spitfires over Essex – the raider crashed into the North Sea and all three crewmen remain missing.

At 18.45 hrs, during 19 Squadron's attack, Pilot Officer Studd of 66 Squadron was also on the scene and joined in, the bomber crashing twelve miles off the

Norfolk coast. Studd's Flight Commander, Flight Lieutenant Howard Frizelle 'Billy' Burton later reported that:

> After the action Flight Sergeant Steere [pilot – 19 Squadron] noticed Pilot Officer Studd to be in difficulties and closed up with him, both aircraft turning towards the shore. When about four miles off the coast at 700ft, steam and smoke started to pour from the engine. Pilot Officer Studd then abandoned his aircraft by parachute. Flight Sergeant Steere reported that the parachute opened perfectly. Flight Sergeant Steere then remained patrolling overhead to guide the lifeboat to the scene. The lifeboat located his parachute first and the pilot about fifty yards away with his head down in the water, apparently dead. The crew tried artificial respiration until reaching the shore, but without effect.
>
> Pilot Officer Studd was removed to Aldeburgh Cottage Hospital and examined. No wounds were discovered and it was reported that death was due to drowning. The Coast Guards state that the pilot's life jacket was not fully inflated. The time taken from abandoning the aircraft to be being picked up was forty-five-minutes.

It was a sad loss, which could have been avoided for want of a fully inflated Mae West – and perfectly illustrates the hazards involved when fighting over the sea.

After landing from that same interception sortie, Squadron Leader Pinkham of 19 Squadron reported to his Station Commander at Duxford, Wing Commander Alfred 'Woody' Woodhall, regarding his squadron's experimental and troublesome cannon-armed Spitfire Mk IBs, referring to the stoppages suffered during this combat by Flying Officer Haines:

> The ejection stoppages experienced were similar in each case: the empty case was not thrown clear of the gun or had bounced back into it, the next round being fed in jamming the empty case with the breech block partly forward. The mark of the breech block was clearly visible on the live round, though rather lower than normal. When firing in action on 19.08.40, Flying Officer Haines had similar stoppages on both guns in aircraft R6882, the port gun firing five rounds and the starboard gun twenty-two.
>
> It would appear that the stoppage is caused by the installation and is due to the effect of the gun being mounted on its side, combined with the small width of the ejection chute. It is not clear how this can be cured until the gun can be mounted the right way up and a belt feed introduced. Further, the magazine is supported on its neck by a magazine positioning stop which is only effective for positive 'G'. If any skidding or slipping or negative 'G' is applied the magazine is entirely supported by the neck. This is thought to have been the cause of the failure at the neck of the starboard magazine in R6776 (author's note: Flight Sergeant Unwin, referring to the action on 16 August 1940, see Volume III) after firing nine rounds in action.

While the cannon issue remained unresolved, Squadron Leader Pinkham also reported on Spitfire X4231, the aircraft armed with both cannon and machine-guns:

> Owing to recent operational commitments it has not been possible to carry out an exhaustive trial of aircraft and the following is merely a report on trials undertaken to date. As far as flying qualities are concerned the difference between this aircraft and a normal Spitfire is not noticeable. Its take-off, climb, landing speed and run are quite normal. It appears to stall at the same speed as the normal Spitfire. It is quite as manoeuvrable as the ordinary Spitfire up to 30,000ft. A test to determine the service ceiling has not yet been carried out, but has already been climbed to 32,000ft. The guns have been fired independently and together and have functioned satisfactorily.

By now, 19 Squadron was losing confidence in the Spitfire Mk IB, owing entirely to the unreliable cannon. The problem was that these aircraft were armed only with two 20mm Hispano-Suiza cannon, so if one – or both – jammed, the pilot was compromised and vulnerable. The squadron, however, had received Spitfire X4231, the first aircraft with the 'B' wing, which included two standard .303 Browning machine-guns in each wing as back-up armament. This combination would, in time, prove favourable, but still this did not yet solve the cannon stoppages. Nonetheless, the cannon was badly needed if the Spitfire was to keep parity with the Me 109E series, and so, for now, 19 Squadron pressed on, further frustrated that being in 12 Group opportunities for action were comparatively rare – and when they came, the cannon let them down.

That night, German bombers were active over England – and so too were RAF day-fighters, pressed into service as night-fighters. Indeed, Fighter Command's final loss of the day was not caused by enemy action but when Pilot Officer Colin Birch, of Northolt's 1 Squadron, inadvertently blundered into the London balloon barrage. Forced to bale out, his Hurricane crashed at Finsbury Park, but fortunately the pilot, who landed on the roof of 28 Gillespie Road, escaped injury.

Throughout the day, although adverse weather impacted upon operations, Coastal Command aircraft had undertaken forty-eight sorties, flying the usual round of anti-invasion and submarine patrols, and reconnaissance sorties in addition to patrolling over twenty-three convoys. At 17.35 hrs, a 206 Squadron Hudson, patrolling a convoy off Lowestoft, engaged a He 111:

> First made attack with front guns … diving on E/A from 2,000ft. The rear-gunner fired two bursts at starboard motor. Smoke appeared and later starboard airscrew became stationary. Another attack with front guns was made and bits of E/A were seen to fall from around cabin. Several hits were registered by the E/A's rear-gunner. Side and rear gunners of our aircraft made concentrated attack on enemy rear-gunner from 150 yards. He then ceased fire. Our crew consider that E/A could not reach coast. Broken cloud prevented steady combat.

The He 111 escaped, damaged.

By day, cloud cover over Germany prevented twelve 2 Group Blenheims completing their sorties to attack oil installations and aircraft facilities; of the remaining five aircraft also sent forth, one attacked a flak position on the Dutch coast while another bombed Flushing airfield. At 08.05 hrs, *Unteroffizier* Richard Woick of 8/JG 54 chalked up his first aerial victory when he intercepted a 114 Squadron Blenheim en route to bomb Bremen; Woick's victim crashed into the sea, one crewman being captured, the other two reported missing.

The Fairey Battles of 12 Squadron, 1 Group, Bomber Command, were deployed to Eastchurch, from where, at 23.00 hrs, five aircraft took off with orders to attach shipping in Boulogne Harbour:

> Pilot Officer Gillett returned after forty minutes due to an unserviceable magneto and leak in petrol union. All aircraft returned safely to base except that flown by Pilot Officer Cook. It has since been reported that the entire crew are prisoners of war. Only one aircraft dropped bombs, the remainder returned with full loads as the target was obscured by cloud [ORB].

Seven Blenheims of 59 Squadron, operating from Thorney Island, set out 'on a night bombing raid on Caen aerodrome. Again, due to thick haze, the target could not be located, except by two, who bombed it. The rest returned with their bombs except one crew: Pilot Officer B. Reynolds, Sergeant Whiting and Sergeant Wilkinson, who were reported missing [ORB].

Blenheim R2995, however, had crashed at Fontaine-Étoupefour, killing the crew, who were buried by the Germans with full military honours at Bayeux.

After dark, in fact, thirty-six Bomber Command Blenheims attacked twenty-one airfields in France and the Low Countries. Two of these aircraft, both of West Raynham's 101 Squadron, failed to return. Twenty-four Wellingtons were tasked with attacking the *Gneisenau* at Kiel, and twelve more were to bomb the Hannover oil refinery and other targets in Germany. Cloud concealed the battlecruiser, so harbour installations were bombed instead, and successes were also reported elsewhere, with several oil facilities set ablaze, and other damage to various targets. Whitleys also carried out successful attacks on German industrial targets, a major explosion occurring at the Zschornewitz power station, and Hampdens caused a massive blaze at the Bordeaux oil plant. No Wellingtons were lost but a Whitely failed to return, and a Hampden forced-landed on the Dorset coast, out of fuel. The strategy of Bomber Command has been covered in previous volumes, but suffice it to say that the Command's commitments were several-fold: attacking the enemy's industrial capacity and communications, airfields and the French ports – especially targeting invasion preparations. What must not be forgotten is that these represented a very great and dangerous effort, by night and day – which was integral to Britain's ongoing preservation.

That *Gneisenau*, and the *Kriegsmarine* bases at Kiel and Wilhelmshaven had featured in Bomber Command's target portfolio was no coincidence. By the end of July 1940, following Norwegian sorties, both the battleships *Gneisenau* and *Scharnhorst*, and the pocket-battleship *Lützow*, were repairing at Kiel, and the 8-inch cruiser *Prinz Eugen* was about to be completed and commissioned there. At Hamburg, construction of the soon-to-be dreaded *Bismarck* was progressing, and similarly *Tirpitz* at Wilhelmshaven, where the *Hipper* was also docked. These were all powerfully destructive ships able to wreak havoc on British convoys, and, indeed, play a part in a seaborne invasion. Consequently the Admiralty had requested that Bomber Command should attack these capital ships at their bases, before they could be completed or repaired, and break out into the open seas. According to Captain S.W. Roskill's official history, *The War at Sea, Volume 1*:

> Raids were started during the first days of July, and continued whenever conditions were favourable throughout the months of August, September and October, during which a total of 1,042 bomber sorties aimed 683 tons of bombs at these naval targets. But the weight of attack which Bomber Command could devote to this purpose on any one night was only some twenty-five to forty heavy-bombers – Hampdens, Whitleys and Wellingtons – and this was insufficient to achieve very favourable results. The *Prinz Eugen* was hit by two bombs of the 1–2 July 1940, the *Lützow* was hit a week later by one which failed to explode, and the persistence of raids, though on a small scale, caused some damage in the dockyards, and so delayed somewhat the progress of construction and repair work. But no damage of an important nature was caused to the ships themselves.
>
> These attacks on the German naval bases were not the only demand made of the RAF to assist the defeat of the enemy's invasion plans and his attacks on our ships and convoys, since aerial minelaying continued to feature prominently in the Admiralty's requests.

The figures quoted by Captain Roskill concerning sorties and the tonnage of bombs dropped, offset against the poor results, provides a graphic illustration of just how inaccurate bombing was, especially by night. The Admiralty's concern regarding these prominent German warships also emphasises the breadth of demands made upon the RAF as a whole – which, as Roskill implies, it was hardly resourced to successfully undertake. Nevertheless, day after day, night after night, Bomber Command's crews were taking the war across the Channel in aircraft which may have been considered 'heavy' at the time, but the bombloads and performance of which were incomparable to the later true, four-engine, heavy bombers such as the Avro Lancaster and Handley Page Halifax.

Daily Home Intelligence Report, 19 August 1940:

The continued success of the RAF still overshadows all other topics of conversation … there is increasing confidence and determination and growing excitement which shows itself almost as exhilaration. In raided areas there is confidence in Civil Defence services and a growing neighbourliness.

Reports from regions – London:

Pride among Civil Defence workers high at being under fire and at efficiency of organisation proved. Young volunteers, unused to sights of physical violence, showing remarkable coolness on handling terrible HE casualties. Neighbourliness proving able to cope with all homeless people … Confusion reported in Piccadilly after crowd had made for large Swan & Edgar shelter to find it was closed on Sundays. Elderly people started panicking and it took several minutes for policemen to disperse crowds to other shelters. Large crowd, particularly of children, at Zoo calm when sirens went on Sunday afternoon … Severe criticism of BBC's feature in 9 pm news after Croydon bombing; e.g. interviewing by Edward Ward of people who had experienced raid. Considered bad propaganda as interviewer 'sounded patronising and people over-excited and either callous or flippant'. Appreciation of Sunday night's Postscript about Merchant Navy [referring to the popular weekly 'Postscript' broadcasts by JB Priestly; see Volume I].

And so, the Battle of Britain went on.

Tuesday, 20 August 1940

In his diary, Mussolini's Foreign Minister and son-in-law, Count Galeazzo Ciano, wrote: 'A speech by Churchill. For the first time in a year I read an English speech which is definite and forward-looking. One can feel that behind the façade of beautiful words and strong affirmations there is a will and a faith.' Indeed there was.

On 'Eagle Day', 15 August 1940 (see Volume II), British Prime Minister Winston Churchill had personally watched the high tension and drama unfolding from the observation gallery of Air Vice-Marshal Keith Park's underground Operations Room at 11 Group's Uxbridge HQ. The Prime Minister was in company with his chief staff officer, General Hastings Ismay, and afterwards was deep in thought as the pair were driven back to Chequers, the Prime Minister's country house in Buckinghamshire. 'Don't speak to me,' Churchill told General Ismay, 'I have never been so moved.' Churchill then said, spontaneously, 'Never in the field of human conflict was so much owed by so many to so few.'

Churchill – soldier, politician, historian, journalist, author, and much more besides – was undoubtedly a complete master of the English language, which, like the rest of Britain, he fully mobilised for 'Action This Day'. On 20 August 1940, with the Second World War nearly a year old, Churchill addressed the

House of Commons at length, an appropriate moment at which, he said, 'to pause on our journey at this milestone and survey the dark, wide field'. The Prime Minister – a skilled and charismatic orator – began by comparing 'German aggression with its forerunner a quarter century ago', opining that 'this war is in fact only a continuation of the last, [but] very great differences in its character are apparent'. In identifying differences between 1914 and 1940, because of air power, Churchill rightly observed:

> The whole of the warring nations are engaged, not only soldiers, but the entire population, men, women and children. The fronts are everywhere. The trenches are dug in the towns and streets. Every village is fortified. Every road is barred. The front line runs through the factories. The workmen are soldiers with different weapons and the same courage. These are great and distinctive changes from what many of us saw in the struggle of a quarter of a century ago. There seems to be every reason to believe that this new kind of war is well suited to the genius and the resources of the British nation and the British Empire ... If it is a case of the whole nation fighting and suffering together, that ought to suit us, because we are the most united of nations, because we entered the war upon the national will and with our eyes open, and because we have been nurtured in freedom.

Churchill's introductory sentiments were clear enough, and he went on, at length, to discuss war aims and review Britain's defences and fighting forces.

> The whole British Army is at home... The whole island bristles against invaders, from the sea or from the air ... As in Nelson's day, the maxim holds, 'Our first line of defence is the enemy's ports'. Now air reconnaissance and photography have brought to an old principle a new and potent aid ... Our Navy is far stronger than at the beginning of the war ... The seas and oceans are open ... I said in the very dark hour two months ago, of continuing the war 'if necessary alone, if necessary for years'. I say it also because the fact that the British Empire stands invincible, and that Nazidom is still being resisted, will kindle again the spark of hope in the breasts of hundreds of millions of down-trodden or despairing men and women throughout Europe, and far beyond its bounds, and that from these sparks there will presently come a cleansing and devouring flame.

The everlasting impact of this significant speech, however, concerned 'The great air battle which has been in progress over this Island [which] for the last few weeks has recently attained a high intensity':

> The gratitude of every home in our Island, in our Empire, and indeed throughout the world, except in the abodes of the guilty, goes out to the British airmen who, undaunted by odds, unwearied in their constant challenge and mortal danger, are turning the tide of the world war by their prowess and

by their devotion. Never in the field of human conflict was so much owed by so many to so few.

This was skilled oration indeed, because here Churchill paid tribute to the RAF aircrews in a David and Goliath scenario, arguably connecting the current struggle, and those fighting in the air, with Shakespeare's Henry V's eve of battle speech: 'We few, we happy few, we band of brothers'.

On 25 October 1415, St Crispin's Day, Henry V's disease-ravaged and comparatively small army defeated the flower of French nobility at the Battle of Agincourt – a victory no one, least of all the bowmen of England and Wales, expected Henry to win. And now, in 1940, there was a direct parallel, clearly not lost on Churchill – whose lines 'Never in the field of human conflict was so much owed by so many to so few' has gone down in history to define the Battle of Britain. With these words, Churchill immortalised the RAF aircrews – but, as we have seen, these brave men were not exclusively 'British'. The RAF now fighting against Hitler's Germany was, in fact, a multi-national – albeit exclusively white – force; men from the Commonwealth: Canadians, New Zealanders, Australians, and even volunteers from still neutral America, and, of course, free airmen from the occupied lands: Poles, Czechoslovaks, Belgians, French and Dutchmen.

Significantly, Churchill continued:

All hearts go out to the fighter pilots, whose brilliant actions we see with our own eyes day after day; but we must never forget that all the time, night after night, month after month, our bomber squadrons travel far into Germany, find their targets in the darkness by the highest navigational skill, aim their attacks, often under the heaviest fire, often with serious loss, with deliberate careful discrimination, and inflict shattering blows upon the whole of the technical and war-making structure of the Nazi power. On no part of the Royal Air Force does the weight of the war fall more heavily than on the daylight bombers who will play an invaluable part in the case of invasion and whose unflinching zeal it has been necessary in the meanwhile on numerous occasions to restrain.

In popular culture, Churchill's speech and reference to the 'few' is assumed to have referred exclusively to fighter pilots – but clearly that was not actually the case. In this narrative we have seen, day by day, how Bomber and Coastal Commands contributed heavily to air operations throughout the Battle of Britain, and Churchill actually paid a greater tribute to 'our bomber squadrons' attacking Germany by night, and concluding that 'On no part of the Royal Air Force does the weight of the war fall more heavily than on the daylight bombers.' Clearly, then, the Prime Minister *fully* acknowledged the contributions of Bomber Command, and especially the daylight bombers of 2 Group, and the reference to 'so few' concerned the RAF as a whole. The Battle of Britain, however, was a defensive battle, much of which was fought over England by Fighter Command and within sight of those on the ground. Consequently, those combats and fighter aircrew epitomised the Battle of Britain, eclipsing, so far as the public was concerned, the less visible efforts of Bomber Command. This is why, no matter what Churchill actually said – and meant – his speech, and reference to the 'few', immortalised Fighter Command's aircrews in the Battle of Britain – ever since known as 'The Few'.

The abridged version of Churchill's speech broadcast by the BBC was, we know from Daily Home Intelligence reports, well-received by the public:

> Morale continues high. The Prime Minister's speech was received extremely well, according to all reports. From Northern Ireland comes the comment that it is the most forceful and heartening he has yet made. Newcastle reports that it has created a strong feeling of confidence. Two Bristol verbatim reports are as follows:
>
>> 'Everyone feels now, come what will, we are top dogs; the past week has shown that we shall win no matter what the slight doubts there were before.'
>
>> 'Bristol has implicit trust in Churchill. If he says things are all right Bristol people know they are all right; if he says they are bad, they know they are bad.'
>
> Weston-Super-Mare in Bristol Region, though, reported 'a feeling that the Premiere was a little too optimistic'.
>
> Londoners were as confident in Churchill as Bristolians, however: 'Churchill's speech yesterday, particularly his reference to the RAF, thought to be completely right – epitomises the feeling of the country.'

The pilots, themselves, though, modest as ever regarding their august achievements, were irreverent; in his memoir, *Spitfire! The Experiences of a Fighter Pilot*, published in 1942 and writing under the pseudonym 'B.J. Ellan', Squadron Leader Brian Lane DFC remarked that:

> 'So few', Mr Churchill said – but no debt as he would have you believe; rather so few so lucky to be able to get on with the job while less fortunate folk looked on and awaited their chance. I think he was really referring to our mess bills, anyway!

Nonetheless, on 20 August 1940, in the House of Commons and via the subsequent BBC broadcast, a legend was born.

Perhaps ironically, given the day's significance in shaping the legend of The Few, cloudy and wet weather much reduced air operations. Indeed, according to 66 Squadron, visibility was down to ten metres, reducing further still in heavy rain to just four. Nonetheless, the enemy's first sorties over England involved reconnaissance aircraft, which were active throughout the morning, as Debden's 257 Squadron reported:

> On their first patrol of a southbound convoy thirty miles East of Clacton, Green Section 'A' Flight sighted a Do 17 flying at about 8,000ft at 0845 hrs. The whole Section gave chase as the Do 17 dived quickly as they caught it up. Green 1, Pilot Officer Mitchell, made successive attacks on the plane which returned fire from its rear guns. One bullet hit the main spar of Green 2, Pilot Officer Capon's Hurricane. Green 3, Sergeant Hulbert was unable to make an attack as the Dornier dived into cloud. Green Section broke off the attack at sea-level as they were short of petrol. They saw a thin trail of smoke coming out of the aircraft's port engine as it flew away. No claim was made [ORB].

By mid-morning, the weather had improved, Flight Lieutenant Ken Gillies, also of 66 Squadron, reporting 5/10ths cloud at 1,000ft and 10/10ths at 19,000ft. Then, elements of *Erprobungsgruppe* 210, now led by Erich Rubensdörffer's successor, *Hauptmann* Hans von Boltenstern, swept in across the North Sea searching for British shipping. It was the unit's first operation since its battering on 'Eagle Day' (see Volume III).

At 10.35 hrs, Flight Lieutenant Ken Gillies had led Red and Yellow Sections of 66 Squadron's 'A' Flight up from Coltishall to patrol off the East Coast. At 10.44 hrs, the Spitfires were at 11,000ft five miles south of Lowestoft when three Me 110s were sighted incoming, dead ahead and 4,000ft above 66 Squadron. Gillies, Red 1, led the Flight to pass beneath the 110s before wheeling round and climbing to port in order to attack from the rear:

> On sighting us enemy went into a steep diving turn to starboard in wide line astern. I led my Section into a diving No 1 Attack on the rear E/A. On breaking away after two bursts of three seconds I noticed E/A's starboard engine slow up. At this point the enemy broke formation and I obtained a good deflection shot on one of the other E/A. No result observed. On turning I then saw No 3 E/A being attacked by another machine of my Section (Red 2, Sergeant Cameron) and noticed E/A's starboard engine aflame. The other two E/A were slowly climbing into cloud cover. No 3 E/A gradually lost height and I re-engaged him. I got a final burst into him as he went into cloud layer at 1,000ft and saw him crash into the sea. I noticed one opened parachute in water 200 yards to rear of crashed E/A. E/A flamed up on hitting the water and there were no survivors.
>
> E/A did not use front guns and rear fire was observed with slight tracer. I did not observe any cannon. E/A camouflage normal dark green.
>
> My aircraft received bullets in oil tank, port wing and rocker box, but no failure of engine occurred and I returned safely.

Gillies claimed an Me 110 destroyed, shared with other pilots of 'A' Flight. The aircraft concerned was a 2 *Staffel* Me 110D, flown by *Feldwebel* Martin Wohlfart, who was killed along with his *Bordfunker*, *Gefreiter* Albert Dietrich.

By early afternoon the cloud had sufficiently dispersed for KG 3 to send twenty-seven Do 17s, escorted by thirty Me 109s, to attack Eastchurch. 65 Squadron was operating from Rochford and was scrambled to intercept the incoming raid, which was at 14,000ft over Canterbury, heading west. At 13.10 hrs over Manston, the enemy was sighted, the Spitfires climbing 4,000ft above while maneuvering to attack from astern.

Sergeant Joseph Kilner, Blue 2:

> Flying in line astern of Blue 1, I was attacked by an Me 109 and forced to break formation, thereupon passing Blue 1 who went into cloud. Shortly afterwards I perceived two Me 109s in front and at the same height (18,000ft) and closed in line astern to about 150 yards without being noticed and opened fire. After about a three second burst the E/A, with pieces falling off, appeared to stagger, burst into flames and dived vertically. Before I could attack the second Me 109 it disappeared into cloud.
>
> As there were no more enemy fighters near me I decided to do a head-on attack on a section of Do 17s which had become separated from the rest. They, however, saw my intention and turned, forcing me to attack from the beam. I saw no result at first and made a second attack from their quarter, allowing one ring deflection. I saw smoke appear from the starboard engine of one and pieces fall from the wing. I broke away for the third attack when I observed six machines which I thought were Hurricanes coming to my assistance. I continued with the attack, receiving return fire from all three Do 17s. In all three attacks I had fired about three two second bursts. On breaking away I found I was being attacked by the six fighters, which were Me 109s. I did a steep diving turn and got on tail of last E/A who dived for cloud. I fired two three second bursts and smoke and what appeared to be flames came from the Messerschmitt, while it dived vertically for the cloud. I broke off the engagement and looked for further E/A but none could be seen. I then dived through the clouds and seeing I was over Calais returned to Rochford.

Sergeant Kilner claimed two Me 109s destroyed and a Do 17 probable – one Me 109 was lost, *Feldwebel* Maul of 1/JG 51 being shot down and rescued from the sea by *Seenotflugkommando* 3. Sergeant Robert MacPherson, who had begun his RAF service as an Aircraft Apprentice before making the quantum leap to fighter pilot, also claimed a 109 probably destroyed. Pilot Officer Kenneth Hart, however, was shot-up, possibly by *Leutnant* Francis Achleitner of 9/JG 3, and crash-landed, unhurt, at Havengore Island, Foulness.

At 14.05 hrs, Flight Lieutenant James Sanders led six Hurricanes of 615 Squadron up from Kenley, followed ten minutes later by the CO, Squadron

Leader Joe Kayll, with five more, all with orders to patrol Tenterden. At 15.00 hrs, the Hurricanes:

> intercepted a Do 17 near Herne Bay. Squadron Leader Kayll attacked a Do 17 and Pilot Officer Young finished it off with enemy crashing near Eastchurch. Pilot Officer Hone attacked another Do 17 which also crashed near Eastchurch. Pilot Officer Eyre attacked a third Dornier and the crew were seen to bale out by Pilot Officer Hone. Pilot Officer Lofts brought down an Me 109 [ORB].

Only one Do 17, in fact, crashed near Eastchurch, so this is an excellent example of how one casualty could be claimed by several pilots and thereby multiplied on the balance sheet.

At 15.15 hrs, nine Hurricanes of 32 Squadron scrambled from Biggin Hill to patrol base before also being vectored to engage the raiders now over the Thames Estuary: 'Pilot Officer Smythe attacked a Do 215 [*sic*] at 10,000ft over the Estuary, getting in several bursts. Pilot Officer Barton confirms that it was damaged [ORB].'

The raid, however, withdrew without bombing its target, and was the day's only large-scale effort. At 15.00 hrs, however, RAF Manston reported being 'attacked by eight Me 109s with cannon and machine-gun fire [ORB].' Being on the coast, close to the enemy, Manston was vulnerable to such low-level snap-attacks, one of which was described by *Oberleutnant* Ulrich Steinhilper of I/JG 52, based at Coquelles and flying a machine-gun-armed Me 109E-3:

> It was clear that many British fighters were used Manston as a forward-base or landing to refuel there after combat. Our signals unit monitored the enemy fighter frequency and from intercepted transmissions we realised that Manston was the scene of much activity – and concluded that a low-level surprise attack should catch many RAF fighters on the ground.
>
> Setting course across the Channel our Schwärme flattened out so we were all at the same height, each Rottenführer with his Rottenhund. Flying practically due South we roared over the coast just East of Margate and within seconds were approaching Manston … I spotted a tanker refuelling a Spitfire quite close to the boundary of the airfield and lined myself up for a shot. Dropping to just three or four metres to minimise deflection, the tanker quickly filled the red illuminated ring of my gunsight. Increasing the pressure on the trigger and button [to fire nose and wing-mounted weapons simultaneously], I felt all for machine-guns begin firing, my airframe vibrating slightly. Grey lines of tracer streaked forwards and focused on the vehicle. I saw the strikes and flashes as the bullets began to hit home and the tanker began to burn. In seconds I had hurtled over it and then turned my attention to two Spitfires, which had been placed out at dispersal, awaiting attention. Again, grey lines streaked out, first tearing up the ground and then concentrating on the aircraft. They both began burning as the tanker erupted into a fireball behind me. Banking

left, we hedge-hopped out of Manston and moments later crossed out over Pegwell Bay – and home.

After Manston was strafed, there was no more action on 20 August 1940 until Red Section of Exeter's 213 Squadron, comprising Flight Lieutenant Jackie Sing and Sergeant Reginald Llewellyn, intercepted three Ju 88s at 18.40 hrs, at 11,000ft over Newton Abbott. According to Sing, as the Hurricanes were sighted, the three bombers went into line astern:

at full throttle and with plugs pulled dived, subsequently stock bombing the railway. As they broke away I attacked the leader but was unable to see my bullets strike the machine, then the rear-gunner ceased firing. The machine was badly damaged but there has been no confirmation of it having crashed. Then I saw another machine heading out to sea and managed to get in two bursts before running out of ammunition, whereupon the rear-gunner of this machine ceased firing suddenly and this machine disappeared into cloud.

Although both pilots claimed Ju 88s destroyed, it appears that all three enemy bombers returned safely to base, although damaged.

Throughout the day, 257 Squadron had continued escorting convoys and carrying out:

precautionary patrols. At 1800 hrs, Green Section took off to intercept raiders approaching a northbound convoy off Southwold. The Section sighted the aircraft above them [1845 hrs] and Green Leader, Flying Officer Mitchell, made three attacks on it, silencing the rear-gunner. Our bag was one Do 215 to Flying Officer Mitchell. No casualties to our side [ORB].

The Dornier was assessed as 'damaged'.

On 17 August 1940, the recently formed Polish 302 Squadron had been made operational at Leconfield under the command of Squadron Leader Jack Satchell. Early in the evening of 20 August 1940, 'B' Flight was scrambled to intercept 'Raid 22'. At 18.53 hrs, the CO took off and hurried after the Flight, joining it over the coast:

I received the order to patrol Hull at 5,000ft. On approaching Hull I observed a twin-engine aircraft flying in an easterly direction below my starboard bow. I dived at once to a position above and slightly behind and saw the German black crosses and at the same time identified the aircraft as a Ju 88. The E/A immediately shot into the clouds endeavouring to avoid me. I followed and got in a short burst using full deflection and both aircraft turned before the E/A went into another cloud. I climbed above this cloud and as the E/A emerged on the far side I got in another burst, and when he emerged a second time I dived and got in a long burst, opening at 300 yards and ceasing fire at about fifty yards, when I had to pull up quickly to avoid a collision. Soon after opening my second burst the rear-gunner ceased fire, as I saw no more tracer. I observed my tracer penetrating the E/A all round the centre of the fuselage, all my attacks being delivered from above and slightly behind. I received a bullet in my propeller. During the attack I observed smoke coming from the E/A's engines, due apparently to over-boosting. The main tactic of the enemy were steep left-hand turns. After I had broken away I observed Green 2 on the E/A's tail for a very short period before E/A went into the clouds. It was not seen again and was presumed to have crashed. This was confirmed later by telephone. At an interview between Flying Officer Robinson, Interrogation Officer, and the four prisoners it was confirmed that the attack from above had set the cockpit on fire. Cloud 5/10. Sun behind … landed 1935 hrs.

The Ju 88 belonged to 8/KG 30 and had been briefed to attack Thornaby, a Coastal Command airfield. One of the crew, in fact, was killed in the combat; another was captured alive but badly wounded and subsequently died. The remaining two saw out the war in captivity. It was an historic combat, being the first aerial victory by a Polish squadron serving in the RAF during the Second World War.

Despite the poor weather, throughout the day sixty-two aircraft of Coastal Command flew fifty-three routine convoy, anti-invasion and submarine patrols, and reconnaissance flights. So bad was the weather, in fact, that only three 2 Group Blenheims were sent forth by day, one of which found itself too exposed over enemy territory owing to a lack of cloud, so aborted, while the other two machines respectively attacked the airfields at Schiphol and Ostend. Owing to the weather, night operations by Bomber Command were completely scrubbed.

Interestingly, at 15.20 hrs, three Blenheims of 236 Squadron had left St Eval in Cornwall to meet the flying-boat *Clare* over Pembroke Dock in South Wales and escort the civilian aircraft to Poole in Dorset. Arriving over Pembroke Dock at 15.50 hrs, 'Pilot Officer Campbell's machine was hit by fire from the ground. *Clare* took-off at 1552 hrs and they escorted it without any further incident to Poole, where they left it at 1700 hrs [ORB].' On 3 August 1940, Captain J.C. Kelly Rogers of British Overseas Airways had taken off in *Clare* on the first British passenger flight to the United States, returning from New York five days later.

Edward Bishop, journalist:

when *Clare* left New York on her homeward journey, her passengers included the first party of American pilots engaged by the MAP to ferry new and repaired aircraft from factory to airfield. America was sending both aeroplanes and non-combatant pilots to fly them. The Atlantic moat … would not quarantine the New World from Europe very much longer.

Wednesday, 21 August 1940

While continuing poor weather over England prevented major raids being flown, *Luftflotten* 2 and 3 nonetheless sent numerous formations of up to three bombers to attack various airfields over a wide front. Inevitably, though, target selection was poor, with aerodromes unconnected with Fighter Command, with Brize Norton, Abingdon and Horsham St Faiths all being on the hit list. On this day, twenty attacks by lone raiders were also made on shipping, primarily in the south-west, while the cruiser HMS *Manchester* was bombed but escaped damage in St George's Channel. Fighter Command, as ever, rose to the challenge – and would enjoy a successful day.

A number of raiders were active by day over Norfolk. At 12.15 hrs, Squadron Leader Douglas Bader was leading a section of 242 Squadron Hurricanes back to Coltishall upon conclusion of yet another tedious training flight when he heard over the R/T Squadron Leader Rupert 'Lucky' Leigh, of Coltishall's 66 Squadron, being vectored to intercept an 'X-Raid'. Without having been instructed himself to do so, Bader broke away and head south-east – towards Yarmouth and the action. Arriving before Leigh's Spitfires, Bader peered through a thin veil of cloud at 8,000ft and saw the silhouette of a Do 17. As Bader climbed through the 'clag', the raider's sharp-eyed rear gunner spotted and opened fire on the rapidly closing Hurricane. Taking aim and being careful not to overtake his target too quickly, Bader briefly returned fire. Nonetheless the 'Flying Pencil' disappeared into thick cloud. Although believing that he had hit the bomber, Bader made no combat claim. At the same time he engaged that lone intruder, 242 Squadron's Blue Section was also in action close-by, with Sub-Lieutenant Gardner, Flight Lieutenant Powell-Sheddon and Pilot Officer Latta subsequently sharing the destruction of a 2/KG 2 Do 17 (which crashed at Conifer Hill, Starston). Several days later, however, Bader was informed by the Coltishall Intelligence Officer that the body of a Do 17 crewman had been recovered from the sea in the area of his inconclusive combat on this day; the dead enemy airman's watch had stopped at the time concerned and on which basis the CO of 242 Squadron was rightly credited with having destroyed this bomber, which, it would appear from German casualty records, was another 2/KG 2 Holzhammer machine, based at Épinoy, nineteen miles south-east of Arras. The crewman recovered was *Leutnant* Ermecke; his three fellow crewmen remain missing.

In the fighting off the East Coast on 21 August 1940, the new Spitfire Mk IIAs of Squadron Leader James McComb's Digby-based 611 Squadron would be the most heavily engaged 12 Group unit:

Cloudy and a cold wind. A day of operations. Blue Section away at 0755 hrs for an hour's fruitless X Raid investigation over Skegness. Red Section at 1200 hrs went off to patrol Mablethorpe at 3,000ft below cloud. They found three Do 215s [*sic*] and attacked them a little offshore, shooting down one for certain, and possibly a second, and landed back at Digby at 1305 hrs. The Intelligence Officer's summary of their reports reads as follows:

'Red Section patrolling Mablethorpe below cloud base. Went to investigate raid X 27. E/A got away and Red Section returned to Mablethorpe. Raid 74, consisting of three Do 215s [*sic*] was sighted off Mablethorpe about 1234 hrs, flying South at 4,000ft but immediately lost in cloud. Re-sighted at 1238 hrs and Red Leader ordered emergency boost to catch up. E/A were flying in tight vic formation which turned East when attacked. Red Leader [Flying Officer Douglas 'Dirty' Watkins] ordered a No 3 Fighter Command attack. He attacked No 2 of enemy formation with a four second burst at 400 yards. No return fire until about seven or eight seconds had elapsed. Red Leader closed to 250/100 yards, firing two bursts which emptied his ammunition and then broke away. No immediate result observed but then No 2 of enemy formation broke away. There were bursts of flame from the fuselage and black smoke as E/A glided down to the South. Finally E/A dived into the sea about eight miles North of Burnham Market, two of the crew having baled out. Red 2 confirms this and a searchlight company confirms that the E/A was seen to crash in flames into the sea.'

This was a KG 3 Do 17, the crew of which were all either killed or never found. Red 2, Pilot Officer Peter 'Sneezy' Brown:

After sighting E/A for the second time I attacked with Leader in echelon port, The E/A were rather close and Red Three (Pilot Officer John Lund) was not quite in position. I attacked No 3 of the enemy formation. After firing for some seconds, black smoke came from the port engine. After finishing my ammunition black smoke was pouring from both engines. I saw my ammunition entering E/A and consider that a number of hits were made. After breaking away I saw the E/A dive towards the sea, two of the crew baled out.

This Do 17, of 4/KG 3, was shared between Brown and Lund; the enemy crew were all killed. The bomber's rear-gunner, however, returned fire, hitting Brown's Spitfire, P7304, and scoring hits in the spinner cap, engine cowling, rudder and wings, bursting a tyre. Watkins' aircraft was hit in the spinner, wings and starboard tailplane, while Lund's machine took hits to the airscrew boss, tailplane and also had a burst tyre, as a result of which his Spitfire tipped onto its nose while landing back at base. None of the pilots were hurt, fortunately, and all three fighters were repairable – Lund's at Digby, while the other two had to be flown to the specialist Supermarine facility at Hamble.

While Red Section was in the air, a further raid was reported and so Yellow Section, led by the CO, Squadron Leader McComb, and comprising Sergeants Alfred Burt and Andrew Darling, was scrambled at 12.55 hrs. At 13.08 hrs, just off Skegness, Yellow Section intercepted a Dornier, head-on, Squadron

Leader McComb had a shot but without any apparent result. The bomber then disappeared into cloud. Two minutes later, the Spitfire pilots once more sighted their prey, as the 611 Squadron Intelligence Officer's report describes:

E/A was then seen 200 yards ahead and 300ft above. A No 1 Attack was attempted. Yellow Leader pulled up onto E/A and gave short burst with deflection at 150 yards. Bullets were seen to go into the wing, near port engine, and Yellow Leader had to break away to avoid ramming. Yellow Section chased the raider out to see but did not see him again. Yellow 2 and 3 did not fire their guns. It was not thought that the E/A was sufficiently damaged to be brought down. On returning, three Do 17s were sighted flying West about fifteen miles East of Mablethorpe. E/A were flying in tight vic formation, speed about 240 mph. Yellow Leader attacked right-hand machine with six or seven seconds burst which silenced the rear-gunner. E/A appeared, from large cloud of smoke, to be fixed so Yellow Leader attacked the middle machine, which was giving trouble tracer from rear-gunner. After a short burst, fire from the rear-gunner ceased and Yellow Leader had a second, longer, burst at very short range into the bottom of his cockpit. Smoke came heavily from starboard engine. Yellow Leader, having ordered Section to ensure attacking before E/A reached cloud, outstripped Yellow 2 and 3 with result that attack ended with a No 1 Attack. Yellow 2 got two short bursts on the middle E/A and Yellow 3 a short burst in E/A No 3 before the formation entered cloud. When re-sighted Yellow 2 got a short burst at 400 yards, with deflection, then lost E/A in cloud. Yellow 3 followed the enemy formation as it was entering cloud and knowing himself to be close, owing to effect of slipstream, gave another burst. Right-hand aircraft of enemy formation was seen to hit the ground and burst into flame after Yellow Leader's attack.

This was a Do 17 of 6/KG 3, which crashed at Bilsby, near Alford; all four crewmen baled out, three of whom were wounded, and all were captured. Although the Spitfire pilots did not see the lead Do 17 crash, the captain of which was *Oberleutnant* H. Schwarz, the *Staffelkapitän* of 6/KG 3, the pilot lost control after a collision with its neighbour, this bomber also crashing near Alford. Schwarz and another crewman were captured, but two others were killed. During this action Squadron Leader McComb's Spitfire was 'extensively damaged. There were bullet holes in the port wing, starboard tailplane, aileron hinge cowling and cooling and hydraulic systems were damaged [ORB].' While Yellow 2 returned to Digby unscathed, Yellow 3's Spitfire was hit in the tailplane and also tipped onto its nose after landing, having hit a chock carelessly left lying around on the airfield.

With enemy bombers still prowling around off the East Coast, at 16.03 hrs Green Section of 611 Squadron's 'B' Flight, led by Pilot Officer Barrie Heath, left Digby to patrol Mablethorpe. This was a section of four Spitfires, Green 2 being Pilot Officer Colin MacFie, Green 3 Sergeant Stephen 'Sandy' Levenson, and, unusually, the Station Commander, Wing Commander Ian Parker, flying the Green 4 position. At 16.14 hrs, Green Section was ordered to investigate Raid X13, and at 16.21 hrs Sergeant Levenson sighted a He 111 some considerable distance ahead. The Spitfires gave chase but Wing Commander Parker soon became lost in cloud and was left behind. Levenson and MacFie attacked, briefly, before losing the bomber in cloud, the latter then sighting the raider again at 16.30 hrs over Spurnhead. For forty miles over the North Sea MacFie chased the He 111 in and out of cloud, firing whenever possible, damaging the bomber, until his ammunition was expended and the German finally disappeared into a bank of cloud.

That afternoon, at 14.57 hrs, further action followed for 66 Squadron, when Yellow Section, comprising Pilot Officers Hugh Kennard, Charles Cooke and Ian Cruikshanks, caught and damaged a Do 17 fifteen miles north-east of Yarmouth. Then, while carrying out an R/T test with Martlesham Heath at 18.15 hrs, Flight Lieutenant Steve 'Squeak' Weaver and Flying Officer Richard Brooker were warned by the North Weald Sector Controller of an enemy aircraft over Ipswich. 'Squeak' sighted a Do 17 flying north of the town, just before anti-aircraft guns opened up. The Do 17 immediately disappeared into cloud but, Flying Officer Brooker regained contact and shot the bomber down, which crashed at Gippeswyk Park, Ipswich. Brooker's machine was also damaged in the combat, the pilot making a crash-landing at Flowton Brook, Bramford, and escaping with minor injuries.

There was also action up in the north-east. At 15.23 hrs, Flight Lieutenant William Riley, commanding 'B' Flight of the Polish 302 Squadron, took off from Leconfield in company with Pilot Officer Stanislaw Chalupa and an unknown pilot, the trio making up Blue Section, to patrol Bridlington at 12,000ft. Having orbited for fifteen minutes, a Ju 88 was sighted and immediately dived for cloud cover:

> Blue 1 [Riley] led the attack from above E/A on its starboard side, opening fire at about 400 yards with burst of five seconds. E/A jettisoned bombs before attack was delivered and during bursts pieces were seen to disintegrate from the fuselage. E/A entered cloud and on emerging after ten seconds Blue 1 again attacked from above and to starboard. Blue 2 [Chalupa] and 3 [unknown] attacked almost at the same time from the beams. E/A again entered cloud with starboard engine smoking, at about 8,000ft, and was not seen again as broken cumulus reached down to about 4,000ft. During attacks ice coated Blue 1's windscreen and he could not see details of E/A.

Pilot Officer Chalupa reported that after this engagement, at 15.50 hrs, he continued patrolling with Flight Lieutenant Riley and spotted an aircraft half a mile away which he identified as another Ju 88:

Having attacked and got in about three bursts from about 150 yards I saw certain objects flying off the aircraft and very much black smoke poured from his port engine. In this state the E/A started to dive and flew into a cloud. Owing to the fact that my engine began to function badly and gave forth white smoke from beneath its cowling I throttled back and tried to glide towards the aerodrome. Being at about 200ft the engine began to vibrate. Being unable to reach the aerodrome I landed on the edge of it without dropping my undercarriage.

Both Ju 88s were accredited as probably destroyed but unconfirmed; in reality, although damaged, these raiders returned to base. At 16.25 hrs, however, slightly further to the north-east, a He 111 was not so lucky when engaged by Green Section of the Catterick-based 41 Squadron, ten to fifteen miles east of Flamborough Head. Having patrolled over Scarborough the Spitfires were vectored towards a bandit just ahead, which was immediately sighted flying into broken cloud. Pilot Officer Edward 'Teddy' Shipman, Green 1, formed the section into line astern and attacked from dead astern:

Return fire from the upper and lower gun positions was observed but with no result. No evasion was noticed. The E/A's starboard fuel tank caught fire and the starboard engine emitted white smoke. The E/A then commenced a steep spiral dive to the right and fell vertically into the sea, the starboard wing breaking off just before E/A hit the water. The E/A sank immediately, leaving a patch of blazing fuel on the water. The crew did not jump and no trace of any survivors was seen.

The enemy crew, of II/KG 53, remain missing.

Perhaps surprisingly, there was little action over the South Coast. On 19 August 1940, 17 Squadron had moved from Debden to Tangmere, 'A' Flight being released the following day while 'B' Flight's turn at readiness passed without incident. At 13.00 hrs on 21 August 1940, however, the whole squadron came to readiness and two interceptions subsequently took place. At 16.15 hrs, the CO, Squadron Leader Cedric Williams, together with Pilot Officers Jack Ross and Harold 'Birdy' Bird-Wilson, shared the destruction of a Ju 88 they caught prowling around just south of Tangmere and which crashed at Marsh Farm, Earnley. Then it was Red Section's turn, led by Flying Officer Count Manfred Czernin (Red 1) and comprising Sergeants Clifford Chew (Red 2) and Leonard Bartlett (Red 3). Czernin reported:

Red Section was ordered to patrol base below clouds at 1645 hrs ... We were given three vectors before going above cloud. We were then over Beachy Head. On going above I perceived E/A about 8,000ft three miles away. I ordered Section into line astern and gave chase. Section delivered an astern attack and put rear-gunner out of action. E/A's speed at first seemed to be about 250 mph but after attack slowed to 160 mph. We then delivered three beam attacks, E/A took no avoiding action but was going down slowly. After fourth attack E/A's starboard engine, which had been smoking, broke into flames. Two of the crew thereupon jumped with their parachutes, which opened, and they landed in the sea. I then approached E/A which was still on an even keel although losing height. I saw behind the cross a red snake-like crest and in front of the cross the number B3 or 33. As we were about twenty miles South, over the sea, I did not think it wise to follow E/A which was obviously going down, and re-formed Section, of which only Red 2 remained as Red 3 had finished his ammunition and returned to base.

Czernin's assessment was correct: this Ju 88, also of II/KG 54, failed to return, its crew all reported missing.

The south-west was also in the enemy's sights on this day of roving raiders. No.236 Squadron was based at St Eval in north Cornwall:

At 1330 hrs the Air Raid alarm was sounded and within two minutes the aerodrome was being bombed and machine-gunned by three Ju 88s. The Squadron hangar was hit by a bomb and badly damaged: one Magister was burned up and five of our Blenheims in the hangar and one at dispersal point were badly damaged. The bomb fell almost in the Orderly Room and wounded the Orderly Room Corporal and two airmen badly. Eight other casualties in the Squadron but not serious. The Squadron HQ offices were destroyed, Maintenance and 'A' Flight office. Squadron HQ was at once moved to dispersal point in two stores vans and tents and the remains of the furniture and office equipment, books and stationery were removed to the new HQ. The Squadron HQ was rather primitive but by next morning the arrangements were completed and the organisation of the Squadron carried on as usual [ORB].

Immediately before the Ju 88s appeared, Pilot Officers Aubrey de Lisle Inniss, Graham Russell, and Stanley Nunn had taken off in their Blenheims to meet a flying boat over Calshot and escort it. At 13.52 hrs, however, they sighted two of the enemy bombing St Eval and immediately engaged the closest raider, getting in:

good bursts with front guns at 400 yards. They chased it to Land's End but it got away in the clouds. Pilot Officer Russell had lost the other two of his formation and saw an E/A dropping bombs on aerodrome so gave chase but lost sight of E/A over Padstow in clouds [ORB].

Three other Blenheims were also airborne when the attack happened, similarly en route to Calshot; Sergeant Reginald Smith's gunner, Sergeant Arthur Piper, fired 100 rounds at one of the bombers but without visible effect. It was a successful raid from the enemy's perspective, indicating the level of disruption that could be achieved – and St Eval was used by Fighter Command. Indeed, on 14 August 1940, 238 Squadron, withdrawn from Middle Wallop, had arrived at St Eval, and were based at this station during the attack:

In company with the Adjutant of 236 Squadron, the Adjutant of 238 Squadron left the Officers' Mess in dignified haste, remarks about the Pied Piper of Hamlyn being passed among those leaving. A bomb went off East of the Mess as they went along the grass corridor at the back, and a stone or fragment broke some of the glass. This acted as boost! The Adjutants of 236 and 238, on getting out, lay under the wall of the Officers' Cookhouse, a point of shelter not well chosen as it was later noticed that the steam heating system was centered there. As a viewpoint it was good, and they saw the aircraft, a Ju 88, let go its bombs at an altitude of about 200ft. The Adjutant of 238 counted five bombs, but his companion thought six, estimated at 40lbs, but later said to be 250lbs. They fell and did not explode for an appreciable time; then the 236 Hangar showed a pall of brown smoke with a centre of black and flame. The pilot was afraid of his job, as he pulled back the stick before letting go. The machine-gunner began firing wildly, and the enemy shot up into the clouds with black boost tails from his engines. The damage done was the roof of the hangar disarranged and a Maggie completely wrecked 'spurlos zerstreut', with the exception of part of the engine. People in the hangar at the time, including the Warrant Officer Engineer of 236 were unharmed. It is worth observing in this connection that the hangar doors were open. Only three craters were found. The other bombs do not seem to have been traced [ORB].

The raid of St Eval was far and away the most successful of the day – but had not caused significant damage.

The Spitfires of 234 Squadron, up from Middle Wallop, were the next 10 Group unit in action, at 14.15 hrs, as the CO, Squadron Leader Joseph 'Spike' O'Brien DFC, reported:

I was leading Red Section on patrol, Angels 8, over Newbury. I sighted one Ju 88 ten miles South of patrol position. I stalked E/A in top of cloud with Red 2 [Flight Lieutenant Cyril Page]. Red 3 [Pilot Officer Bob Doe] had gone below cloud previously to search. E/A sighted us at about 600 yards. I gave him two short bursts at 400 yards as he entered cloud. As he emerged I saw Red 3 on his tail at fifty yards range. I therefore carried out a quarter attack, opening fire at 200 yards. I then lost E/A in cloud but sighted him a couple of minutes later, to my right. I approached him, taking cover in cloud, and suddenly came out of cloud in about 100 yards of him. I opened fire and closed to thirty yards, finishing all my ammunition. A few minutes later, descending through cloud, I saw E/A had crashed and was on fire.

This Ju 88, of I/KG 54, which crashed at King's Sombourne, was shared between Squadron Leader O'Brien and Pilot Officer Doe; the crew were all killed.

Writing after the war, Wing Commander Doe DSO DFC, as he became, recalled that he had actually led Red Section that day, with Squadron Leader O'Brien his Red 2. O'Brien had formerly been a Blenheim pilot on 23 Squadron and Sector Controller at Pembrey; he had only taken command of 234, a Spitfire squadron, two days previously. As the Ju 88 involved had crashed near Middle Wallop, O'Brien and Doe visited the crash-site, as the latter recalled: 'I was sorry that I had afterwards, because some ghoul at the crash informed us that every occupant had at least five bullet holes through his helmet – which brought death a little too close for comfort.'

Although unrecorded in official records, Pilot Officer Doe's Spitfire. X4036, had taken a bullet through the main spar during the engagement, requiring the unharmed pilot to fly the aircraft to Supermarine at Hamble for repair:

> It was a day nearly away from the war, where I could lie back on the grass and watch interceptions going on overhead and sleep in the sun.

> A foreman from the works invited me to his house for a meal … His wife was really motherly and made me feel quite embarrassed by her views of the fighting. It hadn't entered my head that we were doing something that ordinary people could see and admire. It certainly had never occurred to me that we could do anything other than win the war.

Flight Sergeant George 'Grumpy' Unwin, the 'High Priest' of 19 Squadron at Fowlmere felt similarly: 'We were well-trained and just doing our job – it never occurred to us that we could lose.' Flying Officer Frank Brinsden, a New Zealander serving on 19 Squadron, commented:

> So far as we were concerned we were not doing anything out of the ordinary, just what we were there to do and in fact considered ourselves the lucky ones able to hit back at the Germans, who were bombing our people. Indeed, at squadron level I think briefing was sadly lacking and so we were largely unaware of just how crucial the battle we were fighting was.

A 'crucial battle' it was indeed, however, and at 16.50 hrs on 21 August 1940, Red Section of 152 Squadron, up from Warmwell and comprising Pilot Officers Graham Cox, Richard Hogg and Frederick Holmes, struck the next blow for 10 Group:

> Red Section … Encountered a Ju 88 off The Needles. The Section attacked from above and astern … Red 1 opened fire at 250 yards. No 1 Attack was employed. The Ju 88 dived down to about 10ft above the sea and crashed half a minute later. Red 2 [Pilot Officer Hogg] had his aircraft temporarily unserviceable owing to shots from the enemy rear-gunner [ORB].

Which Ju 88 this was cannot be ascertained from surviving German records.

Having been bombed at St Eval, that evening Hurricane pilots of 238 Squadron were able to even the score somewhat. With radar indicating the presence of further enemy aircraft in the vicinity of St Eval, at 17.07 hrs Blue Section, comprising Flight Lieutenant Minden Blake, a New Zealander, and Pilot Officers John Urwin-Mann, a Canadian, and John Wigglesworth, were scrambled to patrol base. At 17.25 hrs, Blue Section intercepted three Ju 88s off Trevose Head, just north of base:

> The enemy was engaged by attack out of the sun and Flight Lieutenant Blake destroyed one Ju 88, Pilot Officer Urwin-Mann destroyed one Ju 88, and Pilot Officer Wigglesworth stated that he discharged all his ammunition into the third aircraft without apparent result. The aircraft attacked by Flight Lieutenant Blake blew up in the air, and Pilot Officer Urwin-Mann followed his Ju 88 down to sea-level. On the way down the crew appeared to throw out everything they could. They also released two streamers. Five men got out after the aircraft reached sea-level. Pilot Officer Urwin-Mann went back an hour or so later but no trace of the crew could be seen. It is not known whether they were rescued [ORB].

These two Ju 88s belonged to *Kustenfliegergruppe* 806, a coastal reconnaissance unit primarily reporting on British ports and shipping movements – and hence why a *Kriegsmarine* officer was a member of each crew. In the case of these two aircraft, both crews were lost.

So ended what was actually a costly day for the enemy: twelve Do 17s and Ju 88s were lost on operations, while others returned to base damaged.

Throughout daylight hours, ninety-two Coastal Command crews flew forty-seven anti-invasion and submarine patrols in addition to various reconnaissance sorties and convoy escorts. By night, Blenheims of 53 Squadron successfully attacked Caen airfield while those of 59 Squadron hit Abbeville aerodrome's petrol dump, and Swordfish dropped mines off the Dutch coast. Bomber Command's daylight operations were hampered by poor weather over the Continent, leading to most aircraft aborting, but airfields were attacked in the Netherlands, Belgium, France and the Channel Islands; a bridge at Paderborn was also hit. The worsening weather, however, led to all nocturnal Wellington, Blenheim and Whitley operations being scrubbed, but Hampdens went ahead with their raids on German industrial targets.

The 'Morale' of the British people, the Daily Intelligence Report, tells us, 'continues high'. One reason was Churchill's famous speech of the previous day, which was 'received extremely well', according to all reports. From Northern Ireland comes the comment that it is the most forceful and heartening he has yet made. Newcastle reports that it has created a strong feeling of confidence. Two Bristol verbatim reports are as follows:

'Everyone feels now that, come what will, we are top dogs; the past week has shown that we shall win no matter what slight doubts there were before.'

'Bristol has implicit trust in Churchill. If he says things are all right, Bristol people know they are all right; if he says they are bad, they know they are bad.'

Some reports received from the south-west, however, (Weston-super-Mare), were more cautious, suggesting that 'the Premier was a little too optimistic'. Morale in London, though, was reportedly 'excellent' and 'Churchill's speech yesterday, particularly his reference to the RAF, thought to be completely right – epitomises the feeling of the country'. North-Midland reports described 'RAF successes' as 'stimulating', while criticising that 'there has been no disclosure of the number of RAF machines destroyed on the ground', and, buoyant though the mood in London was generally, from the capital came doubt 'about the accuracy of German air losses'. Conversely, the Head of the United States Military Mission in Britain, reported back to Washington that the RAF's estimates of German losses were 'on the conservative side'.

Pilot Officer Hugh 'Cocky' Dundas had flown south from Leconfield with 616 Squadron on 19 August 1940, full of joyful enthusiasm following the unit's part in the defeat of *Luftflotte* 5 four days previously. At bomb-damaged Kenley, the mood was more sombre: 'Our arrival coincided with a couple of day's break in the Battle. We sat at readiness throughout the long daylight hours from early morning to late evening. We scrambled once or twice but made no contact with the enemy.'

Things would imminently change for Pilot Officer Dundas and 616 Squadron.

By this time, Fighter Command, and indeed the RAF, was very much changed from the pre-war 'Strawberries and cream and fruitcake for tea' days of the small, professional, service. Starting with the 1936 Expansion Plan, many adventurous and aviation-minded young men from the Commonwealth had taken Short Service Commissions, and these men, from New Zealand, Australia, Canada and South Africa, had already begun changing the RAF's identity, and now volunteers from the occupied lands and America significantly contributed to that process. Indeed, things would never be the same again.

Squadron Leader Peter Townsend:

85 Squadron, like every other, save the homogeneous Polish and Czech units, was a marvellous amalgam of men from Britain and the Commonwealth. Whatever our differences in origin and rank, our view from the cockpit, alone, miles above the earth, was identical. Though we fought wing-tip to wing-tip, each one of us had to fly and fight, and if need be, die alone. It was this sense of isolation and solitude in the air that united us so closely on the ground.

One of those men from the Commonwealth was the legendary South African 'Sailor' Malan, who had led 74 'Tiger' Squadron from Hornchurch on 14

August 1940 to re-fit in 12 Group, first at Wittering, then at Kirton-in-Lindsey. There, the squadron received and trained new pilots, including three former 142 Squadron Battle pilots who, on this day, reported to Squadron Leader Malan; among them was Pilot Officer Roger Boulding:

Operationally, I first flew Fairey Battles with 52 Squadron at Upwood, Kidlington and Benson, then with 98 Squadron at Hucknall before going to France with 142 Squadron as part of the AASF. When things turned a bit sour over there I managed to escape, flying back to England from Dieppe in a Tiger Moth, landing at Hawkinge on 22 May 1940. I remember that on that day Boulogne Harbour was being heavily dive-bombed.

Of course, during the summer of 1940, the RAF needed fighter pilots, to make good losses suffered in France and already during the Battle of Britain, which started in July. I therefore answered the call and, much to my delight, converted to Spitfires ... I was posted to 74 Squadron, the famous 'Tigers', at Kirton-in-Lindsey, where the Squadron was re-forming after involvement in the Dunkirk air fighting and early stage of the Battle of Britain. Our CO was the highly successful fighter pilot and leader 'Sailor' Malan. I first flew a Spitfire the day after my arrival on the Squadron.

Also joining the 'Tigers' that day, from 7 OTU at Hawarden, were two young New Zealanders, Pilot Officers Wally Churches from Auckland, and Wanganui's Bob Spurdle:

Wally and I stood before Sailor Malan and gazed at our new CO with deep respect. 'You pilots will be trained hard in the next few weeks. Your life expectancy will be in direct ratio to your ability to learn ... This is a famous Squadron and I expect you both to remember it. In the last war, Major Mannock won the VC flying for 74. He shot down seventy-three enemy aircraft. Soon you too will have plenty of targets. I'm sure you'll do well!'

Spurdle also remembered, however, how he and fellow colonial Wally Churches were referred to by certain of the British 'Tigers' as 'coloured troops' (this derogatory moniker was also used by the socially elite AAF officers of 601 Squadron, the so-called 'Millionaire's Mob', when referring to regular RAF officers). Spurdle also noted that their fellow 'newbies', namely Pilot Officers Boulding, Franklin and Ricalton, all being British, were 'more readily assimilated' into 74 Squadron. At the time, Britain remained a strictly hierarchical society, and naturally the services reflected this. Spurdle also observed that while 74 Squadron had 'a tremendous élan in the air', it was:

a curiously divided and unhappy unit on the ground. With Malan we would have flown anywhere against anything, but 74's curse was, in my opinion, the presence of several AAF types, who affected longer than regulation hair and tended to treat menials and pilot officers as they must have treated 'fags' at their public schools [younger boys used as servants] ... In a subtle way we 'Colonials' and the new young British recruits, unless 'well connected', were largely excluded from this kind of old boys' club and felt it keenly.

Flight Sergeant George Unwin, 19 Squadron:

I had known Brian Lane since he arrived on the Squadron to command 'A' Flight shortly after war broke out. In the air, we were as one and flew together often. We were friends – but, because Brian was an officer and I was an NCO, so we were segregated on the ground and never socialised.

Sergeant Reg Johnson, 222 Squadron:

Relationships between NCO pilots and officer pilots in our Squadron were formal, based mainly upon respect for each other's abilities and commitments. Of course, many friendships did not last for long due to our heavy losses. Pilot Officer Laurie Whitbread, for example, was an established member of the Squadron when I joined it in April 1940, and during the following weeks and months, he proved himself to be a pleasant and friendly young man. We spent many hours together in conversation at dispersal. We spent many hours together flying in Squadron training, often wing tip to wing tip. There was definitely, in our Squadron and the RAF generally, a social barrier between officer and NCO pilots. Pilot Officer Whitbread, whom I never knew as 'Laurie', overcame this with natural charm, and was at ease with all ranks. He never lost face because of it and we became firm friends. We 'enjoyed' a number of Squadron flying adventures together at Kirton and, of course, suffered a number of more traumatic incidents in at Hornchurch.

And 'traumatic incidents' there were indeed ahead.

Thursday, 22 August 1940

The instructions issued by Air Vice-Marshal Park to his sector controllers on 19 August 1940 underlined the continued concern regarding fighting over the sea – which, given that Britain is an island nation surrounded by water, was hardly surprising. What is mystifying, however, is why provision for an efficient air sea rescue service was not included in the System of Air Defence. Instead, downed airman had to rely upon volunteer lifeboat crews and coincidentally nearby fishing or naval vessels – or the fourteen RAF high-speed launches. Conversely, the Luftwaffe already had its floatplane-equipped *Seenotdienst* rescue service, and enemy aircrew were far better equipped to survive in the water long enough to be rescued, with superior life-preserving vests, fluorescein marker dye, and dinghies. Coastal and Bomber Command crews faced long flights over water by both day and night, causing the latter's chief, Air Marshal Charles 'Peter' Portal, in his unpublished May 1940 dispatch on the Norwegian campaign, to urge the Air Ministry to reduce the strain imposed by long flights over water by providing his aircrews with the best possible distress and survival equipment. In the last three weeks of July 1940, 220 RAF aircrew were either killed or reported missing – many over the sea. This prompted Air Vice-Marshal Park to collaborate with Vice-Admiral Bertram Ramsay at Dover to organise a local rescue service comprising light naval craft, RAF high-speed launches and Lysander aircraft. The value of this combined services approach was rapidly apparent, leading to a significant Air Ministry meeting on 22 August 1940.

Air Publication 3232, which provides a comprehensive history of RAF 'Air/Sea Rescue' during the Second World War, comments thus regarding the significance of this date:

> the Deputy Chief of the Air Staff [Air Vice-Marshal A.T. Harris] called a meeting at the Air Ministry to discuss a draft organisation for rescue craft. This meeting was attended by the Director of Small Vessels Pool [Admiral Sir L.G. Preston] and other Admiralty, Coastal and Fighter Command representatives. It was decided to combine the skeleton rescue organisation run by the high-speed launches of Coastal Command with the rescue functions of the Naval Auxiliary Patrol, and to place RAF rescue craft under the operational control of the local naval authorities. It was agreed that the RAF should be responsible for organising the necessary air search and for informing the naval authorities of the area being searched. Approval was given to the use of twelve Lysander aircraft, already borrowed unofficially from Army Co-operation Command, and which were now to be placed under the operational control of Fighter Command. It was intended that these aircraft should now be stationed at various fighter stations along the coast to conduct searches within a twenty mile radius from the coast, any air search beyond this radius being undertaken by operational aircraft. As a result of these decisions, special liaison officers were appointed to HQ, 10 and 11 Fighter Groups to assist in handling the search operations. Thus, nearly twelve months after the outbreak of war, the first steps were taken towards the formation of an organisation specifically allotted the task of sea rescue.

Clearly, this was a long overdue step in the right direction.

Exactly one month previously, the German labour organisation, *Todt*, had begun work on installations around Calais for heavy artillery pieces. By the end of that month, the first battery, *Siegfried*, was installed south of Cap Gris-Nez. Other batteries of 15, 12, 11 and 8-inch guns were soon situated north of Boulogne, at Calais, and Cap Blanc-Nez. Between 08.00 and 09.00 hrs on Thursday, 22 August, Convoy TOTEM was negotiating the dangerous Dover Strait and fired upon by these German batteries. At first, the sailors assumed they were being attacked by aircraft, but none could be seen. At 08.25 hrs, Squadron

Leader Mike Crossley and four other 32 Squadron Hurricanes scrambled from Hawkinge to protect TOTEM, subsequently confirming that the trouble was actually being caused by shelling from the Germans' long-range guns – a new development indeed.

Sergeant Bill Green, 501 Squadron:

I remember we were patrolling convoys going through the Dover Straits, and one day we were orbiting over this convoy when I saw a huge splash in the middle of it. I immediately suspected that a bomber had crept in, over the top of us, but there was no sign of any aircraft at all; I would have been angry if there had been, because we should have seen it. We spent most of our time in the air 'rubber-necking', which is to say looking through an orbit of 360°, up and down, all the time, constantly, especially the rear, to ensure that we were not bounced by enemy aircraft. Anyway, that evening I learned that the splash was caused by the Germans lobbing their first shell from the French coast.

According to the *Times'* report of the following day, 'The warships escorting the convoy at once laid smoke screens to conceal the convoy from the enemy. Although some shells fell fairly close to the ships, no ship of the convoy or escort was hit or received damage.' Some hundred shells, in fact, were fired at TOTEM, a Berlin spokesman insisting that 'the long-range guns mounted on the Channel and Atlantic coasts were firing merely for practice'. During the day, thirteen Blenheims of 2 Group Bomber Command were sent to attack the gun battery near Cap Gris-Nez and airfields in the Pas-de-Calais but bad weather caused eleven aircraft to abort. Of the two which pressed on, one bombed Merville aerodrome while the other returned with valuable photographs of the enemy's long-range artillery. The batteries failure to damage TOTEM, however, inevitably led to German aerial activity.

At 05.35 hrs that morning, Sergeant George 'Dick' Collett flew with 54 Squadron's 'B' Flight from Hornchurch, led by Squadron Leader James 'Prof' Leathart DSO to Manston, to await events. Radar plots later confirmed enemy air activity over Calais, so between 11.25 and 12.05 hrs, 'B' Flight patrolled Manston as a precautionary defensive measure, but no raid developed. At lunchtime, however, TOTEM was attacked by the Me 110s of precision bombing unit *Erprobungsgruppe* 210, escorted by Me 109s. In response, at 12.35 hrs, 54 Squadron's 'B' Flight was scrambled, and battle was joined off Deal. In the ensuing combat, although no German losses correlate to these claims, 'Sergeant Norwell, at "home" again with his 109s, destroyed one, Pilot Officer Hopkin attacked an Me 110 head-on and destroyed it, and Flight Lieutenant Gribble left a 109 in a somewhat unenviable position – trying to do a flick stall at 500ft [ORB].' 'B' Flight were the only RAF fighters involved in this action, which successfully prevented any damage to TOTEM. 'A' Flight hurried to the scene, scrambling just eleven minutes after 'B' Flight, but arrived to find an empty sky, the fast and furious action already over. Afterwards, the Spitfires returned to Hornchurch in ones and twos – except Sergeant Collett (Spitfire R6708, KL-S) who was missing.

According to a casualty report dated 24 August 1940:

No 54 Squadron were off from Manston to intercept enemy aircraft off Deal. The Squadron became engaged in a dogfight and during the course of this action Sergeant Collett's aircraft was seen diving towards the sea. Since the rendering of signal on 22 August, no news has been received of the missing pilot and the aircraft was presumed lost in the sea.

The 54 Squadron diary added that it was 'believed that he went down with his aircraft, which sank off Deal'.

Sergeant Collett's Spitfire had undoubtedly been shot down by an Me 109 from I/*Lehrgeschwader* 2, which provided *Erprobungsgruppe* 210's escort. The two claims with the best fit time-wise (Continental time being an hour ahead) are those by *Unteroffizier* Werner Götting (1/LG 2) for a Spitfire in the Dover area at 13.35 hrs, his first combat victory, and *Oberfeldwebel* Hermann Staege (2/LG2), for his fourth 'kill' in the same area at 14.05 hrs. In addition to Dick, Sergeant Corfe of 610 Squadron was shot down in combat with Me 109s over Folkestone, crash-landing at Hawkinge, at 14.15 hrs. It is likely, therefore, that these German pilots were responsible for shooting down the two sergeant-pilots, although exactly which is impossible to say.

Immediately, Dick's father was telegrammed with the bad news, the devastating content confirmed by an official letter:

In confirmation of my telegram of today's date, I regret to inform you that your son No 745500 Sergeant George Richard Collett of No 54 Squadron, Royal Air Force, is missing, the aircraft of which he was the pilot and sole occupant having failed to return to its base on the 22nd August 1940, after an operational flight.

This does not necessarily mean that he is killed or wounded. I will communicate with you again immediately I have any further news and would be obliged if you, on your part, would write to me should you hear anything of your son.

In conveying this information to you, may I assure you of the sympathy of the Royal Air Force with you in your anxiety.

As time went on, without further news of his missing son, George Collett's 'anxiety' can only be imagined. Sadly, any hope that Dick remained alive was crushed on 6 January 1941, with the arrival of another official letter:

With reference to my letter dated 22 August 1940, it is my painful duty to inform you that according to a telegram from the International Red Cross,

Geneva, quoting official information from Berlin, your son No 745500 Sergeant George Richard Collett of No 54 Squadron, Royal Air Force, previously reported as 'missing' is now reported 'missing, believed killed in action'.

In conveying this information to you, may I assure you of the sympathy of the Royal Air Force with you in your anxiety.

On 18 February 1942, another letter arrived, confirming that Dick's body had been buried at Haamstede, Zeeland, Holland. This, however, prompted a further enquiry from George, dated 21 February, inquiring as to whether his son had 'crashed in Holland', or had 'his body washed up from the sea on the Holland coast'. The latter had in fact been the case. Eventually, the current had carried Dick across the North Sea, washing the young pilot's remains ashore at Haamstede, on Schouwen Island in the province of Zeeland, where he was buried. The following year, on 14 August 1942, further information arrived, this time from the 'Wounded, Missing and Relatives Department' of the British Red Cross, informing Mr Collett that certain personal effects had been recovered with Dick's body, namely a chequebook, a cigarette case, 'RAF identity paper', two lead pencils, £1.10s, a pocketbook, 'different papers', a calendar and two postage stamps. The letter concluded:

> The Dutch Red Cross have expressly asked us to convey their sympathy to the relatives of our airmen who have lost their lives in Holland, and we should like to tell you of the many intimations reaching us of loyal tributes paid by the Dutch people themselves who have covered the graves with flowers and tend them carefully.

In March 1948, a further communication arrived from the Air Ministry, explaining to Mr Collett that the Graves Registration and Enquiry Service had exhumed Dick from Haamstede, reinterring his remains in the British War Cemetery at Bergen-Op-Zoom, 'where facilities are available' for the 'proper care and maintenance' of graves 'in perpetuity, by the Imperial War Graves Commission'.

Today, the grave of 24-year-old Sergeant George Richard 'Dick' Collett can be found at Bergen-Op-Zoom, some 20 miles north-west of Antwerp, in the British War Cemetery there, immaculately maintained by the Commonwealth War Graves Commission. The cemetery contains the graves of 1,189 identified casualties, 116 known only 'unto God'.

Dick's headstone bears a poignant epitaph:

Beloved son of GL Collett & Elizabeth M Collett
Till We Meet Again

Owing to the weather and *Reichsmarschall* Göring reorganising his fighter groups, Me 109 operations had been significantly curtailed since 18 August 1940. At

13.00 hrs on 22 August, however, Squadron Leader John Ellis DFC led all four sections of 610 Squadron up from Biggin Hill to patrol Folkestone – where the Spitfires were 'attacked from out of the sun by about twenty Me 109s. E/A made one attack and continued their dive into cloud [ORB].' This was a classic tactic of the German fighter pilots, relying on height, sun and surprise, attacking in a single, high-speed, diving pass – and away – aptly described by 19 Squadron's Sergeant David 'Little Boy' Cox as a 'dirty dart'. So fast was the enemy's pass that only Flying Officer Fred Gardiner and Sergeant Ron Hamlyn managed to return fire, albeit without effect. Sergeant Douglas Corfe, however, was shot down in flames, crashing at Hawkinge, although fortunately the pilot was unhurt. It is likely that, like 54 Squadron, 610 Squadron had been ambushed by I/LG 2, *Oberleutnant* Herbert Ihlefeld of 2/LG 2 claiming two Spitfires off Dover at the material time.

At 12.50 hrs, Flight Lieutenant James Sanders DFC scrambled from Kenley with 'B' Flight of 615 Squadron to patrol Deal, where, at 13.15 hrs, Pilot Officer Douglas Hone's 'machine was considerably damaged by what appeared to be a Hurricane [ORB].' Fortunately the pilot was unhurt and safely crash-landed near Deal. Upon return to Kenley, the remainder of 'B' Flight were delighted to discover that the squadron had been released from 13.00 hrs for a full – and rare – twenty-four hours. That evening, however, the Prime Minister and Mrs Churchill visited the station – an occasion 615 Squadron therefore missed, although the Canadian commander of 'A' Flight, Flight Lieutenant Lionel Gaunce, and a non-flying member of the squadron, Flying Officer Stern, remained on site and were introduced. Such morale-boosting visits to RAF stations by VIPs were commonplace throughout the Battle of Britain – most notably by Churchill and Prince George, Duke of Kent, the Honorary Commodore of 500 'County of Kent' Squadron of the AAF and who served as a group captain with Training Command.

The presence of an enemy reconnaissance bomber over the Thames Estuary area during the afternoon of 22 August, however, was ominous. No.32 Squadron's Hurricanes were scrambled to patrol base, Biggin Hill, at 15.15 hrs before being vectored to intercept the snooper. Pilot Officer Rupert Smythe 'attacked a Do 215 [*sic*] at 10,000ft over the Estuary, getting in several bursts. Pilot Officer Barton confirms that it was damaged [ORB].' It would not be long before the raid arising from that reconnaissance sortie would be mounted.

There was also action that afternoon over the West Country and Solent. Exeter's 213 Squadron flying various patrols throughout the day. At 14.45 hrs, the Belgian Pilot Officer Jacques Philippart and Sub-Lieutenant William Moss, an FAA pilot, took off as Yellow Section with orders to patrol Exmouth. Philippart reported that at 15.30 hrs, five miles south of Exmouth he sighted a Ju 88 approaching from the south, which the Hurricane pair attacked: 'The E/A caught fire between the starboard engine and fuselage. He then dived into the sea in a large gliding turn. For members of the crew jumped out but only one parachute opened correctly.'

Pilot Officer Walter Beaumont, flying Green 2 of 152 Squadron, up from Warmwell, reported that at 15.35 hrs:

We saw a Ju 88 about ten miles SW of us when we were over Bristol at 20,000ft. E/A was heading West, very fast. Green 1 gave line astern but I overhauled and passed him in the chase. I closed to exactly 250 yards before opening fire and after first burst E/A starboard engine began to stream white. He then dived below cloud as I broke away. I dived through cloud and came out on the tail and gave another burst. E/A then appeared to be about to forced-land so I waited a while but as he continued low flying at about 50ft I chased and gave another burst from astern and slightly above and had to break away upwards and sideways. As I did so smoke filled my cockpit so I forced-landed two miles from E/A, which crashed and burnt out near Beaford.

This snooper belonged to 3(F)/121, three crew members being captured while the fourth, *Obergefreiter* W. Kuhweide, baled out too low and was killed.

At 16.50 hrs, Red Section of Warmwell's 152 Squadron, Pilot Officers Graham Cox, Richard Hogg and Fred Holmes, caught a lone Ju 88 off the Needles, which was promptly attacked from above and astern. The Ju 88 dived, pulling up just 10ft above the sea – but crashed a few seconds later. At 17.17 hrs, 152's Blue Section was scrambled. Blue 2, Pilot Officer Arthur Watson, became separated in cloud and so climbed to 25,000ft – where he found and attacked a Ju 88 ten miles south of Portland, knocking pieces off the port engine before losing the bomber in cloud at 5,000ft. Meanwhile, Blue 1, Pilot Officer Eric 'Boy' Marrs, and Blue 3, Pilot Officer Charles Warren, attacked a Do 17 'making for the coast at Portland. Both attacked and although they didn't see it crash, the Observer Corps reported a Do 17 in the sea and there is no doubt it was the E/A attacked by Blue 1 and 3 [ORB].'

During the evening, *Major* Adolf Galland, the new *Kommodore* of JG 26, had his first opportunity to lead his new command, the 'Schlageter' *Geschwader* providing an escort to Me 110s of *Erprobungsgruppe* 210 attacking Manston. As the raid was detected while incoming, the Spitfires of 65 Squadron hurriedly scrambled from the airfield. Among the formation was the Polish Waldyslaw Szulkowski, who was about to exact revenge for the death of his friend Flying Officer Franek Gruszka four days before:

I was … Blue 3 when we engaged many Me 109s over Dover at 20,000ft. I became separated from my Section and attacked one of the stragglers. Before he could attempt evasion I fired several bursts from 350 yards, closing to 100 yards, and this E/A burst into flames and crashed into the sea, where I saw it before turning back to base.

Pilot Officer David Glaser was also in action with 65 Squadron:

> I engaged one Me 109 and gave a four second burst from 250 yards, whereupon the Me 109 half-rolled down. I followed, and when it had regained level flight I gave another short burst followed by a second and longer one.
>
> The E/A took no evasive action and during the second burst there was a flash of flames from the port side of the fuselage, and smoke poured out. He then continued in a shallow dive and disappeared into clouds which were at about 10,000ft. Just before he entered cloud I overshot him and did a steep turn above him and observed E/A to be mottled grey, with orange wing tips and the usual black crosses outlined with white. I later found I was over the French coast.

The 109 was claimed as a 'probable'.

The fight, however, was far from one-sided. Sergeant Harold Orchard's Spitfire was seriously damaged when shot-up by an Me 109 over the Channel, although fortunately the pilot was unhurt and returned safely to Manston, as, apparently, did another 65 Squadron pilot whose details have gone unrecorded. Sergeant Michael Keymer, however, had also pursued the enemy back to France, chasing four Me 109s and eventually finding himself over Bazinghen – a village adjacent to the JG 26 base at Marquise. Sergeant Keymer was subsequently reported missing, and remained so, officially, until his grave was identified on 7 August 1946 by the RAF No 1 Missing Research & Enquiry Service:

> before the aircraft crashed the pilot fell out of his cockpit without a parachute. Examination of his body showed a bullet wound in his head, indicating he died in actual combat.
>
> The pilot's body was at first buried at the spot where it fell, and later disinterred and reburied in the village churchyard. The Germans made a cross from the metal of the aircraft on which is printed 'K9909 Star No 2'. The cross is inscribed in German 'Hier Ruht Ein Engl. Flieger Abgesch. 22.8.40' ['Here lies an English airman, fallen on 22 August 1940'].

The report, by Squadron Leader R. Laronde, confirmed that K9909 was the serial number of Sergeant Keymer's Spitfire, and that there was no doubt that he was the airman buried at Bazinghen churchyard, where the grave was 'well cared for'.

It was not until New Year's Eve 1946 that the Air Ministry notified the pilot's mother, Mrs B.W. Keymer, of Bentley, Hampshire, of the discovery and confirmation. To know, at last, that her son was no longer missing naturally gave some solace to her, Mrs Keymer responding on 5 January 1947, that 'It is a great help to know that he cannot have suffered too long and that his burial place is being cared for.'

The German pilots' combat claims arising from the skirmish with 65 Squadron in which Sergeant Keymer was shot down were 100 per cent accurate: *Oberleutnant* Gerhard Schöpfel, the new *Kommandeur* of III/JG 26, and both *Oberleutnant* Hans Krug and *Feldwebel* Wilhelm Philipp of 4/JG 26, all claiming Spitfires destroyed.

However, at 19.00 hrs on 22 August, as 65 Squadron tangled with JG 26 over the French coast, Manston was hit by *Erprobungsgruppe* 210: 'A further attack was made by a squadron of Me 109s and Me 110s. About seven bombs were dropped and hangars in east camp damaged. There were no casualties [ORB].'

At 18.45 hrs, fourteen Spitfires of 616 Squadron had been scrambled from Kenley to patrol base at 5,000ft but, with the action over the Channel and Manston in mind, were soon vectored to patrol Hawkinge at 15,000ft. No enemy aircraft were sighted, however, and so, flying in sections line astern, the squadron was ordered back to base. Over Dover, however, high-flying Me 109s ambushed Green Section; Pilot Officer Lionel 'Buck' Casson's Spitfire was hit in the wing by a 20mm cannon round but he returned to Kenley safely; Pilot Officer Hugh 'Cocky' Dundas had a more traumatic experience:

> Suddenly my aircraft was hit so hard that I assumed a heavy anti-aircraft shell was responsible. Thick white smoke filled the cockpit. I could see nothing, and as the Spitfire went into a spin, I was pressed, hard, against the side of my cockpit. I was terrified and just sat there thinking that this was the end, until a voice in my head told me to open the hood and get out, which I did. Centrifugal force still pressed me into the cockpit and I got stuck, half in, half out. With the ground perilously close I managed to fall clear. My parachute opened and I watched as my Spitfire exploded in a field. I landed a couple of hundreds away from my burning aircraft, my left leg was bleeding and my left shoulder was dislocated.

> The following day I discovered the humiliating truth: I had not been shot down by our own ack ack, as I thought, but by an Me 109 none of us had even seen.

Dundas had probably been ambushed and shot down by *Unteroffizier* Schildknecht of 8/JG 54. It was not a good start to 616 Squadron's Battle of Britain proper, but this scenario was not uncommon for squadrons new to the south-east as Pilot Officer Peter 'Sneezy' Brown of 611 Squadron explained: 'Chasing lone or unescorted formations of bombers about East Anglia or the North was entirely different to the pace of combat in the South. This was entirely due to the presence of Me 109s – and many squadrons found the transition traumatic.'

In this melee, Sergeant Phillip Wareing claimed an Me 109 destroyed, which was confirmed by Flight Lieutenant Denys Gillam, the commander of 616 Squadron's 'B' Flight, and brought the day's daylight fighting to an end.

The Spitfire still lacked cannon, and 19 Squadron's continued frustration with the unreliable Spitfire Mk IB, equipped with two 20mm Hispano-Suiza cannon – is evident from Squadron Leader Phillip Pinkham AFC's entry on 22 August 1940: 'Manoeuvring firing trial. Many stoppages. N(o) B(loody) G(ood)'.

On this day, another new squadron arrived in 11 Group from the North: Squadron Leader Philip Hunter's Defiant-equipped 264 Squadron, which flew in to Hornchurch. After the virtual annihilation of 141 Squadron on 19 July 1940, this decision remains somewhat difficult to comprehend. The tempo of the daylight battle was increasing, and yet the turreted fighter had already proved itself unsuitable as a daytime fighter. Nonetheless, soon after arriving in 11 Group the squadron was up patrolling Manston – fortunately without incident. Unfortunately, this would not last long.

That evening, at 21.00 hrs, the German K5 long-range railway guns near Calais, having failed to hit convoy TOTEM earlier in the day, began shelling the port of Dover. It was estimated that over thirty shells had hit the town, seriously injuring seven civilians, and damaging properties in Maison Dieu Road, Cherry Tree Avenue and Valley Road. The local gasworks was also hit, shutting off the town's supply, and St Barnabas church was also badly damaged – little wonder, then, this south-eastern corner of Kent was known as 'Hellfire Corner'.

Finally, the day fighting closed with an evening attack by five Aalborg-based Ju 88s on Convoy TOPAZ off the Scottish coast, but no hits were recorded.

As usual, Coastal Command had flown the usual round of patrols and reconnaissance flights, and PRU Spitfires reported the presence of barges and fifteen seaplanes in Boulogne harbour – two of which He 59 *Seenotdienst* machines were badly damaged during the day by heavy seas. That night, Coastal Command reached out to attack Luftwaffe airfields in the Pas-de-Calais. No.53 Squadron, based at Detling, was commanded by Wing Commander Hugh 'Jumbo' Edwards, a highly successful oarsman and Olympian, having won two gold medals in a single day, and on this night he led six Blenheims to attack the German aerodrome at St Omer. Taking off just after 23.30 hrs, the Blenheims reached their target at 00.40 hrs, finding a flare path burning brightly on the runway. Despite intense flak from the South, HE bombs and incendiaries were dropped, causing fires which could be seen still burning as the Blenheims re-crossed the French coast over Calais, homeward bound. On leaving the target, however, Pilot Officer Dottridge's 'aircraft was hit in port mainplane, when flying low, and port wing lifted so that starboard wingtip struck ground. Air Observer helped pilot to hold aircraft on level course during flight home [ORB].' It was a lucky escape and all aircraft returned safely. Similarly, four Blenheims of 59 Squadron successfully bombed Dinard airfield and all returned safely. German airfields in the Pas-de-Calais were also harassed after dark by Bomber Command Blenheims, which also targeted the guns at Cap Gris-Nez. Wellingtons once more attacked industrial and railway targets in Germany, and Hampdens sowed mines off Lorient.

Daily Home Intelligence Report, South-Eastern (Tunbridge Wells):

Complains have been received from a number of villages because they have no sirens, and in country districts where there is perhaps not even a village constable there is a feeling that wardens should have more authority. Lorry drivers say that they cannot hear sirens above the noise of their engines … There is discontent among bus drivers and conductors at not being allowed to stop their buses in raids, as some had narrow escapes last Sunday. Country dwellers say the supply of sugar for jam making is considerably delayed. Reference in the press and by the public to the 'All Clear' instead of 'Raiders Passed' lead many Civil Defence workers to believe that if gas is used in air raids, people will remove their masks when the 'Raiders Passed' is sounded.

Friday, 23 August 1940

Again low cloud restricted air operations over England, but the Luftwaffe continued probing and putting the defences under pressure through the use of multiple small formations. Interception of these scattered raids over such a broad front was difficult, especially because cloud assisted the enemy's game of hide and seek. Consequently, such operations imposed a greater strain on the defenders than the Luftwaffe, and on no day during such conditions did Fighter Command collectively fly less than 400 sorties.

At 05.40 hrs, Squadron Leader Mike Crossley led 32 Squadron from Biggin Hill to operate from Hawkinge, landing at 06.00 hrs. At 06.55 hrs, Crossley led the squadron up on an uneventful patrol of base: 'No E/A encountered. Pilot Officer Pfeiffer crashed on landing at forward base [ORB].' Pfeiffer, a Polish pilot, was unhurt in the accident.

On 17 July 1940, 232 Squadron had been formed from elements of 3 Squadron at RAF Sumburgh, located on the southern tip of the remote Shetland Islands, and equipped with Hurricanes. At 08.55 hrs on 23 August 1940, Blue Section, comprising Flight Lieutenant Maurice Stephens DFC (Blue 1), commanding 232 Squadron, and Pilot Officers Joseph Hobbs (2) and Charles Jeffries (3) scrambled to intercept an X-Raid over Fair Isle. Stephens reported that at 09.10 hrs:

I sighted E/A flying West at 3,000ft in broken cloud. I put Blue 3 in line astern and dived to attack … opening fire at 200 yards and closing to fifty yards. I fired a series of short bursts with about half a ring deflection as the E/A swerved and attempted to gain the cloud. The E/A frequently entered cloud and I followed him through, opening fire again when he emerged. When all my ammunition was expended I broke away. Black smoke and flame were issuing from the port engine and white vapour from the starboard. I then went above cloud to drive the E/A down if necessary, and Blue 3 continued the attack. The E/A was observed to dive into the sea sending up a big column of smoke. No wreckage or survivors were visible – a heavy sea was running at the time.

The He 111, however, had returned fire, Stephens' Hurricane being hit by 'Armour Piercing bullets and what appeared to be large calibre cannon. Perspex hood slide shot and hood shattered. No.4 starboard gun mounting shattered. Tailplane front spar shot and bullet holes in rear part of fuselage.' Stephens returned safely to base, but no trace of the He 111 crew, belonging to *Wettererkundung*'s *Staffel* 1, was ever found. The kill was shared between Stephens and Jeffries – and was 232 Squadron's only combat of the Battle of Britain.

The next raider down was at 09.20 hrs when a *Stab* KG 2 Do 17, en route to attack factories in Coventry, fell victim to ground fire and crash-landed at Lodge Farm, Wickhambrook, in West Suffolk – the crew, which included the *Staffelkapitän*, *Oberleutnant* H. Hellmers, were all captured.

Due to the weather over England, things went quiet until 16.05 hrs, when Blue Section of 152 Squadron, comprising just Flying Officer Richard Hogg (Blue 1) and an unknown Spitfire pilot, caught a Ju 88 at 4,000ft ten miles south of Worth Matravers:

> I was Blue 1 … as we crossed the coast going South at 3,000ft we sighted a Ju 88 1½ miles south-east of us. I informed Blue 2. After chasing it for two minutes I saw E/A dive into cloud. I was then at 800 yards. I followed E/A seeing it occasionally in broken cloud, finally I caught it in a clear patch and attacked from the quarter, firing a two-second burst, and again from astern, firing a three-second burst. Blue 2 then attacked. E/A had red crosses outlined in black.

No.152 Squadron records are notoriously poor, and Flying Officer Hogg's personal combat report, quoted above, is scant in detail – so it is surprising that the Ju 88 was claimed as destroyed. This could, however, have been the case, as a 9/LG 1 Ju 88 failed to return from a war flight over England, the crew of which were reported missing. That said, although no combat reports can be found, at 18.36 hrs Green Section of 602 Squadron, up from Westhampnett, 'attacked two separate Ju 88s. Pilot Officer Ritchie being involved in a collision with a Spitfire of another squadron, without serious damage to himself, although the pilot of the other baled out [ORB].' Indicating how impossible the historian's task sometimes is, no record can be found concerning the collision either.

Comparatively quiet though the day was for Fighter Command, it was a busy one for the *Jagdwaffe* across the Channel. Following Göring's Karinhall conference of 19 August, it had been decided to move practically all of *Luftflotte* 3's Me 109s to the Pas-de-Calais, to operate from temporary airfields. This gave *Generalfeldmarschall* Kesselring's *Luftflotte* 2 an overwhelming provision of escort fighters – but even so the Me 109s would only have sufficient fuel for twenty minutes of combat over London, the extreme limit of their range, even flying from the Pas-de-Calais.

RAF intelligence reported on the enemy fighter tactics:

> Escorting fighters are dispersed in various positions relative to the bomber formations they are protecting. During the early phase of the attacks on this country it was usual for the fighter escort to fly behind and several thousand feet above the bomber formation. If our fighters attacked the bombers, the escort would descend and attack them providing that they (the German fighters) were not outnumbered. If our fighters attacked the enemy fighter escort, the latter would usually form a self-defensive circle, thus ceasing to afford protection to the bombers which they were supposedly escorting.

> Heavy casualties suffered by the bombers led to a change of tactics involving an increase in escorting fighters with new dispositions relative to the bomber formations. Fighters were encountered ahead and on both flanks as well as above and behind the bombers and usually flying in closer proximity to the latter. On occasions the individual bomber units were found to be more spaced out with the fighters weaving among them. Accompanying formations of fighters have also been observed acting as remote escort or 'freelance' patrols flying at a great height above, and in the vicinity of, the bomber formations, but they have rarely taken offensive action.

With the amount of Me 109s now buzzing around the Pas-de-Calais and French coast, the invasion fleet being assembled in the harbours of Calais and Boulogne were better defended against air attack. During the early hours, Fairey Battle light-bombers of Bomber Command's 142 Squadron, based at Eastchurch and temporarily attached to Coastal Command, had paid a visit to the latter, but the raid was unsuccessful owing to technical problems and low cloud. Undeterred, at 18.25 hrs, six more of the squadron's Battles took off and attacked Boulogne again. So intense was the flak, however, that results were not observed – then, Me 109s of 6/JG 3 and 2/JG 26 pounced on the bombers. Sergeant Morse's aircraft was 'attacked by a He 113 [*sic*]. He 113 believed to be damaged after firing 300 rounds [ORB].' Pilot Officer Stevenson was also shot-up by a 109, crash-landing near Ashford with a wounded air gunner. Two Battles, however, failed to return, only one crewman of each aircraft surviving to become a prisoner of war; the other four all remain missing. It is reported that the Me 109 of *Unteroffizier* Gottfried Haferkorn of 2/JG 26, who was credited with the destruction of a Battle, was killed in a collision with an unspecified aircraft west of Boulogne, which may have been one of these lost bombers. Four Battles were correctly claimed by the enemy pilots, although two of 4/JG 26 each claimed a Defiant destroyed – but none of that type were involved, 141 Squadron having been withdrawn to Prestwick and 264 Squadron, although operating in 11 Group, just patrolled the Thames Estuary on this day and suffered no loss.

The day and night's other sorties by Bomber and Coastal Command followed the usual pattern, but apart from 142 Squadron's Battles there were no other losses to enemy action.

Daily Home Intelligence Report, London Region:

Reaction of housewives with houses destroyed at first thankfulness for one's own safety, then anxiety about future. Common questions: 'Who will pay for this damage? Where shall we live now? How shall I get my rations as my book is lost?'.

Petty pilfering, especially of fruit and vegetables in abandoned gardens, rife.

Saturday, 24 August 1940

With the host of lethal Me 109s now in the Pas-de-Calais, and the clock ever-ticking towards 15 September 1940 – the date set for unleashing Operation *Seelöwe* – improved weather ensured that, to coin a Churchillian phrase, 'the whole fury and might of the enemy' would now be hurled at Fighter Command. Indeed, as the Prime Minister later wrote, 'In the fighting between 24 August and 6 September, the scales tilted against Fighter Command.' German reconnaissance had confirmed that the majority of 11 Group's strength was now concentrated in the ring of sector stations around London – and it would be against those vital targets that the hammer blow would now fall: the Battle of Britain was entering its most critical phase.

The enemy had also increased the intensity and volume of nocturnal raids. On 16 August 1940, the German pathfinders, KGr 100, was transferred from *Luftflotte* 2 to *Luftflotten* 3 and Fliegerkorps IV, commanded by General Kurt Pflugbeil, based at Vannes. From there, this precision bombing unit was to attack British industry and ports, a most successful attack occurring during the night of 22/23 August 1940, when twenty-three pathfinding He 111s bombed and considerably damaged the Bristol Aeroplane Company at Filton, AA positions and a railway station – the glow of fires and explosions even being visible to the German aircrews through 10/10ths cloud. The following night, 23/24 August 1940, *Luftflotte* 3 began targeting the crucial western ports of Avonmouth, near Bristol, and Liverpool, this attack being delivered by eleven He 111s of I/KG 27. Over 200 enemy bombers, however, are believed to have operated over England that night, and apart from the specialist radio-beam equipped KGr 100's success, the majority of bombing caused little loss of life and no damage to military targets. Nonetheless, not least because Britain's night-fighting defences remained in their infancy, with dedicated and especially equipped aircraft yet to arrive on the scene, this nocturnal activity put the defenders under further pressure: some 160 sorties were flown by RAF night-fighters but only one resulted in contact – an inconclusive combat arising.

As Filton's No.4 Factory smouldered in the cold light of day, after an initially hazy start, the morning of 24 August 1940 was fine and clear. It was not over southern England that the Luftwaffe's first move was made, however, but over the East Coast, between Norwich and Norfolk, at 07.50 hrs. A small force of enemy bombers had managed to slip through undetected by RDF, dropping bombs west of Great Yarmouth, damaging public services. In response, at 07.20 hrs, Flight Lieutenant Howard 'Billy' Burton, the 1936 Cranwell Sword of Honour winner and commander of 'Clickety-Click's' 'B' Flight, scrambled to intercept with Sergeants Arthur Smith and Donald Campbell. The raiders, however, had been and gone before the Spitfires arrived on the scene, Burton recording in his log book that the section had only found a 'friendly Blenheim'.

To the south, simultaneously with the East Coast raid, RDF screens indicated the assembly of two substantial German forces behind Cap Griz-Nez. Immediately, RAF fighters were scrambled to cover the coastal airfields of Hawkinge, Manston, Rochford and Martlesham Heath. One of the enemy formations was then confirmed to have crossed the coast just before 08.15 hrs over Winchelsea, the other, again simultaneously, incoming over Folkestone. Meanwhile, even more enemy aircraft, doubtless fighters ready to cover the bombers' withdrawal, milled about over the Dover Straits. With the raiders' targets still unclear, as a precaution 615 Squadron was scrambled from Kenley, 501 from Gravesend and 56 went up from North Weald, representing a second line of defence should the enemy formations fight their way inland towards London's all-important sector stations. By 09.00 hrs, five further raids, each numbering less than twenty aircraft, crossed the south-east coast between Hastings and the North Foreland.

At 05.10 hrs, the Defiants of 264 Squadron had left Hornchurch to operate from Manston, refuelling there and remaining at readiness. At 08.30 hrs, while still refuelling, the squadron was scrambled to patrol base:

> Flight Lieutenant Campbell Colquhoun had difficulty in starting his engine and was late in taking off. Visibility was not very good and he sighted two aircraft which he took to be Nos 2 and 3 of his Section. They were, however, He 113s [sic] and they immediately attacked and his aircraft (L7013) was hit just behind the turret by an explosive shell which ignited the Verey cartridges. He took evasive action and returned without further damage to Manston. During the patrol other He 113s [sic] dived upon the Squadron but none of our aircraft were damaged [ORB].

The first RAF fighter pilot to engage the enemy, at 08.30 hrs, was Pilot Officer Geoffrey 'Sammy' Allard DFM, who, when flying near Ramsgate at 15,000ft:

> sighted a lone Me 109 at 1,000ft below him which was climbing to join a formation of twenty or thirty Me 109s flying above. Pilot Officer Allard turned to the right and dived and pulled up under E/A: he fired two short bursts at about 250 yards range and saw a cloud of white smoke come from the E/A. The Me 109 then dived out of control with black smoke being emitted and it was finally seen to crash into the sea three miles from Ramsgate. Pilot Officer

Allard dived after E/A, witnessing the crash as he was pursued by some of the other Me 109s. He landed at Croydon 0908 hrs [ORB].

It was believed at the time that Pilot Officer James Lockhart's Hurricane was damaged by the Dover A barrage, but more likely he was the victim of a surprise attack by *Oberleutnant* Josef 'Joschko' Fözö, *Staffelkapitän* of 4/JG 51, who claimed a Hurricane destroyed at the material time, north-west of Dover. The British pilot crash-landed at Hawkinge, wounded, and was admitted to Victoria Hospital, Deal.

Having scrambled from Biggin Hill at 07.58 hrs, the Spitfires of 610 Squadron were also off Ramsgate, Sergeant Ronnie Hamlyn's combat report timed between 08.25 and 08.30 hrs, ten miles south-east of Ramsgate:

I was Yellow 2. I saw three waves of bombers approaching the South Coast. I attacked one of these waves in which there were about fifteen–eighteen Ju 88s at about 300–350 yards. I received a large amount of cross fire but I didn't open fire until 250 yards. I gave a two second burst and saw one Ju 88 dive away from the rest and I watched it crash into the sea. I did not break away, but throttling back an Me 109 overshot me and pulled up right in front at about 150 yards. I opened fire and saw it starting to smoke. I followed it down and saw it also hit the sea.

It was Hamlyn's lucky day – which was far from over.

The remainder of 610 Squadron became split up in the clash, which occurred in a cloudless sky with twenty miles visibility. Sergeant Stanley Arnfield's Spitfire was hit, probably by *Leutnant* Ernst Terry of *Stab* I/JG 51, who claimed a Spitfire destroyed at 08.35 hrs (BST). Arnfield baled out, breaking an ankle in a heavy landing and as a result of which he joined Pilot Officer Lockhart in Deal's Victoria Hospital.

The brief actions fought by 85 and 610 Squadrons off Ramsgate were actually the only contacts reported with these formations of raiders. Bizarrely, considering the apparent number of Ju 88s involved, no targets were attacked, the enemy was merely on reconnaissance – which seemed a huge amount of unnecessary effort. By 09.25 hrs the enemy had withdrawn, and RDF screens were blank – but not for long.

At 09.35 hrs, the Hurricanes of 501 Squadron took off from Gravesend, bound for Hawkinge, and at 10.00 hrs, 54 Squadron's Spitfires left Hornchurch to patrol Dover. By this time reports were incoming from RDF stations that three German formations of up to twenty aircraft each were forming up between Boulogne and Dunkirk, and two small enemy groups were over the Dover Strait. At 10.25 hrs, one raiding party crossed the Kentish coast near Hythe, another between Folkestone and Dover. According to 501 Squadron, the enemy bombers were Dorniers, and 'Red 1 entered into a beam attack on the bombers and the formation was broken up. Enemy jettisoned bombs before turning East [ORB].'

Sergeant James 'Ginger' Lacey subsequently claimed a Dorner damaged, and the Polish Sergeant Anton Glowacki was credited with an Me 109 destroyed north-west of Dover. Another Pole, Pilot Officer Pawel Zenker failed to return. Shot down over the Channel, no trace of the 25-year-old was ever found.

At 09.50 hrs, 54 Squadron had scrambled from Hornchurch, the earlier dawn patrol over base having passed uneventfully. This, however:

> was followed by the first wave of enemy aircraft – approximately 200 strong. The Squadron patrolled Manston and saw large bomber formations but were unable to attack them. They did, however, engage stragglers and 'spotter' aircraft. Pilot Officer Gray destroyed one Me 110; Flying Officer McMullen and Sergeant Robbins each destroyed one Me 109 [ORB].

The engagement took place over Dover, Folkestone and the Channel, Flying Officer Desmond McMullen reporting that:

> I encountered four Me 109s circling at 26,000ft above the coast at Dover. I thought that they were waiting for the bombers to come back so thy could form the protective escort. I followed these round until one became separated from the four and let him get well away. I then followed.
>
> The Me 109 could not have seen me because I attacked from above and astern (range 100 yards closing to 50 yards), and E/A took no evasive action. Large pieces fell off the 109 and black smoke poured from the engine. I followed it down and it crashed into the sea just short of the French coast, near Calais.

No.54 Squadron ORB:

> Flight Lieutenant Gribble put the port engine of an Me 110 out of action. The Squadron Leader dived on being attacked by three Me 109s and on coming up found himself immediately underneath forty Ju 88s in 'Herring Bone' formation. He sprayed the leading five, but did not stay to see the result. The Squadron kept the whole of the fighter escort busily engaged.

Pilot Officer Alan Campbell, a Canadian, was shot-up and wounded, but safely regained base, which the squadron diarist considered to be 'a good piece of work'. Campbell was a lucky man: a bullet had passed clean through one of his flying helmet's two earphones.

Once more, however, the Germans' intention was mystifying, because despite the presence of many bombers, still no major attack occurred. Soon after these formations withdrew, RDF indicated large enemy formations over the Dover Straits – which made no immediate offensive move. The 11 Group Controller, however, had squadrons patrolling the coastal airfields of Hawkinge, Manston and Rochford, and the port of Dover. By 11.30 hrs the Germans were flying west, and so 264 Squadron's Defiants were scrambled from Hornchurch to reinforce the Manston patrol, while 65 Squadron went up from Rochford to relieve the Hurricanes of 151 Squadron, also operating from Rochford, which had been patrolling the Manston area. Before their relief arrived, however, at 11.30 hrs 151 was bounced over Ramsgate by 'Twelve Me 109s with a few He 113s [*sic*] thrown in [ORB].' The enemy fighters were from the northerly escort fighters, comprising the whole of JG 26, led by *Major* Adolf Galland, which, together with other fighters to the south, protected the bombers situated between them. Flight Lieutenant Dick Smith was shot-up, fortunately returning his damaged fighter safely to base, but two Hurricanes were destroyed: Pilot Officer Kenneth Debenham was shot down in flames and baled out, badly wounded, later requiring reconstructive surgery at East Grinstead's Royal Victoria Hospital, and Sergeant Gordon Clarke, who crash-landed at Plumford Farm, Ospringe, and admitted to hospital with wounds which kept him out of action until 6 October 1940. The damage was done by III/JG2 6's *Oberleutnant* Joachim Müncheberg, *Kapitän* of 7/JG 26, and *Leutnant* Gustav 'Micky' Sprick of 8/JG 26.

The southerly German fighters were engaged by Squadron Leader John Ellis's 610 Squadron, which had scrambled at 10.35 hrs, for the second time that morning, with orders to patrol Biggin Hill, then Gravesend before being vectored to Dover. At 11.35 hrs, the Spitfires tangled with six Me 109s of JG 51; having already scored earlier in the day, Sergeant Ronnie Hamlyn, Yellow 2, struck again:

> I was attacked while in formation over Dover. After a short dogfight I got on to the Me 109's tail and he at once flew to France. I followed and while I was chasing him I saw another dogfight between two Spitfires and one Me 109. The Me 109 went down smoking badly but carried on flying, eventually going into the sea off Cap Gris-Nez. By this time I had got within range of the Me 109 I was chasing but did not open fire until I had crossed over the coast into France, after about three more bursts I saw it go out of control with smoke pouring out and watched it crash in a field. I did not experience any AA fire while over France. The Me 109 I saw crash into the sea was destroyed by Flying Officer Lamb – Yellow Leader.

The Me 109 destroyed by Sergeant Hamlyn was very likely a machine of II/JG 51, the pilot of which who forced-landed at Marquise, and that shot down by Flying Officer Peter Lamb probably *Unteroffizier* Kroll of 9/JG 51, who was killed. A 'probable' was claimed by Pilot Officer Eric Alduous, but these successes were not without loss to 610 Squadron: Pilot Officer Donald Gray was shot down and crash-landed, wounded, near Shepherdswell (although the confused timings of German combat claims makes it impossible to be certain who was responsible) and admitted to Waldershare Hospital.

AA gunners in Dover reported that the formation now overhead comprised thirty Ju 88s and their Me 109 escort. The guns banged away but two bombs exploded in Dover – one causing minimal damage in Malvern Meadow, while the other scored a direct hit on 31 Avenue Road. With 54 and 501 Squadrons in action overhead and the defending gunners firing one round after another, the resulting search party miraculously found a 6-month-old baby still alive in the debris, along with 6-year-old Pearl Tallent and 19-year-old Ruby Tallent. Ruby, the baby's mother and Pearl's sister, sadly, was dead. The nearby civilian airport was also damaged, as was Ramsgate's civil airfield, which was hit by sixty bombs. Heavy damage too was caused in Ramsgate town, which was hit by 150 bombs. The raiders then withdrew; however, although by 11.45 hrs south-east England was clear of the Luftwaffe, incoming threats were continuous and German aircraft were constantly over the Dover Strait – their intentions, of course, unknown to the 11 Group Controller. Indeed, the Group's Senior Fighter Controller, Wing Commander Lord Willoughby de Broke, commented that:

> The Group Controller's job was like a glorified game of chess, only infinitely more exciting and responsible as so much was at stake. The Germans would frequently put up 'spoof' raids with the deliberate intention of 'foxing' our controllers, so that squadrons were ordered to patrol lines only to find that the plots faded away as enemy aircraft dispersed back to their bases in northern-France. Our squadrons then had to land and refuel and sensing this, the Germans would follow their 'spoof' raid pretty quickly with a genuine one, which necessitated putting up fresh squadrons to meet it while others were refuelling.

This was exactly the scenario at 12.30 hrs – five enemy formations were identified between Dunkirk and Boulogne, but what were they doing? Were they a distraction, or assembling for a major raid? These were questions without answers.

At 11.30 hrs, Squadron Leader Phillip Hunter led the Defiants of 264 Squadron from Hornchurch with orders to patrol Manston, and at 11.50 hrs, Flight Lieutenant Alan Putt, commanding 'B' Flight, led 501 Squadron to patrol Hawkinge. Other coastal stations, however, also required protection, and so at 11.45 hrs, Squadron Leader John 'Tubby' Badger led a flight of 43 Squadron up from Tangmere to patrol base, while elements of Croydon's 111 Squadron, operating from Martlesham Heath, were up covering that forward airfield. Precious little time was given to react to attacks on these targets, and so these patrols were vital to their defence.

Just after 12.30 hrs, three German formations crossed the Kentish coast, two over Deal, one at Dover. Two of these raids were 'spoofs', however, and turned back to France soon afterwards – neither were engaged by RAF fighters. The remaining raid, comprising Ju 88s of KG 76, escorted by Me 109s of JG 51, headed for Manston.

Having patrolled over that aerodrome for an hour uneventfully, at 12.30 hrs, Squadron Leader Hunter had led Red, Blue and Green sections to:

pancake at Manston for a quick refuel, while Yellow Section remained above. At 1240 hrs Red, Blue and Green sections took-off to join Yellow Section, but before they had time to join up Manston was attacked by twenty Ju 88s escorted by Me 109s and He 113s [*sic*]. A Squadron Attack was impossible as sections had not had time to join up. It was found impossible to attack the Ju 88s in their dives, so individual combats developed as the enemy flattened out [ORB].

Pilot Officer David Whitley and his air gunner, Sergeant Robert Turner, of Yellow Section, were already up over Manston when the attack came in, as the pilot later reported:

> I saw twelve Ju 88s diving on Manston in a converging attack. I chased one and got under his port wing and started firing. His starboard engine then caught fire and the port engine issued forth smoke. My gunner saw the E/A burning hard and diving steeply. I was then attacked by Me 109s and received a cannon shell in the tail.

Taking evasive action, Pilot Officer Whitley retuned his crippled Defiant safely to base.

According to 264 Squadron records, Ju 88s were also claimed destroyed by Squadron Leader George Garvin and Flight Lieutenant Robert Ash, and Sergeants Edward Thorn and Fred Barker; a Ju 88 was claimed as damaged by Flying Officer William Knocker and Pilot Officer Frank Toombs.

Pilot Officer Eric Barwell, Green Leader, and his gunner, Sergeant Martin (no other details known), had urgently scrambled just before Manston was attacked, and dived to intercept the Ju 88s as bombs were released from 4,000ft, 'And was attacked by five He 113s [*sic*]. I got astern of the He 113s and fired 120 rounds at the second. It immediately burst into flames and dived into the sea.'

None of these claims can be confirmed, but the oil system of 6/JG 51's *Oberfeldwebel* Fritz Beek's Me 109 was damaged, forcing him to land in a field near East Langdon – the war for him being very much over, as he became a prisoner of war.

No.264 Squadron, however, had lost three aircraft and crews in the engagement. Pilot Officer Whitley confirmed having seen the Defiant of Pilot Officer Joseph Jones and William Ponting crash into the sea during the clash with Me 109s off Ramsgate – both remain missing; similarly, Flying Officer Ian Shaw and Sergeant Alan Berry had disappeared over the sea. Squadron Leader Phillip Hunter, and his air gunner, Pilot Officer Fred King, who had hurriedly taken-off just before the attack, and who 'had been in every engagement in which 264 Squadron have taken part, were last seen by the other pilots of Red Section chasing a Ju 88 at maximum throttle towards France: No news has so far been received of them [ORB].' Sadly, nor would it be.

Just after Manston was bombed, 501 Squadron's Hurricanes, diverted from their patrol of Hawkinge, arrived on the scene:

> The enemy fighter escorts were late in attacking our aircraft and the Squadron accounted for two Ju 88s [*sic*] destroyed [Pilot Officer Gibson and Sergeants Lacey and Glowacki] and two damaged [Flying Officer Witorzenc and Pilot Officer Dafforn], and one Me 109 destroyed [Sergeant Glowacki] [ORB].

Unfortunately, none of these pilots' personal combat reports appear to have survived, and, again, nor do German casualty records cross-reference – yet again illustrating the difficulty of reconstructing these events given available records are frequently contradictory or, indeed, incomplete. No.501 Squadron, however, had been able to attack the Ju 88s [*sic*] because 264 Squadron was occupying the Me 109s.

By 24 August 1940, Sergeant Green had just over eight hours flying time on the Hurricane:

> We were scrambled and vectored towards Manston. We were just pulling in behind the raiders, to attack, when I was hit by AA fire. My windscreen immediately became covered with black oil, and the engine was coughing. I turned away, back towards Hawkinge, realising that I was a non-combatant from that point onwards, pumped the undercarriage down and managed to land with a half-dead engine, which was only running some of the time. I put the aircraft down on Hawkinge but discovered that so much damage had been done to my undercarriage that the aeroplane finished up on its nose, with me looking almost vertically down at the ground. Anyway, I was safe and sound, not injured in any way, and continued flying. I must say that I was, and am, no hero. I was very mindful of the very dangerous activity in which we were engaged, and mindful that I could be seriously wounded or killed at any time. My overriding recollection is that while in the air I was very vigilant, very aware of the dangers of being attacked from behind or above.

In his log book, Sergeant Green recorded the incident as a 'Nasty prang'.

Manston, though, had been badly hurt:

> 1250 hrs: A very heavy bombing attack was made on the Station. There were seven fatal casualties, and one enemy aircraft was brought down by ground defences. Living quarters were badly damaged, and the presence of a number of unexploded bombs made it necessary temporarily to vacate the area. Later it was decided to evacuate permanently all administrative personnel and those not required in connection with Station defence and servicing of aircraft. Accommodation for evacuated personnel was found in Westgate [ORB].

Still, German aircraft maintained a presence over the Dover Straits, keeping the defenders on full alert in anticipation of further attacks – but which plotted formations would be 'spoofs' or actual raids? There was no way of knowing until it happened, so between 13.00 and 15.00 hrs, 11 Group's pilots flew approaching 100 sorties. The only squadron to engage the enemy during that time, though, was 32 Squadron, which had scrambled from Hawkinge to patrol base at 14.30 hrs. At 15.00 hrs, the Hurricanes clashed with elements of JG 26, at 20,000ft four miles north-west of Dover.

Flight Lieutenant Peter Brothers DFC:

> I was leading Blue Section ... when we were attacked by about twelve Me 109s which had been circling above us for some time. As we climbed up to them they climbed away and kept their distance until an opportune moment, when they dived on us. I fired short bursts at two or three and then lost them owing to blacking out. I climbed up to 20,000ft and engaged them again, and, managing to get onto the tail of one, I gave him two three second bursts. Part of his starboard wing came away and he dived into the sea about ten miles SE of Dover. I followed him down, then returned to base.

Sergeant Donald Aslin damaged an Me 109 which 'made off with smoke pouring from it [ORB]', but the balance sheet was even: two Hurricanes were shot down. Flying Officer Rupert Smythe – whose RAF career began as an Aircraft Apprentice in 1934 – was shot up and crash-landed at Lyminge; wounded, the pilot was admitted to Hammersmith's Royal Masonic Hospital. The Polish Pilot Officer Karol Pniak was shot down over Dover Harbour, and baled out safely (as so often happens, the sequence of this day's events are confused in the 32 Squadron ORB, but the chronology is correctly sequenced here); it would be literally minutes before he was back in action.

As 32 Squadron returned to Hawkinge, at 15.15 hrs, four more enemy formations were plotted by RDF gathering over the French side of the Channel, as usual between Dunkirk and Boulogne. No.54 Squadron was up over Hornchurch with an hour's petrol remaining, and 65 Squadron was in the Dover area, having been airborne for twenty minutes. Hawkinge was being covered by 501 Squadron, and 615 was up over Kenley. Fifteen minutes later it was clear that two major threats had developed: '30+' heading towards the Kentish coast at Dungeness, while a larger force approached the North Foreland and Essex. Two formations of fighters remained over the central Straits before milling around over coastal Kent between 15.50 and 16.15 hrs, thereby covering the bombers' withdrawal.

At 15.40 hrs, when patrolling over Greatstone, New Romney, 501 Squadron sighted the more southerly German formation, of some thirty Ju 88s and their fighter escort, inbound towards London at 13,000ft. Both the Hurricanes and enemy fighter escort positioned themselves with the sun behind them before a general skirmish began, during which 501 Squadron claimed the destruction of four Ju 88s, another damaged, plus an Me 109 destroyed and one damaged, although these claims cannot easily be confirmed from the German records available. Having pursued the enemy inland, however, Pilot Officer Keith Aldridge one of 501's original auxiliary pilots, was shot down and baled out near Maidstone, suffering burns and a broken arm.

At 16.05 hrs, 32 Squadron went up on patrol from Gravesend, the formation including Pilot Officer Pniak, who had already survived being shot down and baling out less than two hours previously. The Hurricanes clashed with some of the fighters milling about the coast, awaiting the bombers' homeward flight.

Sergeant William Higgins, 32 Squadron:

The Squadron intercepted from twelve to twenty Me 109s off Folkestone. Each pilot took on one of the enemy, a dogfight ensuing. I attacked an Me 109 at about 300 yards range, remaining on his tail for several minutes. Continually the rounds struck the E/A, then finally a gentle dive resulted in the Me 109 hitting the water, still in the gentle dive, about ten miles out to sea off Folkestone. I did not see the pilot bale out and saw no movement where the aircraft sank.

Pilot Officer Anthony Barton chased an Me 109 to France, damaging it, and Pilot Officer Keith Gillman attacked another which 'blew up and fell in the sea'. A 'probable' was claimed by the remarkable Polish Pilot Officer Pniak, who was himself shot down for the second time that day:

I was flying No 3 of Blue Section when we met twelve Me 109s at about 20,000ft. They were above and attacked us. I was attacked by an Me 109 from head-on and above. I circled round on his tail and closing to 150 yards gave him two-two second bursts. He started to smoke from the engine, I followed him and gave him two more bursts, much black smoke came from this aircraft and he was diving. Just after this I felt my engine vibrating and saw smoke coming from the engine and right wing; flames also appeared from the right wing. I switched everything off and put my aircraft into a dive to land, but when I reached 5,000ft the flames were so big that I turned my plane on one side and jumped. I landed very fast because my parachute was not properly open and full of big holes. I landed three miles NW of Hawkinge. My ankle and knee were injured and I was taken to hospital.

It was a lucky escape – Pniak would be out of action now until early September 1940.

The skirmish with elements of JG 26 also cost 32 Squadron two other Hurricanes: Pilot Officer Eugene Seghers, a Free Belgian volunteer, was shot down and baled out into the sea, from which he was fortunately rescued, his aircraft crashing at Tedders Lee, near Hawkinge. The Squadron's CO, Squadron Leader Mike Crossley DFC was also shot-up and crash-landed near Lyminge, fortunately unhurt.

Meanwhile, the raid intercepted by 501 Squadron had pressed on inland towards its objective: RAF Hornchurch, to which 600 Squadron had been withdrawn following the virtually continuous attacks on Manston. AA guns opened up, but the enemy was not intercepted by fighters before hitting its target. The attack, however, achieved poor results owing to the station's spirited AA barrage: 'The attack on Hornchurch was abortive – 100 bombs were dropped but only about six fell inside the boundary, causing slight damage to the perimeter track [ORB].'

Fortunately, Hornchurch's Spitfire squadrons, 54 and 65, were already airborne when the raid came in, but at 15.40 hrs, as the Germans approached, 264 Squadron – or what remained of it – was scrambled to patrol base. Seven Defiants hurriedly took-off, two of which collided on the ground, such was the panic, as bombs were already exploding on the airfield when the remaining five fighters took off. Some miles northeast of Hornchurch, contact was made with a large formation of Ju 88s and Me 109s:

> Squadron Leader Garvin attacked the main formation and succeeded in destroying two Ju 88s by overtaking and converging attacks. Pilot Officer Welsh attacked a straggler some 400 yards behind the main formation and shot it down in a crossover attack, he also damaged an Me 109, which attacked with two others. Pilot Officer Young, separated from the main formation, found a solitary He 111 which he destroyed in an overtaking attack. Flight Lieutenant Banham and Pilot Officer Goodall combined in damaging a Ju 88, which they last saw diving towards the London balloon barrage [ORB].

Pilot Officer Harold Goodall, Red 2, reported that having followed Squadron Leader George Garvin:

> I saw a formation of Ju 88s. I carried out a No 1 Attack from the port side, firing several bursts. The enemy aircraft started to dive, issuing forth white to black smoke. I followed him through cloud and found him underneath. I attacked him from the front and saw bursts entering the cockpit. The enemy aircraft dived away very steeply. I was unable to follow him down.

The bomber was awarded as a 'damaged', shared with Flight Lieutenant Arthur Banham. Yet again though, the Defiants did not escape unscathed: Pilot Officer Richard Gaskell was shot down over Hornchurch by a 109, his gunner, Sergeant William Machin, dying of wounds. In a single day, therefore, 264 Squadron had lost four Defiants and six aircrew killed – a third of the unit's operational strength. This bode not well for the now leaderless squadron's continued operations from Hornchurch.

Following the attack, the raiders withdrew across north Kent where, when fifteen–twenty miles north of the Isle of Sheppey, they were intercepted by Red, Yellow and Blue Sections of 610 Squadron, which had scrambled from Biggin Hill just ten minutes previously. The Spitfires, however, were unable to penetrate the fighter screen to attack the bombers, Me 109s subsequently being claimed destroyed by Flying Officer Stanley Norris and Sergeant Aubrey Baker, while Pilot Officer Joe Pegge claimed a probable. Beyond doubt, however, it was Sergeant Ronnie Hamlyn's lucky day, having already been credited with the destruction of three enemy aircraft:

> I was Yellow Leader, on taking-off we started to fly towards Gravesend but on reaching 5,000ft we saw AA fire over NE London, so we changed course. At about 12,000ft I first sighted about twenty Ju 88s heading in a westerly direction. I led my Section towards them but I saw a bunch of Me 109s just above me so I pulled up and attacked one. After two bursts smoke started pouring out and he fell away, out of control. I was just about to break away when I saw tracer bullets passing me. I at once turned sharply and saw my No 3 being attacked by an Me 109, so I attacked it. As it started to pull up, I gave another burst and it started smoking. After another burst it caught fire and went down with pieces falling off it. The last I saw of the Spitfire, my No 3, was that he was still diving, out of control.

Sergeant Hamlyn was awarded two Me 109s destroyed, making him, with five enemy aircraft now so accredited, an ace in a day – a feat for which he would receive the DFM. Yellow 3, Pilot Officer Claude Merrick, who had only flown his first operational sortie ten days before, crash-landed at Fyfield, wounded, and was admitted to Ongar Hospital.

Six Spitfires of 54 Squadron, led by Squadron Leader James 'Prof' Leathart DSO, had taken off from Hornchurch at 14.55 hrs and headed towards Dover. According to Pilot Officer Hillary Edsall, Red 2, at 15.15 hrs the Spitfires became embroiled in a dogfight with Me 109s at 22,000ft over the port, after which he claimed an Me 109 destroyed – which he had set on fire and pursued across the Channel at 2,000ft, leaving the stricken machine at the French coast. At 15.43 hrs, Pilot Officer Charles Stewart, a New Zealander of the same squadron, was shot down in the combat over Dover and baled out, his Spitfire crashing at Kingsdown, near Deal. Stewart landed in the sea but was horrified when, after fifteen minutes of immersion, an ASR launch failed to see him and turned away. So followed the most anxious forty-five minutes of his young life, until, fortunately, another launch appeared and rescued him.

While their own home station of Hornchurch was being bombed, 65 Squadron, operating from Rochford, was first to engage the second raiding formation, at

15.35 hrs over – according to the Australian Flight Lieutenant Gordon Olive, commander of 'A' Flight – the 'Thames Estuary area', at '18–22,000ft':

> I was patrolling with my Flight, following 'B' Flight, when we were instructed to intercept enemy raid. I saw about forty–eighty bombers heavily escorted by fighters. Some of the fighters were above us. We climbed to 28,000ft and attacked down-sun. On my first attack I fired a full deflection on an Me 110, which immediately threw out clouds of white smoke, apparently glycol. I last saw it diving about 10,000ft below, still throwing out smoke but could not observe it further, and opened fire on the rear one which tried to fire from a gun in his tail. I could not observe the effect of my fire as I was being attacked by five Me 109s from above. I managed to outclimb them and attack the rear Me with my remaining ammunition, but observed no results.

This report raises questions, however. The report above refers to an attack on an 'Me 110' – but the actual claim was for a probably destroyed Me 109. Similarly, Pilot Officer Kenneth Hart claimed an Me 109 probable – and yet page 2 of his personal combat report also refers to having attacked an 'Me 110' – once more illustrating the conflicting information in official records. Indeed, confusion generally surrounds this raid, because although the Home Security Daily Summary refers to another attack on Manston at 15.39 hrs, no mention of such is made in the Station ORB. We do know, however, that the Me 110s and Me 109s of *Erprobungsgruppe* 210 had flown down to operate from Calais-Marck that morning before taking off at 14.15 hrs for another *Gruppe*-strength attack on Manston – which it subsequently bombed and left a shambles.

At 15.30 hrs, as a precautionary measure, the Hurricanes of 615 Squadron had scrambled from Kenley:

> The Squadron sighted fifteen He 111s at Thameshaven about 1550 hrs. Squadron Leader Kayll shot down one which Pilot Officer McClintock finished off. It crashed near Hornchurch where Pilot Officer McClintock landed and met the German pilot. The crew were taken prisoner and the aircraft destroyed [ORB].

This was a machine of 9/KG 53, which crashed and exploded at Clay Tye Hill, Bulphan.

A damaged He 111 was also claimed by Pilot Officer Sydney Madle, and Pilot Officer David Evans attacked another, noting black smoke resulting, leaving the bomber losing height. Pilot Officer John Gayner chased a He 111 to Chelmsford and shot it down, the raider, also of 9/KG 53, crashing in flames at Langford Grove Road, Langford, near Maldon, Essex. Four of the crew were killed while one baled out, wounded, and was captured. Upon return to Kenley, Gayner's Hurricane was covered in oil from the Heinkel, and had a bullet through the propeller spinner. Pilot Officer Keith Lofts hit an Me 109, which went into a spin but was not seen to crash. 615 Squadron's only casualty was Pilot Officer Douglas Hone, whose glycol tank was holed by return fire, forcing him to land near Melpham, fortunately uninjured.

After 54 Squadron's earlier engagement over Dover, Pilot Officer Henry Matthews, Yellow 2 of 54 Squadron, reported that at 16.00 hrs:

> After an engagement with Me 109s over Dover I attempted to re-join my Squadron over Manston, but failed. Proceeding home alone, I saw straggling formation of ten Me 109s and He 113s [*sic*] approaching Southend from the East. I attacked the rear aircraft of this formation, making a stern attack, using slight deflection as the aircraft swerved. The E/A belched forth smoke and was seen descending in an obviously uncontrolled dive towards the sea.

At 15.45 hrs, 56 Squadron had received no order to scramble from Rochford – but Squadron Leader Manton's pilots needed no encouragement when Southend's air raid sirens began wailing and enemy aircraft began passing overhead. At 16.05 hrs, at Angels 12, ten miles east of Bradwell, Flight Lieutenant Steve 'Squeak' Weaver, leading Yellow Section, engaged the raiders:

> I saw many E/A flying east very high over the Thames, I tried to lead the leader of the Squadron to them. However, with my Yellow Two, Pilot Officer Mounsden, I became separated from the Squadron and being unable to climb up to these E/A climbed over Rochford to about 15,000ft. I then saw two separate formations flying east, one approximately approaching Bradwell, and one further north. Both were approximately twelve aircraft each. Utilising the sun, I flew parallel to and above this formation, keeping to the south. When nearly level, I turned in and selected the extreme left-hand aircraft. There was no apparent fighter escort. I opened fire at 250 yards and closed to about thirty yards, firing the whole time. I saw bits fall off this E/A. I then broke away and saw him falling out of control, two people jumping out by parachute. Pilot Officer Mounsden saw E/A hit the sea. I then climbed up and delivered another attack, on the E/A Pilot Officer Mounsden had damaged (white smoke pouring out). Owing to intense cross-fire, I used up all my rounds at about 400 yards, with no apparent effect. There was a type of rear gun fire I have not encountered before, and it appeared as a cluster of tracer, only fired once by each E/A I attacked. It was not cannon and I was not hit by it. I received two hits on my aircraft, one of which pierced the oil tank, front centre-section spar, right through self-sealing petrol tank, out the other side and through rear spar.

This Heinkel belonged to 9/KG 53 and ditched in the sea of Brightlingsea. Three of the crew remain missing, but two others baled out and were captured by an RN launch. 'Squeak's' wingman, Pilot Officer Maurice Mounsden, damaged an Me 109, and Pilot Officer Kenneth Marston destroyed another. Returning to North Weald late that evening, the Hurricane pilots found their home station had been badly knocked about, bombing having caused 'considerable material damage', although not to any vital installations. Sadly, ten soldiers had been killed when their air raid shelter took a direct hit.

This enemy formation was also hit over Chelmsford by the Hurricanes of 111 Squadron, which had scrambled at 15.25 hrs from Debden's satellite airfield at Stapleford Tawney, with orders to patrol Chelmsford at 20,000ft. At 16.00 hrs, this squadron also entered the fray:

> AA barrage in the vicinity of North Weald drew attention to the position of the enemy bombers. Yellow Section, led by Sergeant Dymond, made a head-on attack, followed by attacks from astern – the He 111 was seen to crash near de la Haye reservoir (author's note: Abberton), two of the crew baled out [ORB].

This was another 9/KG 53 aircraft, returning from the Hornchurch raid, three of the crew believed to have drowned in the reservoir, while a fourth was captured:

> Blue 3, Sergeant Brown, who was flying in the box on Yellow Section … noticed a number of Me 109s approaching from astern and broke away to attack these, damaging one and preventing an attack on Yellow Section. Red 1 and 2 attacked the bombers without any apparent result but Red 3, Sergeant Wallace, broke away and climbed to meet a formation of Me 109s diving down on the Section from astern. They broke up and he delivered a two-second burst on the leader from head-on and below, and saw his tracer on the target and smoke issuing from the port wing. Unfortunately the Squadron consisted of only eight aircraft and in its depleted state was unable to press home attacks on the bombers owing to interference from the enemy escort fighters, which drew off several of our Hurricanes from their attacks on the bomber formation [ORB].

With 11 Group's squadrons either engaged or refuelling, 12 Group had been called upon by Air Vice-Marshal Park for assistance, 19 Squadron consequently having taken off from Fowlmere in a '"panic" … at 1545 hrs. Vectored onto formation of approximately fifty enemy bombers, Me 110s and Me 109s.' North Weald had been bombed at 15.40 hrs, five minutes before 19 Squadron were scrambled, and twenty minutes before they arrived. On this occasion, as on 15 August 1940, 11 Group had clearly requested 12 Group's assistance too late. Flight Lieutenant Brian Lane DFC led fourteen Spitfires in haste towards the trouble, describing the subsequent action in his combat report:

> At approximately 1600 hrs over North Weald, AA fire was sighted to the East and I turned towards it, at the same time sighting a number of enemy aircraft above at about 15,000ft. I climbed up and at approximately 1610 hrs got astern of a ragged formation of about forty Me 110s and Do 215s [sic] with an escort of approximately ten Me 109s above and to the rear. The Me

110s were at the rear of the Do 215s. I approached from below and from the sunward side, and almost got within range when Me 110s sighted us and turned towards us. A dogfight ensued and I opened fire from below and astern of the nearest Me 110 but was forced to break away as tracer appeared over my head from an enemy aircraft astern of me. This tracer appeared to be hitting the enemy aircraft that I was firing at, but I observed no result. I got below another Me 110 and fired with slight deflection at the port engine and observed a large part of the engine or mainplane fly off. Enemy aircraft dived down and I observed it crash in sea. No rear fire was experienced from the Me 110s. The Me 109s appeared to be painted yellow on upper surfaces and pale blue below with yellow roundels around all the markings, including those on underside of mainplane. Me 110s had normal camouflage. After the fight I observed a lone Me 110 flying East with its port engine out of action. I attacked but had no ammunition left. I flew alongside the enemy aircraft which immediately opened up flat out. There appeared to be no gunner in the rear cockpit.

Lane must have been as relieved and surprised on equal measure when his cannon suffered no stoppages, considering how problematic the weapon had been to date. Meanwhile, Green Section of 'B' Flight, comprising Flying Officer Dennis Parrott and Pilot Officers Ray Aeberhardt and Eric Burgoyne, 'made contact with the Me 109s above and the main formation … No success, but drew their attention from "A" Flight [ORB].'

Sergeant Bernard 'Jimmy' Jennings, was flying in Flying Officer Frank Brinsden's Yellow Section, when, at 16.00 hrs over 'Mouth of Thames Estuary':

I attacked four Me 110s in fairly wide formation. My attack was from slightly above. My first burst at the nearer Me 110 knocked off the top of his starboard engine and propeller. He went down in a vicious engine turn to starboard. I dived under the remaining nine E/A and turned to starboard, then to port, climbing to regain height. I attacked a single Me 110 and after a fairly long burst saw a piece of his tail fall off the starboard side, complete with starboard section of his rudder. I turned to port to find him since he swung round. Dived to port and saw two Me 110s in front of me. I fired a burst but only with my starboard gun – my port gun had jammed. One Me 109 passed between my sights and the Me 110. I broke away, since he had apparently come down after me, and I looked round for any more from above but did not see any. I attacked another Me 110, but my starboard gun stopped and I came home. I did not hit this Me 110.

Jennings' port cannon had stopped after firing thirty-seven rounds, the port at sixty; he was credited with two Me 110s destroyed.

At 15.40 hrs, the Hurricanes of 151 Squadron had scrambled from Rochford and vectored towards North Weald, the Station Commander, Wing Commander Victor Beamish DSO AFC, and the unit's new CO, Squadron

Leader Eric 'Whizzy' King, in the formation. Previously, King had briefly flown as supernumerary with 249 Squadron at Boscombe Down, during which time, on 16 August 1940, he had been a member of Flight Lieutenant James Nicolson's section patrolling over Southampton, the outcome of which was all three Hurricanes being bounced by Me 109s and shot down; Pilot Officer Martyn King, the youngest of The Few, was killed; Nicolson baled out badly burned and later received Fighter Command's only VC of the Second World War for his 'signal act of valour' that day; Squadron Leader King was shot-up but made it safely back to base. After 151 Squadron's Canadian CO, Squadron Leader John Gordon, was shot down and badly burned on 18 August 1940, King was among those squadron leaders serving as supernumerary to gain experience of current operations and combat conditions, and waiting in the wings (literally) to receive their own command. So it was that on 21 August 1940, Squadron Leader Eric King took command of 151 Squadron, replacing the wounded Gordon. King flew on operations immediately, but temporarily – and sensibly – took a back seat in the air, as had Squadron Leader Graeme 'Minnie' Manton, a similarly combat inexperienced officer who had taken command of 56 Squadron, and let a more experienced 'chap' lead in the air. So it was that around 16.00 hrs on 24 August 1940, 151 Squadron also intercepted the raiders after they had bombed North Weald, 151's CO flying as Red 3:

> The Section Leader put us in line astern and we attacked the extreme port side bombers first from the beam, then dead astern. I fired a burst from the beam and then a five second burst from dead astern, aiming at the port engine. A Me 110, coming from the beam, attacked, a cannon shot hit propeller … As I broke away I saw black smoke coming from the port engine. This was seen by Wing Commander Beamish, who was following. I glided down and landed on one wheel at base.

A 'Do 215' [*sic*] was awarded as 'damaged'.

Wing Commander Beamish claimed two Dorniers damaged, and commented:

> I suggest that in view of the enemy fighters circling round the flanks of the bombers at the same level that all our fighters should go to the same level and decide then how best to combat the fighters circling the bombers and to then attack the bombers. It is suggested that to dispatch our fighters to attack higher enemy fighters is a waste.

Beamish was right: the height advantage was vital, and frequently RAF fighters were either being ambushed from out of the sun by high-flying Me 109s, or attacked while clawing for height over south-east England, the enemy having already achieved high altitude on the flight from France. Moreover, the heights at which RAF fighters were ordered to patrol were often too low, failing to acknowledge that Me 109s were inevitably lurking much higher in the sky. Fighter sweeps could be ignored, as they were only dangerous if defending fighters were scrambled to intercept – but fighters escorting bombers had somehow to be dealt with, because otherwise little or no execution could be effected against the bombers. It was a vexing issue, one which really came down to the speed of events involved and climbing performance. It took, for example, even the new Spitfire Mk IIA nearly six minutes to climb to 20,000ft, over nine to 30,000ft, and nearly seventeen to 40,000ft – and time was of the essence.

Returning to the action over North Weald during the afternoon of 24 August 1940, having intercepted the '150+' strong formation of He 111s, Do 17s, Me 110s and Me 109s, in addition to the claims by Squadron Leader King and Wing Commander Beamish, according to the 151 Squadron ORB, Flying Officer Kenneth Blair probably destroyed a He 111, Flight Lieutenant Richard Smith an Me 109, and Pilot Officer John Ellacombe bagged a He 111 'confirmed'. The petrol tank of the Canadian Pilot Officer Irving Smith's Hurricane was pierced by return fire during the interception, although the pilot was unhurt and returned safely to base.

Despite the efforts of the all defending fighters, however, North Weald was hit – and both that aerodrome and Hornchurch, which had also been bombed, were important Sector Stations. The RAF North Weald ORB recorded the damage:

> Enemy consisting of thirty to fifty Do 215 [sic] accompanied by up to a hundred He 111 & Me 110 Bombers were above cloud at 15,000ft. in very close formation of sections of three in line astern. Waves of Me 110 were stepped up above bombers which were encircled by other Me 110 at same level; travelling at about 200 mph. Bombers broke cloud and bombed N. WEALD from about 15,000ft.
>
> 150–200 bombs were dropped. Airmen's Married Quarters & Officers Married Quarters suffered severely. Powerhouse badly damaged. Majority of bombs fell along main EPPING-ONGAR road. Damaging water supply and gas mains. A number of delayed action bombs dropped; some exploring on following day; remainder blast with by Demolition Squad. Casualties nine killed ten wounded; the killed and majority of wounded were in a shelter which suffered a direct hit.

Although more successful for the enemy than the Hornchurch raid, the runway and station's communications remained unscathed – and so RAF North Weald remained operational.

By 16.30 hrs, the sky over south-east England was at last devoid of enemy aircraft, Kent and Essex having been under attack continuously, one way or another, for eight hours. The daylight fighting was now over in those counties – it was Hampshire's turn next.

At 15.45 hrs, while the fighting was happening around North Weald, RDF indicated that *Luftflotte* 3 was assembling large formations over Cherbourg. The defenders' reaction was swift: at 15.55 hrs, 17 Squadron's 'A' Flight scrambled from Tangmere to patrol base at 15,000ft, and by 16.10 hrs both 234 and 609 Squadrons were up from Middle Wallop, the former vectored to the Isle of Wight, the latter specifically to St Catherine's Point, the islands most southerly tip – the Spitfires thereby providing an advance defensive screen. Furthermore, at 16.10 hrs, 'B' Flight of 249 Squadron scrambled from Boscombe Down to patrol the Solent between Portsmouth and the Isle of Wight, and at the same time, a flight of 43 Squadron's Hurricanes were sent up from Tangmere to help deal with the incoming '"X" Plot' [ORB].

Although there was a row brewing between 11 and 12 Groups (the former charging the latter with failing to make sufficient haste to protect Air Vice-Marshal Park's airfields, and 12 accusing 11 of hogging the action and requesting reinforcement too late – which, as we have seen, was a justifiable criticism), it is noteworthy that three of the squadrons (234, 249 and 609) scrambled to meet the latest incoming threat over the 11 Group area belonged to 10 Group. Throughout the entire Battle of Britain, Air Vice-Marshal Sir Quentin Brand's 10 Group would work in perfect harmony with 11 Group; why this was not happening between 11 and 12 Groups was complex – and will shortly be investigated as our narrative progresses.

The incoming raid approaching the South Coast was huge. According to the after-action report by Luftwaffe intelligence officer *Hauptmann* Genst, twenty-five Ju 88s of I/KG 51 started up at 14.30 hrs (BST), followed by twenty-one of III/KG 51 at 14.50 hrs – forty-six bombers with a formidable fighter escort: sixty-three Me 109s of JG 53, sixty-nine of JG 2 and seventy-one of JG 27, along with forty-four Me 110s of ZG 2, and fifty-five of ZG 76 and V/LG 1 – 203 Me 109s and ninety-nine Me 110s.

The bombers approached their target – Portsmouth dockyard – at 16,000ft via the eastern side of the Isle of Wight, without being intercepted. According to Genst, I/KG 51 hit the docks at 16.20 hrs (BST) with twenty-eight SC500 (Kg), thirty-six SC250 bombs, and eight Flambombe 250 incendiaries. Three minutes later III/KG 51 dropped nine SC1000, six SC500 and thirty-six SC250. Great damage was caused to both the northern and southern districts of the city, and blocking the railway line between Portsmouth and Southsea.

No.234 Squadron, however, was patrolling over the Isle of Wight at 20,000ft and missed the Portsmouth raid, engaging instead a formation of fifty Me 109s at 16.30 hrs; Pilot Officer William Gordon of 'A' Flight:

I was Yellow 3 ... when we sighted E/A at about 17,000ft. I attacked an Me 109, giving a short burst from 250 yards. I then closed to fifty yards and saw ammunition in his wings explode and smoke pouring from engine. I broke away and followed the E/A further out to sea. On turning back to land I was attacked by another formation of Me 109s. I dived straight down and got away through superior speed.

The tail of Gordon's Spitfire was hit by a single bullet.

Squadron Leader Joseph 'Spike' O'Brien DFC, commanding 234 Squadron, also claimed an Me 109 destroyed in the clash, while the Polish Pilot Officer Zbigniew Olenski claimed a 'probable', and New Zealander Pilot Officer Keith Lawrence damaged an Me 110. No.234 Squadron's Pilot Officer Janusz 'Zura' Zurakowski was shot-up by an Me 109, but safely crash-landed on the Isle of Wight and was unhurt.

No.609 Squadron, however, were somewhat frustrated – and vulnerable. On previous days, Tangmere and the airfields around Portsmouth and Southampton had been hit by Ju 87 dive-bombers – and RAF Controllers had no way of knowing that the losses inflicted on the type had led to the *Stuka's* withdrawal from the arena. Consequently, as a precaution in case the incoming raids were Ju 87s, 609 Squadron was positioned over Ryde at just 10,000ft – at 16.40 hrs the Spitfire pilots finding themselves '5,000ft below a large formation of bombers and fighters, right in the middle of our own AA fire, and down-sun.' The Squadron was attacked and fortunate to sustain no further casualties other than two aircraft damaged, one of which was a "Write-off" [ORB].' Neither pilot of the damaged Spitfires, namely Flight Lieutenant Frank Howell and the American volunteer Pilot Officer Andy Mamedoff, were hurt and both pilots returned safely to base. It was I/JG 53 which had done the damage to 234 and 609 Squadrons, *Hauptmann* Hans-Karl Mayer, *Staffelkapitän* of 1/JG 53, *Leutnant* Alfred Zeis of *Stab* I/JG53, and *Oberleutnant* Günther Schulze-Blanck of 4/JG 53 all claiming Spitfires destroyed.

An incident of friendly fire occurred at the same time 609 Squadron was attacked by JG 53. At 16.50 hrs over Thorney Island, Hurricanes of 1 (RCAF) Squadron mistook three 235 Squadron Blenheims for Ju 88s; two were badly damaged and crash-landed back at base, their crews unhurt, but the third was shot down into the sea off Bracklesham Bay, the crew killed. A tragedy indeed – but an easy mistake to make, especially with Ju 88s active in the vicinity.

At nearby Tangmere, 17 Squadron had been on readiness since 13.00 hrs when 'A' Flight scrambled at 15.55 hrs to patrol base. The CO, Squadron Leader Cedric Williams, reported combat at 16.50 hrs, ten miles off Selsey Bill:

> Seeing six or more aircraft apparently diving on aerodrome I ordered Blue Section to remain above and led the remainder of the Squadron down to investigate. I identified the aircraft as Hurricanes, and then saw at 5–6,000ft above me to the SE eight – ten E/A but too far away to chase. Climbing to 10,000ft I saw one He 111 making for France and losing height. Red Section attacked and I gave E/A two three second bursts in a beam attack, turning to quarter. I then turned and made a frontal quarter attack with a long burst, my fire going into the nose and port mainplane. I saw pieces falling away from the latter. After breaking away I saw a long white streak on the water which I thought might have been smoke or foam in the approximate position in which the E/A would have been.

The He 111 was awarded as destroyed, and shared with Pilot Officer Leonard Stevens, Red 2. No He 111s are known to have been active in the area at this time, although an Me 110 of 5/ZG2 crashed in the Channel after combat that day, one crewman later being rescued by the *Seenotdienst.*

Boscombe Down's 249 Squadron had been ordered, like 609 Squadron, to patrol the Isle of Wight at the suicidal height of 10,000ft. Some 100 Ju 88s, Me 110s and Me 109s were reported over the island by 249 at 17.20 hrs, flying between 15,000 and 20,000ft, as the Canadian Flight Lieutenant Robert Barton reported:

> I was Blue 1 ... Blue Section sighted E/A at 19,000ft, proceeding South. I fired a head-on attack at an Me 109... then turned away to attack others. A few seconds later saw E/A diving towards sea emitting white vapour. The E/A were much too far above for us to make an effective attack.

The Me 109 was claimed as 'conclusive', and others were claimed destroyed by Pilot Officers Richard Wynn and James Meaker.

So ended the daylight fighting – the heaviest raid so far on Portsmouth, inflicting the highest number of casualties so far in an air raid on Britain since the beginning of the war: 154 dead, including many naval personnel, and 237 injured.

Bomber Command operations, however, had been thwarted throughout the day by unfavourable weather conditions over enemy occupied Europe. Of nine 2 Group Blenheims which set out to attack airfields in the Netherlands, only five found and bombed their targets. By night, Blenheims attacked more airfields, starting fires at several in northern France, a direct hit on hangars at Bourges being noted. The heavy and dangerous German batteries around Cap Gris-Nez and shipping at Zeebrugge were also attacked. Heavier bombers continued their raids on industrial targets in Germany and Milan, which included successful attacks on Messerschmitt's Augsburg factory and Stuttgart's Daimler-Benz plant – important targets indeed; a Whitley failed to return from the Augsburg raid. Coastal Command's sorties followed the familiar pattern of convoy patrols, reconnaissance and mine-laying, while 142 Squadron's Battles made a persistent attack on enemy invasion barges and *Seenotdienst* seaplanes at Boulogne in the face of heavy AA fire.

Daily Home Intelligence Report (Cardiff):

> Many believe that our news is true only 'insofar as it goes'. There is, however, general credence of the RAF and enemy plane losses.

Night of 24/25 August 1940

The night of 24/25 August 1940 was a most significant one – notwithstanding the fact that overall, the night was typical of the enemy's nocturnal operations to date. The Luftwaffe intruded over a broad front, ranging far and wide from South Wales to Teeside. At 21.00 hrs, thirty-four bombs were dropped on RAF St Athan, east of Cardiff, rendering the station unserviceable. Fortunately, though, this base was unconnected with Fighter Command other than it was home to an operational training unit converting pilots to the Hurricane fighter. KG 27 and I and III/LG 1 raided the port of Bristol with forty-four He 111s and Ju 88s, but apart from damage to the suburbs of Avonmouth, most bombs fell harmlessly in open country. After midnight, Birmingham's Castle Bromwich area was targeted, but again, little damage was caused to the all-important, Spitfire producing, CBAF, the Moss Gear Company and Fort Dunlop. Coventry, Swansea, Portland and Poole were also subject to harassing attacks. RAF day fighters, pressed into night-time service along with the night-fighting Blenheims of 10 Group's 604 Squadron, based at Middle Wallop, patrolled over Britain but caught not one glimpse of a raider – the aim of which was only upset by AA fire and searchlights.

No.12 Group possessed two Blenheim-equipped night-fighter squadrons: 23 Squadron, at Collyweston, near Stamford, and 29 Squadron at Digby. Serving with the latter was a certain 20-year-old Pilot Officer Bob Braham, who intercepted a raider over the Humber in the early hours of 25 August 1940:

> I sighted bandit in searchlights at 0120 hrs, travelling at 180 mph–200 mph at approx. 8,000ft. E/A turned steeply and unsuccessfully to evade searchlights. I carried out astern attack. Smoke started coming from aircraft after my last burst. My Air-Gunner, Sergeant Wilsdon, fired two short bursts at 50–100 yards range which were effective. There was no enemy fire observed. The enemy most probably did not see my aircraft and only appeared to be trying to avoid searchlights. E/A seen descending with smoke and sparks issuing forth. Combat took place above 3/10ths cloud, visibility good.

Immediately after the combat, 'It was later reported by searchlights that they saw an aircraft on fire coming come down in the sea [29 Squadron ORB].' Initially, the bomber's destruction was claimed by AA gunners, but the evidence from 'searchlights' led to Pilot Officer Braham being awarded the enemy aircraft as destroyed, 'probably' being, according to the 29 Squadron ORB, 'a Heinkel'. It was an historic occasion, in fact, being the first of twenty-nine confirmed victories that would make Braham the most outstanding RAF night-fighter pilot of the war. Identified by Braham as either a He 111 or a Do 17, no enemy loss is apparent in German records, however.

Before midnight, enemy bombers had been active over Essex and Greater London, bombs being dropped on Islington, Tottenham and the docks at

Millwall, where big fires were reported. After midnight raids increased, crossing the Sussex coast over Beachy Head. The air raid warning had wailed across the City of London and East End at 23.08 hrs – the sixth such alert that day. Enemy bombers now approached central London – but in the enemy camp there was confusion. Previously, Hitler had personally forbidden attacks on London without his express authorisation. Frustrated at the Luftwaffe's apparent inability to smash Fighter Command in short order, however, Göring had berated his *Kampfflieger* to 'Hammer at the enemy by day and night to break his nerve' – adding that he personally would approve attacks on the cities of London and Liverpool. As noted earlier, in doing this Göring overstepped the mark – which had not gone unnoticed by OKW. Consequently on 24 August 1940, OKW chief *Generalfeldmarschall* Wilhelm Keitel signalled a reminder that 'Attacks against the London area and terror attacks are reserved for the Führer's decision.' London, however, had already been hit – not least by *Erprobungsgruppe* 210's raid on Croydon airfield, which it had mistaken for Kenley on 15 August 1940. Now, things were about to go seriously awry; suddenly, at 00.20 hrs, HE bombs hit St Giles, Cripplegate, and incendiaries rained down upon dwellings in adjacent Fore Street – in Central London's so-called 'Square Mile'. A lone German bomber had made a navigational error and in so doing made history: these were the first bombs on London since 1918 and set in motion a catastrophic chain of events.

The 'Brandbombe' was an incendiary weighing between 1–2kg; a 13.5-inch long magnesium cylinder filled with thermite – which burned hot enough to melt steel – fitted with a three-vaned aluminium tail that would ignite upon impact by a percussion charge. Hundreds of thousands of these evil devices would be dropped on Britain from containers holding as many as 700 Brandbombe – which were devastating to property. Crashing through roof-tiles and often becoming lodged in attics and floorboards, the burning magnesium set fire to everything around. In a matter of minutes, the first London Fire Brigade (LFB) units, from Redcross Street and sub-stations, arrived in Cripplegate and Fore Street – where they found a serious situation. Two-hundred water pumps, each with a six-man crew, would be used that night to extinguish the blaze in Fore Street – as the professional fire-fighters of the LFB fought the flames shoulder-to-shoulder with volunteers of the recently forced Auxiliary Fire Service (AFS). This was actually the first fire that the majority of auxiliaries had seen – and yet the majority of pumps, heavy and trailer, belonged to the AFS. It was a shocking sight, and baptism of fire indeed. Worse, however, was to follow.

In 11 Group, Air Vice-Marshal Park also had two Blenheim-equipped night-fighter units: 600 Squadron, which remained in the process of reorganising at Hornchurch after being bombed out of Manston, and 25 Squadron, operating from Martlesham Heath but actually engaged on daylight convoy patrols. At 00.10 hrs, however, Flight Lieutenant James Sanders DFC of 615 Squadron took off alone to try to intercept a raider, which he did at 01.30 hrs:

I climbed above the clouds and toured the South Coast waiting for searchlights to expose an E/A. Soon I spotted an He 111 miles away and proceeded to intercept. When low enough I lowered undercarriage to produce drag to avoid colliding with E/A. Four short bursts, of about three seconds each, set both engines on fire; he half-rolled and dived over the vertical, probably in the sea. The rear-gunner put in some effective fire at me, damaging my port wing slightly; he seemed to fire with four guns. Attacks were from astern below, firing 15° up to 8,000ft.

The enemy bomber belonged to Villacoublay's 9/KG 55 which was on a reconnaissance sortie, primarily concerned with RAF Harwell, a Bomber Command training base near Abingdon in Oxfordshire, and exploded a mile out to sea off Hastings; all but one of the crew were killed or missing, the survivor was taken prisoner. Almost immediately after the crash, Sanders saw another He 111 caught by searchlight beams, which he attacked and damaged – a feat of arms recognised by a praiseworthy signal from Air Vice-Marshal Park himself. Other Hurricane pilots of 11 Group, however, prowled the night sky unsuccessfully.

That night, the Do 17 crews of KG 1 had been briefed to attack the oil storage tanks of the London and Thames Haven Oil Wharves Ltd on the north bank of the Thames Estuary. Somehow, a navigational error was made and instead the West India Docks – twenty-five miles west of the intended target – was bombed. Located in the Isle of Dogs, on the Thames' famous 'S' bend, like St Giles and Fore Street, the West India Docks were within the City of London. Incendiaries set fire to two warehouses, the resulting blaze threatening the whole surrounding area. Already committed with the serious fires at St Giles and Fore Street, the LFB and AFS soon had all appliances and firemen in the locality fighting these fierce fires. The two major fires burning in the West India Docks required 170 pumps and 8 fireboats to extinguish the flames – and before this night a 30-pump blaze was considered a major incident. With cinders blowing downwind across the East End from these blazes, the LFB also attended forty-eight smaller fires. As dawn broke, steam rose from the charred remains of St Giles, Fore Street and West India Docks. Countless firefighters had experienced their first major incident and had contained the fires; fortunately none of these brave men were killed, but many had been injured by the usual hazards: burns, falling masonry and roof slates.

According to Hanson Baldwin, the *New York Times*' military correspondent, this accidental bombing of Central London was 'One of the greatest miscalculations in history'. Indeed, it was on that one night that the Germans arguably lost any chance of achieving their objective of aerial supremacy over southern England.

Sunday, 25 August 1940

Hitler and Göring were furious about the bombing on Central London. The Luftwaffe chief signalled *Major* Joseph Knobel, KG 1's Operations Officer: 'Report forthwith which crews bombed the London prohibited zone. The Supreme Commander [Hitler] reserves punishment of commanders concerned by transferring to the infantry.'

The damage, however, had been done – and could not be reversed. 'Nothing impressed or disturbed Hitler,' Churchill wrote, 'so much as his realisation of British wrath and will-power' – and there would be reprisals. Indeed, Churchill remembered that 'The War Cabinet were much in the mood to hit back, to raise the stakes, and to defy the enemy. I was sure they were right.'

The Air Staff, however, was lukewarm regarding the idea of a retaliatory raid on Berlin, a distant target as opposed to those of much greater military significance closer to home. As we have seen, Bomber Command had kept up nocturnal raids on oil refineries, factories, naval bases, communications and airfields in Germany – but had not bombed the German capital. Nonetheless, Churchill got his way: with only a few hours to prepare the operation, Berlin was to be attacked that very night. Immediately, preparations for the raid began.

By day, German reconnaissance aircraft prowled far and wide over Britain, although surprisingly, considering the fair weather, albeit with a low cloud base of 2,000ft, it was not until late afternoon that a major raid developed. This came from *Luftflotte* 3, and unlike some previous major attacks, did not coincide with a raid in similar strength further east by *Luftflotte* 2.

At 16.40 hrs, RDF detected a large enemy formation of over 100 aircraft was moving north-east along the Cherbourg peninsula – but a few minutes later the raid appeared only a third of that size, owing, as it later transpired, to have separated into sub-formations. Three of these, each of 30+, following each other closely, were bound for Portland, while a fourth of similar size, further west, penetrated as far as Yeovil, home of Westland Aircraft, but this important target was not attacked, suggesting that these were flank-covering fighters. As the enemy progressed across the Channel, the 11 Group Controller was understandably primarily concerned with protecting the likely targets: the fighter airfields of Tangmere, and both Warmwell and Middle Wallop in 10 Group, both sector controllers being alerted immediately. It was clear that the raid's direction of travel was Portland, and that, therefore, 10 Group's area was the target and the early RDF detection, given the distance the enemy had to travel, provided Fighter Command plenty of time to scramble squadrons and prepare a reception committee in strength.

The first to scramble were twelve Hurricanes of 17 Squadron from Tangmere, ordered to patrol base at 15,000ft. Seven minutes later, twelve Spitfires of 152 Squadron roared skywards from Warmwell and headed to their patrol line, west of Portland at 17,000ft. Between 16.55 and 17.00 hrs, no less than fourteen 609 Squadron Spitfires took-off from Middle Wallop, to patrol base at 15,000ft. At 17.00 hrs, the Spitfires of Westhampnett's 602 Squadron were scrambled and five minutes later all twelve Spitfires were airborne and heading for Portland. Also at 17.00 hrs ten 213 Squadron scrambled from Exeter, the ten Hurricanes ordered to cover Warmwell at 22,000ft; at 17.10 hrs, thirteen 87 Squadron Hurricanes also scrambled from Exeter, bound for Portland, the extra aircraft being flown by the Station Commander, the ever-keen and popular Wing Commander Johnny Dewar DSO DFC. Finally, 234 Squadron also fielded thirteen aircraft, the Spitfires scrambling from Middle Wallop to patrol base at 17.15 hrs. Thus, sixty-two 10 Group fighters and twenty-four of 11 Group – a total of eighty-six fighters – were now airborne and ready for action. This represented perfect cooperation between 10 and 11 Groups – and a substantial reaction to the incoming threat – with the squadrons involved all ordered to take-off with, according to the AHB narrative, 'all available strength'.

The raid was actually substantially larger than the '100+' estimated by RDF. When enemy formations were incoming over England, of course, the men of the Observer Corps could visually track them, cloud and visibility permitting, and report numbers – but over the sea there was no such facility. On this occasion twenty-eight Ju 88s of II and III/KG 51, and nine more of I/KG 54, were bound for Warmwell – escorted by masses of fighters: all three *gruppen* of both JG 2 and JG 53 – the latter yet to move to the Pas-de-Calais – and the Me 109s of III/JG 27, some with a roving brief, swarmed around the bombers, which were closely escorted by Me 110s of I and II/ZG 2, III/KG 76, and V(Z)/LG 1. To those watching from the ground on what was a clear day, the sky must have appeared back with German aircraft.

By 17.15 hrs it was clear that the raid was heading directly to Portland, rather than dog-legging to Tangmere, suggesting that the naval base or, more likely, the airfields at Warmwell and Middle Wallop were threatened. Consequently, 17 Squadron was diverted from patrolling Tangmere and instead vectored to Portland, 213 Squadron was also ordered to cease patrolling Warmwell and head for the same area, and 609 moved forward from patrolling Middle Wallop to cover Warmwell. Five minutes later the raid was over Portland, and two minutes after that the hellish cacophony of the AA barrage opened up.

Sergeant Ernest Snowden of 213 Squadron had hurriedly refuelled at Exeter before making haste to join his squadron patrolling over Warmwell, reporting that, at 17.15 hrs, 14,000ft over Warmwell:

I intercepted a large formation of Ju 88s and was shot from behind by an Me 109 as I shot down a Ju 88. I gave him [the Me 109] two bursts as he climbed up across my bows, and crashed into the sea off Swyre. This was confirmed by soldiers of the Royal Artillery at Burton Bradstock. The Ju 88 crashed into the sea further East, and officers of the Durham Light Infantry at Burton Bradstock saw a Hurricane or Spitfire put a final burst into him at

1,000ft. He was already on fire when this aircraft made its attack. I forced-landed at Burton Bradstock.

The Ju 88 was an aircraft of II/KG 51, the crew of which were all killed, although it is impossible to be certain which Me 109 Snowden destroyed, with III/JG 2, II and III/JG 53 all losing fighters destroyed over the sea. Snowden's Hurricane was badly damaged but the pilot was unhurt.

Flight Lieutenant James Strickland, leading Blue Section of 213 Squadron's 'B' Flight, mixed it with German fighters over Warmwell and Portland:

> Sighted about sixty Me 110s and Me 109s at about 18,000ft. Dived to the attack and got in one short burst at an Me 110 who slowed down considerably and his port engine started smoking. Had to break away as they started to form a circle. Patrolled by myself about half a mile inland of circle and found twenty Ju 88s. Managed to get in one burst from below and astern but no damage noticed. Followed a 109 down to sea-level, which crashed, and started to patrol about quarter of a mile off Chesil Beach. An Me 109 came and tried to formate on us – then realised his mistake and went out to sea as fast as he could. I pulled everything and managed to catch him up and shot him down in flames into the sea. The pilot tried to bale out but his parachute failed to open. I gave him three short bursts and presume he must have been armoured. His starboard petrol tank was alight and bits fell off him – then he abandoned aircraft at about 7,000ft.

An Me 109 and a 110 were also claimed destroyed by Sergeant Reginald Llewellyn, and another 110 was accredited to Pilot Officer Jacques Philippart – but the Belgian pilot was missing, shot down into the sea, as was Pilot Officer Harold Atkinson. The damage had been done by Me 109 pilots of *Stab* I and 1/JG 53, who claimed eight Hurricanes destroyed during the operation.

Warmwell, however, was bombed, with two hangars being damaged and the Sick Quarters destroyed by fire; communications were also disrupted and not restored until noon the following day. Ray Johnson was there:

> We armourers of 152 Squadron were working on the airfield when we saw about a dozen twin-engine aircraft approaching Warmwell at 8–10,000ft and drop their loads. It was all over in a matter of minutes. They were pretty accurate: the hangar and a number of aircraft were either destroyed or damaged, and then delayed action bombs kept exploding for the next few days. There was also a number of casualties among the ground personnel. As practically all our waking hours were spent at the dispersal point at the wooded end of the airfield, for years after in any panic our standard warning call was 'Away to the woods!'

Fortunately most of 152's Spitfires were airborne:

Warmwell was bombed and afterwards, between 1720–1725 hrs, about twenty Ju 88s, thirty Me 110s and forty Me 109s were encountered West of Portland. The engagements became a collection of dogfights in which Pilot Officer Marrs (Black 2) destroyed an Me 110, Pilot Officer Beaumont (Green 2) destroyed an Me 109, Sergeant Barker (White 2) destroyed an Me 109 and Flight Lieutenant Thomas (Blue 1) probably destroyed a Ju 88. Flying Officer Deansley and Pilot Officer O'Brian went up from Warmwell when it was bombed but did not engage [ORB].

Hauptmann Hans von Hahn, *Staffelkapitän* 7/JG 53:

The Spitfires approached in a long string of pearls, peeled off as if on training flight and were about to carry out a textbook attack on our bombers. We roared into them from above; they now forgot all about the bombers and instead a wild dogfight began. They tried to force us inland, but in short order they lost three of their number, which went down in flames into the sea. Then they made off and I latched onto the last one. First its canopy flew off, then it wobbled oddly during one burst, went straight down belching smoke and flames – and then it was nothing more than a tiny white speck of foam.

Two of 152 Squadron's pilots were lost in this action: Pilot Officers Richard Hogg and Timothy Wildblood – the former one of two brothers killed while flying Spitfires during the war, the latter a former Cranwell King's Cadet – both being reported missing over the Channel.

The Spitfires of 609 Squadron were also in action over Warmwell, at 17.20 hrs, in which the squadron ORB described as 'a big tea-time party with 100 plus'. Squadron Leader Horace Darley put the squadron into line astern, and engaged the enemy – Pilot Officer David Crook was the last in line:

I shall never forget seeing the lone line of Spitfires ahead, sweeping round and curling round at terrific speed to strike right into the middle of the German formation. It was superb! The onslaught split up the Huns immediately and they scattered all over the place with Spitfires chasing them right and left.

Squadron Leader Darley, 'Sorbo Leader':

When three miles North of Holton Heath was told to investigate bandits West of Swanage, Angels 15. Immediately afterwards saw a large force of unknown E/A at 20,000ft over Portland. Warned Squadron, turned into the sun and began to climb. Yellow 1 then warned me of E/A below but I could not see them and told Yellow 1 to go ahead. Immediately afterwards saw fifteen–twenty E/A under right wing at 15,000ft, and dived after them. I opened fire at one Me 110 which was banking away from me, giving me a full plan view. I gave a three-second burst turning from full deflection into a quarter from 250 yards to 50 yards. E/A went into a vertical dive and crashed about two miles South of Warmwell. I engaged another Me 110 but found I was being fired upon from behind. I dived down and after coming up saw a circle of twenty 109s and 110s four miles out to sea South of Warmwell at 20,000ft. Climbed into sun and saw line astern of four 109s. Selected last and began gentle dive. Another 109 dived down in front of target aircraft and so I fired at him instead, two-second burst from 20–100 yards, dead astern. E/A fell into sea four miles off coast South of Warmwell. I tried to pick off some more from this circle but had to dive to evade E/A on my tail. After coming up for third time saw E/A going South and so I returned to base ... Lot of German R/T chat but no controlling voice as previously heard.

The Me 110 destroyed by Darley belonged to 1/ZG2 and was also attacked by the American volunteer Pilot Officer Eugene 'Red' Tobin. The enemy aircraft crashed at Winfrith, East Chaldon, both *Leutnant* Karl Westphal and *Unteroffizier* Josef Brief were killed. Tobin, having pulled considerable 'G' in an 18,000ft dive 'blacked out colder than a clam and realised I was too low to be any good to my motor. I came home [ORB].' In total, 609 Squadron claimed two Me 109s destroyed, five Me 110s destroyed and four probables. The Spitfire of the Polish Flying Officer Piotr 'Osti' Ostaszewski-Ostoja, was badly damaged by cannon fire from an Me 110 over Swanage, the pilot crash-landing but overrunning the runway at Warmwell owing to damaged flaps, writing-off the aircraft; the pilot was 'slightly wounded in the arm and nastily battered on the head by his windscreen but made a quick recovery [ORB]'. Pilot Officer Crook's Spitfire was also damaged by a 110 but he returned to base and was unhurt.

During the early part of the Battle of Britain, the morale of 609, an AAF squadron, had suffered badly owing to casualties. These losses, however, had been made good, with replacement pilots arriving from the RAFVR and occupied lands, causing Squadron diarist Flying Officer John Dundas, a pre-war auxiliary and journalist in peacetime, to observe: 'the Squadron was becoming cosmopolitan. One might think that this heterogeneity would interfere with team-work or morale, but this was not so.' Since those early days, 609 had also recorded several highly successful combat results; Dundas knew why: 'Under Squadron Leader Darley's quietly firm and competent leadership the Squadron gained steadily in skill and confidence and remained a veritable "Band of Brothers" [ORB].'

As 609 Squadron had engaged the enemy over Warmwell and Portland, the Hurricanes of 87 Squadron were approaching the action. On 15 August 1940 the CO, New Zealander Squadron Leader Terence Lovel-Gregg, had been killed in action; he was succeeded in command on 24 August 1940 by Squadron Leader Randolph Mills DFC, a former pre-war aircraft apprentice and veteran of the Norwegian campaign. As Mills was new to the battle over south-east England, however, 87 Squadron was led in the air on this interception by a previous CO and Exeter's current Station Commander, Wing Commander Johnny Dewar DSO DFC:

Led squadron to patrol Warmwell at 10,000ft, as ordered. Sighted AA bursts over Portland, but no aircraft. Then sighted a large enemy force coming westwards, along coast. Selected squadron of Ju 88s least escorted, and led in on a quarter attack. Fired about 800 rounds. As I pulled away, I saw the E/A smoking. Flight Sergeant Badger, who was following, saw it burst into flames. It must have fallen near Lulworth. Later confirmed by Observer Corps that one fell there.

I continued my turn on pulling away, and met about ten 110s head-on, taking a fleeting burst at the last one. By the time I had turned around again, I could see no aircraft near me. Beyond Lulworth there was a huge circle of wheeling aircraft. Every now and then, one dropped out, smoking. The bombers seemed to be making out to sea. Very high over Portland way a white 'Verey' light was fired. I flew, climbing towards the coast, turning now and again, to sweep the sky above. During one of these turns I almost collided with an Me 109 turning in the opposite direction. I started to pursue as he went past me, and saw that he was the leader of four. They did not appear to have seen me, so I joined them in the rear. Unfortunately their high speed prevented me from getting closer than about 600 yards, and although I had +9 on the boost, I could not catch up. As they turned, however, I slowly gained. When about 300 yards away, I opened fire on the rearmost in short bursts. He immediately turned more steeply than the rest, and increased speed, but not before vapour came pouring from him. His manoeuvre carried him to the front of the others and I had to break off action with him. Last seen, he was diving at about 45°, slightly banked, and may also have come down near Lulworth, on land or in the sea. Fumes were pouring from him. I suspect he carried armour, as I fired at least 800 rounds, with almost dead astern shots. The others quickly climbed out of reach. I was greatly handicapped by lack of speed. Seeing no further activity and being short of ammunition, I returned to base without seeing any of my squadron since the first encounter.

I consider that greater effect would be achieved from an attack, and less losses suffered, if we patrolled in larger numbers, if possible two squadrons going together. Twin-engine bombers can take terrific punishment from the rear and their own shooting has greatly improved. I consider it a mistake to attack from the rear if any other method is possible. With fighter escorts, only fleeting attacks can be made, making it difficult to obtain conclusive results.

Dewar's observations were pertinent: in due course Air Vice-Marshal Park would favour employing two squadron formations, as we will see.

No.87 Squadron made multiple combat claims, amounting to four Ju 88s destroyed, six Me 110s destroyed and one probable, three Me 109s destroyed and three damaged, and Pilot Officer Roland 'Bee' Beamont claimed a 'Do 17 probably destroyed [sic] [ORB]'. These claims, of course, in the heat and chaos of battle, were inevitably exaggerated, however. One 87 Squadron pilot failed to return, Sergeant Sidney Wakeling, who was shot down and killed, his Hurricane crashing at New Barn, just north-west of Dorchester.

At 17.45 hrs, Squadron Leader Alexander 'Sandy' Johnstone, up from Westhampnet and leading the Spitfires of 602 Squadron, 'between Swanage and Portland sighted a solid mass of enemy aircraft at 15,000ft between Dorchester and the coast, total number was estimated at 200/300 Do 17s [*sic*], Me 109s and Me 110s [ORB]'. The Spitfires, however, had the advantage of sun behind them, and Johnstone led 'A' Flight down to attack the bombers, getting in one pass,

> before the fighters were among us, after which the sky became a maelstrom of bombers, fighters and escorts swooping and swerving all over the shop. The air waves reverberated with shouts of 'Look out behind you!', 'I've got one!' or simply 'Jezus Christ!', as planes were locked in individual battles.

The squadron went on to claim a total of seven Me 110s, three Me 109s, and a Do 17 [*sic*] destroyed – which was also somewhat optimistic. Squadron Leader Johnstone recalled the scene back at Westhampnett after the battle:

> Some of the lads got back before me and Westhampnett was bubbling with excitement by the time I landed. Refuellers and armourers were already hard at work turning the aircraft round, while Henry [squadron IO] buzzed about like a bee on heat, frantically trying to piece together what had happened.

There were two Spitfires missing, however: Flying Officer Hugh Coverley had been shot-up and baled out near Dorchester, and Sergeant Mervyn Sprague had also been shot down, baling out over the sea; both pilots were safe, but neither would survive the Battle of Britain. At the material time, both *Oberleutnant* Helmut-Felix Bolz of 5/JG 2 and *Oberleutnant* Hans 'Assi' Hahn of 4/JG 2 both claimed Spitfires over Dorchester, and *Feldwebel* Emil Clade of 7/JG 27 became an ace, recording his fifth aerial victory, a Spitfire, West of Portland.

Finally, as the bombers continued to withdraw, Squadron Leader Cedric Williams, a Cranwellian, led the Hurricanes of 17 Squadron into action at 17.45 hrs, meeting a gaggle of covering Me 109s and Me 110s milling around at 15–20,000ft, ten miles south-east of Weymouth.

Pilot Officer Geoffrey Pittman:

> Red Section [Squadron Leader Williams – 1, Pilot Officer Pittman – 2 and Sergeant Bartlett – 3] was flying in a westerly direction when I saw about fifteen–twenty Me 110s. Red 1 put the Section into line astern and attacked a straggler at 17,000ft. The Me 110 then dived down in a southerly direction. The Section was out of position for an organised attack and Red 1 broke away to the right and upwards. Before following Red 1 I delivered a stern quarter on E/A, firing for about two-seconds. No result was seen from this attack. Red Section then flew on the port side at about 800ft distance – overtaking in preparation for a head-on attack.

The Me 110, however, was extremely dangerous when so attacked, considering two forward-firing 20mm MG FF cannon and four 7.9mm MG17 machine-guns were nose-mounted; Pittman continues:

> The E/A suddenly turned into us just as we were passing and opened up with intense front cannon and gun fire. The Section pulled round hard to starboard and upwards to avoid E/A. We then made a slow left-hand turn onto the E/A. Red 1 delivered a head-on attack. When Red 1 was about 100 yards from E/A his port wing disintegrated into hundreds of small pieces. He then flicked over into a left-hand spin and went straight into the sea, nobody jumping out. The Me 110 then dived down with a stream of smoke from the port engine and went into a left-hand spin and crashed into the sea. This last action took place at 10,000ft, five – six miles south-east of Portland Bill.

It was an eye for an eye. The damage to Squadron Leader Williams' wing provides a graphic example of the 20mm cannon's destructive power. The CO was never seen again.

AC1 Geoff Gwillam, 17 Squadron: 'It was a great shame when Squadron Leader Williams was killed. He was very popular with all of us, even us "Erks" on 17 Squadron. He definitely wasn't one of those snobby officers; very approachable with time for everyone.'

No.17 Squadron's Flight Lieutenant Alfred Bayne, the commander of 'B' Flight, was also shot down over Portland, and having safely baled out of his Hurricane was fortunate to be rescued from the sea unhurt.

Like other RAF squadrons in this chaotic air battle, potentially involving nearly 400 aircraft in total, 17 Squadron's combat claims were optimistic. Nonetheless, three Me 110s and a 109 were claimed destroyed along with various 'probables'. As the unit lamented the loss of its Boss that evening, a congratulatory signal was received from Air Vice-Marshal Park: 'Warm congratulations on their grand results this afternoon.'

The enemy had successfully bombed Warmwell, although the station remained operational. The presence of so many escorting fighters suggests that heavy fighter opposition was anticipated; the defenders, consequently, were only able to claim the destruction of just four Ju 88s – while no less than thirty-six enemy fighters were considered destroyed. In reality, only one Ju 88 failed to return and another crash-landed, damaged, back at base; six Me 109s were lost with two more also returning badly shot-up, but the Me 110s had suffered: six were destroyed and seven returned to France damaged. The RAF squadrons involved had lost nine fighters, six pilots being killed and one wounded, while one forced-landed near the coast and another crash-landed back at base, both badly damaged.

The next action of the day also involved a 10 Group squadron, namely 92 based at Pembrey in South Wales, and specifically Flight Lieutenant Robert

Stanford Tuck, who reported a combat with a 'Dorner 17 or 215' at 18.10 hrs, 15 miles south of St Govan's Head:

While on patrol at 10,000ft over the burning oil tanks at Pembroke above 10/10 cloud, I was instructed by Dewdrop to investigate an aircraft bombing a ship six miles South of St Govan lightship. On coming down through cloud at 4,000ft ... a further six miles South I sighted a twin-engine aircraft circling above a ship. I immediately proceeded towards it as fast as possible and identified it as a Do 17, or possibly a 215. I carried out one beam attack of two-seconds' fire, then found myself in the astern position and gave him four seconds from 150 yards and observed large pieces fall off him, and bright flashes from each motor. By this time he had climbed into cloud so I opened up at full throttle and entered cloud on the same course as the E/A had done. A few seconds after entering cloud I heard several loud cracks on my aircraft. I knew immediately that I was being hit by enemy bullets, but still could not see the E/A. However, I eventually saw him over my leading edge about 20ft below me. I pulled quickly to one side and back into the astern position and from extremely close range, i.e. about twenty-five yards astern, I gave him a two-second burst. By this time my engine was giving off thick clouds of smoke so I decided to break off the engagement and make for land, as E/A had obviously hit me in a serious place in the engine. On coming out of cloud I found myself approximately fifteen miles SSW of St Govan's Head. As the engine was getting so very hot and smoke thicker, I decided to switch off the motor and glide for land. I just managed to make it and crash-landed just inland of the cliffs.

'Lucky' Tuck was wounded in a leg, but nonetheless had survived yet another narrow escape. Five ships had been attacked in St George's Channel before the Spitfire appeared, one being sunk and another set ablaze. The bomber concerned, of the coastal reconnaissance unit 1/606, was destroyed by Tuck, the crew of three all killed.

Next, the action shifted to south-east England, RDF detecting 30+ inland of Cap Gris-Nez at 17.55 hrs. Unlike the Warmwell raid, however, there was little initial reaction by Fighter Command. At 18.15 hrs, Pilot Officers Alan Eckford and Anthony Barton of 32 Squadron, up from Hawkinge, were already patrolling near Dungeness when they sighted a Hs 126 reconnaissance aircraft, which, immediately dropped to sea-level and made for France upon spotting the Hurricanes. Keeping a wary lookout for enemy fighters, Eckford managed a three-second burst, damaging the snooper, before losing sight of the Henschel and breaking off the pursuit. Then, at 18.20 hrs, Squadron Leader Mike Crossley scrambled from Hawkinge with six other 32 Squadron Hurricanes with orders to patrol Dover. For the past ten minutes, RDF had indicated 100+ starting to cross the Dover Strait – so it is surprising that the seven Hurricanes of 32 Squadron were not scrambled until 18.20 hrs, followed by twelve Spitfires of Kenley's 616 Squadron three minutes later, twelve more of 610 Squadron from Biggin Hill at 18.52 hrs, and seven of 54 Squadron not until 19.10 hrs. In anticipation of an attack on RAF Hawkinge, air raid warning Red was sounded there at 18.35 hrs. The incoming threat, however, was essentially a fighter sweep, the whole of JG 26 being led by *Major* Adolf Galland, and elements of JG 54; although the Do 17s of 3/KG 76 were present, no bombs fell on the mainland.

No.32 Squadron had been ordered to patrol Dover, where, at 18.45 hrs, five miles off the Kentish coast, 'Twelve Do 215s [*sic*] escorted by about thirty-six Me 109s were intercepted at 14,000ft south of Dover. Squadron Leader Crossley shot down a Do 215 in flames and sent an Me 109 spinning into the sea [ORB].'

Pilot Officer Jon Proctor:

> I was leading Yellow Section on the right of the Leader when the E/A were sighted. We attempted to cut them off in an attempt to run for the French coast. I attacked the escort fighters with the rest of the Section and the formation split up into several dogfights. One Me 109 settled onto the tail of one of our aircraft so I gave a burst at 15° deflection from astern. The E/A dived and climbed up to a stall-turn but I followed all the while except when recovering from a spin. After my final burst the E/A dived straight down towards the English coast and crashed in flames, four miles SE of Cap Gris-Nez. I followed it down then went home to rearm.

It is likely that the Hurricane which Proctor had seen attacked was flown by either Pilot Officer Jack Rose, who was shot down, baled out and was fortunate to be rescued from the sea unharmed, or Pilot Officer Keith Gillman – who was missing. Gillman, according to his Casualty File, was last seen at 18.50 hrs, three miles south of Dover – his hometown – it being 'thought that he was following an enemy aircraft out to sea'. Sadly, the 19-year-old Hurricane pilot, who would appear in flying kit on the front cover of *Picture Post* on 31 August 1940 – an iconic image – was never seen again. It is likely that 32 Squadron's two casualties had fallen prey to *Leutnant* Josef Bürschgens of *Stab* III/JG 26 and *Leutnant* Ludwig Hafer of *Stab* I/JG 26, both of whom claimed Hurricanes over that Channel that fateful evening. Pilot Officer Gillman's loss, in fact, reduced 32 Squadron's pilot strength to just eight – little more than a flight; forty-eight hours later the squadron would be withdrawn to Acklington, in 13 Group, to rest and rebuild.

Strangely, the enemy did not press on inland over Dover, but skirted round to the east, around Deal and headed towards Manston.

No.54 Squadron was in action at 19.00 hrs:

A very quiet day until the evening, when about 100 E/A approached Dover and district. The Squadron, patrolling Manston, became separated and Green Section was suddenly attacked by twelve Me 109s. Pilot Officer Howes saved the situation by passing the information of their presence just in time to enable to Section to take evasive action. Pilot Officer Colin Gray destroyed one of these and Pilot Officer Matthews attacked four 109s over Dover, shooting one down into the sea [ORB].

The Me 109 attacked by Pilot Officer Colin Gray 'caught fire, blew up and broke in two. The tailpiece fell separately. This aircraft fell near a searchlight post near Faversham and its destruction is confirmed by them.' The 109, of *Stab* I/JG 54, crashed at St Nicholas-at-Wade, killing the pilot, *Oberleutnant* H. Held, the Gruppe Technical Officer.

Pilot Officer Michael Shand, also, like 54 Squadron's Kiwi aces Colin Gray and Al Deere, a New Zealander, was flying only his second operational sortie that evening when he was shot down by a 109, crash-landing, wounded at Brook End, Birchington.

Back at Hornchurch, there was good news for 54 Squadron: '"Al" Deere was awarded a Bar to his DFC – the first member of the squadron to achieve this distinction, he has shot down eleven enemy machines, shared in the destruction of another three and probably destroyed a further three. Heartiest congratulations [ORB].'

Returning to the fighting on the evening of 25 August 1940, the twelve Spitfires of 616 Squadron, ordered to patrol Maidstone, were also in action at 19.00 hrs: 'Before reaching Maidstone the squadron ordered over Canterbury to intercept Raid 21, consisting of fifteen–twenty Do 17s flying in vics at 15,000ft, escorted by fifteen–twenty Me 109s in staggered line astern at 16,000ft and 20,000ft, above and behind. The Squadron was immediately broken up by Me 109s [ORB].'

Pilot Officer Jack Bell:

The Me 109s turned to meet us and a general dogfight occurred, when we were about to go in and attack the bombers. I fired a short full deflection burst at an Me 109 which was on the tail of a Spitfire – no known results – and later chased a 109 out to mid-Channel, firing a total of about twelve seconds in four bursts. I noticed a few stabs of flame coming from it as I broke away in cloud, this might have been exhaust. I noticed my incendiary entering E/A.

Bell claimed the 109 as a probable. Flying Officer George Moberley was awarded a 109 destroyed, and Sergeant Marmaduke Ridley a Do 17 destroyed. There were casualties, however. The Spitfire clashing with the Me 109s II and III/JG 26. Sergeant Phillip Wareing, who had destroyed a 109 three days before, chased a 109 across the Channel, recording hits, but was himself hit by German coastal flak and forced to bale out, becoming a PoW (the intrepid pilot would, however, escape from Oflag XXIB at Schubin in 1942, returning home via Sweden). Sergeant Thomas Westmoreland, however, was shot down and killed over the sea and remains missing.

Meanwhile, 610 Squadron was being shadowed over Dover by twelve Me 109s of JG 26, which the Spitfires climbed to attack. Many years later, Sergeant Bob Beardsley recalled:

> We received a scramble to patrol Dover–Folkestone and on approaching the coastal area saw a number of Me 109s crossing inbound at 90° to our course. I had a wild burst at a 109 crossing me at 90° full deflection and was immediately hit by fire from another on my tail, which affected my aileron control. Not being able to sustain effective action I returned to Biggin Hill, where I was congratulated on my first 'kill', which my No 1 confirmed, in flames – and I didn't see it happen!

According to the 610 Squadron ORB, the 109 hit by Beardsley flipped over onto its back in a vertical dive, its crash being witnessed by Flying Officer Peter Lamb (although there is little doubt that he actually saw the 109 crash destroyed by 54 Squadron's Pilot Officer Colin Gray). Flying Officer Thomas Gardiner, however, was shot down and baled out, his Spitfire crashing near Sandwich; the pilot was admitted to Waldershore Hospital, slightly wounded. Sergeant Claude Parsons reported seeing 'a green streak in the water off Dover at 19.54 hrs, he circled round until the pilot was picked up by a motor boat [ORB]' – this most likely being 32 Squadron's Pilot Officer Rose, who that day had been issued a pack of dye which he stitched to his Mae West life preserver – sadly, 32 Squadron's missing pilot, Pilot Officer Keith Gillman, had not done so.

This was a strange raid, given that no bombing apparently took place. Seven German aircraft were *claimed* destroyed, two of them bombers – the actual casualties being one Do 17 and an Me 109 destroyed, with another of the latter crashing back at base. Fighter Command's casualties were five aircraft lost, with two pilots killed, one wounded and one captured, in addition to one aircraft damaged.

So ended the day-fighting on 25 August 1940.

That day, Adela Curtis, leader of the Christian Contemplatives' Community at St Bride's Farm, Burton Bradstock, Dorset, published her advice regarding furthering Britain's war aims in *The Two Edged Sword*: 'We are to summon each enemy leader by name. For cumulative effect the message should be spoken three times – "Adolf Hitler! Adolf Hitler! Adolf Hitler! Hear the truth!"' It is not thought that this appeal had any effect on the Battle of Britain or the Second World War's outcome…

As ever, Coastal Command had protected shipping and carried out reconnaissance sorties, in addition to a raid by six Blenheims against Cherbourg's oil tanks. Seven of the eighteen 2 Group Blenheims sent to attack targets in the Netherlands were forced to abort owing to unsuitable weather, the remainder attacking various targets, including a low-level raid on the airfields at Bergen and Texel.

So far, the war had barely touched Berlin, a popular saying there being 'Friends, do enjoy the war, the peace will be dreadful!' – and the German civilian population was confident of victory.

Frau Else Wendel: 'Everything was fine for Germany … we waited feverishly for the invasion … at the time we did not hate the English; we were rather sorry for them when we thought of the thrashing they were going to get.'

The war, however, was coming to Berlin – that very night.

In response to the bombing of Central London, of 102 Wellingtons, Whitleys and Hampdens on operations that night, many were attacking Berlin, and specifically legitimate targets including the Siemens factory and Klingenberg power station. When the air raid sirens wailed across Berlin, the German public were barely alarmed, disbelieving that they were about to be attacked, it was impossible, they thought: Germany had all but won the war. Then bombs exploded.

Accurate bombing, however, was prevented by thick cloud covering the enemy capital, and a strong headwind made the return journey a struggle for the Hampdens, operating at the extremity of their endurance: three simply disappeared and three more ditched in the sea. Only a handful of bombs fell within Berlin's city centre, destroying a summer house in the suburb of Rosenthal and injuring two civilians. Most bombs fell in the countryside, falling on Stadtgüter – state owned farms – inspiring more banter: 'The British are now trying to starve us out!'

Nonetheless, for all the bravado, as the American journalist and war correspondent William L. Shirer, who was in Berlin that night, wrote: 'Berliners are stunned. They did not think it could ever happen.'

Hitler was bewildered that Churchill should have authorised a raid on Berlin which in practical terms achieved nothing – but had poked the hornets' nest sufficiently to turn the destructive power of what was effectively the mightiest and most accomplished air force in the world against London. The raid shocked the Germans – and would soon lead to the pivotal turning point in the Battle of Britain.

Monday, 26 August 1940

Pilot Officer William Walker, 'B' Flight, 616 Squadron, Kenley:

It was still dark when the orderly awoke me with a cup of tea at 0330 hrs that morning, just two days after my twenty-seventh birthday, which had passed unnoticed amid the current level of activity and excitement. I drank my tea slowly and gradually awakened to another day. It seemed such a short while since we had been stood down the previous evening, at about 2100 hrs, and after which a few beers refreshed our spirits before bed. However, I dressed and went down to breakfast, always a quiescent occasion at the unearthly hour of 0400 hrs! The sound of aero engines could be heard in the distance, indicating that the groundcrews were already busy. One was so accustomed to the drone of engines that it passed almost unnoticed amid the clatter of cups and plates.

Following breakfast I joined other pilots outside the Mess. We all climbed aboard a lorry and were driven to dispersal, to remain at readiness, where a hut and a few tents constituted 616 Squadron's base. A few days earlier the Duke of Kent had visited us at our modest location to wish us well.

That day I was allocated Spitfire R6633, and was to fly in Yellow Section, led by Flying Officer Teddy St Aubyn, a former Guards officer. The plane stood within fifty yards of our hut and so I walked over and placed my parachute in the cockpit with the straps spread apart and ready for wearing immediately I jumped in. Two of the groundcrew stood by the plane with the starter battery plugged in. I walked back to the hut as the sun rose and added a little warmth to a chilly start. Pilots sat about either reading or exchanging the usual banter that had become routine. We had spent many months in this way, which was now a way of life. At 0800 hrs our second breakfast arrived at dispersal, and was just as fulfilling as our breakfast of four hours earlier: coffee, eggs, bacon, sausages and toast to replenish our undiminished appetites.

And so, in a scene repeated at airfields throughout the land that morning, 616 Squadron settled down and anxiously awaited the next call to action.

During the previous night, III/KG 55 had despatched ten He 111s to attack such targets as Portsmouth, Southampton, Aldershot, Bristol and the airfields at Abingdon and Worcester. According to the Fliegerkorps V intelligence report submitted by an *Oberleutnant* Schonbeck to *Luftflotte* 3 HQ, the latter, elementary flying training base RAF Perdiswell, had been bombed by two He 111s, which reported 'heavy fires' arising in buildings – although no such damage occurred. Indeed, the majority of these nocturnal raiders did not see the effect of their attacks, presumably owing to cloud.

Inevitably, the first RDF plots that morning concerned German reconnaissance aircraft, five in total, all of 3/(F)121, which returned to report on activity at Warmwell and Chickerell airfields in Dorset (the latter an obscure FAA base inland of Chesil Beach, used by aircraft involved with gunnery training at the Lulworth ranges), Weymouth Bay, Portland and Pembroke. A Do 17 of 3/(F)31 bombed St Eval airfield, reporting bombs exploding on the runway and beyond the perimeter, and at 11.03 hrs a He 111 bombed RAF Harwell in Oxfordshire, a Bomber Command training base.

By 11.30 hrs, however, all RDF indications were that a major raid was assembling behind Cap Gris-Nez – and as the enemy's target was Folkestone, events developed quickly. By 11.39 hrs, three German formations were heading towards Dover. The only RAF fighters airborne, however, were those of 616 Squadron's 'B' Flight, Blue and Yellow Sections, which had scrambled at 11.03 hrs to intercept the He 111 attacking Harwell – Blue Section sighting the bandit 'just above cloud at 7,000ft, but it dived into the cloud and disappeared [ORB]'. Yellow Section was then ordered to 'pancake' back at Kenley, while Blue Section was vectored to Dungeness in search of a rogue balloon at 10,000ft.

Meanwhile, at 11.40 hrs the 11 Group Controller scrambled the Defiants of 264 Squadron from Hornchurch, followed two minutes later by the Spitfires of 610 Squadron from Hawkinge, both ordered to Dover, and at 11.46 hrs, Yellow Section of 616 Squadron took-off from Kenley, hastening to find Blue Section over Dungeness, and at 11.49 hrs the Hurricanes of 56 Squadron scrambled from North Weald to patrol Manston.

Pilot Officer William Walker:

> The telephone rang in the dispersal hut and a shout of 'Yellow Section, scramble! Patrol Dungeness/Dover Angels 20!' sent me running to my plane. I leapt onto the wing and was in the cockpit, parachute strapped on, within seconds. I pressed the starter and the engine fired immediately. The groundcrew removed the plug from the cowling and pulled the remote starter battery clear. I waved the chocks away and taxied the aircraft, followed by my Section Leader, Flying Officer 'Teddy' St Aubyn and Sergeant Marmaduke Ridley, to the end of the runway for take-off. Within minutes Yellow Section was airborne. We headed East, climbing quickly and passing through cloud, reaching our patrol course in some fifteen–twenty minutes.

The Spitfires of 610 Squadron, operating from nearby Hawkinge, were already in action, engaging the enemy at noon:

> Red, Yellow, Blue and Green Sections engaged about eight Me 109s which were bombing Folkestone at 5,000ft … Squadron Leader Ellis attacked a 109 from astern and above, the E/A burst into flames and plunged into the sea 400 yards off Folkestone. Flying Officer Wilson confirms this. Flying Officer Lamb delivered a No 1 Attack against a Do 215 [sic] flying home out to sea off Deal at 1,000ft; after a burst of eight seconds the starboard engine of E/A began smoking, rear-gunfire ceased, E/A was losing height and pilot was picked up twelve miles South of Dover. Flying Officer Wilson chased an Me 109 and gave it a deflection burst, the E/A went into a steep dive towards France, another burst and the E/A started smoking and went right in – no wreckage or pilot were seen, merely the splash and rings. Sergeant Hamlyn attacked an Me 109 at 9,000ft with two long bursts, saw it start to smoke and turn downwards. He then attacked another Me 109, set the cockpit on fire, finally the whole fuselage was in flames and it was seen to crash into the sea one mile off Folkestone by Sergeant Parsons. Sergeant Ramsay fired three short bursts at an Me 109, the E/A emitted a cloud of black smoke and vanished

into cloud. After a few seconds our pilot followed it through the clouds and saw E/A blazing on the ground West of Folkestone [ORB].

Unfortunately, 610 had suffered casualties. Having flown his first operational sortie just two days previously, Sergeant Frank Webster was shot-up and killed when crash-landing his blazing Spitfire at Hawkinge. Sergeant Peter Else was attacking an Me 109 when hit by an unseen assailant from astern, forcing him to abandon his machine – as he did so another burst of fire raked his Spitfire, shattering his forearm. Having landed by parachute on Hawkinge airfield, Else was admitted to the Kent and Canterbury Hospital where his left arm was amputated above the elbow in a life-saving operation.

At 12.20 hrs, between Hearne Bay and Deal, the Defiants of 264 Squadron, alone, intercepted twelve Do 17Zs of 7/KG 3, based at St Trond in Belgium, heading for Manston, heavily escorted by fifty Me 109s of JG 3.

Flight Lieutenant Arthur Banham, commanding 'B' Flight:

I was Red Leader 264 Squadron, when approaching Dover at 12,000ft we sighted twelve Do 17s in vics line astern and I opened fire at the leading bomber of last section. I saw my gunner get in a long burst at 100 yards; I then broke away and turned in towards the leading section and get a long burst in at 100 yards on No 2 of first section. I was then hit myself near the cockpit and my machine was on fire. I lost control, and telling my gunner to jump, as I turned aircraft on its back, I fell out and was picked up in the sea. Sergeant Thorn and gunner confirm seeing second Do 17 I fired on go down in flames.

Shot down by a 109, Flight Lieutenant Banham, rescued after ninety minutes in the sea, was luckier than his gunner, the 27-year old 'Brummie' Sergeant Barrie Baker – who remains missing.

Flight Lieutenant Ernest Campbell-Colquhoun was Yellow 1:

On patrol approaching Dover at 11,000ft I saw nine Do 17s in three vics. Approaching enemy aircraft from starboard side I carried out several attacks from beam. I saw one Do 17 break formation and commence a shallow dive, smoking from starboard engine. I returned to base owing to gun stoppages.

Pilot Officer Harold Goodall, Yellow 2:

When over Manston at 11,000ft we climbed up to attack a formation of nine Do 17s. During this climb and before we were in range of the Do's, I was attacked by an Me 109 from behind and above. My gunner got in two short bursts and appeared to hit the Me 109, which dived away and was not seen again. Immediately after this I attacked a Do 17 with an overtaking beam attack at 250 yards, and got in two fairly long bursts at point blank range. Pieces fell from the starboard engine which burst into flames. Just as the machine went into a dive one of the crew baled out. I saw the machine go down in flames.

I immediately attacked another Do 17, which had broken formation and my gunner got in a short burst which appeared to hit. I saw the Do 17 dive into cloud and lost it as I was being attacked by Me 109s. I landed with three guns jammed and damage to my machine.

One Do 17 was accredited as destroyed.

Pilot Officer Ian Stephenson, however, was 'set on fire by a 109 and baled out. He was picked up in the sea and later taken to Canterbury Hospital with minor injuries. His gunner, Sergeant Maxwell, is missing [ORB].'

The 264 Squadron ORB also reports:

Pilot Officer Hughes in his first engagement with the enemy successfully destroyed two Do 17s by converging attacks. Sergeant Thorn and Sergeant Barker put up a magnificent show by destroying two Do 17s in the action, and while attacking a third machine they were attacked by an Me 109 and their machine developed oil and glycol leaks. Taking evasive action, they spun away and were preparing to make a crash-landing near Herne Bay when the Me 109 again attacked them at 500ft. The aircraft caught fire but before crashing Sergeant Barker fired his remaining rounds into the enemy which crashed a few fields away.

From German records, we know that a German *experten*, *Hauptmann* Günther Lützow of *Stab*/JG 3 claimed two Defiants in this combat, recording his eleventh and twelfth victories, while *Oberleutnant* Friedrich-Franz von Cramon, also of *Stab*/JG 3, claimed a Defiant as his second kill.

By now, the Hurricanes of 56 Squadron had appeared on the scene – fortunately for 264 Squadron, because the Defiants' losses would otherwise undoubtedly have been higher. Unable to catch the bombers, 56 Squadron took on the escorting fighters, Pilot Officer Ken Marston reporting the action taking place over Westgate-on-Sea:

I was flying Red 2. I saw the first Me 109 about 2,000ft below me, coming from the north-west. I managed to drop on his tail about 100 yards behind him. He attempted to evade me but I got in a short burst, his port radiator and cowling flew off. The E/A then turned on its back and I saw the pilot's head and shoulders out of the cockpit. The machine then dived steeply into the cloud. I followed him through the cloud but the first thing I saw was another Me 109 on the tail of a diving Boulton-Paul Defiant. I dived with full throttle and got about seventy yards behind the Me 109 at a height of 50ft behind him. I gave him a short burst and saw a flame appear from beneath the cockpit. Then the aircraft crashed about 100 yards behind the Defiant, which had forced-landed with wheels-up [Sergeants Thorn and Barker]. The crew of the Defiant got away from their machine and were picked up by an army tender. The position of the crash was approximately five miles due South of Reculver Church, near Herne Bay.

I then returned to the position where I came out of the cloud and saw below me a burning wreck in a crater by a farm, approximately three miles south-west of Westgate-on-Sea. I looked around for a parachute but could not see one. I then returned to base.

The Me 109 involved was a fighter of 4/JG 3, which crashed on Chislet Marshes, south of Grays Farm, Reculver, at 12.25 hrs; the pilot, *Unteroffizier* W. Finke, was killed.

The other Me 109 destroyed by Marston was a 6/JG 3 machine which crashed on Shuart's Marshes near St Nicholas-at-Wade – the pilot, *Unteroffizier* Fritz Buchner, would remain missing, buried in the wreckage of his fighter until recovered, from a depth of over 30ft, by aviation archaeologist Peter Dimond in 1984.

No.56 Squadron's Pilot Officer Maurice Mounsden also claimed a 109 destroyed in the action, but two Hurricanes were shot down: Pilot Officer Bryan Wicks baled out, unhurt, over Canterbury, his Hurricane crashing into the river Stour, and Sergeant George Smythe forced-landed at Courtsend, Foulness; *Oberleutnant* Lothar Keller (1/JG 3) and *Oberfeldwebel* Robert Olejnik (2/JG 3) each claimed a Hurricane destroyed.

Meanwhile, Blue Section of 616 Squadron had not found the balloon they sought over Dungeness – sighting 100 Me 109s at 12.30 hrs instead. The Spitfires were immediately hit hard by JG 51 over Dover. The commander of 'B' Flight, Flight Lieutenant Denys 'Kill 'em' Gillam, was the only 'South Yorkshire' pilot to bring his guns to bear:

On arriving at 10,000ft we were ordered to intercept two 40 plus raids. We climbed to 11,000ft and discovered about 100 Me 109s all around and above us. I ordered line astern and we formed a circle. One Me 109 appeared on Blue Two's tail, so I turned on to it and fired at it down to 4,000ft. I then followed it through cloud and on coming out saw the aircraft hit the water straight ahead.

Gillam was also the only pilot of 'B' Flight to return to Kenley unscathed.

Blue Section's Flying Officer George Moberley was shot down and killed, his Spitfire crashing into the Channel; Flying Officer Roy Marples was shot-up and crash-landed at Adisham and was also admitted to the Kent & Canterbury Hospital, suffering from shell splinters in his legs – wounds which would keep him out of the war until 7 November 1940; Sergeant Percy Copeland crash-landed his Spitfire near Wye, also wounded, and sent to Ashford Hospital, and Flying Officer John 'Jack' Bell forced-landed at Bekesbourne but was fortunately unhurt.

Yellow Section of 616 Squadron arrived over Dungeness and were immediately ambushed by JG 51. Flying Officer Teddy St Aubyn's Spitfire was hit in the coolant system, the pilot, a former Grenadier Guards officer, crash-landing on Eastchurch airfield; Sergeant Marmaduke Ridley crashed near Dover and was killed.

Major Mölders himself, leading all three *gruppen* of JG 51 on a *freie hunt*, as usual attacked from behind and slightly below, a blind-spot, and aimed at Pilot Officer William Walker's Spitfire R6633:

When the 109s hit us I banked steeply to port, towards a 109, but suddenly my machine was raked with bullets. I never even saw the one that attacked me. The flying controls ceased to respond and a sudden pain in my leg indicated that I had been hit. Baling out seemed to be a sensible option. My two comrades of Yellow Section had both vanished.

I pulled back the hood and tried to stand up but realised that I had not disconnected the radio lead, which was still plugged in, and had to remove my helmet before I was free to jump. The aircraft was still banking to port, so jumping out was easy. I was still at 20,000ft and pulled the ripcord immediately. A sudden jerk indicated that all was well and that I was on my way down. I looked around but could not see a single aircraft. Below there was 10/10ths cloud. I had no idea where I was. It seemed to take ages to reach the clouds and passing through I realised that I was still over the Channel. Thinking that I would soon land in the sea prompted the thought that I had better remove my heavy flying boots. I did this and let them fall. I watched them spiral down for what seemed like ages and then realised that I was much higher than I thought. I inflated my Mae West and eventually landed in the sea. I easily discarded my parachute and could see the wreck of a ship sticking out of the water a few hundred yards away and swam to it. I reached it and climbed on, sitting there for about half an hour until a fishing boat came alongside and I clambered aboard. I was now extremely cold from my immersion and wet clothes.

The fishermen gave me a cup of tea, well laced with whisky, as we headed for land. When about two miles offshore an RAF launch came alongside and I was transferred to it. By this time the tea concoction had worked quite disastrously on my cold stomach. Fortunately there was a loo aboard to which I retired, with some relief. I was still enthroned when we reached Ramsgate Harbour. An aircraftman kept knocking on the door and enquiring whether I was okay. It was some time, however, before I was able to emerge! I was carried up the steps to a waiting ambulance, by which time quite a crowd had gathered and gave me a cheer as I was put in the ambulance. A kind old lady handed me a packet of cigarettes, so I decided that being shot down was perhaps not such a bad thing after all!

This had been a catastrophe for 616 Squadron. Since having arrived at Kenley a week previously, seven out of fifteen Spitfires had been lost, four pilots killed and four more wounded. The squadron diarist, clearly a master of the understatement, recorded this action as 'a most unfortunate engagement'.

Pilot Officer Lionel 'Buck' Casson:

Having arrived at Kenley with the replacement Spitfire on 24 August 1940, the following day Tom Murray and I were loaned to 615 Squadron, a Hurricane unit with which 616 shared Kenley, because they were short of pilots and we both had experience on Hurricanes. After 616 was badly mauled on 26 August 1940, however, we had to return to 616, which was also rapidly running out of pilots.

Pilot Officer William Walker:

I was driven to Ramsgate Hospital, which had been badly bombed, where doctors tried to remove the bullet in my foot. This proved too great an undertaking, so I was put to bed; I was absolutely freezing cold and it was a further five–six hours until I felt my circulation returning.

Returning to the fighting on 26 August 1940, as the Me 109s withdrew, the Spitfires of 54 Squadron engaged them at 12.20 hrs, over the Channel off Deal and Dover.

Flying Officer Desmond McMullen:

I was one of a formation of four and saw at least twelve E/A above us and there were many more below. I dived down and chased one over Canterbury. There was a dogfight and he disappeared. Returning to Dover, I encountered a lone Me 109 and gave it a three second burst at a range of 200 yards, closing to 100 yards, with slight deflection. The E/A burst into flames and fell, probably into the sea.

The New Zealand ace Pilot Officer Colin Gray, and Pilot Officer Eric Edsall, also claimed Me 109 'probables'; 54 Squadron suffered no losses.

Given the lack of warning, however, the RAF fighters had been unable to prevent Folkestone being bombed – and the town had suffered. Salter's Laundry in Park Farm suffered two direct hits, killing three people – 60-year-old Charles Holloway and two teenage girls: 17-year-old Louise Hart and 19-year-old Annie Todd. Another teenager, Ethel Harris, 18, was seriously injured.

Mrs Christine Nash was working in the Laundry's office:

I heard aeroplanes flying over very low but thought they were ours until just afterwards there came a scream of bombs. I threw myself forward over my desk to protect my head as best I could and said a little prayer. Then there were two terrific explosions. I was covered with glass, wood splinters and plaster. When it seemed a little quieter I began to move my arms and legs. Glass had cut me in several places but I eventually managed to crawl out from beneath the debris. As I emerged from the wreckage I could hear machine-guns. The thought crossed my mind that they would see me because I was wearing a light blue frock – but then I met rescuers.

Houses adjacent to the devastated laundry were also damaged, and across town a whole row of houses was reduced to rubble by a stick of bombs, and 16 Lower Sandgate Road collapsed, trapping the occupant, Mrs Morrison, who had sheltered beneath the stairs. PC Spain of Folkestone Police disregarded his own safety to burrow through rubble and rescue her – for which courageous act he would receive the George Medal. George Knight, a 79-year-old, was sat in his potting shed at the allotments in Archer Road when a bomb exploded, making a crater 20ft deep – the pensioner was killed instantly.

As the raid withdrew, the RAF fighters landed to refuel and rearm – but before their places on aerial patrol lines could be taken by fresh squadrons, a raid came in and bombed Broadstairs, and at 13.00 hrs another raid dropped bombs near Ramsgate. No damage was caused to military targets.

By 14.30 hrs, RDF was plotting another major assembly of German aircraft over Dover, the three forces involved numbering sixty, twenty and twelve 'bandits', all of which, by 14.50 hrs, were clearly making for the Thames Estuary. Further to the south-west, 501 Squadron was patrolling over Hawkinge – but this raid was approaching the aerodromes in Essex. The 11 Group Controller reacted by scrambling 65 Squadron from Rochford at 14.38 hrs to intercept the threat north of Manston, reinforced there by 615 Squadron which took-off from Kenley at 14.45 hrs, while at the same time 1 (RCAF) Squadron hurriedly took-off from North Weald to patrol base.

As the raiders progressed, it was clear that this was another major raid, and so further squadrons were scrambled: at 14.50 hrs 85 Squadron left Croydon to patrol base before being vectored towards Maidstone; at 15.00 hrs 111 Squadron left Martlesham Heath to patrol Chelmsford; two minutes later 56 Squadron went up from North Weald to cover Colchester, and at 15.10 hrs, 54 Squadron scrambled from Hornchurch to patrol over Manston. It was a sizeable force – but, even so, 11 Group requested assistance from 12 Group. Consequently, at 15.10 hrs twelve Hurricanes of 310 (Czech) Squadron scrambled from Duxford with orders to patrol North Weald, and five minutes later Flight Lieutenant Wilf Clouston of 19 Squadron led 'All available aircraft in air in a panic take-off [ORB]' from Fowlmere to patrol Debden. Quarter of an hour before, however, combat had already been joined over Whitstable, from which point on the defenders fought a running battle between the Isle of Sheppey and Colchester.

The first of the defending squadrons to engage was Squadron Leader Joe Kayll's 615, over Whitstable at 15.00 hrs. Unfortunately no individual combat reports appear to have survived, and the ORB is scant in detail: 'Squadron was sent up to intercept raid and sighted enemy over Thames Estuary. Enemy surprised.'

According to the AHB narrative, the Hurricanes, for once, had the advantage of height, being at 19,000ft with the enemy – Me 109s – 1,000ft below. Moreover, the Hurricanes were perfectly positioned between the enemy and sun – as a result of which surprise was complete. Four Me 109s were claimed as destroyed, in addition to several others probably destroyed or damaged – but the enemy clearly recovered and counter-attacked quickly because three Hurricanes were shot down: Pilot Officer John McClintock baled out off Sheerness and was rescued from the sea unhurt; the Canadian commander of 'A' Flight, Flight Lieutenant Lionel Gaunce DFC, was shot down in flames over Herne Bay, baled out and was also picked up – he was admitted to Herne Bay Hospital suffering from shock. Pilot Officer Douglas Hone was shot-up but made it back to land, crash-landing at Rochford wounded by cannon shell shrapnel necessitating treatment at Southend Hospital. As is commonly the case, especially with so many aircraft involved, it is difficult to be sure which German pilots were responsible, but both *Oberleutnant* Helmut Kühle and *Feldwebel* Karl Ruttger of 3/JG 52 recorded their first victories, Hurricanes, in this area and at the material time.

At 15.20 hrs, 111 Squadron ran into the most northerly raiders, bound for Debden: 150 Do 17s, Me 110s and Me 109s heading east, 15,000ft over Maldon. The previous day, David Bruce had been promoted to acting flight lieutenant and given command of 'B' Flight, which he led into action on 26 August 1940 at the head of Blue Section:

> I led my Flight into attack on enemy bomber formation after Red Section had attacked. After firing short burst I found myself with an Me 109 on my tail and bullets had struck both main planes, port aileron control and fuselage. I did a steep turn to the right and then attacked an Me 110 from head-on with a two-second burst. E/A went down in a vertical dive and wreckage was found at Marks Tey.

This was a machine of 4/ZG26, the crew of which were killed; Bruce, however, was unhurt and returned his damaged Hurricane safely to base.

Flying Officer Peter Simpson, leading Green Section, followed Blue in to attack the Do 17s, but the Hurricanes were in turn assailed by the fighter escort. Breaking downwards, Simpson 'saw a Dornier flying East just above cloud. Green 2 made a head-on attack and I followed with one from the beam, closing to fifty yards. E/A went into the clouds, I followed and saw it emerge from under cloud base and crash into the ground near Great Bentley.'

This was not, however, a 'Dornier' but an Me 110C-4 of 9/ZG26, which dived vertically and exploded on impact, killing the crew, at Crabtree Farm, Great Bentley; Flying Officer Simpson shared the kill with Sergeant Thomas Wallace, who had attacked the same enemy machine. It was a good result for 111 Squadron, which had damaged the enemy before their target was bombed. Back at base, twelve bullet holes counted in Flight Lieutenant Bruce's aircraft, and Sergeant Raymond Sellars was found to have been shot down, crashing near Brightwell Church, Martlesham Heath, sufficiently shocked and injured to be hospitalised and out of the battle until mid-September.

Hurricanes of 56 Squadron also joined the action over Great Bromley and Great Bentley, engaging at 15.25 hrs. Pilot Officer Fraser 'Barry' Sutton, Green 3, made several inconclusive attacks on the main enemy formation before spotting an Me 109 diving beneath him on a reciprocal course. The Hurricane pilot:

> half-rolled to follow him but lost him in cloud. In the ensuing climb from my dive I found myself on the tail of an Me 110. I broke away to the left as he was turning leftwards, also I got in a short deflection shot at about 100 yards. The E/A broke away very steeply to the left and I came in on his tail, continuing to fire at same range, closing to thirty yards. E/A was now smoking from both engines and I had to break away owing to his slipstream. I followed him through cloud and saw him in a field on fire near Tendring, south-east of Bromley. Pilot Officer Westmacott confirms this and the crash was also witnessed by two Intelligence Officers who salvaged the wreckage.

This Me 110 was, in fact, the 9/ZG26 machine down at Great Bentley, which 111 Squadron's Flying Officer Simpson and Sergeant Wallace had also had a hand in destroying. No.56 Squadron's Pilot Officer Innes Westmacott also claimed an Me 110 destroyed, this believed to be the 4/ZG26 machine also claimed by Flight Lieutenant Bruce of 111 Squadron and which crashed at Great Tey. A Me 110 'probable' was also claimed by Flight Sergeant Fred 'Taffy' Higginson DFM.

RAF Debden, to the north-east of London, however, was hit by this northerly German force with 100 bombs and many incendiary devices, scoring direct hits on the runway, Sergeants' Mess, NAAFI, MT Yard and stores. Electricity and water supplies were severed; four airmen and a civilian driver were killed.

The Hurricanes of 310 Squadron had hurried from Duxford as fast as they could, led by their English CO, Squadron Leader Douglas Blackwood, whose Czech 'shadow', Squadron Leader Sacha Hess, was also in the formation. Having taken off from Duxford at 15.10 hrs, the 12 Group fighters arrived at 12,000ft over the North Weald area, some thirty miles to the south, and sighted the enemy at 15.35 hrs – after Debden had been bombed and the enemy was retreating to the south-east.

Squadron Leader Douglas Blackwood:

> As mine was the only aircraft fitted with VHF I was unable to give orders for any particular attack. I dived in from astern and opened fire at about 600 yards, closing to about 200 yards when I broke away owing to return fire from the rear of the formation. On second attack I noticed one Dornier slightly separated from the formation so I attacked from astern and gave it a long burst

at about 30–250 yards. The E/A wobbled and seemed to take slight evasive action but may have been out of control. I then smelt something burning and noticed that my starboard main tank was blistering on topside of the wing. I broke off the attack and realised that my petrol tank was burning inside. About ten seconds later the tank burst into flames so I undid my straps and disconnected my oxygen tube etc. I turned the aircraft on its back and fell out. I landed in a stubble field without any damage to myself.

Blackwood was credited with a 'Do 215' [sic] destroyed, his own aircraft crashing at Maldon. Similarly, the Czech Pilot Officer Vic Bergman was also shot down by return fire, baling out safely over Clacton. Pilot Officer Emil Fechtner – who could speak no English – also claimed a bomber destroyed, his Hurricane being hit in the wings and left tyre during the exchange, although fortunately the pilot landed safely. Flight Lieutenant Gordon Sinclair, one of Blackwood's two English flight commanders, attacked a Do 17 over Clacton and was hit by return fire, also returning safely to base. Another Czech, Sergeant Edward Prchal, claimed a Dornier destroyed over the sea but was severely shot-up by an Me 109 and crash-landed at Upminster; slightly wounded, the pilot was treated at Ely Hospital.

Squadron Leader Blackwood had issues with his VHF radio, rendering him – absurdly – unable to communicate with the rest of 310 Squadron's pilots, whose aircraft were fitted with High Frequency (HF) sets; had he been able to issue orders, the action may well have been more successful. Nonetheless, these were 310 (Czech) Squadron's first recorded victories.

Earlier that morning, Squadron Leader Eric McNab had led the Hurricanes of his 1 (RCAF) Squadron from Northolt to operate at North Weald for the day, from where the Canadians had scrambled at 14.45 hrs to patrol base. Five minutes after 111 Squadron had intercepted, 1 (RCAF) sighted '25+ Do 215s' [sic] at 14,000ft north-east of North Weald, this being the second and middle enemy formation which had crossed the Essex coast at the mouth of the Blackwater, flying north-west; McNab reported:

I climbed into the sun to about 18,000ft and gave order echelons starboard. I engaged outside left-hand aircraft, opening fire at 400 yards with a six-second burst closing to 200 yards. I felt my aircraft get hit and fired a few more rounds before breaking away. I thought my aircraft was on fire as the cockpit was full of smoke and prepared to jump. As I flattened out I saw the E/A I had fired at fall past me in a vertical dive and on emerging through the cloud I saw this aircraft hit the ground. Directly after, I saw an aerodrome and decided I could land, which I did.

In total, the Canadians claimed three Dorniers destroyed and three more damaged, which were 'credited to the Squadron as a whole [ORB]'. All three were from 7/KG 2 and were confirmed – one exploding over Thaxted, another crashing at Wimbish, and the third forced-landing at Whepstead. In response, Flying Officer Jean-Paul Desloges was shot up and returned his damaged Hurricane safely to base, but Flying Officer Robert Edwards was shot down and killed, crashing at Little Bardfield – the squadron's first fatality of the Battle of Britain. Nonetheless, the Hurricanes had done well, their successful attack on the bombers made possible because 'A formation of escorting fighters was drawn off by a squadron of Spitfires [ORB]' – providing a perfect example of the two RAF fighter types working in harmony. The Spitfires were those of 65 Squadron, up from Rochford.

When 65 Squadron met the enemy over Manston, these raiders were withdrawing westwards towards Ramsgate. The Spitfires had wisely climbed to 30,000ft and had the advantage of height and sun. The Australian Flight Lieutenant Gordon Olive reported that the bombers were protected by:

> eighty–120 heavy fighters [Me 110] in three or four formations thirty–forty strong. 'B' Flight attacked, being the leading flight, whereupon the fighters formed a 'defensive circle' of about thirty aircraft. I remained approximately 3,000ft above this mass, awaiting a chance to attack at the first opportunity. It then occurred to me that by remaining in a threatening position I could keep this formation circling indefinitely, thus detaching them from their escort duties. I remained in this position for some twenty minutes when the fighters tried to break up and fly East. I immediately attacked the ear and shot one Me 110 down in flames [confirmed by Sergeant Orchard]. The E/A re-formed the circle. I then went back to my position above and after firing every time the fighters broke their circle I returned to refuel and re-arm.

Olive had executed perfect tactics; 65 Squadron claimed a Do 17 destroyed and a probable, and two more Me 110s damaged – for no loss.

No.85 Squadron's Hurricanes were patrolling Maidstone when 'At 1520 hrs near Eastchurch fifteen Do 215s [*sic*] were sighted flying in stepped-up vic formation at 15,000ft and escorted by approximately thirty Me 109s flying at 5–10,000ft higher [ORB].' This was the most southerly raid, which Squadron Leader Peter Townsend DFC led his pilots to attack:

> First attack on Dorniers executed from starboard on lowest and leading section, head-on attack. Leading section of Dorniers broke away. Engagement became general but three or four pilots with me concentrated on Dorniers which were separated. A series of attacks, astern and quarter, executed. First Dornier went down in controlled nose-dive, seen by Pilot Officers Allard and Worrall to pancake at Rochford. It was attacked before landing by Spitfires … Pilot Officer Worrall states that the pilot of the Dornier volunteered information that his instruments and starboard engine were put out of action above cloud (i.e. when attacked by aircraft of 85 Squadron) and caused his

descent to Rochford. This Dornier is therefore claimed as a complete victory for 85 Squadron, in spite of attacks by Spitfires.

Having suffered losses and it being obvious that more defending fighters would intercept if the raid continued to its intended target of Hornchurch, the bombers then wheeled about, withdrawing south-east, randomly jettisoning bombs over Eastchurch, Detling and Maidstone.

Townsend continued:

> Remaining two Dorniers closed formation. Finally, after repeated attacks, left-hand one broke away. Followed it through clouds. It made out to sea on port motor only, thought better of it and now with bits falling off it pancaked near Eastchurch. AA fire from the ground had no effect on this Dornier which is claimed by 85 Squadron. Third Dornier last seen losing height and flying vaguely around. This one seen to crash in sea fifteen miles East of Foulness by Sergeant Howes.
>
> During attacks on Dorniers, I noticed no attempt by Me 109s to molest us although one or two pilots report being attacked in a half-hearted way by Me 109s, one of which Flying Officer Woods-Scawen claims as a probable.

The Me 109s were cautious because the pilots were operating at the limit of their fuel endurance. This raid had seen fighter sweeps in advance of KG 2 and KG 3's advance, meaning that when the bombers were intercepted the single-engine enemy fighter pilots were acutely conscious of their remaining petrol. Their subsequent unwillingness to enter the fray given critical fuel stakes, therefore, deprived the bombers of close protection – leading to recriminations across the Channel and a further call from the *Kampgeschwarden* for less free-chasing by Me 109s and closer escort instead.

No.85 Squadron's Pilot Officer John 'Paddy' Hemingway, however, an Irishman from Dublin (and at the time of writing, May 2023, the last known surviving member of The Few at 102), was shot down over Eastchurch by an Me 109. As his stricken aircraft dived vertically at 400 mph, the 21-year-old pilot managed to safely take to his parachute, landing, unhurt, while the Hurricane piled into the Fobbing Marshes – where it would remain until recovered by enthusiasts from a depth of 32ft in 2019.

The first Do 17 destroyed by 85 Squadron, attacked while crash-landing by Spitfires of 65 Squadron, belonged to 2/KG 2 and came to a grinding halt in the centre of Rochford airfield; the crew of four were all wounded, one badly, and captured. The second Do 17, which came down two miles south-west of Eastchurch, belonged to the *Gruppenkommandeur* of I/KG 2, *Major* M. Gutzmann, who was captured unhurt along with two other crewmembers; the fourth man was killed. The third bomber cannot be identified in Luftwaffe records.

While 12 Group's 310 Squadron had arrived over North Weald after Debden had been bombed, as we have seen the Hurricanes engaged the enemy, claiming two bombers destroyed. No.19 Squadron, however, 'did not contact the enemy [ORB]'. No.12 Group's failure to prevent Debden – only some fifteen miles south-east of Fowlmere – being bombed drew fire from 11 Group.

Sergeant David Cox, 19 Squadron:

> As we of 19 Squadron were patrolling at 10,000ft and above 10/10ths cloud, we did not see the raid which actually came in at 1,000ft. It appears that the Observer Corps had accurately reported the raid at 1,000ft, but 11 Group assumed this to be a mistake and so sent us off at Angels 10. The subsequent intelligence reported claimed that Debden had been damaged because 'the Spitfires from Fowlmere were too slow in getting off the ground' but that was certainly not the case.

According to the official AHB narrative, the raid approached above cloud, which was between 5,000–7,000ft, before gliding through them to attack Debden. No.19 Squadron, therefore, must have arrived overhead at 10,000ft while the raiders were descending through the cloud and therefore invisible to the Spitfire pilots. Arguably, had 19 Squadron been called earlier it would have been well placed to intercept the Germans before Debden was bombed. Air Vice-Marshal Park was furious and this latest event did nothing to improve the worsening antipathy between 11 and 12 Groups.

Pilot Officer Teddy Morton, 'Ops "B"' Controller at Duxford:

> The 11 Group controllers definitely called for 12 Group too late. By the end of August there was a certain amount of hostility between the respective operations' rooms. 11 Group accused us of being too late, we said that they called for us too late. Whenever 12 Group squadrons arrived after the action, we would suffer sarcastic remarks from the 11 Group Controller. The situation was not good.

But why, though, was 12 Group not being requested in a more timely manner – when no such scenario existed between 11 and 10 Groups? The 10 Group bases at Middle Wallop and Warmwell, being close to the South Coast, required much less warning to get airborne; this, combined with the fact that the enemy had a long sea crossing from Cherbourg, meant RDF provided earlier indications of an assembling threat. Conversely, the Duxford-based squadrons, over thirty miles north of London, and some fifty north-west of Harwich, required more time to scramble and cover the distance to the combat zone – the problem being that because *Luftflotte* 2 was much closer, in the Pas-de-Calais, RDF gave less warning of a raid approaching and therefore time for the 11 Group Controller to realise that a raid was sufficiently strong to request 12 Group support – and ask for those reinforcements, which then had to be scrambled. Indeed, even when RDF showed a raid assembling behind Dunkirk, Calais or Cap Gris-Nez, the 11 Group Controller could only rely upon experience and guesswork to identify which formations were feints, which were pure fighter sweeps (which approached very quickly), and, indeed, anticipate what the intended targets were – none of this assisted by the Luftwaffe often flying a dog-leg course in order to further confuse the harassed defenders. It must also be remembered that 12 Group had its own defensive responsibilities to the industrial Midlands and the North – and *Luftflotte* 5's massive north-eastern raid of 15 August 1940, which for all Fighter Command knew might be repeated, emphasised that these commitments, and the need to maintain fighters north of 11 Group, were essential. It must also be understood that the Battle of Britain was an unprecedent aerial conflict and therefore the first time the 'System' was so tested. Everyone was still learning – on the job. Certainly, as we will in due course explore, the long-standing enmity of Air Vice-Marshal Leigh-Mallory towards Air Vice-Marshal Park, and indeed Air Chief Marshal Dowding, although a factor, is far too great a simplification of the situation at this stage of the fighting to explain away why 11 Group was calling for 12 Group too late. The frustration on both sides was becoming palpable – but would only get worse.

Wing Commander Alfred 'Woody' Woodhall, Station Commander and Chief Controller, Duxford:

In those early days, RDF information was not very accurate, particularly regarding height and numbers of aircraft, and of course there was a time lapse of several minutes before the information reached the Sector Operations Room. The Sector Controller therefore had to use intelligent guesswork to direct his fighters on an intercepting course, and to position them up-sun, above the enemy. To begin with, the operations table in 12 Group only extended to the north bank of the Thames, and enemy plots were only passed to us when they reached this point. In 11 Group, however, enemy plots were received while the enemy was still over France. Command Operations Room had the whole picture, of course, but, in my opinion, there was insufficient liaison between 11 and 12 Groups.

Luckily, Wing Commander Victor Beamish, the Sector Commander at North Weald, was a good friend of mine, so I extended our operations table to the south and as far into France as St Omer; as soon as North Weald was informed of enemy activity we kept the tie-line telephone open, and the plots were passed from North Weald to Duxford. In that way we obtained earlier warning, but in spite of this, we were frequently scrambled too late because we were not allowed to fly over 11 Group territory unless asked for by them. It was frustrating to see an enemy raid plotted on our board, obviously going for a target in No 11 Group, then to wait on the ground, with the pilots in their cockpits for 15–20 minutes, and finally to be scrambled too late to get into the fight.

Flying Officer Frank Brinsden:

During late August 1940, we of 19 Squadron, up in 12 Group, always felt a bit cheated as we always seemed to be late off the ground and therefore late to intercept; we often arrived over the battle zone only to find all gone home. It was exasperating.

The situation between 11 and 12 Groups would only get worse as the battle progressed.

Another vexing issue was the enemy's penchant for splitting into two formations over the English coast, each heading for a separate target, thus confusing the Observer Corps and meaning that although the first defending fighters scrambled generally intercepted over the coast, subsequently scrambled squadrons frequently missed the enemy. Air Vice-Marshal Park provided his controllers the solution on this day:

Our fighter squadrons are frequently engaging greatly superior numbers because other squadrons despatched fail to intercept owing to accidents of cloud and inaccuracies of sound plotting by ground observers. To enable Group and Sector Controllers to put all squadrons in contact with the enemy, formation leaders are to report approximate strength of enemy bombers and fighters, their height, course and approximate position immediately on sighting the enemy. A specimen R/T message would be 'Tally Ho! Thirty bombers, forty fighters, Angels 20, proceeding North Guildford'. These reports should enable us to engage the enemy on more equal terms and are to take effect from 27 August.

As we have seen, neither Air Vice-Marshals Park or Brand were averse to meeting the enemy in strength whenever possible – contrary to later assertions by 12 Group – and this new instruction, going forward, would mean that defending forces could be more accurately controlled and intercept in greater numbers.

By the time *Luftflotte* 2's three formations withdrew from the 11 Group area on the afternoon of 26 August 1940, however, having only materially bombed Debden, *Luftflotte* 3 was already assembling a major raid, having earlier sent two aircraft on a reconnaissance of the Solent and Portsmouth area. At 16.00 hrs, RDF, rather late, detected 100+ already sixty miles out across the Channel from Cherbourg, 30+ to the Cherbourg peninsula's west, moving north, and a few minutes another a similarly sized force in the same area. By 16.10 hrs, the larger formation was just thirty miles south of the Isle of Wight. This was once more directed at the Portsmouth dockyard, involving three He 111s of *Stab/* KG 55, twenty-three of I/KG 55 and twenty-five of II/KG 55 – with a huge fighter escort provided by Jafü 3: sixty-three Me 109s of JG 2, seventy of JG 27, seventy-eight of JG 53, along with twenty-five Me 110s of ZG 2, thirty-six of ZG 76 and five more of V/LG 1.

In response to this great incoming threat, at 16.00 hrs 11 Group scrambled six Hurricanes of 43 Squadron from Tangmere to patrol base, and from the nearby Westhampnett satellite, between 16.10 and 16.15 hrs, ten 602 Squadron Spitfires hurriedly took-off with orders to patrol over Portsmouth – the Controller having correctly guessed the raid's intended target. Simultaneously, ten Hurricanes of 615 Squadron were sent off from Kenley and also vectored to Portsmouth. These fighters were supported by 10 Group, which scrambled six Spitfires of 234 Squadron from Middle Wallop to patrol base at 16.10 hrs, twelve Hurricanes of Boscombe Down's 249 Squadron at 16.15 hrs to cover the Isle of Wight, while seven of 213 Squadron took-off east from Exeter at 16.20 hrs to patrol Warmwell, and at 16.25 hrs twelve 609 Squadron Spitfires left Warmwell for Portsmouth – the two groups fielding a combined force of 63 fighters against 276 German fighters, which outnumbered the RAF pilots by over 4:1, and 51 bombers. Again, the enemy approached Portsmouth east of the Isle of Wight, the bombers' western flank and rear covered by waves of fighters, with more above; the eastern was rarely given the same attention as the western flank because 11 Group squadrons further east could be tied down by diversions or incursions by *Luftflotte* 2.

At 16.20 hrs, Squadron Leader John Badger, Green 1, was leading 43 Squadron south-west of Selsey Bill when 'Massed formations' of He 111s, Me 110s and Me 109s were sighted, between 15,000-25,000ft:

When over Thorney Island gave 'Tally Ho!' and bandits were seen approaching Portsmouth. Sections were in line astern so I flew Squadron across path of enemy and turned to meet them head-on. I ordered sections to echelon to port. Green Section, which was heading West, for the leading vic of three and arrived within range almost in line abreast. I gave a two–three-second burst and then broke away. I saw one bandit fire a signal light and immediately waves of 109s and 110s swept down on us. The port engine of the E/A at which I had fired was emitting dense white smoke. There were so many enemy fighters about that it was impossible to attempt further coordinated attacks and we had to stand on the defensive. I climbed after the main formation and saw Green 2 [Sergeant Hallows] attacking a straggler. I joined in and noticed one engine had already stopped. E/A made for cloud but we followed him through and came out above base. After further attack E/A lowered undercarriage. At this point many other Hurricanes joined in the battle and E/A landed one-mile East of Ford. I think this E/A was crippled by Green 2 and about to make a forced-landing before I joined in. The E/A bomber formation held tight and crossfire was most intense.

The destruction of the He 111, of *Stab* I/KG 55, was shared between Squadron Leader Badger and Sergeant Hallowes, and crashed at 16.30 hrs, crash-landing at Helliers Farm, Wick, near Littlehampton; *Oberleutnant* Ignatz Krenn and his crew were captured. Hallowes claimed another He 111 destroyed in the engagement, as did the New Zealander Pilot Officer Harold North, a 4/KG 55 machine which crashed at West Brook Farm, Waterlooville, four of the crew being captured; the observer, *Unteroffizier* Oskar Shufft baled out too low and was killed. The Belgian Pilot Officer Albert van den Hove d'Ertsenrijk claimed a 109, the pilot of which, from 2/JG 2, *Oberleutnant* Hans-Theodor Grisebach, baled out and was captured, his fighter crashing at Blendworth, near Horndean. D'Ertsenrijk was shot-up, however, fortunately returning to base unhurt, but Pilot Officer Roy Lane was shot down in flames over Wittering and baled out badly burned. Pilot Officer Clifford Gray was also shot down, over Bosham, and also baled out, his right arm wounded.

No.602 Squadron's Spitfires intercepted the raid at 16.20 hrs, 15,000ft over Selsey Bill.

Sergeant Cyril Babbage, Green 2:

I followed Green 1 climbing to attack fighters and got separated. I saw one Me 109 on the tail of a Spitfire and attacked from dead astern and as he turned away used deflection shot. He just fell into spin from the turn and went down with large quantities of black smoke coming from engine. I am confident from the colour and quantity of smoke that this E/A was probably destroyed.

I then attacked centre aircraft of three Do 215s [*sic*] in vic formation which was one of several such formations making out to sea, adopting dead astern attack opening at 300 yards and firing until my ammunition was exhausted. I saw my bullets striking this E/A but observed no other damage. Heavy crossfire was experienced from all these bombers, and as I broke away downwards to the left I was struck by a cannon shell, probably from an Me 109 and had to bale out because my aircraft was on fire.

Sergeant Babbage's Spitfire, X4188, went into the Channel – from which the pilot was lucky to be rescued and brought ashore at Bognor Regis, where he was admitted to the local hospital. Babbage was credited with a 109 probably destroyed, Sergeant Andrew McDowell a He 111 destroyed, Squadron Leader Sandy Johnstone damaged another, and Sergeant Basil Whall two; Pilot Officer Ellis Aries incorrectly claimed a 'Do 17' destroyed. Flying Officer Charles MacLean was shot-up, however, and crash-landed at Tangmere – admitted to Chichester's Royal West Sussex Hospital, his wounds were so bad that his right leg was amputated. The Spitfires had clashed with 1/JG 53, *Hauptmann* Hans-Karl Mayer subsequently claiming Sergeant Babbage as his sixteenth victory east of Portsmouth, and *Leutnant* Albrecht Zeis hitting Flying Officer MacLean, his fourth victory, north-east of the port.

Squadron Leader Joe Kayll's ten 615 Squadron Hurricanes, having made all haste from Kenley, were also engaged over Selsey Bill at 16.30 hrs: 'Large formations were sighted. Squadron Leader Kayll damaged a He 111 for certain, Flying Officer Eyre damaged a Ju 88 [*sic*]. One section chased what turned out to be Blenheims [ORB].' Fortunately the Blenheims, probably of a Coastal Command squadron, were recognised as friendly before any damage was done. 615's Flying Officer John Gaynor was shot down, crashing near Hambledon and admitted to Idsworth House Hospital with minor facial injuries.

During this action over and off Portsmouth, the German ace and *Staffelkapitän* of 3/JG 2, *Oberleutnant* Helmut Wick, destroyed two Hurricanes, chalking up his twenty-first and twenty-second victories, and *Unteroffizier* Walter Ebert of 8/JG 2 recorded his first, a Hurricane; which of these aircraft were those shot down of 43 or 615 Squadrons, though, is impossible to say.

The final RAF squadron to engage was 234 Squadron, at 17.00 hrs, south of the Isle of Wight, the Spitfires led by that stalwart Australian Flight Lieutenant Pat Hughes:

> As Cressy Leader was on patrol and ordered to Portsmouth. Intercepted eight Me 109s 2,000ft above and three miles behind. My Section formed astern and attacked the leading eight, who immediately split up into sections of two aircraft each. I attacked the leading two aircraft and fired a burst of five seconds at the rear one, which caught fire and dropped vertically. The second aircraft had climbed and was shooting from above but on turning he dived away but was caught by a long burst from dead astern when he pulled out. This aircraft caught fire but stayed in the air for several minutes. The pilot jumped out near what seemed to be an ordinary auxiliary launch, painted dark grey and blue. This boat opened fire at me at 2,000ft range, then moved towards the pilot in the water. I climbed towards the coast and on the way three Me 109s approached and one shot at me from about 1,000 yards, but I had no ammunition. The aircraft all appeared to have red spinners in the first section of eight aircraft.

The second aircraft destroyed by Hughes was flown by *Leutnant* Roos of 6/JG 53, who was unhurt and rescued from the sea.

Pilot Officer Bob Doe: 'I was Red 1 and chased E/A (Me 109) from ten miles south of Swanage. Dived from above and went behind at angle of 30°. Pilot slumped over controls and aircraft went straight in.'

Two pilots from 5/JG 53 were lost in action off the Isle of Wight and continuing nearly to Cherbourg: *Leutnant* Berwanger and *Feldwebel* Holdermann, both of whom were killed – but whether shot down by Hughes or Doe cannot be said with any certainty. Indeed, *Unteroffizier* Ackmann of 9/JG 27 and *Leutnant* Hoffman of 7/JG 2 also failed to return from this operation and were presumed to have been shot down over the Channel.

No.234 Squadron's Pilot Officer Patrick Horton, a New Zealander, was shot-up by a 109 and crashed back at base, wheels-up, fortunately unhurt, and similarly Sergeant Michael Boddington's Spitfire was damaged by another 109 forcing him to land near East Grinstead.

The other 10 Group squadrons, 213, 249 and 609, neither saw or engaged the enemy.

During this sharp action against overwhelming odds, three Hurricanes and a Spitfire had been destroyed, a Hurricane and three Spitfires damaged; no pilots had been killed but five were wounded, two of them seriously. This was, however, a costly operation for *Luftflotte* 3. KG 55 had lost four He 111s and their crews, and seven Me 109s failed to return. The *Luftflotte* 3 after action intelligence report records strong fighter opposition but ineffective AA fire, confirming that Portsmouth was hit: it was, but surprisingly little damage was caused, bombs only hitting Fort Cumberland and a minor gas works while most fell harmlessly on Hayling Island and in Langstone Harbour. In fact, owing to the target being concealed by dense cloud, many of KG 55's He 111s returned to base with their bombloads intact. On this occasion, however, the Luftwaffe fighter pilots' combat claims were delusional: sixteen Spitfires and a Hurricane were claimed destroyed, giving OKL planners the impression that the raid had been much more successful than it actually was.

That evening, *Seenotdienst* He 59 seaplanes were active over the Channel, seeking survivors from the day's fighting. At 18.37 hrs, 'B' Flight of 602 Squadron were scrambled from Westhampnett to seek such an intruder, which was destroyed by Pilot Officer Paul Webb twenty miles south of St Catherine's Point – thus bringing the day-fighting to a close. Luftwaffe's bombing had achieved little, with only Debden having been successfully attacked. The fighting had cost Fighter Command thirteen Hurricanes destroyed and ten damaged, with one pilot killed and nine wounded; three Defiants were lost and another damaged, with two of their pilots and an air gunner wounded, plus two of the latter missing; ten Spitfires had been destroyed and five damaged, three pilots killed and seven wounded – a total of twenty-six fighters destroyed and sixteen damaged, four pilots killed and two air gunners missing, and eighteen pilots and an air gunner wounded.

Squadron Leader Peter Townsend DFC, 85 Squadron:

Of the twenty pilots I led to Croydon on 19 August 1940, fourteen, including me, were shot down within the next two weeks, two of them twice. The number itself looks insignificant; never, in fact, did the RAF lose more than a few dozen fighter pilots in a day. Yet during those crucial weeks such losses, especially in experienced pilots, began to spell defeat. As reinforcements, came pilots from other commands, from the Navy too, and the flying schools – the latter boys barely past their teens, brave as lions but tenderfeet. Our battle was a small one but on its out depended the outcome of the western world.

On 26 August 1940, Park reported to HQ Fighter Command, summarising the fighting thus far:

[1 ...] The heaviest casualties to pilots and aircraft were experienced among reinforcing squadrons that had been formed in the North since the outbreak of war. During the past two months' fighting over our own territory, our former experience has been confirmed, as will be seen from the figures given below.

2. In order to keep our casualties in pilots and fighter aircraft to a minimum, especially during the next critical month, it is strongly recommended that only highly trained and experienced eight-gun fighter squadrons be sent from northern groups to exchange with depleted squadrons in the South of England, because of the German practice of employing fighter screens and close escorts to mass formations of bombers in this part of the country.

3. The marked difference in results shown in the table below can hardly be due to the difference in standard of fighting efficiency of northern groups. It is thought probably to be due to the fact that 13 Group have always made a practice of selecting squadrons for temporary duty in the South from among their most experienced squadrons, because of the appreciation of the heavy fighting up to date in the South of England:

Squadron	Period under 11 Grp	Enemy Aircraft Destroyed	Own Casualties Kld.	Msg.	Wnd.	Total
41	26/7 – 8/8	13	–	1	–	1 (13 Group)
152	12/7 – 4/8	4	–	–	1	1 (13 Group)
602	17/8 – date	26	–	1	1	2 (13 Group)
266	12/8 – 21/8	9	2	4	–	6 (12 Group)
616	19/8 – date	8	–	6	1	7 (12 Group)

4. Sector commanders have commented favourably on the high standard of flying and fighting efficiency of several of squadrons of 13 Group that have been sent South on exchange or on temporary duty during the past few months.

And so the daylight battle wore inexorably on.

During the day, Coastal Command's operations had followed the usual pattern, and that evening six Blenheims of 59 Squadron successfully bombed petrol and oil storage tanks at Cherbourg. Adverse weather conditions over the Continent led to fourteen of sixteen 2 Group Blenheims aborting, just two bombing airfields in the Netherlands. By night, the incredibly brave crews of Bomber Command continued taking the war to Germany and Italy, long and dangerous flights, but fortunately only one Hampden of 61 Squadron was lost, having run out of fuel. After forced-landing on the North Sea island of Vlieland, the crew were captured and their aircraft repaired and flown to Germany for evaluation at Reclin.

Daily Home Intelligence Report:

> London has come through a weekend of extensive raids with courage and
> calmness ... East Enders experiencing screaming bombs for the first time
> expressed great fear but did not panic. Those in shelters remained, but said it
> sounded as if the bomb was falling right on top of them. Still far too many
> people go sight-seeing after the first ten minutes in shelters. No absentees
> today from large Silvertown factory in spite of employees' sleepless nights
> and experience of bombs. Local people impressed by vigour and efficiency of
> fire-fighting at Docks. Delayed action bombs causing apprehension in these
> areas. Exaggerated rumours of casualties and damage rife ... Maltese refugees
> in Kensington hotel appear to be bored and aimless. Do not seem to make
> full use of adjacent park to take their babies in.

Tuesday, 27 August 1940

On the night of 26/27 August 1940, bombing was widespread, beginning
at 21.25 hrs. Until after 03.00 hrs the raids were continuous on targets in
the Midlands, Devon, Bristol and South Wales. At 02.31 hrs, the He 111 of
Major Willibald Fanelsa, the *Gruppenkommandeur* of III/KG 1, was hit by
AA fire during a mission to attack factories in Coventry, and abandoned by
the crew, who were all captured; the aircraft crashed and burned out at Manor
Avenue, Caterham. On 17 August 1940, 145 Squadron had been withdrawn
from Westhampnett to Drem, and at 03.25 hrs on this dark night Flight
Lieutenant Finlay Boyd was patrolling east of St Abb's Head when drawn to
that area by bomb-bursts and searchlight beams. The Hurricane pilot 'sighted
and engaged one He 111, giving it six short bursts and no return fire was
noticed after the second burst. The E/A was lost in the darkness [ORB].'
Such were the frustrations of night-fighting without specialist aircraft and
airborne interception radar, and flying at night during the blackout was
in any case inherently dangerous, and that in itself took a toll of Fighter
Command's pilots and aircraft. At 01.00 hrs that night, for example, Pilot
Officer Charles Chetham, a Hurricane pilot of 1 Squadron, was patrolling
over Buckinghamshire when dazzled by searchlights, losing control and being
forced to bale out. Patrolling from St Eval in an antiquated Gloster Gladiator
biplane, 245 Squadron's Sergeant Robert Thomas wrote off his aircraft when
hitting trees during a dummy landing approach. Both pilots were fortunately
unhurt – but dawn would find twenty-five civilians dead with fifty-six seriously
injured and twenty-one slightly so.

What, though, were the pilots' thoughts regarding this critical aerial battle?

Pilot Officer Tim Elkington, 1 Squadron:

> One day, a hot day, we were returning from a patrol and flying low over Beachy Head with our cockpit hoods slid back. Down below, farm labourers were burning stubble, and the smell of wood smoke was in the air. I thought 'That smell's England, that is – and worth fighting for.'

Squadron Leader Peter Townsend DFC, 85 Squadron:

> Obviously, we knew we had to win; but, more than that, we knew we could not lose. I think it had something to do with England. Miles up in the sky, we fighter pilots could see more of England than any of England's defenders had ever seen before. Beneath us stretched our beloved country, with its green hills and valleys, lush pastures and villages clustering round an ancient church. Yes, it was a help to have England below. She was behind us too. When, at the end of the day, we touched down and slipped out for a beer at the local, people were warm and wonderfully encouraging. They were for us, the fighter boys, who had once been the bad boys, who supposedly drank too much and drove too fast. Now people realised that, on the job, we were professionals. They rooted for us as if we were the home team, and we knew we had to win, if only for them.

Pilot Officer William Walker of 616 Squadron, shot down over the Goodwin Sands the previous day, remained in Ramsgate Hospital – but not for long:

> It was decided that I be moved, still with a bullet lodged in my ankle, to RAF Hospital Halton. En route we stopped off at Kenley so that I could collect my belongings, and the driver took me to dispersal so that I could say farewell to any remaining pilots. It proved a sad occasion, however, as the Squadron had suffered severe losses and very few pilots actually remained operational.

Nobody in Fighter Command complained when 27 August 1940 turned out to be one of the month's quietest days. This provided an opportunity to, among other things, rotate and rest some squadrons and personnel. No.65, for example, was stood-down at Hornchurch and began moving north, to Turnhouse in Scotland, via Church Fenton, its place in 11 Group taken by 603 Squadron.

Sergeant Jack Stokoe, 603 Squadron:

> Only a year before the Battle of Britain began, my contemporaries and I were pursuing our civilian careers while learning to fly with the VR in our spare time. The majority of us were 18 or 19 years old. Being aircrew, when called up, in September 1939, we were automatically given the rank of sergeant, which at first caused some dismay among the ranks of professional sergeants, many of whom had taken twenty years to reach that exulted rank!

Most of us only had fifty or sixty hours flying on elementary types like Tiger Moths and Magisters when we were called up. After a brief spell at ITW to instil some discipline into us, we had about 100 hours on Harvards at FTS, which included a few trips actually firing guns. We were then posted to an OTU, in my case Aston Down, converting there to Spitfires before being posted to an operational fighter squadron – with just ten to fifteen hours on Spitfires recorded in our log books.'

603 was an auxiliary squadron, and there were only three of us NCO VR pilots. By the time we went to Hornchurch I had seventy hours on Spitfires, so counted myself most fortunate as I could easily have gone straight from OTU to a front-line fighter squadron – as so many young pilots did – and in which case I would not have rated my chances of survival very highly. I had even already seen, although not engaged, German reconnaissance bombers over northern Scotland.

As the pilots of 603 Squadron prepared to move south, there was great excitement, Pilot Officer Richard Hillary recalling how the 21-year-old Pilot Officer Noel 'Broody' Benson was 'hopping up and down like a madman. "Now we'll show the bastards! Jesus will we show 'em!".'

At Turnhouse, 'B' Flight of 603 Squadron had been detached to operate from the nearby airfield at Montrose – where the pilots had formed a close association with the local children. As 'B' Flight's Spitfires left for Hornchurch, each pilot dived, one by one, and roared over the hamlet where their young friends lived. On the road, the children had spelt out two words in white rocks: 'Good luck'.

Pilot Officer Richard Hillary: 'Twenty-four of us flew South ... eight were to fly back.'

No.32 Squadron was also relieved, at Biggin Hill, and flew north to Acklington, its place taken by 79 Squadron.

Flight Lieutenant Peter Brothers, 32 Squadron:

Of our pre-war pilots, who were experienced chaps, there were some who had been shot down and baled out unhurt, or burnt, or wounded, or both, but none were killed. Our losses were the 'new boys' who never had the time or opportunity not only to learn or be taught the tricks of the trade, but also to know the performance advantages and limitations of their aircraft and how to exploit them. Tragically, they often paid the ultimate price for this inexperience.

On 27 August 1940, an angry Air Vice-Marshal Park issued instructions to 11 Group controllers concerning 'Reinforcement from 10 and 12 Groups'. While 10 Group had provided every assistance and fully cooperated, Park charged that 'the same desire' had not been shown by 12 Group, despatching their squadrons to locations other than that instructed by the 11 Group controller

– leading to failures to intercept the enemy. On two occasions, the 11 Group Commander charged, referring to the incidents involving 19 Squadron on both 19 and 26 August, 'our airfields were heavily bombed'. In both cases, however, the available evidence firmly points to 19 Squadron having made all haste to exactly where instructed – but arriving late owing to time and distance. Park continued that when offers of help had proactively been extended by 12 Group, Leigh-Mallory's fighters had not patrolled where requested. From this point on, therefore, 11 Group Controllers were ordered to direct requests for 12 Group assistance only when incoming raids were 160 plus, and not to talk direct to 12 Group HQ at Hucknall, but to the Command Controller at Fighter Command HQ. Park decided that such a system would mean 'obtaining assistance' would be 'a little slower', but would ensure that 12 Group's fighters 'are in fact placed where they can be of most assistance'. Park also wrote and complained about 12 Group to Fighter Command's SASO, Air Vice-Marshal Douglas 'Strath' Evill – who did nothing. Had he placed the matter before Air Chief Marshal Dowding, and had the AOC-in-C intervened decisively at this early stage, subsequent sorry events may well not have happened. It is safe to say, however, that it was on this date that relations between 11 and 12 Groups broke down.

This was a time of real crisis and great stress. Air Vice-Marshal Park's subsequent report made clear the situation with his airfields:

Contrary to general belief and official reports, the enemy's bombing attacks by day did extensive damage to five of our forward aerodromes, and to six of our seven sector stations. The damage to forward aerodromes was so severe that Manston and Lympne were on several occasions for days quite unfit for operating fighters.

Biggin Hill was so severely damaged that only one squadron could operate from there, and the remaining two squadrons had to be placed under the control of adjacent sectors for over a week. Had the enemy continued his heavy attacks against the adjacent sectors and knocked out their operations rooms or telephone communications, the fighter defences of London would have been in a parlous state during the last critical phase, when heavy attacks have been directed against the capital.

The sector operations rooms have on three occasions been put out of action, either by direct hits or by damage to GPO cables, and all sectors took into use their emergency operations rooms, which were not only too small to house the essential personnel, but had never been provided with the proper scale of GPO landlines to enable normal operations of three squadrons per sector. In view of this grave deficiency, arrangements were made to establish alternative sector operations rooms within five miles of each aerodrome, and work is now proceeding on the highest priority.

At several important aerodromes and sectors, enemy bombing has put out of action the station's organisation by destroying telephone communications, buildings etc. Fortunately the enemy switched his raids from aerodromes onto industrial and other objectives, and gave a short respite during which the station organisation at bombed aerodromes was completely reorganised.

The attacks on our fighter aerodromes soon proved that the Air Ministry's arrangements for labour and equipment to quickly repair aerodrome surfaces were absolutely inadequate, and this has been the subject of numerous signals and letters during the last four weeks.

On this occasion, however, Dowding did not support Park's criticism of the Air Ministry, as he had in the past, stating in his own covering report that 'although the scale of attack certainly exceeded the capacity of the works organisation existing at the outset, this was rapidly strengthened, and I do not wish to express any dissatisfaction with the measures taken to effect this improvement.' Park's report, nonetheless, offended the DCAS, Air Vice-Marshal Sholto Douglas, convincing him that the commander of 11 Group should be replaced – and antipathy between Douglas and Park pre-dated the Second World War by many years. The whole thing was already getting out of hand, and was not being dealt with decisively by the High Command – in fact, the vexing matter was not being dealt with at all. Things would soon take a turn for the worse.

During the day, in the absence of any major raids, enemy reconnaissance aircraft remained active over England.

At 10.03 hrs, Flight Lieutenant Minden Blake, a New Zealander who was acting squadron commander of 238 following Squadron Leader Fenton being wounded on 8 August 1940, took-off from Exeter with Pilot Officer Brian Considine to patrol base. Flying at cloud-level, in the hope of catching a snooper hopping in and out of cloud, at 10.20 hrs, four miles south of Plymouth the Hurricane pilots sighted a Do 17 of 3(F)/31 flying north from a direction of Plymouth, which they chased into cloud, attacking it and disabling the starboard engine:

It was subsequently found at Tavistock having made a forced-landing. Three persons were taken from the machine and made prisoner, and later Flight Lieutenant Blake and Wing Commander Harvey went to Tavistock to see the aircraft, which was full of holes. This aircraft was probably a photo-recce aircraft as a large camera was found inside. It had possibly been photographing the punitive damage at St Eval the previous night, when the enemy set fire to the false flare path, and put bombs on it until an early hour of the morning. Sixty-two craters were reported, and the damage may have appeared enormous to an aircraft whereas in fact the heather was duly cleared and a barren heath put in the way of being well and truly ploughed for future crops [ORB].

Further east, at 11.25 hrs, Flight Lieutenant Edward 'Jumbo' Gracie and Flying Officer Innes Westmacott of 56 Squadron were patrolling from North Weald when, 'in mid-Channel chased a Do 17 or 215 and shot it down, three of the crew baling out [ORB]'. This was a Do 17 of 3(F)/10, shot down near Cap Gris-Nez and was also intercepted by Hurricanes of 501 Squadron, up from Gravesend. The enemy rear-gunner returned fire, however, holing the glycol tank of 501's CO, Squadron Leader Harry Hogan, who managed to return safely to base.

At midday, *Luftflotte* 2 mounted a raid on Folkestone, so Squadron Leader John Ellis and the Spitfires of 610 Squadron were scrambled from Biggin Hill to intercept:

> The Squadron climbed to 15,000ft when enemy fighters were spotted above and below us. I ordered sections of four aircraft to deal with the fighters above while I took my Section of four to attack the aircraft bombing Folkestone from 5,000ft. It looked to me as though the Me 109s were bombing as I saw no enemy bombers.
>
> My No 2 and I attacked a pair of Me 109s from astern and above, taking them both by surprise. Immediately after I had opened fire a large piece of exhaust manifold flew off the 109 and hit my wing. As I broke away I saw the E/A burst into flames and plunge into the sea 400 yards off the beach at Folkestone. This is confirmed by Flying Officer Wilson.

There can be no doubt that this Me 109 was destroyed but no such loss appears in German casualty returns – yet again confirming that these documents cannot be as comprehensive and accurate as is widely accepted by researchers.

Fifteen minutes later, the action shifted to 10 Group; at 12.20 hrs Green Section of 152 Squadron, comprising Flight Lieutenant Peter O'Brien, a Canadian, and Pilot Officer Walter Beaumont claimed a He 111 destroyed west of Portland. The Spitfires were at 12,000ft, the Heinkel 2,000ft below, which the Spitfires dived and attacked from astern. 'A chase followed in and out of cloud and eventually the E/A dived into the sea.' This was not, however, a He 111, but a Ju 88 of 4/KG 4. Pilot Officer Beaumont – by profession a teacher and the first member of the RAFVR – was shot down in the action and baled out eight miles off Portland, later being rescued from the sea.

Just before 13.00 hrs, 213 Squadron was patrolling from Exeter when, inexplicably, Sub-Lieutenant William Moss lost control of his Hurricane and crashed into the sea – he was never found.

At Tangmere, 'A' Flight of 17 Squadron were released while 'B' remained at readiness, Flight Lieutenant Alfred Bayne, Pilot Officer David Leary and Sergeant George Steward scrambled at 14.20 hrs 'to intercept raid and sighted and attacked Me 110 "Jaguar". After attack, port engine was out of action, with white smoke pouring from it. E/A was last seen 50ft above sea level thirty miles out to sea and Blue Section claimed it as a probable enemy casualty [ORB].'

On this day, Coastal Command escorted no less than 20 convoys in addition to the 60 anti-invasion patrols, U-boat hunts, and reconnaissance sorties undertaken by nearly 100 aircraft. Five E-boats were attacked off Cherbourg by a 59 Squadron Blenheim, without any apparent effect, and cloud prevented three 142 Squadron Battles noting the result of their attack on E-boats at Calais. No.248 Squadron, based at Sumburgh, however, reported that 'Pilot Officer Arthur, Sergeant Cox and Sergeant Ringwood failed to return from a recco of southern section of Norwegian coast. No W/T received from time of take-off [ORB].' The Blenheim had, in fact, been caught by Me 109s and shot down into the sea by *Leutnant* Heinrich Setz of 6/JG 77 – the crew were all killed.

Yet again, 2 Group's Blenheims were frustrated by unfavourable weather in their efforts to attack enemy airfields, only one of fourteen aircraft pressing on to attack a ship off the Dutch coast. The PRU lost a Hudson, hit by flak over Cuxhaven, which ditched in the North Sea – two of the crew were rescued but one remains missing. By night Bomber Command Wellingtons, Whitleys and Hampdens attacked various German industrial and naval targets, including Kiel, Frankfurt, Wilhelmshaven and the Messerschmitt factory at Augsburg, as well as an aircraft factory in Turin, Italy. Hampdens also sowed mines off Lorient. Just one aircraft was lost: a 149 Squadron Wellington which failed to return to Mildenhall from Kiel, its crew later being reported as prisoners.

That evening, Pilot Officer Walker was still on the road to Halton from Kenley by ambulance: 'By the time we arrived at Halton it was almost 22.00 hrs, a fourteen-hour journey. Having not eaten since breakfast I was starving. Although the kitchens were closed at that late hour, a wonderful night nurse produced a wonderful and appropriate meal: scrambled eggs!'

Wednesday, 28 August 1940

Concerned with daytime losses to his *Kampfgeschwardern*, *Reichsmarschall* Göring now implemented a new policy authorising nocturnal raids in strength. *Luftflotte* 3's KG 55 was temporarily transferred exclusively to night bombing and briefed to attack Liverpool and Birkenhead on the night of 28/29 August 1940 – the first of four consecutive night-time attacks – while twenty-three Do 17s of *Küstenfliegergruppe* 606 and eight He 111s of the specialist *Kampfgruppe* 100 attacked the Gloster Aircraft factory at Hucclecote, near Gloucester, sub-contracted by Hawker to produce Hurricanes. With the vast majority of *Generalfeldmarschall* Sperrle's Me 109s transferred to *Luftflotte* 2, the Pas-de-Calais now positively bristling with German fighters, his *Luftflotte* 3 in fact turned, temporarily, to night bombing. Meanwhile, *Generalfeldmarschall* Kesselring's *Luftflotte* 2 was to fling all its might and wrath at 11 Group.

For the wounded Pilot Officer William Walker, his trials and tribulations continued at RAF Hospital Halton:

After breakfast, doctors appeared and attended to the officers in my large ward of twenty beds. Nobody came to see me, however, and apart from my wound getting rather painful, I was starting to worry about gangrene. The previous forty-eight hours had been rather traumatic to say the least, so my concern was not entirely unjustified!

At noon the head doctor, a group captain, did his rounds. As he passed my bed he asked what I was in for. I told him that I had a bullet in my leg. He said 'Oh yes, and who is looking after you?' When I told him that I had yet to see a doctor despite having arrived the previous night, I thought that he was going to have a convulsion! He literally exploded and his wrath remains a vivid memory. Never were so many doctors torn off a bigger strip. It was action stations from then on, and within just ten minutes I was in the operating theatre.

When I regained consciousness, the surgeon was beside my bedside. He said, 'I think you may like to have this', and handed me an armour-piercing bullet. He then told me that as he was prising open the bone in my leg to extract the bullet it shot out and hit the ceiling of the Operating Theatre! I still possess the bullet today as a cherished souvenir.

Fortunately my sense of humour never quite left me, and when a doctor later asked how my accident happened I assured him that I was not the victim of an accident, but of a determined attempt on my life by a German fighter pilot!

For William Walker, the Battle of Britain was over.

As ever, the day began with German reconnaissance aircraft snooping around – but then, at 08.19 hrs RDF indicated an enemy formation of 20+ between the Somme's mouth and Cap Gris-Nez. The previous day, 79 Squadron had moved from Acklington to Biggin Hill, from where, at 08.25 hrs, Squadron Leader John Heyworth led his Hurricanes to patrol Hawkinge; at 08.30 hrs twelve 264 Squadron Defiants left Rochford to patrol Dover at 12,000ft, and five minutes later Squadron Leader Joe Kayll scrambled from Kenley leading eight other 615 Squadron Hurricanes, also heading for Dover. By that time, 08.35 hrs, two more German formations, of 3+ and 12+, were detected over the same area as the first. At 08.45 hrs, the raiders crossed the Kentish coast north of Dover – Do 17s of I and II/KG 3 heading for Eastchurch, a 16 Group Coastal Command station, and He 111s of II and III/KG 53 targeting Rochford. Escort was provided by Me 109s of JG 26 and JG 51.

At 08.55 hrs, eleven Hurricanes of 501 Squadron were scrambled from Gravesend to patrol Canterbury, and nine Spitfires of 616 Squadron were ordered up from Kenley to patrol Tenterden – as the enemy's route was further to the north-east, however, the latter would be the only squadron scrambled not to engage the enemy.

The first RAF unit to sight the Rochford-bound enemy was 79 Squadron, which, complying with Air Vice-Marshal Park's instructions at 09.00 hrs, reported He 111s and Me 109s at 16,000ft inland of Folkestone – 1,000ft higher than the Hurricanes, which climbed hard to intercept. Having attacked the bombers from astern, Pilot Officers George Nelson-Edwards and Owen Tracey, a New Zealander, both claimed He 111 probables. Then, inevitably, the Me 109s of I/JG 26, flying high cover, pounced on the Hurricanes. In the ensuing melee, Flight Lieutenant Rupert Clerke probably destroyed an Me 109, but the aircraft of Flight Lieutenant Geoffrey Haysom, a South African, was hit in the coolant system, forcing him to land at Appledore – the pilot was unhurt.

At 09.00 hrs, the Hurricanes of 615 Squadron engaged 'Raid 27' over Sandwich, attacking the Do 17s heading for Eastchurch; Squadron Leader Joe Kayll attacked the leading bomber head-on but was forced to break away when attacked by a 109. Green 1, Flying Officer Anthony Eyre 'attacked the formation from out of the sun ... a beam attack on No 2 in the third section ... E/A broke away downwards with his starboard engine on fire and a large hole blown in his starboard wing.' Pilot Officer Sydney Madle, however, was hit by the bombers' crossfire, writing off his Hurricane in a crash-landing at Throwley and later being admitted to Hothfield Hospital with a cut eye.

The formation of He 111s was attacked at 09.15 hrs by the Defiants of 264 Squadron, patrolling Dover at 12,000ft:

Twenty He 111s were engaged near Folkestone, heavily escorted by German fighters. The Squadron attacked but was split up by the Me 109s and the crossfire from the Heinkels. One of the He 111s was destroyed by Pilot Officer Carnaby, his first engagement, and one damaged by Sergeant Lauder. Squadron Leader Garvin had a fuse blow in his turret and while Flight Lieutenant Ash was replacing it, his aircraft was hit by a cannon shell and caught fire. Both baled out, but Flight Lieutenant Ash was dead when found. Squadron Leader Garvin suffered minor injury. Pilot Officer Whitley and Sergeant Turner, one of the most successful crews in the Squadron, were killed when their machine crashed and burst into flames. Pilot Officers Kenner and Johnson crashed and were killed. Pilot Officer Bailey made a forced-landing after being shot down by an Me 109. Both he and his gunner, Sergeant Hardy, were unhurt. Eight machines returned to Hornchurch. Only three were serviceable [ORB].

Again, the damage had been executed by high-flying Me 109 escorts – this time *Major* Adolf Galland and his JG 26 *Stabschwarm*, which hit the Defiants in a high-speed pass. East of Canterbury, Galland destroyed one of the hapless turret-fighters, his twenty-third victory, while *Oberleutnant* Walter Horton recorded his first two aerial combat successes.

Meanwhile, 501 Squadron was hurrying towards Canterbury and the East Kent coast – when even in the heat of battle there was time for a little black humour, as Sergeant Bill Green's log book records: 'Patrolled Southend at 3,000ft. Attacked by Hurricane just below cloud base until out-turned same, to see grinning face of Flying Officer [Peter] Hairs. [Bags of cold sweat.]'

When battle was joined, the Hurricanes took on the Me 109s, Pilot Officer Byron Duckenfield, Flight Sergeant Paul Farnes, and the Polish Sergeant Anton Glowacki each claiming one destroyed, and Pilot Officer John Gibson damaged another. No.501 Squadron suffered no casualties in this sharp action.

Rochford escaped serious damage largely because of the intense barrage returned by the airfield's AA gunners, but Eastchurch was hit, the runway being damaged, two Battles destroyed with three more damaged; fortunately, however, there were no personnel casualties and restricted flying continued. As the enemy retired east then south-east, the gunners at Manston and Dover opened up but there were no further interceptions by 11 Group. Afterwards, the He 59 ambulance seaplanes of *Seenotflugkommando* 3 were active over the Channel, leading to 'A' Flight of 79 Squadron, now operating from Hawkinge, scrambling at 11.00 hrs to intercept one of these machines which Flight Lieutenant Clerke destroyed fifteen minutes later mid-Channel. At 11.30 hrs, four Hurricanes of 79 Squadron's 'B' Flight similarly scrambled from Hawkinge, sharing in the destruction of a second floatplane over the Channel at noon.

By then, RDF was already providing early warning of a renewed assault by *Luftflotte* 2: twenty-seven II/KG 3 Do 17s escorted by JG 3's Me 109s. Again, the target was Rochford. At 12.13 hrs, 54 Squadron's Spitfires were ordered up from Hornchurch to patrol Manston, and at 12.20 hrs, 615 Squadron scrambled from Kenley to patrol Tenterden. By 12.25 hrs, three sizeable German formations were over the French coast between Dunkirk and Boulogne, the southerly force crossing the Dover Strait and then the Kent coast over Dungeness less than five minutes later. At 12.27 hrs, 'A' Flight of 603 Squadron, freshly arrived at Hornchurch from Turnhouse the previous day, scrambled to patrol Canterbury, and a minute later 56 Squadron scrambled from North Weald to cover Rochford. The remaining two plots combined into one raid and crossed the North Foreland at 12.35 hrs.

The first of the defending squadrons to engage was 54 Squadron, over Manston at 12.30 hrs. Squadron Leader James 'Prof' Leathart DSO:

> I sighted twenty-four Do 17s at 16,000ft over Manston. I dived to make a head-on attack on the leader but I was going too fast and couldn't get my sights on him. Pulling up again, I found a single Do 17 going home. I gave it a quarter attack from starboard and the E/A crashed into the sea off North Foreland.

Leathart had shot down a bomber of 6/KG 3, which ditched in the sea, the four-man crew all being wounded and captured. The 54 Squadron ORB expanded upon the action:

> Do 17s in a 'herring bone' formation, He 113s [*sic*] and Me 109s all attacked. It was a day for the 'old hands'. We congratulate Squadron Leader Leathart on shooting a Do 17 down into the sea in a commendably economic way (420 rounds only). Sergeant Norwell added to his bag of Me 109s with one probably destroyed. Flight Lieutenant 'Al' Deere also got a probable and Flight Lieutenant George Gribble sent a 109 into the sea; he also attacked twelve He 113s [*sic*] in line astern – successfully altering their formation. Later in

the combat Flight Lieutenant Deere had to bale out; this is an art in which he is rapidly becoming expert!!

On this particular sortie, Deere, that tough ace from New Zealand, was leading 54 Squadron with its new CO, former Olympic hurdler and medallist, Squadron Leader Don Finlay, who was flying as his No.2 due to lack of combat experience. The Spitfires had climbed to 33,000ft, 'the highest,' Deere later recalled, 'we had ever been'. Advised by the Controller that he should soon sight the enemy 'any moment now', Deere wrote 'See them? We couldn't avoid them, they covered the whole sky ahead.' While attacking a 109, over Detling at 13.00 hrs, Deere was shot-up by a Spitfire, which he saw clearly and could only have been a member of his own squadron. As we have seen previously, such 'friendly fire' incidents were common – for both sides. Indeed, Robert Götz, a young KG 55 air gunner, when recalling the previous day's Portsmouth raid wrote that on the return flight when 'an Me 109 came closer to us it was immediately fired upon by our defensive armament as it could scarcely be distinguished from a Spitfire'. Fortunately for Deere, he survived the experience and used up another of his 'Nine Lives': 'At one stage during this patrol, Flight Lieutenant Gribble and Sergeant Norwell were flying so low that the former shot a cow when attacking his 109, and the latter found a piece of tree sticking to his plane!! [ORB].'

The next 11 Group fighters in action were the Hurricanes of Squadron Leader Graeme 'Minnie' Manton's 56 Squadron. At 12.40 hrs, Squadron Leader Manton attacked the Rochford-bound raiders over the Thames Estuary. The CO went after the fighters with Red and Green Sections, while Yellow, led by Flight Lieutenant Steve 'Squeak' Weaver, and Blue Sections took on the bombers. Weaver, Yellow 1, opened 56 Squadron's assault on the bombers, firing from close range – but his Hurricane was damaged by return fire. Breaking away, Weaver forced-landed at Scocles Farm, Eastchurch, walking away unhurt. Pilot Officer Michael Constable-Maxwell, however, crashed in flames at West End, Herne Bay, slightly injured. In response, Flight Lieutenant 'Jumbo' Gracie claimed a Do 17 destroyed; Sergeant Clifford Whitehead a probable, and Sergeant Peter Robinson one damaged. Pilot Officer Peter Down and Flight Sergeant Frederick 'Taffy' Higginson claimed Me 109s destroyed and the vanquished Constable-Maxwell a probable.

Over Tenterden at 12.50 hrs, 615 Squadron engaged Me 109s, Squadron Leader Kayll and Flying Officer Eyre both claiming enemy fighters damaged; all of the eight Hurricanes returned safely to Kenley – the squadron had fought hard, and this would be its last combat of the Battle of Britain.

At 12.55 hrs, 1 Squadron, up from Northolt to patrol Hornchurch, ran into Raid 27 over Rochford:

flying in formations of five patrolled by fighters at 20,000ft. During the ensuing action two Do 215s [*sic*] were seen to crash, one at Rochford and the other out to sea near the Tongue Lightship; another was seen to be flying low down, and damaged, protected by bombers. No pilot made any individual claims but the casualties were claimed collectively by the whole Squadron [ORB].

Two Dorniers were claimed destroyed and another damaged.

Five minutes after 1 Squadron went into action over Rochford, Squadron Leader 'Uncle' George Denholm's 603 Squadron engaged twelve Me 109s at 22,000ft and twenty miles west of Canterbury, the CO reporting:

I was at the same height and got onto the tail of an Me 109, followed it through cloud, and fired at eighty yards range with a two-second burst, firing 240 rounds. The E/A went into a vertical dive with a long trail of white vapour, which I thought was glycol fumes. After that I did not see the E/A again.

This damaged 109 was 603's only claim in this, the newly arrived squadron's first sortie from Hornchurch.

At that sector station, feelings were running high among the few survivors of 264 Squadron: reports having been received that the body of the squadron's senior air gunner, Flight Lieutenant Robert Ash, shot down earlier in the day, had been found riddled with bullets – the implication being that he had been machine-gunned while descending by parachute. Despite the battering received, and only having three serviceable fighters left, 264 Squadron was determined to avenge Ash's death:

At 1245 hrs a large enemy formation was reported approaching Rochford. Permission was sought for the three serviceable machines to take-off. This was refused by Operations. At about 1300 hrs, the Section was ordered to scramble. Enemy aircraft were then almost overhead at 18,000ft. The Section was just airborne when four sticks of bombs dropped across the aerodrome. One of our aircraft was slightly damaged. It was too late for the Section to engage the enemy [ORB].

Unsurprisingly, at 18.00 hrs, a signal was received at Hornchurch withdrawing 264 Squadron from the frontline – the defeat of the Boulton-Paul Defiant as a day-fighter was complete. Since arriving at Hornchurch less than a week ago, the squadron had suffered six pilots and air gunner killed, eight missing – including the CO, Squadron Leader Hunter DSO, and five more wounded. On 1 September 1940, the handful of survivors would return to Kirton-in-Lindsey, Air Chief Marshal Dowding – who had disputed the Defiant turret-fighter concept from the outset – thereafter officially setting the type aside for use as a night-fighter. Underpowered and relying upon coordinated attacks with pilot and air gunner acting in concert, the type was completely unsuited to the high-speed cut and thrust of modern air combat. In any case, even single-seater fighter squadrons arriving from the North found the increased tempo of battle in the South traumatic.

Squadron Leader George Denholm, 603 Squadron:

> We had to learn quickly when we arrived in 11 Group. I determined that we would never be 'bounced' from above, which is to say taken by surprise by a high-flying enemy. I would therefore fly on a reciprocal course to that provided by the Ground Controller, until reaching 15,000ft when I would turn the Squadron about, climbing all the time. That enabled us to usually see the enemy flying inland, beneath us, giving us the advantages of height and surprise. It was never possible to deliver more than one concerted attack as a Squadron, because after the initial contact we all split up, fighting our own individual battles. After action, the Squadron would return in ones and twos. I would then wait for an hour before chasing up the fates of any missing pilots. Sometimes we might receive a telephone call from a pilot who had landed at another aerodrome, for whatever reason, or forced-landed a damaged aeroplane, or baled out. Other times we would receive notification from the police or army that a pilot was safe, perhaps in hospital. Or we would receive bad news. Or there would be no news at all, which was worse.

Pilot Officer Richard Hillary wrote: 'At the time, the losing of pilots was somehow extremely impersonal; nobody, I think, felt any great emotion as there simply wasn't time for it.'

Squadron Leader Harry Hogan DFC, 501 Squadron:

> Some of our replacement pilots were straight from OTU, and these we tried to get into the air as soon as possible to provide a little extra experience, but we were just too tired to give them any dogfighting practice at all. They were all very green, youngsters who were completely bewildered and lost in action.

Sergeant Norman Ramsay, 222 Squadron:

> People missing or killed at that stage of the battle meant little to me. I joined 222 from 610 Squadron at Biggin Hill, after we had lost ten, yes ten, pilots, so I was well used to disappearing faces. Having been shot down myself I had learned to survive, to get the experience necessary for survival.

Sergeant Bernard 'Jimmy' Jennings, 19 Squadron:

> Casualties? Well, when it came to that sort of thing we just didn't talk about it much, didn't dwell upon that sort of thing. It was just a case of 'Old so and so's copped it', and that was it.

Squadron Leader Peter Townsend DFC, 85 Squadron:

> Those days of battle were the most stirring and most wonderful I have ever
> lived, all the more so because they were lived in the midst of death – which was
> never far away, a few minutes or inches, maybe, so it was all the more exalting
> to be alive. Though our numbers dwindled steadily, no one ever believed he
> would be next to die.

During the afternoon of 28 August 1940, both Squadron Leaders Denholm
and Townsend would be in action again – duelling with enemy fighters high
over Kent.

With so many Me 109s now concentrated in the Pas-de-Calais, the rest
of the day, for the first time, consisted purely of a succession of high-altitude
fighter sweeps by formations of between a dozen and thirty or so Me 109s. In
response, various 11 Group squadrons were scrambled and engaged the enemy
in skirmishes between Canterbury and Dover. That afternoon, Churchill,
accompanied by his bodyguard, Inspector Walter Thompson, visited Dover castle
on a snap inspection of the underground naval and coastal artillery headquarters
deep underground in bomb-proof casements. From the castle, the Prime Minister
had a ringside seat of the fighting overhead, and watched a demonstration of
Parachute and Cable anti-aircraft contraptions – used successfully at Kenley
ten days before – fired from Admiralty Pier.

Inspector Walter Thompson:

> While at Dover Castle an alert sounded … the battle went on over our heads
> … two German planes came down in the sea, perhaps half-a-mile from where
> we stood … It thrilled us to see the enemy in flames, hurtling down at terrific
> speed, to meet the rock-hard sea with a splash, a roar, a hiss and a fountain
> of exploding waters.

Among the RAF fighters in action above the Prime Minister and his escort
was 610 Squadron, up from Hawkinge, Flight Lieutenant Joe Pegge reporting
that at 16.15 hrs:

> I was Red 2 in 'A' Flight … patrolling just beneath a thin layer of cloud at
> 18,000ft. AA bursts indicated the position of about fifteen Me 109s. I climbed
> into the cloud and through it and saw more Me 109s above. I dived through
> the cloud and saw three Me 109s with yellow cowlings and wingtips below
> me. I selected the near one, which was about fifty yards away and gave it a
> short burst, seeing tracer enter fuselage upon which it caught fire and went
> down, being confirmed by Sergeant Parsons … Attack was made from above,
> rear and slightly from starboard side.

Although not seen to crash, the Me 109 was confirmed as destroyed. According to the 610 Squadron ORB:

> Sergeant Hamlyn fired a few bursts at am Me 109 which went straight down, Sergeant Manton seeing this aircraft crash inland and catch fire … Sergeant Bamberger fired at a 109 which turned over on its back, black smoke pouring from the engine … Sergeant Chandler fired without visible effect at a twin-engine aircraft larger than a fighter which also had a yellow nose.

Inspector Thompson:

> Driving from Dover to Ramsgate, we saw a fighter plane shot down and Churchill immediately asked our driver to take us as close to the point where it would crash as we could get. We arrived at the spot. Churchill jumped out and proceeded on foot with me at his side. This was an unnecessary risk as the Germans did a great deal of strafing and always shot off whatever they still had aboard before scooting for home again. Firemen had arrived just before us. Flames were shooting up. We had not been able to determine whether it was a German fighter or one of our own. 'I hope to God it isn't a British plane', Churchill remarked as he walked right up to the blazing craft.

In the battle above, 610 Squadron had lost a pilot: Pilot Officer Kenneth Cox. That day, Squadron Leader John Ellis, commanding 610 Squadron, wrote to Cox's father – but the Orderly Room suffered a direct hit shortly afterwards, the mail was destroyed and never posted. Consequently, Mr Cox chased up the matter, having received no specific information regarding his son's fate, to which Squadron Leader Ellis replied on 5 December 1940:

> The Squadron was operating from Hawkinge at the time and on the afternoon of the 28th August we were ordered up to patrol between Dover and Folkestone at 15,000ft. I was leading the Squadron and we patrolled immediately below the cloud base which was at 15,000ft. After we had been up for twenty minutes fifteen Me.109s were sighted diving through the cloud between Dover and Deal, we immediately turned towards them and engaged them behind Dover. A general dog-fight ensued, some below and some above cloud, the cloud being very thin. I saw Kenneth, who was flying in my section, engage an Me.109 and I last saw him diving steeply down on the enemy's tail with his guns firing. Directly after this however the enemy aircraft I was chasing pulled up through the cloud and in following I naturally lost sight of your son. No other pilots in the Squadron saw Kenneth shot down or crash so it is difficult to say exactly what happened to him. I can only surmise that another 109 got on his tail while he was firing at the first one or he was shot down in a subsequent dog-fight.
>
> I had only known Kenneth for a short time but he impressed me by his great enthusiasm for flying and fighting and his well above the average skill

and experience as a pilot. This was only his second or third encounter with the enemy and it was a great tragedy and loss to the Squadron when your son who so obviously had the makings of a first-class fighter pilot lost his life so early on.

I should like to take this opportunity of expressing to you on behalf of the whole squadron, both Officers and Men, my very deepest sympathy in your sad and irreparable loss. But Kenneth died fighting, defending his Country and we are proud to have had him in 610 Squadron.

Pilot Officer Cox's Spitfire had exploded in mid-air over Stelling Minnis, Sergeant Baker of Canterbury Police reporting:

Footnote by PC 331 Clayton. The time of crash was 16.25 hours. The plane had been in combat and while flying at about 2,000ft in the direction of RAF Station Hawkinge suddenly disintegrated in the air. The pilot came down with the main part of the fuselage. There was no fire. Guarded by military until arrival of RAF party from Hawkinge.

The cause of the explosion was unknown but it has since been suggested that this was due to the highly pressurised oxygen bottle (and/or, perhaps, the two compressed air cylinders) situated behind the cockpit. Whatever happened, it was not the crash-site of Pilot Officer Cox's Spitfire that Churchill visited but, as Inspector Thompson recalled: 'To the relief of us all, we found it was a German and the pilot had baled out.' This was *Leutnant* Landry of *Stab* I/JG 3 'Udet', whose fighter crashed at Church Farm, Church Whitfield – Churchill's response being 'Good! That's another on the long list!' The enemy pilot, apparently shot down by 610 Squadron's Sergeant Hamlyn (whose relevant combat report is unfortunately missing from those preserved by The National Archives), landed safely but was mortally wounded and died on 23 September 1940.

Thirty miles to the south-east, over Dungeness and the Channel, Squadron Leader Peter Townsend's Croydon-based 85 Squadron was also in action against Me 109s with yellow wingtips, having quite a combat:

The Squadron approached from the sun but were spotted at the last moment by E/A who appeared not to be anxious to engage and broke formation in all directions. Six Me 109s and one Me 110 destroyed. Squadron Leader Townsend gave a two to three-second burst, E/A rolled over and dived steeply, seen going down by Flight Lieutenant Hamilton and Pilot Officer Gowers, both of whom saw black and white smoke coming out of the aircraft. Squadron Leader Townsend reported his position at about twelve miles North of Lympne. This confirmed by Maidstone Observer Corps who received a report at 1646 hrs that an Me 109 had crash-landed at R.8167, pilot being taken prisoner [no Me 109s forced-landed in England as a result of this action, and the only two enemy airman captured both baled out, their Me 109s being the only German fighters to actually be shot down and crash in Kent that afternoon].

Pilot Officer Allard attacked E/A at 200 yards closing to twenty yards and it caught fire and dived vertically into the sea, two to three miles outside Folkestone Harbour. Witnessed by Pilot Officer English. He then fired several short bursts from 250 yards at another Me 109 which was making for France, E/A dived and flew at twenty feet from the sea, but engine failed with black smoke coming out, position was then about five miles North of St Inglevert...

Pilot Officer Hodgson chased E/A from 17,000ft down across the Channel, to twenty feet above sea-level. Fired several bursts and saw pieces falling off and only one third of rudder left. E/A going very slowly when last seen and emitting much black smoke. Pilot Officer Hodgson had to turn back when five miles north-west of Cap Gris-Nez owing to lack of ammunition, but he was certain that E/A was finished...

Flying Officer Woods-Scawen attacked E/A from quarter following to astern and got in two long bursts. Black smoke and what appeared to be petrol from the wing tanks poured out of E/A and it dived down vertically. He followed it down for several thousand feet and left it when it was obviously out of control. It was believed to have crashed near Dungeness and this was confirmed by Maidstone Observer Corps who reported an Me 109 in the sea off Dymchurch at 1640 hrs.

Sergeant Walker-Smith attacked an Me 109 and the port petrol tank was seen to explode, and then went into a steep dive. At that moment Sergeant Walker-Smith was fired at and had to take evasive action, but immediately afterwards dived and saw a large explosion in the sea and black smoke. Pilot Officer Hodgson confirmed having seen an Me 109 dive into the sea at this point.

Pilot Officer Gowers attacked an Me 1110 from astern and saw bullets entering, but it went into a shallow dive towards the French coast and got away. Pilot Officer Gowers used all his ammunition and definitely damaged E/A.

No.85 Squadron had suffered no loss and was undoubtedly responsible for bringing down the enemy aircraft the Prime Minister and his party had watched crash into the sea. Four pilots of 5/JG 3 and one of 7/JG 3 ditched or crashed into the Channel, all of whom were later rescued by the *Seenotdienst*.

No.54 Squadron's patrol was extended to the Canterbury, Manston and Ramsgate area, but by 16.40 hrs the Spitfires were also in action over Dover; Flight Lieutenant George Gribble DFC:

I was over Dover at 30,000ft when I encountered two Me 109s at 25,000ft with yellow noses. I attacked one of them, giving it one long burst at a range of 250 yards, closing to fifty yards. I saw the pilot bale out. There was no evasion on the part of the enemy.

Pilot Officer Colin Gray DFC claimed a 'damaged Curtis Hawk' [*sic*] but the squadron's new CO, Squadron Leader Don Finlay, was shot down and wounded, baling out to be admitted to the hospital set up at Leeds Castle while his Spitfire plunged into Westbere Lake, near Canterbury.

Tellingly, the 54 Squadron diarist commented 'that 54 Squadron rarely operates below 25,000ft these days'. This would become a common feature of Spitfire operations going forward, owing to the Supermarine fighter's superior high-altitude performance – a tiring and very physical undertaking for the pilots involved, who were often patrolling several times a day or more.

By now, with German fighters roaming hither and thither over Kent, combats were ongoing between the Thames Estuary and Dover. The Spitfires of 603 Squadron were also up at high altitude, Pilot Officer James Morton reporting his combat as having occurred at 17.00 hrs, east of Canterbury:

As No 2 of Yellow Section, flying sections line astern in a southerly direction over Canterbury at 24,000ft I observed about eight Me 109s 2,000ft above and on port beam 800 yards away. E/A crossed over us … I pulled up onto one E/A's tail but stalled. On recovery I observed another to the NE of me. I approached and attacked a 109 pursuing a Spitfire. He emitted a long trail of white smoke and dived for cloud. I followed and found him diving SE over the Channel. At 6,000ft he flattened out a little and I got within range, firing two bursts, during the second of which flames came rom behind the cockpit. I left him at 4,000ft burning fiercely and still diving steeply East, as I was approaching the French coast. I returned at sea-level.

Pilot Officer Ronald Berry was at 27,000ft:

When approximately over Dover the Squadron split up on sighting several Me 109s. Looking above, three Me 109s crossed my bow in line astern. Shortly after, on my beam, an Me 109 was firing and I immediately whipped up my aircraft and round and found myself on his tail, and at close range pumped lead into it until it opened into a heavy cloud of smoke. On turning again, another Me 109 was attacking from quarter astern. I steep turned to the right and got on his tail and he dived. I followed him and attacked, some bits fell from E/A. As my ammunition was expended I broke off combat and returned to base.

Pilot Officer George 'Sheep' Gilroy also claimed a 109 destroyed, and Flying Officer Brian Carbury, a New Zealander, damaged one. No.603 Squadron, however, new to the fighting over 11 Group, lost two pilots: Flight Lieutenant John Cunningham and Pilot Officer Donald MacDonald were both shot down by Me 109s over Dover and never seen again, very likely shot down by *Oberleutnant* Rudolf Ziegler of *Stab* II/JG 54, and *Oberfeldwebel* Karl Hier of 5/JG 64, who both claimed Spitfires destroyed over Dover. Pilot Officer Ian Ritchie was shot-up, but returned his damaged Spitfire to Hornchurch.

Hurricanes of 56 Squadron were also engaged over Dover and Hawkinge at around 17.00 hrs. Initially the squadron had been ordered to patrol Canterbury at 10,000ft, but given the presence of high-flying German fighters Squadron Leader Manton's pilots climbed much higher – and were at 18,000ft over Ashford when the enemy was sighted.

Flight Lieutenant 'Squeak' Weaver:

> [E/A were] milling round in a circle, but came down on us as we climbed [over Dover], a dogfight ensued, E/A breaking away in twos. I chose the rear of a pair of E/A and carried out a beam attack, firing from below and to one side a burst of twenty rounds from each gun at about 200 yards. E/A's nose dropped a little and the pilot jumped out. I saw him hurtling through the air but did not see his parachute open. This was about five miles inland from Dover. Seeing no other E/A and receiving the order to land, I returned to North Weald.

Weaver had shot down *Oberfeldwebel* Artur Dau of 7/JG 51, whose aircraft crashed at Garden Wood, Poulton Farm, South Alkham, the time of the crash recorded as 16.55 hrs; the enemy pilot was captured unhurt.

Sergeant George Smythe DFM attacked the same Me 109 as Weaver, independently, and was also accredited with a destroyed kill – another example of how one casualty could be multiplied on the balance sheet. During his attack, however:

> I was attacked from the rear by another Me 109. I fired a final burst at the E/A in front and broke away. As I was breaking away a cannon or large-bore bullet passed through the hood, over my head, through the windscreen, the armour plated cowling over the gravity tank and the petrol tank itself. I was immediately drenched with petrol and became semi-conscious. I baled out, landing about two miles from Hawkinge. On arriving at Hawkinge I was informed by the Duty Pilot that the pilot of the E/A I had attacked baled out as well and landed in the vicinity of the aerodrome. I received a few minor scratches on my face from glass from the armoured windscreen.

Pilot Officer Barry Sutton, however, was not so lucky: shot down by a 109 over the Thames Estuary, the 21-year-old Hurricane pilot baled out and was admitted to Canterbury Hospital, badly burned.

Having taken-off from North Weald at 15.55 hrs on a 'Fighting Patrol', Squadron Leader Eric 'Whizzy' King and six other 151 Squadron Hurricanes were bounced by Me 109s of II/JG 3 over the Ashford area at 16.35 hrs. Two Hurricane pilots were shot down: Pilot Officer John Alexander baled out, badly burned, his Hurricane crashing into a bungalow at Godmersham, between Ashford and Canterbury; Sergeant Leonard Davies was also wounded, crash-landing at Eastchurch. Interestingly, among the German fighter pilots claiming victories over the Thames Estuary, Rochester and Ashford area at that time was the flamboyant and narcissistic *Oberleutnant* Franz von Werra of *Stab* II/ JG 3, who claimed no less than three Hurricanes between Ashford and Rye around 16.30 hrs (BST), adding to the Spitfire he claimed west of Rochester at 16.10 hrs. Quite a feat of arms, four RAF fighters destroyed in a single sortie – if all of the claims were true, which is far from likely. The lion-cub-owning von Werra would later become infamous as the only German prisoner to escape Allied custody during the Second World War – and when interrogated, in due course, embarrassed by certain of his fanciful claims – on this occasion increasing his score to eight.

This was a hard-fought afternoon in the skies of Kent, 11 Group not yet having decided to ignore these high-flying sweeps – which were only dangerous if defending fighters were scrambled to intercept them. And that is exactly what the Germans wanted.

At 18.36 hrs, ten 603 Squadron Spitfires, led by Squadron Leader George Denholm, took off from Rochford on the day's fourth patrol. Me 109s were still intruding, and exactly an hour after take-off, at 20,000ft, ten miles west of Manston, the Spitfires clashed with ten Me 109s. Denholm singled out an Me 109, attacking from astern before following the German fighter in a dive, firing again:

> after the second attack, it appeared to be in difficulties. I was then able to make two quarter attacks and the pilot, who had been heading for France, turned back towards the coast and glided down to land. I saw him hit high tension wires and crash in a field West of Dover.

In what was 603's only claim in this short cut-and-thrust action, Denholm had shot down *Feldwebel* Shöttle of 1/JG 54, whose forced-landing went awry upon hitting the cables at Copt Hill Farm, Capel; having ultimately crashed in flames, the pilot was captured. No.603 Squadron, however, had suffered another pilot killed: Pilot Officer Noel 'Broody' Benson – who only the previous day arrived at Hornchurch having enthused at how the squadron 'would show 'em'. Sadly, Benson never had a chance: at 20.30 hrs he was shot down in flames, crashing near Tenterden, by *Leutnant* Hans-Erich Heinbockel of *Stab* III/JG 54 (who mistakenly claimed a Hurricane).

Martin Hayes was a much younger cousin of Pilot Officer Benson's:

> After being bombed out in Headingly, Leeds, as a family we moved to the Yorkshire countryside about twenty miles the other side of Harrogate, to the small village of Great Ouseburn. My great-uncle Joe and great-aunt Daisy lived there with their youngest daughter, Margaret. Joe was the local 'Doctor Benson', having retired years ago from the Indian Army. They lived in a wonderful old house located opposite the village church with extensive

grounds going down to the small burn or river at the bottom of their land. They had a large tree covered plot devoted to chickens, vegetables and the old stable housing pigs, pets of Margaret's.

My grandmother, mother and myself frequently drove there through the country lanes to visit for supplies. Early in the war our visit coincided with a rare visit from their son, Noel Benson, an RAF pilot on 603 Squadron, recently issued with Spitfires. Previously, he had patrolled in the slow and cumbersome Fairey Battle light-bomber, so to be converted to Spitfires was, for Noel, heaven indeed. He had stopped by staying overnight, after landing at Linton-on-Ouse airfield, an airfield just three miles away from his parents' house. He was en route to Hornchurch and wanted to drive his new MG sports car which his parents had given him for his twenty-first birthday, because having been stationed up in Scotland he'd not had the opportunity.

The following morning we rose early for breakfast and I sat on his knee to share his scrambled egg. He then left for Hornchurch. It was the last time we ever saw him.

Noel Benson is buried in the churchyard of St Mary's, Great Ouseburn, across the road from the family home.

Wednesday, 28 August 1940 had seen the *Luftflotte* 2 depart from its usual tactics, and the morning's bombing achieved little. The afternoon and early evening fighter sweeps, however, were costly for certain squadrons, not least 603 Squadron. Thanks to Lord Beaverbrook and MAP, the flow of replacement aircraft was never an issue – but the problem was the comparative inexperience of squadrons fresh to 11 Group in dealing with the Me 109. Air Vice-Marshal Park's sector commanders felt that larger formations may overcome these shortcomings, and that combat experienced pilots from other groups should be posted to 11 Group squadrons should their strength fall below fifteen operational pilots. What Fighter Command could not know, however, was that the enemy was preparing its major assault on 11 Group's airfields.

Up in 12 Group on 28 August 1940, Air Vice-Marshal Leigh-Mallory began sending 611 Squadron's Spitfires from Digby to the Duxford Sector, to operate out of the Fowlmere satellite with those of 19 Squadron, while the Hurricanes of the new Czech 310 Squadron remained at readiness at nearby Duxford. Duxford was 12 Group's closest station to London and therefore offered the greatest chance of action. The move also increased the chances of 12 Group fighters successfully responding to an assistance call from 11 Group by operating closer to the action. Meanwhile, 66 and 242 Squadrons remained relatively inactive further north at Coltishall. For Squadron Leader Douglas Bader, not being in the thick of the action – and the limelight – was intolerable. His squadron had trained hard, drawn blood, and was bursting with high morale. Like a caged tiger, Bader sulked and ranted to anyone within earshot about Fighter Command's apparent stupidity in not committing 242 Squadron to the battle raging further south. No.11 Group, however, was complying perfectly with the strategy decided by Air Chief Marshal Dowding – and it was working.

Across the Channel, *Oberleutnant* Ulrich Steinhilper of I/JG 52 was among the Me 109 pilots gathered in the Pas-de-Calais. Based at Coquelles, operating from a former potato field hastily converted 'into a first-class fighter base', the young officer from Stuttgart found Dunkirk and Calais, following the British evacuation, like 'a vast military supermarket', where 'virtually anything you wanted could be found in or around the harbours and beaches'. Upon arrival at his new base and seeing all the abandoned vehicles and equipment, Steinhilper had wondered whether 'there was really anyone left in England to fight'. Now, after flying a number of operations, he knew there was indeed – and the first cases of battle fatigue – *Kanalkranheit* or 'Channel Illness' were beginning to show among the German aircrews. Resulting from a combination of chronic stress and extreme exhaustion, the first cases were isolated, this nervous reaction manifesting itself in stomach upsets, sickness, loss of appetite, irritability – and an increase in the consumption of cigarettes and alcohol. Unlike Fighter Command, the Luftwaffe did not rotate and rest units, so the pressure was relentless. For some senior men, strings were pulled to get them rest – causing deep resentment. The *Kommandeur* of Steinhilper's *Gruppe*, *Hauptmann* von Eschwege, for example, was awarded an Iron Cross First Class and sent away for an appendix operation – which, because battle fatigue had yet to be understood, was the excuse doctors used to get pilots a few weeks out of the line. Before taking his leave of I/JG 52, von Eschwege explained that he would not be returning after convalescence but going to a staff job at *Luftflotte* 2 HQ. According to Steinhilper, 'There was uproar among the pilots' because of what was an undeserved decoration and 'because he was being rested while we remained at the sharp end of things … It was not the last time strings were pulled for some of the more senior officers.' *Hauptmann* Wolfgang von Ewald replaced the unpopular von Eschwege but 'inherited quite a disconsolate brood of fighter pilots'. Clearly, Britain was not the pushover *Reichsmarschall* Göring anticipated.

Admiral Sir Charles Forbes, Commander-in-Chief of the RN, however, was frustrated; increasing shipping losses and concentration of much of the Home Fleet's strength in the South causing concern. Forbes argued that offensive strikes against enemy-held coastal bases would lead to the Germans dispersing their forces and therefore be unable to consider a seaborne invasion. While the threat of invasion remained imminent, however, such forays were prohibited by the War Cabinet. Forbes also warned that the new battleship *Bismarck* and other *Kriegsmarine* forces would support the proposed invasion – although in reality *Bismarck* was incomplete. Both enemy cruisers had been disabled during the Norwegian campaign, and the Germans' intention was to deploy their most important naval forces to attack the Atlantic shipping routes, and, in the event of Operation *Seelöwe* setting sail, create a northerly diversion. The truth was that *Gross-Admiral* Raeder and the *Oberkommando der Marine* (OKM) were disappointed that the Luftwaffe had failed to prioritise attacks on RN bases and the Home Fleet – the decimation of which the *Kriegsmarine* considered equally important to defeating the RAF. It was a vexing time indeed for both sides.

Daily Home Intelligence Report:

> Morale is much the same today ... The air war remains the chief topic of conversation and optimistic faith in the RAF is still the highest common factor of conversation. There are, however, complaints that we are not doing enough in the way of bombing Berlin objectives, and there is a demand that Berlin should be bombed yet more heavily.

That night, Berlin was the primary target of the Hampden force, fourteen aircraft attacking the Siemens and Halske factory, where explosions and fires were reported, and Wellingtons also went to the 'Big City'. A railway north of Berlin, an oil storage facility at Nordenham and the Berlin railway were also attacked. An 83 Squadron Hampden, based at Scampton, ran out of fuel returning from Berlin, having been airborne for nine hours; the pilot, Flight Lieutenant Jamie Pitcairn-Hill DSO, managing to ditch off Skegness alongside a North Sea trawler which rescued the crew.

Thursday, 29 August 1940

Estimates regarding how many German bombers were active over England on this first night of *Luftflotte* 3's nocturnal attacks vary from 200–340, but nonetheless this was the greatest nocturnal attack so far: by dawn, 37 civilians had been killed and over 100 injured. Five Fighter Command Blenheim night-fighter squadrons and certain day-fighters patrolled Britain's dark skies but despite the number of intruders not one interception occurred. The matter would become an increasingly vexing one for Fighter Command.

The day would be a comparatively quiet one, again permitting certain changes to Fighter Command's Order of Battle.

The decimated 264 Squadron, having suffered grievous losses, was no longer operational and so the hapless Defiants were replaced at Hornchurch by the Spitfires of Squadron Leader John Hill's 222 Squadron. As the latter unit's ORB put it, over the forthcoming days 222 would be 'very positively engaged in operations'. At Kenley, Squadron Leader Joe Kayll's 615 Squadron, which had fought long and hard, was at last relieved when 253 Squadron flew in from Prestwick.

No.253 Squadron, which had re-formed in October 1939 and equipped with Hurricanes, had seen action during the Fall of France, after which it had been withdrawn to Kenley, so was no stranger to the famous fighter station. Squadron Leader Tom Gleave had been a pre-war fighter pilot and flying instructor, having formerly served as Bomber Liaison Officer at Fighter Command HQ, and his association with 253 had begun on 2 June 1940. A week after joining the squadron Gleave was given command – but promotion, not battle, was in the air for Tom Gleave, who was notified that he was to become an acting wing commander at the HQ of a new Fighter Command Group, 14, responsible for defending northern Scotland and, in particular, the all-important naval base at Scapa Flow in the Orkneys. This was not considered good news by Gleave; he knew that at nearly 32 years of age it was highly unlikely he would be given another operational command at squadron level, and would therefore be denied the opportunity to see aerial combat – and that, of course, is what Squadron Leader Gleave had spent years of his life training and preparing for. The prospect of leaving 253 Squadron, however, was cushioned by the fact that Gleave knew and approved of his successor: Squadron Leader Harold Morley Starr, whom he had previously known as a pupil pilot: 'A very charming fellow, efficient and full of the right ideas', and 'overjoyed at receiving his first squadron command.' A great consolation to Gleave was that 253 Squadron 'took to [Starr] immediately', reassuring him that the 'fine fellows' he had previously commanded were in good hands.

For a few days, Squadron Leader Gleave remained at Turnhouse, handing over to the new CO, where the pair were interviewed by 13 Group AOC, Air Vice-Marshal R.E. 'Birdy' Saul – who informed Gleave that before taking up his new staff appointment with 14 Group, he would be spending the interim at 13 Group HQ, 'to learn something about operations'. Gleave, however, robustly argued that he 'had already acquired some knowledge of the subject' and 'pleaded with him' for permission to instead remain with 253 Squadron, as supernumerary. The impassioned Squadron Leader explained that he was desperate to meet 'a Hun at close quarters', and felt that having impressed upon 253 Squadron what they were going to do to the enemy once met, he felt that he was otherwise 'slipping off without the opportunity of showing them I was willing to practice what I preached'. Saul put the matter before the AOC of the new 14 Group, Air Vice-Marshal Henderson, who in due course agreed. As Squadron Leader Starr had no objection, Gleave remained with 253 Squadron as 'vice', and 'life once again took on a rosy hue'.

On 23 August 1940, Gleave was on leave but recalled: 'Come back immediately'. Upon return to Turnhouse, he discovered that 253 Squadron had been posted to Prestwick, on Scotland's West Coast, and that the move had to be completed early the next day. This was no mean feat, and the station became a veritable hive of activity. Over the next week life continued much the same at Prestwick for 253 Squadron, until Gleave – having just returned from leave and feeling depressed that his extension of service with 253 Squadron was likely to end any day now, still without having engaged the enemy – took an unexpected telephone call: 253 Squadron was to fly south the following morning, 29 August 1940, to relieve 615 Squadron at Kenley in 11 Group. Gleave could hardly believe his ears – but was then told that he was not to go with them, but instead was required at 13 Group HQ. Bereft, Tom implored the Sector Controller 'do something about it', and nothing of 'it' was ever heard again: Squadron Leader Tom Gleave was going to war at last.

On 253 Squadron's last night at Prestwick, there was an air of celebration, the officers inviting the NCOs to their Mess for a 'scrum'. A cushion improvised as a rugby ball, and after several vigorous tussles the series was declared a draw, the party eventually breaking up after 'a final drink'. Considering subsequent events, and the carnage 253 Squadron was about to have visited upon it, one cannot help but be reminded of the Duchess of Richmond's ball in Brussels on the eve of Waterloo…

En route to Kenley, 253 stopped to refuel at an RAF base where they met pilots from 615 Squadron doing likewise before pressing on to Scotland. According to Gleave, 'They had a lot to tell us, and their experiences did much to make our chaps all the more-keen to get down into the battle zone.' Of 253 Squadron's arrival at Kenley, Gleave wrote of helpful briefings, meeting old friends, and, being 'full of enthusiasm'. At the earliest opportunity after their arrival on 29 August 1940, 253 Squadron 'volunteered to stand-by with a flight, and our offer was accepted, so we made up two sections and stood-by'.

At 16.00 hrs that afternoon, Squadron Leader Gleave and his composite flight of seven other Hurricanes was scrambled to patrol base at 2,000ft, Tom leading in Hurricane P2361, SW-X. An hour later the Hurricanes returned to base, their patrol uneventful. Then, at 22.20 hrs, Squadron Leaders Gleave and Starr flew a nocturnal patrol, in formation, of thirty minutes, 'To check on night-flying facilities.' It had been a long day, but a quiet one, compared with previous days, from the perspective of enemy air activity: several German formations had crossed the Kentish coast that afternoon, penetrating as far as Westerham and Maidstone, but the operation was over in an hour; during the evening, enemy fighters swept around Dover, but again these were over quickly. Both sides had lost nine fighters. The pattern of German air activity, however, suggested that the following day was likely to be busier. Indeed, dawn on 30 August 1940, brought fine weather, and it was on that day that the Battle of Britain entered its most critical phase, with the enemy concentrating even heavier attacks on 11 Group's all-important airfields. No.253 Squadron, although more than just keen and confident, was about to discover just how ferocious the fighting was over southern England – and meet the lethal Me 109.

The previous day, 11 Group's controllers had been lured into reacting unnecessarily to the enemy's otherwise harmless high-altitude fighter sweeps, and had lost a number of aircraft and pilots as a result. Air Vice-Marshal Park was determined, therefore, that this would not happen again. After a quiet morning, soon after 15.00 hrs the Germans eventually played their hand: a small number of Do 17s, being used as bait, which would not be assisted by a complete covering of cloud over south-east England, droned across the Channel covered high above by the most enormous phalanx of fighters so far – a staggering 500 Me 109s and Me 110s.

At 15.15 hrs, 11 Group scrambled nine Spitfires of 603 Squadron from Hornchurch on a 'defensive patrol'; twelve Hurricanes of 85 Squadron took-off from Croydon at 15.21 hrs to patrol Hawkinge; fourteen Spitfires of 610 Squadron left Biggin Hill at 15.30 hrs to intercept the incoming raid approaching from the South, and, having been brought to readiness at 15.22 hrs, half an hour later eleven Spitfires of 616 Squadron scrambled from Kenley and headed for the trouble.

The first of the defenders to engage was 610 Squadron, at 15.50 hrs over Mayfield, a running battle developing to the coast:

> The enemy bombers were engaged at varying heights from 18,000ft to 20,000ft over Mayfield. They were broken up and last seen returning to the French coast. Cloud 10/10ths at 10,000ft … Flying Officer Lamb opened fire at one Me 'Jaguar' coming almost head-on, Sergeant Baker saw this aircraft crash [ORB].

A 'Jaguar' was an unofficial term for the Me 110, usually referring to the fighter-bomber version; no Me 110s were lost this day, however, and certainly none fell on British soil, so whatever Baker saw crash it was not the enemy aircraft engaged by Lamb.

> Flight Lieutenant Lamb fired two or three short bursts at one Me 'Jaguar', the starboard engine of the E/A smoked badly and it disappeared into clouds. Sergeant Beardsley delivered a stern attack on a Do 215 [*sic*] on the port side of an enemy formation and fired five bursts of about 100 rounds each at a range of 250–150 yards. After the first two bursts no fire was met with fire from the E/A which was badly damaged, pieces flying off and holes appearing all over it. It went down in a series of short, jerky, dives and seemed definitely out of control. Sergeant Chandler attacked a straggler from abeam with four long bursts which definitely damaged the Do 215. Pilot Officer Aldous followed a Do 215 down to near the top of the clouds and fired a long burst from abeam when the E/A was turning, it dived steeply into the clouds at 10,000ft and was not seen again. Pilot Officer Pegge attacked another Do 215, giving it a short burst from above and behind, saw pieces come off the fuselage. Sergeant Baker attacked an Me 'Jaguar' from the rear and slightly to port and underneath. He gave a three-second burst from 200 yards, which caused white smoke to issue forth, the E/A healing over into a dive. He then attacked a Do 215 from about the same position as before and fired two bursts of about three seconds each, which caused the E/A to go into an over-the-vertical dive [ORB].

The foregoing combats illustrate just how hard German bombers were to shoot down with eight rifle-calibre machine-guns – none of the Do 17s were actually destroyed. Sergeant Aubrey Baker, however, was shot-up by return fire and wrote off his Spitfire when crash-landing at Gatwick – the pilot was unhurt. Sergeant Edward Manton, sadly, was shot down and killed, his Spitfire crashing on the Great Wigsell Estate, Hurst Green in Surrey.

The cloud covering had prevented the Do 17s bombing whatever their intended target was, and it also caused problems for certain defending squadrons. No.85 Squadron were initially ordered to patrol Hawkinge at 15,000ft but then ordered below cloud, reducing height to 4,000ft – before being informed by the Controller of enemy aircraft in their vicinity, between 15,000–20,000ft, and sent up to intercept. This put Squadron Leader Townsend's pilots at a serious disadvantage, although at 16.00 hrs eighteen bombers and thirty Me 109s were sighted much lower down, at 7,000ft, albeit still with a height advantage. Townsend led the Hurricanes in pursuit, still climbing, the enemy formation climbing to 16,000ft. Over Beachy Head, more Do 17s and escorting fighters were seen, 85 Squadron estimating the combined enemy strength being 200 to 300 aircraft. In compliance with Air Vice-Marshal Park's recent instructions, Townsend reported the enemy's location and disposition, and requested back-up.

In view of the overwhelming number of enemy fighters, Townsend turned 85 Squadron into the sun and away from the main enemy fighter force, intending to attack from above and out of the sun – but twelve Me 110s had shadowed 85 Squadron and now curved round to attack the Hurricanes from astern:

> Squadron broke away and circled again, E/A then appeared unwilling to engage in spite of vastly superior numbers, and stuck closely together. Periodically one or two would leave the main mass and dive, but this was clearly in order to trap an unwary pilot. One or two of the Hurricanes accepted the bait in spite of warning and were promptly set upon.
>
> After ten minutes of playing a waiting game, five Me 109s dived in front of the Squadron and Squadron Leader Townsend was able to get in a five second deflection burst at one, causing black and white smoke to come from its belly, and a piece, possibly the roof, to fly off. E/A stalled and was then seen to crash somewhere North of Hastings and North of Battle [ORB].

This was a 4/JG 3 Me 109E-1 which crashed at Lodge Field, Green Farm, Hooe; the pilot, *Oberleutnant* J. Kipper, baled out but fell dead at nearby New Lodge Farm.

> Flight Lieutenant Hamilton chased an Me 109 which was firing at a Hurricane. The E/A broke off attack and started to rejoin formation, when Flight Lieutenant Hamilton got in a seven second burst and the Me 109's engine caught fire and it dived down vertically into the sea, out of control [ORB].

Very like, the Canadian Flight Lieutenant Harry 'Hammy' Hamilton, a Canadian, had killed *Oberleutnant* Floerke of 3/JG 3, who crashed into the Channel and was never seen again. After breaking away, 'Hammy' was unable to attack the main enemy formation as by then it was retiring south and mid-Channel.

Sergeant Glendon Booth attacked a 109 from astern at 100 yards range, pursuing his target as it emitted black smoke, continuing to fire until ten miles out to sea off Eastbourne; the enemy fighter was last seen at 500ft, still smoking, and losing height. Sergeant John Ellis, however, was shot-up, his cockpit and engine both damaged, the latter stopping. Electing to glide down to a forced-landing, at 13,000ft the Hurricane burst into flame, Ellis baling out safely at 10,000ft. The pilot floated down to land at Brigden Hill Farm, Ashburnham, his aircraft impacting just 100 yards away. Sergeant Francis Walker-Smith's Hurricane was hit by a 20mm cannon round when at 14,000ft, but this pilot also took to his parachute, wounded in a foot, having descended to 1,600ft and experiencing a complete loss of throttle and rudder controls; the aircraft went in at Underwood Farm, near Etchingham, while the injured pilot alighted at Hawkhurst.

No.85 Squadron saw 'no other friendly fighters' in this engagement excepting 'one Spitfire seen to descend in flames [ORB]'.

That Spitfire seen in flames was that of 610 Squadron's Sergeant Manton.

Further east, at 16.00 hrs the nine Spitfires of 603 Squadron were led into action by Squadron Leader Denholm over Deal; the South African Pilot Officer Basil 'Stapme' Stapleton reported that:

we sighted enemy fighters [eighteen Me 109s] just South of Deal. Pilot Officer Read and I broke away from the Squadron to engage two Me 109s who were circling above us. Pilot Officer Read engaged the first and myself the second. After firing short deflection bursts the Me 109 which I had attacked went straight down out of my sight with smoke issuing from the engine. I then broke away and climbed into the sun.

The Me 109 was awarded as 'damaged', while Flying Officer John Boulter and Pilot Officer Colin Pinckey both claimed German fighters destroyed; Pilot Officers William 'Bill' Read and Richard Hillary each claimed 'probables'. The squadron's only casualty was Flight Lieutenant Fred 'Rusty' Rushmer, commander of 'B' Flight, who was slightly wounded when shot-up by a 109 and forced-landed at Bossingham.

No.616 Squadron's eleven Spitfires, up from Kenley, sighted thirty Me 109s 'pass very high overhead' while climbing to Angels 10. When up at 17,000ft, ten more 109s were seen orbiting Kenley and Biggin Hill before turning for the coast. The Spitfires dived and attacked, the enemy pilots, doubtless concerned about fuel reserves, 'sheared off towards France. Flight Lieutenant Gillam chased, attacked and destroyed one Me 110 within five miles of French coast [ORB].' The Spitfires landed back at Kenley without suffering any casualties – a confidence-boost after the 'unfortunate engagement' of three days previously.

In these afternoon skirmishes, just one Spitfire was lost – but pilots of II and III/JG 3 claimed seven of the type destroyed, and 4/JG 53 claiming a single Hurricane.

The German fighter sweeps were not yet over, however, so the skies of Kent would not be clear of 'bandits' for long. At 18.10 hrs, ten 603 Squadron Spitfires scrambled from Hornchurch to patrol over Manston; six minutes later, eleven 85 Squadron Hurricanes once more scrambled from Croydon to patrol Maidstone, where they were vectored towards Dungeness, and between 18.25–18.30 hrs, twelve Hurricanes of 501 Squadron scrambled from Gravesend.

Sadly, an avoidable tragedy followed for 85 Squadron, which:

> climbed to 24,000ft and were then joined by a Spitfire and a Hurricane, which both began weaving behind flank sections. Warned of presence of E/A some miles to the North, Squadron wheeled to attempt interception, still accompanied by Spitfire and Hurricane [the latter probably a 501 Squadron aircraft]. While circling, Red 3, Pilot Officer Hodgson, suddenly shouted warning that enemy aircraft were behind. These turned out to be three Me 109s – the leader of which was not identified until he was within range on account of the previous presence of the Spitfire and the strong resemblance at a certain distance of a Spitfire to an Me 109 front view.
>
> On receipt of warning Squadron circled steeply left. Red 3 saw tracer ammunition passing close-by and … saw cannon shell explode on Red 1's tail unit [Flight Lieutenant Hamilton], blowing most of it off. Red 1 was also seen to lose starboard wing-tip. He flicked over on his back and fell straight to earth. A Hurricane was later seen in flames on the ground which was presumed to be Red 1. His body was subsequently found near Winchelsea [ORB].

Flight Lieutenant Hamilton, shot down by *Oberleutnant* Martin Rysavy of 2/JG 26, crashed near the ruins of Camber Castle on the foreshore at Rye, 85 Squadron's only response being made by Pilot Officer James Marshal, who sent an Me 109 plunging towards the Channel ten miles off Dungeness. The 109 was not seen to hit the water due to thick haze, but was accredited as destroyed.

Townsend, understandably, was furious at Hamilton's loss and hastened back to base to submit a scathing report on the matter for immediate dissemination 'to all interested parties'. Many years later, Group Captain Townsend, as he became, was still angry:

> Our Hurricanes were in open, or search, line astern formation, covered by a section of three tail-end Charlies. The appearance of Hillary's Spitfire, which from the front looked not altogether dissimilar to the Me 109, caused us confusion in identifying the enemy when we were attacked over Winchelsea. Hillary might have known better. We lost Flight Lieutenant Hamilton, a Canadian and a superb flight commander, purely because the Me 109s were identified a fraction of a second too late.

Pilot Officer Hillary had become separated from his own 603 Squadron, which was in action over Manston, as Flying Officer Brian Carbury, leading Green Section, reported: 'We went into line astern, Green 2 and 3 attacked individual E/A. I climbed and saw two Me 109s climbing below, so carried out a long frontal attack with slight deflection. A long burst and the E/A smoked and then blew up.'

Carbury then 'returned to base having lost the rest of formation' – which, of course, is what Hillary should have done. Finding himself further south after the action over Manston, Hillary, having most of his ammunition left, climbed, searching for 'friendly Spitfires but found instead a squadron of Hurricanes flying round the sky at 18,000ft in sections of stepped-up threes but with no rear-guard. So I joined on.' Taking aside that Hillary's action was well-intentioned but ill-advised, the other primary issue here is the limitations of the airborne radio in use – as explained in detail previously in this narrative. Because Hillary could only communicate with his own squadron and Sector Controller, he was unable to notify 85 Squadron of his presence – a good reason for clearing off out of it when separated to avoid confusion. Had the later VHF set been in service this would not have been an issue, because cross-squadron communication then became possible. But it was not – yet. And Hamilton was dead. Hillary, however, was also surprised and shot down during I/JG 26's attack, crash-landing, unhurt, at Lympne, later describing the experience as 'the most amusing though painful'.

Prior to his escapade over Dungeness, Hillary claimed a 109 destroyed, as did Flying Officer Colin Pinckney, the latter then being shot down himself, baling out with his face and hands burnt; his Spitfire crashed at Dymchurch. He was the fourth 603 Squadron pilot to be shot down that day. In response, in addition to Carbury's claim, two more Me 109s destroyed and two probables were also claimed by 603.

Sergeant Bill Green of 501 Squadron had just returned to from a brief leave with his wife, Bertha, earlier in the day:

She had given me some socks, and on 29 August 1940, I left her at Whitchurch, in the Magister, wearing my brand-new socks, picked Sergeant Peter Morfill up, then the pair of us returned to Gravesend, where we had to be by mid-day, to go on readiness straight away, which we did. I recall that there was very low cloud, so I wrote to my wife, telling her how much I loved her, how much I'd enjoyed being with her, how much I missed her, and telling her not to worry because the weather was too bad for there to be any flying that day. I had no sooner written the letter than we were scrambled.

We went up through the cloud, late afternoon, early evening, formated above it and were vectored down to Deal. Once over Deal – codenamed 'Red Queen' – at 20,000ft we were told to orbit and 'Look out for 200 "Snappers"' – 109s – coming in. I remember that when Squadron Leader Hogan got the vector, he said, somewhat whimsically, 'Come on, boys, come to Deal with me'

– not using the codename. There we were orbiting, vigilantly and vigorously searching the sky all around us – when suddenly there was a crash, broken glass, and a gaping hole in my windscreen, slightly larger than a tennis ball, and immediately I was covered with liquid of some sort. My control column was useless, it was connected to nothing. I realised that my aeroplane was finished. So, I slid back the hood, although I may have already had it back, because I think that at the time we were told that one of our colleagues had been hit and seen going down, on fire, clawing at the canopy, which was stuck fast; he crashed and was killed, so with that in mind, I'm sure my hood was already back. I pulled the pin of the Sutton safety harness, got as far as being on my knees, up on my seat in a semi-crouched position, when I was either sucked out or the aeroplane blew up, I don't know which. But I was suddenly out, rolling over and over, and I heard my flying boots go past my ear. My legs were spread-eagled, so I frantically grabbed around for the ripcord, eventually found it after what seemed like a long time – and pulled it. I saw something white do two eccentric circles, going away from me, upwards. This had no significance until the main canopy came straight up between my legs. I rolled forward, into this unopened parachute. I realised that the parachute should not have come out between my legs but behind me, so I then tried to push the parachute back between my legs. I remember thinking about my wife, who I had seen that morning, and I suppose that I was now contemplating my end, thinking 'I wonder if she will wonder if I wondered, as I was falling, what my end was going to be like.' Then I remember thinking that she would realise, as I realised, that everything would go black, and that would be it. I kept struggling with this parachute until eventually there was a jolt, then a secondary jolt. I grabbed the rigging lines – having seen one part of the parachute disappear I thought the whole lot might be going! I was then hit by this enormous silence that one experiences – having fallen through the air from perhaps 16,000ft, at 140 mph, with the rustling of the parachute around my ears all that way – when one experiences when floating down by parachute. The silence – caused by my parachute opening at almost literally the last second – hit me more than any noise I've ever heard. I just shook my head and thought 'Gosh, that was close!' Left and above me there were trees, higher than I was, and there were electricity cables level with me, and I thought 'Gosh, I'm near the ground!' The only thing I knew about parachuting was that I had to bend my knees, which I did – bang – I hit the ground. I sat there, on this sloping field, full of thistles and cowpats, and there I sat, in my stockinged feet, having lost my boots, thinking 'Oh dear, I've got to go and walk through this awful field in my bare socks.' I then pulled my parachute towards me, to examine the cords and see what had gone on, and found that the pilot parachute had been severed about nine inches from where it joined the main canopy, the thin attaching cords having been severed by shrapnel. So, when I pulled the ripcord, the pilot parachute shot off into space, leaving nothing to pull the main parachute out of its pack. In 1995, I visited the crash site for the first time since the event, and worked out, from the height of trees and the electricity cables, that my parachute had eventually opened at just 150ft – or, in other words, 1½ seconds from certain death.

Sergeant Green's Hurricane crashed at Ladwood Farm, near the village of Elham, close-by Hawkinge airfield. Kent; Bill landed at Mill Hill Farm, Elham:

I was rescued, if that's the right word, by two fellows who came running down from the nearby farmhouse with shotguns. They quickly recognised that I was British and took me back to the house for a cup of tea. I was collected by a couple of army people who motored me back to Hawkinge. I had collected some wounds in my right leg, and in my right knee there was a hole where a bullet had passed completely through, a perfectly round hole. I was taken to Station Sick Quarters and the Medical Officer there started to poke around in this hole, with a long steel needle, and I remember just passing out. I was then invited to go into the Officers' Mess by my Flight Commander, Flight Lieutenant John Gibson [a New Zealander], or 'Gibbo' as he was known to us, and I learned that he had been shot down at exactly the same time, but that his parachute had opened in the orthodox fashion. He had floated down gently from a great height and was conjecturing where he might land, and thought 'Oh, I won't be far from Hawkinge', but then thought, 'Oh, I think I should land just about on the airfield.' Then 'Oh crikey, I'm going to overshoot the airfield, looks like I'm going to land in Folkestone, hope I don't hit a church spire and end up suspended 150ft above the ground … I'm going to overshoot Folkestone, I'm going to land on the beach. Wonder if it's mined?' Then he realised he was going to hit the water, some miles out, and got picked up by an RAF ASR launch. He would say that he hit the water at 7.30 pm, and I know that I was in the farmhouse drinking tea at 7.10 pm. I was about eight miles from the coast, he was some miles off the coast, so that tells you the difference between a perpendicular fall, in a non-operating parachute, and drifting out to sea in an offshore breeze from a height of 20,000 or 16,000ft. The time difference is also indicative.

The next day, I was taken to Station Sick Quarters at Gravesend, and then to Woolwich Hospital, where my wounds could be attended to. I was then sick for some weeks, and didn't fly again with 501 Squadron.

Sergeant James 'Ginger' Lacey shot down the Me 109 which had got Gibson, and the latter also claimed a 109 destroyed before being knocked out himself.

At 18.00 hrs, the Spitfires of 610 Squadron had scrambled from Biggin Hill to patrol Hawkinge, over which Sergeant Bob Beardsley claimed a 109 probable, and Sergeant Aubrey Baker one destroyed. These were the only 610 Squadron pilots to engage, for no loss.

This, at last, brought the daylight action to a close, during which 11 Group had lost five Hurricanes destroyed, one pilot killed and another wounded, the Spitfire force suffering the loss of two Spitfires, two more damaged, a pilot killed and one wounded. *Luftflotte* 2's fighter losses, however, amounted to some eight Me 109s destroyed and two damaged, plus an Me 110, damaged; four Me 109 pilots had been killed, one was missing and one captured. For 11 Group, although not without loss, it had been a good day, overall.

Daily Home Intelligence Report:

> There is no noticeable decline in morale, although in London particularly there is some depression mainly brought on by lack of sleep.

South-eastern (Tunbridge Wells):

> Air Raids in this region are frequently followed by the rumour that gas has been used ... Anxiety is still being caused through lack of news of men reported missing after Dunkirk. There is grumbling over the time taken for special army allowances for high rent and medical fees to come through.

That night, while Bomber Command continued taking the war to legitimate targets in Germany, as many as 250 German bombers were active over England in waves of 100 at a time. *Luftflotte* 3 continued to target South Wales, Liverpool and Manchester. Just one of the raiders was brought down, when Pilot Officer Alan Wright of 92 Squadron, up on a nocturnal patrol from Bibury, caught and destroyed a 3/KG 27 He 111 over Bristol; the enemy crew all baled out safely and were captured, their aircraft crashing at Hale.

The following day would prove a significant one in the Battle of Britain – not least for the Poles of Northolt's 303 Squadron and 12 Group's irascible Squadron Leader Douglas Bader, CO of the Canadian 242 Squadron, all of whom were frustrated by the lack of action.

Squadron Leader Ronald Kellett, CO, 303 Squadron:

> We had all learned certain Polish words: 'Klapy' = flaps, and 'potwozie' = undercarriage, so in the air we could remind the pilots of these needs. The rumour circulated that the Poles were so keen to land that they failed to put the undercarriage down – typical schoolboy humour imparted to high places. I would have none of this, as they were very quickly being converted to Hurricanes and had retractable undercarriage for the first time.
>
> There was an incident that illustrated the problem of language and non-communication. A principle of the dispersal of aircraft was that no aircraft should be nearer than, say, twenty yards from the next, and on seeing two aircraft wing tip to wing tip, I ordered a Polish airman to start one so that it could be taxied to another place. There was a certain amount of gesticulating which I ignored. I should have noticed that the air pressure for the brakes was nil, but once the aircraft was started I taxied onto the slope of the taxi-track. I tried the brakes to turn the aircraft but they didn't work – and within seconds the eight-ton aircraft had crashed into one of the dispersal huts, destroying its propeller and not improving the hut either! As chance would have it, the Command Accident Officer was just walking to dispersal and witnessed the

event. He told me not to report the accident, saying there were too many to deal with and that he quite understood the reason.

An awkward thing happened. The men and NCOs were paid but the officers, strangely, were not. Gieves, the outfitters, had come to fit their uniforms but the authorities had not decided as to their pay. Of this I was unaware, but assuming they would get RAF pay, I drew my own cheque at my private account, against which the Accounting Officer paid them the money. When the second month's pay was due, this process had to be repeated, but the accountant still held the cheques and said he could not continue the arrangement. I decided that if the third month was the same, I would draw my own cheque on the Bank of England and instruct my bank to collect. I hadn't spent eleven years in the City for nothing and knew that the Bank of England would accept some responsibility.

At this time we received visits from the Air Minister, Lord Sinclair, who discoursed in French with the Poles and showed himself to be the sincere, good and unselfish man he was. This visit was entirely informal. Indeed, a little later Churchill turned up as an area near Northolt had been bombed that night and he wanted first-hand knowledge of the damage. He was in great form and full of vigour. We expressed regret at the civilian damage and loss of life; 'In these times', he said, 'they must learn to put up with it.' I was able to mention the matter of officers pay – it was not, after all, the Crimean War. 'They must be paid,' he said. Furthermore, within six hours of the receipt of the money, all loans were repaid and my cheques torn up. He also said, 'I value the commander of a fighter squadron today as much as a Cabinet Minister, but don't tell them.' However, he was off to his work within minutes, but had done a great deal for morale and certainly showed none of the anxiety he must have felt.

During the training period I had, with the agreement of General Ujesjski, recruited more pilots from the Polish collecting depot at Blackpool and think we had about thirty-two operational pilots in the Squadron. It was therefore possible for each pilot to be on duty twenty-four hours on and twenty-four off. We changed over at one o'clock. No pilot on duty was allowed to leave the Mess, early bed and early rising, the Squadron being on readiness from half an hour before sunrise until half an hour after sunset. We suggested to the ground crews that they should do the same but British and Polish NCOs replied that while our pilots were in the air they wanted to remain on duty, and so it was. I don't believe any Squadron had better NCOs or aircraft maintenance than 303.

The Group Captain offered my Squadron an old lorry as a dispersal wagon – I said that would not do and that I should use my own Rolls-Royce, an old, open, four-seater. It would have been bad for morale to use an old lorry when other squadrons had cars, even though not Rolls-Royces. The car was looked after as well as the aircraft and proved to be an excellent morale factor, arriving at dispersal from the Mess with as many as twelve pilots in it.

We soon started Squadron training in fighter tactics. It was soon clear, however, that the four or so attacks laid down by Fighter Command were unworkable, as the R/T orders could not be understood. Instead, we perfected one attack only and each battle was made to fit the attack, i.e. not the method of attack to suit the battle.

It is often said that Air Chief Marshal Dowding was remote and detached from his pilots, but Ronald Kellett writes that during the Battle of Britain, which, while the Poles trained, was in full swing, he was to 'receive many visits from him and Air Vice-Marshal Park'. The matter of fighter tactics, however, provoked a sharp reaction when discussed with the Commander-in-Chief:

These matters were discussed with Dowding on his various visits, but above all he asked 'Have you shown them the bloody wall where we shoot pilots who kill their own side?' I replied that certainly the Poles practised aircraft recognition and reminded him that these men had seen the real thing in Poland and France.

The wait for more of 'the real thing' was nearly over.

Friday, 30 August 1940

At airfields all over 11 Group the dawn chorus was not one of peaceful birdsong but the roar of countless Merlin engines warming up, ready to power RAF fighter pilots into the battle once more. As always, even before first light, fighter stations were a hive of activity as bleary-eyed pilots, awoken at an unearthly hour, arrived at dispersal to fly the dawn patrol or await events. None knew what the day would bring – and for some this sunrise would be their last.

Across the Channel, there were similar scenes – and *Generalfeldmarschall* Kesselring's preparations were now complete, the weather was fine – and the Battle of the Airfields was now on. Indeed, great urgency was attached to this renewed assault, given that time was marching on. On this day, the OKH sent *General* Ernst Busch's 16th *Armee* detailed operational instructions for Operation *Seelöwe*. This represented a draft of what became the final plan, to which more parachute landings would be added. The role of the 16th *Armee* role was to embark from the 'invasion ports' between and including Rotterdam and Calais, landing on a 'broad front on the Folkestone-Hastings section of the coast'. The importance of the 'speedy capture of the dock installations at Dover' was emphasised, which would be assisted by the simultaneous landing of *Fallschirmjäger* on high ground above the port. The 9th *Armee* was to land simultaneously with 16th, between Bexhill and Worthing, the role of both formations in this first wave being to establish bridgeheads and expand them to make a connected and broad landing ground for disembarkation of the reinforcing second wave, provided by Army Group B. The Luftwaffe's role was made clear: 'The Luftwaffe will destroy the British Air Force and the armament production which supports it, and it will achieve air superiority.'

This, then, was no longer Hitler playing Brinkmanship or Air Fleet Diplomacy; the Germans were seriously pursuing the objective of launching Operation *Seelöwe* – and about this let there be absolutely no mistake. Indeed, by 21 July 1940 Hitler had realised that with Britain not climbing down, invasion represented the most likely means of ending the war that autumn – and as previously discussed Germany needed a swift victory over Britain. Nonetheless, Hitler fully acknowledged the great difficulties involved, and mollified the concerns of the OKM and OKH by the assurance that Operation *Seelöwe* would not proceed unless the 'overwhelming results' he required from the aerial campaign were achieved. Hitler, therefore, regardless of the pessimism of the OKM and OKH, was now enthusiastic about the prospect of invading southern England – and the ever-vain and boastful *Reichsmarschall* Hermann Göring and his Luftwaffe had to deliver. All eyes were now on *Generalfeldmarschall* Albert Kesselring's *Luftflotte 2*.

No.253 Squadron's first full day at Kenley began with curious enemy activity, formations of up to 'twenty plus' bandits flying towards Dover, shortly before 08.00 hrs, but none actually crossed the coast. This effort was intended to lure the 11 Group Controller into scrambling his squadrons, which would then be back on the ground, refuelling and rearming when the main raids came in. Wise to such subterfuge, only one section of RAF fighters reacted, the remainder staying firmly on the ground. Between 09.15 and 09.30 hrs, three more enemy formations approached Dover, and this time two 11 Group fighters were sent up to patrol the coastal airfields at Hawkinge and Rochford respectively. At 10.30 hrs, however, the situation had clearly changed: three enemy formations of around twenty each were up over Calais, and another, numbering 'fifty plus' further south, above Tramecourt. This enemy air activity, then, was the real thing, representing a significant threat – to which the 11 Group Controller lost no time in responding.

At 10.25 hrs, a flight of 501 Squadron's Hurricanes were scrambled from Hawkinge to patrol base, before being vectored to Dover at 10.50 hrs. At that time, the rest of 501 Squadron took off, to patrol base. No.603 Squadron's Spitfires were off from Hornchurch at 10.35 hrs, to patrol Canterbury, and a minute later the Hurricanes of 85 Squadron raced off from Croydon, Dover bound. At 10.45 hrs, 610 Squadron's Spitfires went up from Biggin Hill, also ordered to Dover. At 10.30 hrs and 10.40 hrs respectively, 1 Squadron was sent off from Northolt, and 56 from North Weald, but their orders are unknown, and those two squadrons did not subsequently engage. At 11.00 hrs, fifty more German aircraft were plotted over Cap Griz-Nez, and those detected over Tramecourt headed towards Dungeness, prompting more RAF squadrons to be scrambled: 253 Squadron from Kenley at 10.55 hrs, 151 Squadron from Stapleford five minutes later, and 234 Squadron's Spitfires were sent from Middle Wallop in 10 Group to protect Northolt.

This was, of course, the opportunity 253 Squadron had been waiting for. At 10.50 hrs, Squadron Leader Harold Starr sped off from Kenley, leading five 'A' Flight Hurricanes.

Pilot Officer Alan Corkett remembered that:

We were well aware of the urgency ... In the circumstances Squadron Leader Starr did not wait for the Squadron to form up on the runway but took off immediately. Pilot Officer DNO Jenkins was flying on Starr's port side as No 3, and I was flying in the second Section of three aircraft as No 2 [starboard side] to the Section Leader. As the leading Section became airborne the Controller ordered 'Buster', which means we were to go flat-out.

'Raid near Redhill'. We were, of course, at full throttle in the take-off climb. The leader ordered us to open out and individual aircraft flew wider on their leaders and my Section moved well out to starboard of the leading Section.

At 10.55 hrs, Flight Lieutenant Cambridge followed with 'B' Flight, an attack on Biggin Hill, Croydon and Kenley appearing likely by that time, and Squadron Leader Starr's formation was recalled from Maidstone to patrol base.

At 11.03 hrs, the first raid, target Farnborough, was incoming over Dungeness and proceeded towards Tonbridge. Seven minutes later, 85 Squadron sighted and reported fifty He 111s over Bethenden, above which were many Me 109s. Squadron Leader Peter Townsend led his Hurricanes inland before turning to attack out of the sun, taking the glass-nosed bombers head-on. The surprise and savagery of this attack dispersed the Heinkels, after which individual dogfights took place. 85 Squadron's CO attacked an Me 110 which was 'last seen twenty miles South of Beachy Head with black and white smoke coming from port engine but aircraft still under control [ORB]'. Off Ramsgate, Pilot Officer William Hodgson, a New Zealander, claimed two Me 110s destroyed, having already damaged a He 111 in the initial charge. Sergeant Geoffrey Goodman shot down a 110 which he saw ditch in the Channel, and claimed a 'probable'. Pilot Officer Sammy Allard DFM claimed two He 111s destroyed, both of 5/KG 1, one crashing at Mannings Heath, the other at Lingfield. Pilot Officer Patrick Woods-Scawen claimed a 110 destroyed near Dover as the enemy withdrew, and Pilot Officer Charles English damaged a He 111, and Sergeant Glendon Booth an Me 110. At 11.40 hrs, Pilot Officer James Marshal, however, was shot-up and baled out, fortunately unhurt, his Hurricane crashing at Smarden; *Oberfeldwebel* Werner Machold of 1/JG 2, who claimed a Hurricane at exactly that time, possibly being responsible.

As the enemy were dispersed, a running battle back to France developed, and more enemy formations were incoming, threatening Biggin Hill, Kenley and Hornchurch. Consequently, at 11.10 hrs, Squadron Leader John Hill's 222 Squadron – freshly arrived from Kirton only the previous day and joining the other two Spitfire squadrons at Hornchurch, 54 and 603 – scrambled to patrol Gravesend. Five minutes later 54 Squadron went up to patrol Billericay.

At 11.10 hrs, Sergeant Bob Beardsley of 610 Squadron attacked a He 111 near Hawkinge, later recalling with wry amusement:

it was heading for home. I was short of ammunition after a scrap with a couple of escort fighters, but as one engine was smoking badly I followed up and put the other engine out. I followed it down until it landed off Hythe and a couple of aircrew got out onto the wing root. Three Hurricanes who had arrived later claimed a third each!

Other 610 Squadron pilots brought the Squadron's 'bag' in this action to four He 111s destroyed, an Me 109 destroyed, an Me 110 probable and a Do 215 [*sic*] also probably destroyed.

At 11.20 hrs, 501 Squadron engaged over Dungeness, claiming two He 111s destroyed, an Me 110 probable and another damaged. West of Dover, at 11.25 hrs, 603 Squadron's Pilot Officer James Morton claimed a 110 probable and one damaged, but the CO, Squadron Leader 'Uncle' George Denholm, was shot down and forced to bale out of Spitfire L1067, XT-D:

While my recollections of some personal experiences in 1940 is still quite vivid, sadly my log book was destroyed in a fire several years ago, and there is no means of pinning memories to any particular aircraft except L1067, which was my 'personal' aircraft up to 30 August 1940, when we parted company. The painting of names and emblems on our aircraft was unofficial and purely personal – L1067 was my 'Blue Peter' [after the horse of that name which won the Derby in 1938/39].

Fortunately, 'Uncle George' was unhurt, the Spitfire plunging into marshy land at Snargate. 603's Sergeant Alfred Sarre's Spitfire was also shot-up, but, also unharmed, he returned safely to Hornchurch.

At 11.25 hrs, 43 Squadron, up from Tangmere, began a running battle with various raiders in the skies of Kent, Sussex and Surrey, during which a 'He 113 [*sic*]' was claimed destroyed – but a recent replacement pilot, fresh from OTU, Sergeant Dennis Noble, was shot down by an Me 109 over the Sussex coast and killed when his Hurricane crashed near the junction of Portland and Woodhouse Road in Hove.

At 11.30 hrs Squadron Leader Tom Gleave was leading 253 Squadron's 'Emergency Section' up from Kenley, comprising Pilot Officer Colin 'Dopey' Francis and Flight Lieutenant George 'Bruno' Brown, joining those fighters of 253 Squadron already airborne over Kenley and heading south; eight Spitfires of 616 Squadron also left Kenley at 11.30 hrs and were vectored towards the Thames Estuary. At the same time, significantly, assistance having been requested from 12 Group, the Spitfires of 19 Squadron left Fowlmere to reinforce the Hurricanes of 79 Squadron which were patrolling over their home station

A delayed action bomb explodes at Bibury airfield in Gloucestershire on 19 August 1940, on which day a flight of 92 Squadron's Spitfires became operational there, having relieved Hurricanes of 87 Squadron. On the same day, the airfield was subjected to a low-level bombing and strafing attack by a Ju 88. (*Historic Military Press*)

The same site in February 2023, during a site investigation by Stephen Clark and the author.

The Spitfire pilot of 92 Squadron, in black flying overalls and carrying his parachute, looks less perturbed by the explosion than the airman hiding beneath the lorry! (*Historic Military Press*)

AC2 Arfon Jones, aged 19, of 92 Squadron's Defence Section, who returned fire at the Ju 88 – but was killed by the nose-gunner. (*via Arfon Owen*)

Arfon Jones' grave at Dylais Higher (Brunbedd) Cemetery, South Wales. (*Nevin Williams*)

Sergeant Sidney Wakeling of 87 Squadron at Bibury in August 1940 – killed in action 25 August 1940.

By August 1940, the flow of Polish pilots with good English had increased to RAF fighter squadrons – and were welcome reinforcements. This in Pilot Officer Franek Surma, who joined 151 Squadron at Stapleford Tawney on 15 August 1940 – and claimed a He 111 probable on 30 August 1940.

A He 111 crew, shot-up over England, consider damage to their aircraft after crash-landing in France.

Flight Lieutenant Ken Gillies of 66 'Clickety-Click' Squadron prepared for a patrol.

Do 17s of KG3 immediately before taking off for an attack on England.

Sergeant George 'Dick' Collet of 54 Squadron, killed in action on 22 August 1940.

Bill Gulland displays the flying log book of his Spitfire pilot uncle, Sergeant Collett.

Pilot Officer Peter Down of 56 Squadron scrambles from North Weald in August 1940.

Flight Lieutenant Peter Brothers of 32 Squadron at Hawkinge, August 1940.

Flight Lieutenant Pat Hughes, an Australian and flight commander serving with 10 Group's 234 Squadron.

Sergeant Bill Green of 501 Squadron on the happy occasion of his marriage to Bertha; he was shot down over Elham of 29 August 1940 and lucky to survive, having baled out very low.

Bomb damage at St Giles-without-Cripplegate Church. The rector of St Giles-without-Cripplegate, which is located on Fore Street within the modern Barbican complex, examines damage to the church caused at the start of the Blitz in 1940. The rear of the image is date-stamped as having been first published on 26 August 1940. Located on Fore Street, within the modern Barbican complex, St Giles-without-Cripplegate Church was one of the first buildings within the City of London to be badly damaged during the war – in this case during a raid on the evening of 24 August 1940, before the official start of the Blitz. (*Historic Military Press*)

Bomb damage at St Giles-without-Cripplegate Church. Air Raid Precautions workers entering St Giles-without-Cripplegate, which is located on Fore Street within the modern Barbican complex. Original caption dated 31 August 1940. (*Historic Military Press*)

A Boulton-Paul Defiant turret-fighter of 264 Squadron – the type suffered horrendous casualties and was withdrawn from the daylight battle. (*Andy Long*)

A flight of 264 Squadron Defiants on patrol – the bravery of their crews is beyond doubt.

Pilot Officer Harold Goodall of 264 Squadron, who survived the carnage of 26 August 1940 only to be killed in action on 8 October 1940. (*Andy Long*)

Sergeant-Observer Robert Bett Mirk Young, Pilot Officer Goodall's air gunner. (*Andy Long*)

The grave of Sergeant Young, a New Zealander, at Northwood Cemetery.

Hurricane pilots of 501 Squadron at Gravesend.

Pilot Officer William Walker, a RAFVR pilot flying Spitfires with 616 'South Yorkshire' Squadron at Kenley. Shot down in combat with Me 109s on 26 August 1940. Walker baled out with a bullet in his ankle and rescued from the Goodwin Sands.

Amongst the successful German Me 109 pilots on 26 August 1940 was Hauptmann 'Joschko' Fözö, *Staffelkapitän* of 4/JG 51, seen here describing his latest success.

William Walker and the author in 2000, pictured with the bullet extracted from the pilot's ankle.

No.616 Squadron suffered heavy casualties flying from Kenley. Pilot Officer Lionel 'Buck' Casson survived, but was shot down over France on 9 August 1941, spending the remainder of the war in captivity.

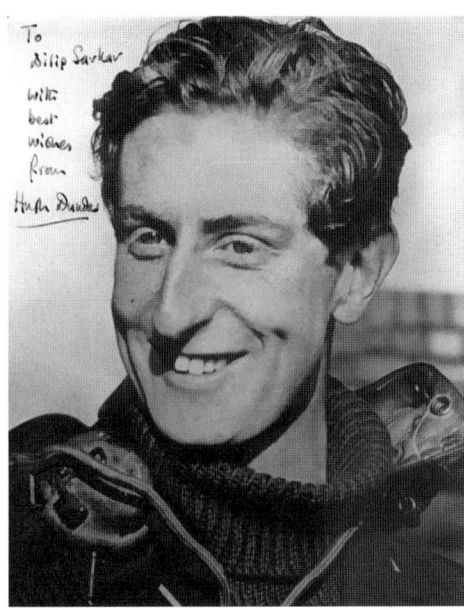

Pilot Officer Hugh 'Cocky' Dundas, also of 616 Squadron, survived being shot down and wounded on 22 August 1940; he survived the war as a highly decorated fighter ace and group captain.

AC1 Bob Morris was an 18-year-old engine fitter on 66 Squadron, which relieved 616 Squadron on 3 September 1940 – finding the station 'a shambles'.

Bader's theory was supported by Duxford's Station Commander and 'Boss' Controller, Wing Commander A.B. 'Woody' Woodhall (left) and his 12 Group AOC, Air Vice-Marshal Sir Trafford Leigh-Mallory (centre), leading to creation of the controversial 12 Group or Duxford Wing.

Exhaustion: Flight Sergeant Fred 'Taffy' Higginson DFM, 56 Squadron, at readiness.

Boredom: Squadron Leader Douglas Bader and pilots of 242 Squadron, whiling away their time in 12 Group – desperate for action. On 30 August 1940, 12 Group assistance was requested by 11 Group, 242 subsequently fighting an action Bader believed was far more successful than it actually was and which led to him arguing that he should lead a wing of several 12 Group squadrons into action over the south-east.

Above: 30 August 1940 was also a significant for the Polish 303 'Kosciuszko' Squadron, led by Squadron Leader Ronald Kellett (standing on wing) – whilst on a bomber affiliation exercise, Flying Officer Ludwick Paszkiewicz destroyed a Me 110, recording the unit's first victory. Later that day, the Squadron was made fully operational.

Left: Flying Officer Ludwick Paszkiewicz was killed in action on 27 September 1940, and buried at Northwood Cemetery.

Below: At Duxford, pilots of the Czech 310 Squadron await the next call to scramble.

Hurricane pilots of 32 Squadron at Hawkinge.

When Biggin Hill was heavily bombed on 30 August 1940, Sergeant Helen Turner continued working her switchboard – next to the Armoury – for which act of valour she received the MM.

On 30 August 1940, Corporal Elspeth Henderson also maintained communications – whilst the Operations Room disintegrated around her – and was also decorated with the MM.

ACW1 Edna Button, an Australian, was amongst the dead at RAF Biggin Hill on 30 August 1940 – and was one of three WAAFs to lose their lives during the Battle of Britain. (*Ken Back*)

AC1 John Joseph Jackson, an engine fitter on 610 Squadron, was also amongst the fatal casualties at Biggin Hill on 30 August 1940, pictured here with his wife, Hilda, and daughter, Hazel; he would never meet his youngest daughter, Jacqueline – born a week after her father's death in action.

Squadron Leader Tom Gleave of Kenley's 253 Squadron, shot down and horrendously burned on 31 August 1940.

Angela Lodge, Tom Gleave's daughter, displaying her late father's cigarette case – which was with him when he was shot down on 31 August 1940.

Fighter pilot superstar: Pilot Officer Keith Gillman of 32 Squadron on the front cover of *Picture Post*, 11 August 1940: he was reported missing over the Channel, within sight of his home town of Dover on 25 August 1940.

On 30 August 1940, Flight Lieutenant Geoffrey Matheson, commander of 222 Squadron's 'A' Flight was shot down and crash-landed near Sittingbourne Paper Mills – and had a lucky escape when his Spitfire exploded shortly after he vacated it. Wounded, the pilot is seen here with two soldiers surveying the wreckage of his fighter.

The Polish Squadron Leader Zdzislaw Krasnodebski of 303 Squadron – shot down and badly burned on 6 September 1940.

Flight Lieutenant Percy 'Squeak' Weaver, a pre-war pilot on 56 Squadron, reported missing on 31 August 1940 – the very day his DFC was announced.

Paul Weaver proudly display's his august uncle's DFC.

Many NCO pilots flew and fought in the Battle of Britain, which is still not that widely known to the general public. This is Sergeant Jack Stokoe, an RAFVR pilot flying Spitfires with 603 'City of Edinburgh' Squadron of the AAF at Hornchurch. Stokoe became a decorated fighter ace and survived being shot down in flames over Leeds Castle on 2 September 1940. Note that his top button is undone – the sign of a fighter pilot.

A traction engine flattening repaired sections of Hornchurch's runway on 1 September 1940, damaged in the previous day's heavy raid. The Spitfire in the foreground, X4278, is the 222 Squadron machine in which Flying Officer John Cutts was shot down and killed in, and the 603 Squadron aircraft adjacent, X4277, is the Spitfire in which Pilot Officer Richard Hillary was shot down on 3 September 1940, grievously burned.

A 222 Squadron Spitfire lies wrecked at Hornchurch following the heavy raid of 31 August 1940.

On 2 September 1940, Pilot Officer Tony Woods-Scawen of 43 Squadron was shot down and killed, and buried in Hawkinge Cemetery; his elder brother, Flying Officer Pat Woods-Scawen of 85 Squadron, had been shot down and killed the previous day; both brothers were decorated with the DFC.

Pilot Officer Richard Hillary of 603 Squadron, shot down and badly burned on 3 September 1940, and who left behind his classic, soul-searching, memoir *The Last Enemy*. Sadly, Hillary was killed in a flying accident whilst converting to twin-engined Baufighters.

Squadron Leader Phillip Pinkham AFC, commander of 19 Squadron, shot down attacking German bombers over Kent on 5 September 1940; he baled out, wounded, and was found dead.

Flight Lieutenant Willie Rhodes-Moorhouse of 601 'County of London' Squadron, AAF, attending the investiture of his DFC at Buckingham Palace, on 3 September 1940, with his wife, Amalia, and mother, Lynda. On 11 August 1940, Amalia's brother, Richard, had been killed in action with 601 – and three days after this happy occasion in London her husband would suffer the same fate.

Dilip Sarkar with the scroll commemorating the sacrifice of Flight Lieutenant Rhodes-Moorhouse, and his medals (including the Battle of Britain Clasp incorrectly displayed on the Aircrew Europe Star, instead of the 1939–1945 Star). These precious artefacts are preserved by the pilot's nephew, Rupert Ryle-Hodges.

Like the Spitfire and Hurricane, the Me 109 was designed and intended as a short-range interceptor, not as a long-range escort fighter. With only minutes of fuel to spare for combat over London, the German pilots were ever-mindful of their fuel states – many only just making it back to France.

"IF YOU DON'T BELIEVE ME, HERE ARE THEIR PROPELLORS"

Both sides overclaimed, but Fighter Command's claims were often wildly exaggerated.

An unknown German airman at Hawkinge Cemetery – believed to be one of two Me 109 pilots of 7/JG 26 shot down on 6 September 1940.

AC1 Harry Burridge, of Worcester, killed when Manston was heavily bombed on 24 August 1940.

Twenty-year-old Harry Burridge's grave in St John's Cemetery, Worcester.

Above and Below: Whilst escorting the Manston raid on 24 August 1940, the oil system of *Unteroffizier* Fritz Beek's 6/JG 51 'Yellow 10' was damaged in combat, forcing him to land in a field on the West side of the A258 Dover to Deal Road near East Langdon, where the he was captured.

Today, the scene remains virtually unchanged at East Langdon. (*Mary Bean*)

Beek's 'Yellow 10' was later put to good use promoting the Spitfire Fund – seen here displayed outside Worcester's Shire Hall. The 'Faithful City's' 'Fighter Fund' was launched in July 1940, being amongst the very first, ultimately funding two Spitfires, P9845 and P9846, City of Worcester 'I' and 'II'.

All photographs Dilip Sarkar Archive unless otherwise indicated.

of Biggin Hill. Simultaneously, bombs began falling – not on airfields but randomly in the Chislehurst, Bromley and Orpington areas, and did so for the next twelve minutes.

No.253 Squadron ORB:

at 18,000ft, near Redhill, they saw three formations of bombers escorted by thirty fighters, Me 110s and Me 109s.

'B' Flight at once attacked the bombers, which included He 111s, Do 215s and possibly Ju 88s but observed no results, with the exception of Pilot Officer Nowak [Green 3] who probably destroyed a Do 215. 'A' Flight, which was behind and below, followed in the attack and Yellow 3 [Pilot Officer Greenwood] fired all his ammunition into a He 111 which forced-landed, four of the crew seen climbing out.

This was a landmark moment: 253 Squadron's first confirmed aerial victory since arriving at Kenley, an He 111H-2 of 5/KG 1, which had bombed Farnborough and forced-landed at Haxted Farm, Lingfield, at 11.35 hrs. One of the crew was killed, the other four captured.

The 253 Squadron ORB continues:

A series of individual fights took place, chiefly with Me 110s and Me 109s which had come to the rescue of the bombers.

Blue 1 [Flight Lieutenant Cambridge] delivered a beam attack which developed into a quarter attack. Finally, when the Me 110 was in a gentle dive with port wing streaming smoke, he gave it a long burst from astern, causing the starboard engine to pour out black smoke and driving the aircraft into a steep dive. When Flight Lieutenant Cambridge pulled out of his dive, the E/A was still going straight down.

Blue 2 [Pilot Officer Samolinski] attacked an Me 110 from above and astern, silenced the rear-gunner and saw his bullets entering wings and fuselage, sending it down in a spiral dive. He made a similar attack on a second Me 110, silencing the rear-gunner.

Blue 3 [Sergeant Innes] made a head-on attack from 800–75 yards. As he broke away he saw parts breaking off the machine, which then rolled over and dived towards the ground.

Pilot Officer Corkett recalled:

Suddenly, the raid was clearly seen, ahead and above us, flying left to right. Almost at once, two aircraft [Me 110s from the escort] broke away and dived (in echelon) towards the port side of our formation. 'Jenks' aircraft was hit and as it dived steeply to port I saw either smoke or glycol vapour streaming from the underside of the fuselage. I do not know whether 'Jenks' baled out.

It was now that Squadron Leader Gleave led his Emergency Section into attack the Me 109s at 11.45 hrs, three to four miles west of Maidstone, Flight Lieutenant Brown on his right (No.2), Pilot Officer Francis to his left (No.3). The sky was full of Me 109s. Gleave later reported engaging fifty:

At 17,500ft, large formation of 109s sighted travelling SSE. Attacked from sun into E/As' flank. Attacked one Me 109 at angle of 20° to line of flight – 175 yards range – with four second burst. Shot appeared to enter fuselage near cockpit and engine cowling. Tracer appeared to spiral fuselage and come aft, believe this was shattered Perspex. E/A turned on back and dived vertically down.

Tracer and cannon passed either side of me. And I dipped, turning right and left, and pulled up. No sign of No 2 or No 3. E/A crossed my sights at 120 yards range. Gave him four second burst. Column of black smoke burst from what appeared to be leading edge of starboard plane, about 3ft from wing root. E/A turned across my path and dropped into dive, leaving long column of black smoke in his wake. Pulled up to avoid collision with this E/A and nearly collided with another 109, which flew straight across my sight at 60–70 yards range. Gave him three second burst. E/A pulled the nose up, appeared to lose speed rapidly and fall out of sky as though stalling into a dive. Gave him another short two-second burst to help him on. Cockpit appeared empty but saw no body leave aircraft. Turned towards sun to evade tracer and cannon.

An Me 109 passed just to the right and slightly ahead. Gave him all I had at seventy-five yards range. Shot appeared to go slap into underpart of cockpit and fuselage. E/A rolled on back, flew inverted for a few seconds and then went into a vertical dive, still going all out. Dived from scrap to throw off 109s on my tail. No sign of No 2 or No 3, both missing. Returned to aerodrome.

This was truly extraordinary shooting – especially considering it was Squadron Leader Gleave's first experience of a mass fighter combat. Back at Kenley, he reported having 'accounted for four Me 109s', officially claiming all four 'Probably destroyed'. Not having 'seen them break up, catch fire, or crash' however, 'they could not be counted as destroyed', so the squadron Intelligence Officer credited Gleave with 'two probables and two possibles'. In his log book, though, Gleave wrote, in red ink 'Later converted to four confirmed by 11 Group and confirmed by Fighter Command HQ.' Given that only two Me 109s actually crashed in south-east England that day, and considering the number of Fighter Command claims for 109s destroyed, it is difficult to understand, it must be said, on what evidence this conversion was based. Nonetheless, whether or not these four 109s were destroyed, probably destroyed or damaged, it was quite some feat and a spectacular entré into the cut and thrust of air fighting. In total, after this engagement, according to the ORB, 253 Squadron claimed three Me 110s destroyed, two Me 109s probably destroyed, one Me 110 damaged, one He 111 destroyed, and a Do 215 probably destroyed. This, though, was sadly not without loss.

Back at Kenley, news was soon received that Flight Lieutenant George Brown had been shot down by a 109 and had forced-landed near Maidstone, injuring his legs and a shoulder. Pilot Officer Colin 'Dopey' Francis was missing, however, and according to Squadron Leader Gleave, a few days later he heard that Francis 'had been found; he had crashed and received fatal injuries ... I like to think that "Dopey" got one as he was the youngest in the Squadron and a likeable chap.' Certainly, at 19, Francis was very young, but he was not actually found until 23 August 1981, when his Hurricane, L1965, was recovered by the Tangmere Aviation Museum from its crash site at Wrotham in Kent; Pilot Officer Colin Dunstone Francis was eventually laid to rest at Brookwood on 29 September 1981.

Twenty-one-year old Pilot Officer D.N.O. 'Jenks' Jenkins, who Pilot Officer Alan Corkett had witnessed being hit, was also missing. News was soon received that, according to 253 Squadron's official report on the casualty, his Hurricane, P3921, 'Was seen to crash from a great height. The pilot must have been killed instantaneously.' The aircraft had crashed at 11.20 hrs, in Butlers Dene Road, Woldingham, on Surrey's North Downs, between Oxted and Warlingham; Squadron Leader Gleave wrote:

'Jenks' was missing, and that overshadowed everything. Soon afterwards we heard that he had tried to bale-out, but something had gone wrong and he had plummeted to earth. When his bloodstained parachute was returned to the Station the next day, we found that he had made no attempt to pull the rip-cord. He must either have been badly wounded, or hit something getting out. 'Jenks' was one of our best pilots and his death was a bitter blow to the Squadron, the kind that breeds hate.

In this action, the Hurricanes of both Squadron Leader Harold Starr and the Polish Pilot Officer Wlodzimierz Samolinski were both damaged, although fortunately both pilots were unhurt and returned safely to Kenley. Squadron Leader Tom Gleave recalled that Starr's:

engine had been hit by an armour-piercing shell – with curious results. A neat hole a little less than half-an-inch in diameter had been made in the front of the port rocker cover, and, when it was lifted off, a small, solid, bullet of much less calibre was found lying harmlessly inside!

No.222 Squadron had patrolled Gravesend as ordered before being sent to the north-west of Dover. There, 'Ten Me 109s were contacted by "B" Flight. No combat took place but Sergeant Hutchinson was shot at from behind and forced-landed about one mile from Hornchurch [ORB].'

Sergeant Iain Hutchinson:

> It was the first time we had engaged the enemy since our arrival at Hornchurch
> only the previous day, and was the usual scenario: the Me 109s were higher
> and knew exactly what they were doing, while we were just learning the ropes.
> I didn't even see the one that hit me; I doubt any of us did.

Like 253 Squadron, also freshly arrived in 11 Group, as the day wore on it
would be a tough one for 222, as the pilots adjusted to the incomparable pace
and violence of combat over 11 Group.

Me 109s also gave the hapless 616 Squadron trouble again: over West Malling,
as the Spitfires dived to attack a formation of eighteen retiring Do 17s, Me 109s
attacked the squadron from above. In the ensuing dogfight, Pilot Officer Donald
Smith claimed a 109 destroyed, but Flying Officer Jack Bell was shot-up; badly
wounded, he was killed when his Spitfire crashed and burned out at West
Malling – he was the fourth pilot lost by 616 Squadron in ten days.

At 11.50 hrs, 79 Squadron intercepted He 111s some twenty miles south of
Biggin Hill, claiming six bombers destroyed and a probable, and an Me 110
damaged. Over Reigate, Pilot Officer Edward Morris, a South African and,
like the legendary 'Sailor' Malan a former 'Botha Boy', having been a merchant
navy cadet, collided with a He 111 of 5/KG 1, causing him to bale out. The
Hurricane pilot landed unhurt at Dorking, his aircraft crashing at Brockham;
the German bomber involved crashed and exploded at Capel.

To the north-east, over the Thames Estuary area, 151 Squadron fared not well,
making no claims but losing its new CO, Squadron Leader Eric 'Whizzy' King,
at 11.51 hrs, whose 'body was found in a burned-out Hurricane near Rochester'.
Undoubtedly ambushed by an Me 109, nobody even saw what happened.

By midday this first major raid was over, and an hour later the skies of south-
east England were devoid of enemy aircraft. Biggin Hill had been subjected to
a high-level attack, damaging the runway, but the airfield remained operational
and the Farnborough-bound raid failed to locate its target. The RAF squadrons
involved believed that great execution had been meted out to their tormentors,
some fourteen bombers and as many German fighters being claimed destroyed.
Although some combats had taken place over the sea, meaning that the wreckage
of four He 111s and two Me 109s down over land were no reflection of total
enemy losses, the claims were inevitably exaggerated; eight RAF fighters and
five pilots had so far been lost.

After a two-hour lull, several hours of attacks followed, simultaneously, against
multiple targets in an effort to overwhelm the defences.

At 14.40 hrs until 15.00 hrs it appeared that an attack was imminent, so
six 11 Group squadrons were scrambled. Just after 15.00 hrs, Lympne was
'lightly attacked', according to the AHB narrative, and a *freie hunt* swept inland
to Redhill – where, at 15.00 hrs, Flight Lieutenant Gillam and 'B' Flight of
616 Squadron were patrolling at 16,000ft; Sergeant Hopewell:

I was Blue 3 ... we were ordered to scramble to Angels 15. When we reached that altitude we noticed AA gun-fire bursting to the right of us. We climbed up to 22,000ft and encountered 25–30 Me 109s painted yellow from 'prop' spinners to rear of engine. Blue 1 [Flight Lieutenant Gillam] ordered me into line astern. We dived into enemy and I saw one 109 go down in flames, spinning, shot by Blue 1. I noticed one Me 109 coming round on Blue 1's tail. I attacked, giving him two bursts of two-three seconds. The aircraft burst into flames on the port side near the root of the main-plane. I immediately pushed my nose down and saw Blue 1 doing the same.

Flight Lieutenant Gillam: 'I was Blue 1 when we were attacked by 109s. I took one off Blue 3's tail. I shot at it down to 12,000ft, it just went on diving. I finished my ammunition and left it. Blue 3 saw the 109 still diving vertically at 4,000ft.'

The Me 109 was awarded as a 'probable', and Sergeant Hopewell's as 'destroyed'.

The Me 109s then crossed out over Beachy Head and back to France; 616 Squadron suffered no loss.

The intention of such sweeps was to force the 11 Group Controller to commit squadrons to long periods of patrolling in strength, so that when the major raid came in, many of those defending units were on the ground being refuelled and rearmed. When, an hour later, the big raid came in, certain squadrons had only twenty minutes to land and be replenished before scrambling again – testimony to the groundcrews' efficiency.

At 15.40 hours, three large German formations crossed in over Dover, heading NNW, thereby threatening both sector stations south of the Thames Estuary, and Hornchurch north of it. At 15.55 hrs, 603 Squadron was scrambled from Hornchurch and sent forward to patrol Manston, and at 16.05 hrs 501 Squadron took-off from Gravesend to patrol base and Chatham. At 16.05 hrs 151 Squadron left Stapleford to intercept a raid incoming over the Thames Estuary, and at 16.22 hrs, 616 Squadron scrambled from Kenley with orders to intercept the same raid of 30+ over Eastchurch.

Having scrambled from Hornchurch at 14.30 hrs to patrol Rochford, twelve Spitfires of 222 Squadron were already airborne when the raid came in, on their second sortie of their first full day in 11 Group. Diverted to Lympne, at 16.10 hrs over Canterbury twenty-five He 111s were sighted flying at 15,000ft, escorted by twenty-five Me 109s and Me 110s. As Squadron Leader Hill led the Spitfires to attack the bombers, 'the enemy fighters retaliated. One Me 110 shot at by Pilot Officer Vigors was reported to have been out of control [ORB].' This success, however, was short-lived: although the squadron was well-positioned, the number of enemy fighters was overwhelming. Pilot Officer John 'Chips' Carpenter was shot down over Rochford, taking to his parachute, his Spitfire crashing in flames near Cherry Orchard Lane; Pilot Officer William Assheton was shot-up over Canterbury, crash-landing on Bekesbourne airfield, and similarly Sergeant Sidney Baxter brought his damaged Spitfire down to land at Eastchurch.

At 16.20 hrs, 151 Squadron intercepted the same raid over the Thames Estuary. Having converted to Hurricanes, the Polish Pilot Officer Franciszek 'Franek' Surma, who saw action during the ill-fated Polish campaign flying PZL IIc fighters with the 121 Eskadra, had been with 151 Squadron just ten days when he now opened his account:

> eight Hurricanes of 151 Squadron in two sections of three and two aircraft just above us. The E/A were approaching us from the sea and we dived at the first bomber from the beam and continued down beneath them. After this attack I saw one He 111 turn away to the right and make for the sea. I was below and I climbed after him and fired a short burst under him. There was no return fire and I closed in and gave a longer burst from direct astern as the enemy was by then down to about 6,000ft and continuing in a series of slow turns towards the sea. I consider the crew were either injured or dead.

In the same interception, Pilot Officer William Patullo claimed a Do 215 [*sic*], and Flight Lieutenant Kenneth Blair a Ju 88. The Polish Sergeant Felicks Gmur, however, was missing, it being subsequently confirmed that he had been shot down and killed when his Hurricane crashed at Jacks Hatch, Epping Green. Pilot Officer John Ellacombe was also shot down and 'pancaked his machine and returned to the Squadron [ORB]'.

The Hurricanes' attack forced most of the enemy to jettison their bombs, bombs falling randomly on Billericay, Hadleigh and South Benfleet. Other bombing formations, however, continued droning north-west.

By 16.30 hrs the eight 616 Squadron Spitfires had climbed to 23,000ft over the Thames Estuary when they were attacked by Me 109s. Pilot Officer 'Buck' Casson:

> After going in to attack enemy fighters near Eastchurch, I lost the remainder of the Squadron. As I knew enemy aircraft were still in the vicinity, I climbed to 3,000ft and patrolled over the Thames Estuary. Suddenly I saw about twenty-five He 111s flying South with an escort of Me 110s behind them and about 2,000ft above. I manoeuvred for a frontal quarter attack on two bombers that were flying together on the outside of the formation and dived at them from the sun. I fired two long bursts which appeared to damage the starboard engine, which started smoking, and broke away to the right. The other machine may be slightly damaged as some of my ammunition must have hit it. I then dived away as the fighters saw me and were coming round to attack.

In this combat, Flight Lieutenant Gillam, who was leading the squadron, claimed an Me 109 destroyed and two damaged, and Sergeant Hopewell destroyed another.

Flight Lieutenant Denis Gillam: 'By that time we had suffered a lot of casualties. In that engagement we suffered no loss – which was certainly a boost to our morale.'

At the same time 616 engaged over Eastchurch, Spitfires of 603 Squadron also fought Me 109s, which were escorting bombers, the latter flying at 20,000ft. Pilot Officer Robin Waterston reported that at 25,000ft over Deal: 'I saw three Me 109s in a vic at the same height as myself. I attacked the nearest one to me on the starboard quarter, firing a short burst. The Me 109 dived steeply then caught fire and crashed in the Medway.'

The combat was reportedly 'North of Canterbury'. Flying Officer Brian Carbury DFC also claimed a 109 destroyed, last seen with a stationary propeller, trailing white vapour and gliding towards the East Coast. Sergeant Alfred Sarre was shot-up for a second time on this day when attacked by a *schwarm* of Me 109s:

> I turned into them and opened fire. I was unable to see the result of my fire as my machine fell into a violent spin. On landing by parachute I was met by Flying Officer [illegible] of West Malling, who had witnessed the combat through field glasses, and said he had seen a 109 fall away and enter a steep dive but had not seen the E/A crash.

At 16.30 hrs, and for the next fifty minutes, Spitfires of 54 Squadron were variously in action between Thameshaven and Billericay. Over the latter, Pilot Officer Eric Edsall reported that Red Section:

> sighted a large formation of Do 215 [*sic*] in a large vic, escorted by Me 110s at same level and above. One Me 110 I engaged with a two-seconds deflection shot and saw pieces flying off. I then attacked a straggling Do 215 ... Both engines stopped and one of the crew baled out, and the aircraft crashed at Thorpe Bay and exploded.

This victory, actually a He 111 of II/KG 53, was shared with Flight Lieutenant Desmond MacMullen. A probable 'Do 215' was also claimed by Flight Lieutenant Al Deere DFC.

At 16.25 hrs, 'A' Flight of 79 Squadron scrambled from Biggin Hill to reinforce the squadrons fighting over east Kent and 'saw a lot of Me 109s but as they were 2,000ft higher the CO did not order attack. Only Pilot Officer Bryant-Fenn attacked alone and fired 1,920 rounds, one damaged [ORB].'

Such was the scale of fighting, in fact, that Air Vice-Marshal Leigh-Mallory, whose 12 Group 19 and 310 Squadrons were already patrolling over 11 Group's airfields at Debden and Biggin Hill, decided to send one of Coltishall's squadrons to Duxford, where it would remain at readiness. Squadron Leader Douglas Bader's 242 Squadron, therefore, at last flew south to Duxford, but while en route was – for reasons unknown – recalled. Bader, who had brooded, sulked and stormed about 12 Group's lack of action, was exasperated. Upon return, he immediately harangued the Controller over the telephone, who, a short while later, ordered 242 Squadron off again. Arriving at Duxford without further incident, Bader and his Canadians settled down to await the call to action that they were so desperate for.

At 16.20 hrs, sixty He 111s of I/KG 1 and II/KG 53, escorted by Me 110s, had crossed the coast north of the Thames, by-passing the combats occurring over the south bank. Anticipating an attack on Hornchurch, the 11 Group Controller requested reinforcements from 12 Group. At 16.23 hrs, therefore, Wing Commander Alfred 'Woody' Woodhall, Duxford's Station Commander and 'Boss Controller', scrambled 242 Squadron. At long last, Squadron Leader Bader led fourteen Hurricanes off from Duxford, heading south with orders to patrol North Weald at 15,000ft.

The enemy formation next showed its true intention; I/KG 1 headed for the Vauxhall Motor Works and aerodrome at Luton, while II/KG 53, being the larger of the two raiding parties, began fighting its way to the Handley Page aircraft factory at Radlett. At 16.25 hrs, 56 Squadron was scrambled from North Weald, and 1 Squadron from Northolt. At 16.55 hrs, two Spitfires of 222 Squadron were sent up from Hornchurch, while Squadron Leader Harry Hogan's 501 Squadron's Hurricanes had already scrambled from Gravesend. At 16.50 hrs, while flying east over Chatham, 501 Squadron sighted a large force of He 111s, sub-divided into *staffeln*, each in an arrowhead pattern. According to the squadron's combat report:

> The bombers were at 15,000ft and flying West, South of the Thames Estuary towards London. Stepped up behind them were formations of Me 109s and 110s. The enemy aircraft turned north over Southend, and the squadron circled around them, attacking the second vic head-on. This broke up, and one He 111 jettisoned its bombs. Another was pursued by two of our fighters and landed on the water near the *Girdler* lightship. Another crashed in Southend. Our aircraft were not attacked by fighters, which were some distance behind'.

Shortly after take-off, 1 Squadron sighted six enemy aircraft 'North of London', which it prepared to attack, but fortunately recognised them as Blenheims before any gun buttons were thumbed. Upon breaking away, Squadron Leader David Pemberton's pilots saw the enemy formation: 'thirty to forty bombers protected by a similar number of fighters, in no standard formation from 12,000 to 25,000ft'. No.1 Squadron's subsequent attack was carried out with each pilot acting independently; Sergeant Henry Merchant:

> I was No 2 of Red Section and upon sighting enemy followed my Section Leader in line astern. After attacking a Do 17, which was in company with another E/A, an Me 110 dived on me from astern. Breaking away, I shook him off, and then saw ahead a single He 111K. Climbing and going ahead, I attacked from the beam. On the second attack the port engine stopped. At this moment a Hurricane from another squadron dived on the rear of the He 111

and got in a burst. Again attacking from the front I got in a long burst, and a man jumped by parachute. A further two parachutists jumped after about one minute, as I put in another burst. The aircraft dived down and crashed in the middle of a road near a cemetery to the east of Southend.

The He 111 claimed by Marchant crashed at Lifstan Way, Southend; it was the same raider claimed by 501 Squadron, another example of how one actual enemy loss became two, as it were.

No.1 Squadron's Pilot Officer Pat Hancock:

I pursued the main body of enemy aircraft. One He 111 was lagging behind. I gained height and prepared to attack it. Before doing so, however, a Spitfire did an astern attack of about five seconds duration. I then went in and fired several long bursts at each engine in turn. I observed smoke, oil and flames coming from each engine. I did not follow the aircraft to the ground as a vic of Me 110s appeared to be attacking me. I evaded them and returned to base.

Again, the He 111 attacked by Hancock is also believed to have been that which came to grief at Lifstan Way. The Spitfire mentioned was no doubt one of the two 222 Squadron machines involved: Flying Officer John Cutts and Sergeant Phillip Davis also claimed a He 111 'probable' in that area.

No.1 Squadron's Sergeant Arthur Clowes claimed a He 111 that 'emitted smoke and some flames', reporting that on his second pass the bomber's 'perspex nose exploded' – this too being the Lifstan Way raider. Another shared kill was the 5/KG 53 He 111 that crashed at Colne Engaine, near Halstead: this bomber was first attacked and damaged by 1 Squadron's Pilot Officer Peter Matthews before being finished off by 56 Squadron's Flight Lieutenant 'Jumbo' Gracie. The North Weald Station Commander, that indomitable Irishman Wing Commander Victor Beamish, was flying with 56 Squadron and claimed an Me 110 'probable' during this engagement. No.1 Squadron's CO, Squadron Leader Pemberton, attacked an Me 110 'in company with a Hurricane of "LE" squadron', which was one of two 110s that crashed at Ponders End, to the east of Enfield. 'LE' were the code letters of Squadron Leader Bader's No.242 Squadron. This is significant.

Romantic and exaggerated accounts of this action claim that 242 Squadron was ordered to patrol North Weald at 15,000ft but instead climbed to 19,000ft, Squadron Leader Bader flying twenty miles west of his allotted position so as to have the sun behind him. Consequently attacking from the sun, 242 Squadron executed the perfect 'bounce'. The 242 Squadron combat report, however, offers a slightly different view:

Squadron 242 was ordered at 1623 hrs from Duxford to patrol North Weald at 15,000ft on a vector 190°, just north of North Weald. They received a vector of 340°. Three aircraft were noticed to the right of the formation, so the Squadron Leader detached Blue Section to investigate.

These three aircraft were almost certainly some of the Blenheims reported by 1 Squadron, and the changing vector was in response to the enemy's changing course. The Coltishall Intelligence Officer, Flight Lieutenant Maybaum, continued his report:

> Green Leader then drew attention to a large enemy formation on their left so the rest of the squadron turned and saw a vast number of aeroplanes flying in an easterly direction. These were recognised to be from 70–100 E/A, twin-engine and in tight formation, stepped up at 12,000ft, after which there was a gap of 1,000ft, then another swarm of twin-engine machines stepped up from about 15,000ft to 20,000ft.

The foregoing report indicates that Squadron Leader Bader actually complied with instructions, his own report confirming this, adding that '242 Squadron had the height advantage on the lower group and as it was obviously impossible to attack all the enemy it was decided to attack down sun on the lower group.'

Maybaum continued:

> Green Section were ordered to attack the top of the lower formation; Red and Yellow Sections were ordered into line astern. It seemed impossible to order any formation attack. The Squadron Leader dived straight into the middle of the formation closely followed by Red 2 and Red 3; the packed formation broke up and a dogfight ensued. Squadron Leader Bader saw three Me 110s do climbing turns to the left and three to the right. Their tactics appeared to be to climb in turns until they were nearly stalling above the tail of Squadron Leader Bader's aircraft. Squadron Leader Bader fired a short burst into the Me 110 at practically point-blank range and the E/A burst into flames and disintegrated almost immediately. Squadron Leader Bader continued his zoom and saw another Me 110 below and so turned in behind it and got a very easy shot at about 100 to 150 yards range. After the E/A had received Squadron Leader Bader's first burst of from two to four seconds, the enemy pilot avoided further action by putting the stick violently forwards and backwards.
>
> Squadron Leader Bader got in another burst and saw pieces of the enemy's starboard wing fly off; then the whole starboard wing went on fire and the E/A went down burning in a spiral dive. Squadron Leader Bader then saw in his mirror another Me 110; he did a quick turn and noticed five or six white streams coming out of forward-firing guns; the E/A immediately put his nose down and was lost, but subsequently seen far below. Squadron Leader Bader saw nothing around him, called Duxford and was told to land.

Red Two, Pilot Officer Willie McKnight, went into attack with Squadron Leader Bader, getting behind an Me 110 and opened fire at 100 yards, the enemy aircraft bursting into flames and crashing. After a beam attack on a formation of He 111s, Red 2 turned the tables on an Me 110, which had attacked him from behind, chasing the enemy machine from 10,000 to 1,000ft: from just thirty yards, McKnight opened fire; the 110 crashed at Enfield Sewage Farm, Ponders End. After the initial Section attack, Red 3, Pilot Officer Denis Crowley-Milling, damaged a He 111, which Pilot Officer Norris Hart confirmed having seen go down in flames. Yellow 1, Flight Lieutenant Eric Ball, emptied a third of his ammunition into an Me 110, which Pilot Officer Noel Stansfield also attacked, the 110 going down with both engines on fire – and so it went on, with many more claims by 242 Squadron's elated pilots.

This was what Squadron Leader Bader and 242 Squadron had been desperately waiting for: an opportunity to engage the enemy in numbers. As indicated by the foregoing, however, there were other squadrons involved in this combat and which also recorded victories. Due to the high numbers of engaging fighters, various pilots had independently attacked and claimed the same German aircraft, which became duplicated on the balance sheet. In the heat of the moment, however, the relatively inexperienced 242 Squadron had been oblivious to the presence of other RAF fighters and so believed that 242 – and 242 alone – was responsible for this successful interception. In total, 242 Squadron claimed seven Me 110s destroyed and three probables, and five He 111s destroyed.

At the time, 242 Squadron's combat claims were accepted unconditionally, it being the result that Air Vice-Marshal Leigh-Mallory craved for 12 Group, and Squadron Leader Bader for 242 Squadron. Indeed, the AOC 12 Group signalled 242 Squadron: 'Heartiest congratulations on a first class show. Well done 242.' The CAS added his congratulations: 'Magnificent fighting. You are well on top of the enemy and obviously the fine Canadian traditions of the last war are safe in your hands.' It was, in fact, an unprecedented signal. The Undersecretary of State for Air sent a similar message. Certainly the destruction of twelve enemy aircraft for no loss would have been remarkable – had it been accurate. There was clearly much more afoot here. No.242 Squadron was Canadian; although loyal to the Crown, Canada had not rushed to join Britain in declaring war on Nazi Germany, debating the issue for a further week, the country's mood differing markedly to that of 1914. Just as their legless commander Douglas Bader was newsworthy, so too was 242 Squadron important to the propagandists. This was, in fact, the propagandists' first opportunity to trumpet the contribution of Canadian fighter pilots.

Sebastian Cox, Head of the MOD AHB, confirms that:

> Air Intelligence, perhaps because of its relative inexperience in the field, was certainly too ready to accept RAF claims at face value. In the period 8 August to 16 August 1940, the defences claimed 501 enemy aircraft confirmed as destroyed, and a further 231 probably destroyed, when the actual scale of loss was only 283.

The romantic legend surrounding the story of Douglas Bader also claims that the raid in question was turned about by 242 Squadron before it reached the Handley Page factory. This is not true. The majority of RAF fighters, low on ammunition and fuel, actually disengaged some ten miles before the bombers reached their target where, hampered by accurate and heavy AA fire, the bombardiers' aim was poor; little damage was caused and work on the new Halifax bomber was unaffected (the other raiding force, however, hit the Vauxhall works hard, killing fifty-three people).

From Bader's perspective the world was suddenly aglow. As far as he and his pilots were concerned, they alone had broken up a determined enemy attack and inflicted numerous losses upon the raiders without loss themselves. No.11 Group squadrons did not make claims like this, leading Bader to conclude that he, above all others, including both Air Chief Marshal Dowding and Air Vice-Marshal Park, had the right idea. Feverishly, he set pen to paper, scribbling a report on the action entitled 'Fighter Tactics v Escort and Bomber Formations'. Given that 11 Group's squadrons had been in action daily, sometimes several times a day and often against even bigger enemy formations than that intercepted by 242 Squadron, this is astonishing:

> At the suggestion of the Intelligence Officer I am writing a report on the tactics employed on 30 August against a large formation of enemy bombers and twin-engine escort fighters. It has been suggested this report may be of interest in view of the warning signal from 11 Group of increased casualties suffered in that Group due to enemy tactics of tight formation with bombers and escort fighters intermingled, and the good fortune enjoyed by 242 Squadron of complete immunity from damage to aeroplanes or personnel. In regard to the second point it must be appreciated that luck definitely played a part since any squadron leaving an engagement without any damage cannot claim all credit for cleverness in flying etc.
>
> ...It appears that bombers escorted by twin-engine fighters can be dispersed by shock tactics of the sudden arrival of a Hurricane or Spitfire in their midst, preferably out of the sun ... It was anticipated (and the fight in question proved it) that if a squadron of Hurricanes or Spitfires met a large enemy bomber formation (provided there were no single-engine fighter escorts) the Hurricanes or Spitfires would have the advantage (in spite of numerical inferiority) if the enemy formation could be broken up, and provided the squadron started with the height advantage. In any case, the primary object is achieved if the formation is broken because it ruins the enemy's chance of accurate bombing, and even if one's own squadron's successes in E/A shot down is slight, the E/A are scattered in small groups or singly and other fighters which are certain to be at hand can pounce of them.

Bader concluded that 'as far as 242 Squadron is concerned the attacking and fighting conditions were very favourable'. They were indeed. Not only had the Controller perfectly positioned the Hurricanes to strike from the sun, but, perhaps even more importantly, there were no Me 109s engaged. Flying very high, the 109s would undoubtedly have bounced the Hurricanes lower down – possibly with disastrous consequences.

Bader later described subsequent events:

> When we were writing up our combat reports afterwards, Leigh-Mallory rang me up and said 'Congratulations, Bader, on the Squadron's performance today'. I said 'Thank you very much, Sir, but if we'd had more aeroplanes then we would have shot down a whole lot more.' He asked what I meant and I explained that with more fighters our results would have been even better. He said 'Look, I'd like to talk to you about this,' so I flew over to 12 Group HQ at Hucknall and told the AOC what I thought. He agreed and created the 'Duxford Wing', under my leadership and comprising 19, 242 and 310 Squadrons. Leigh-Mallory said to try the idea and see what we could do.

Leigh-Mallory, of course, had been told by Dowding on a number of occasions regarding how he expected squadrons to be deployed. That Leigh-Mallory had a penchant for large formations has already been evidenced. Given 242 Squadron's apparently all-conquering victory of 30 August 1940, and the newsworthy Squadron Leader Bader's huge enthusiasm for his idea, Leigh-Mallory clearly saw the prospect of a 12 Group wing as a means of getting his squadrons into the battle proper – even if such tactics were contrary to the System and the requirements of his AOC-in-C. That he was prepared to go ahead with this suggests a degree of confidence, indicating the level of Leigh-Mallory's political support at the Air Ministry – not least from the CAS and DCAS. There was much more to this decision than Douglas's simple explanation to his biographer and brother-in-law Wing Commander 'Laddie' Lucas: 'We were learning... We were all learning. That was the point.' That may well have so for Squadron Leader Douglas Bader, only recently returned to the service, but it did not apply to Dowding and Park – who knew exactly what they were about and had immense experience. Brave as a lion though he undoubtedly was, and an immense inspiration to many, in his blazing desire for action and glory, Bader was naïve.

That 242 Squadron wildly over-claimed on 30 August 1940 is a demonstrable fact, possibly in the ratio of 4:1. The attack was not, therefore, as successful as believed. Moreover, not one 242 Squadron report on the action mentions the presence of fighters from other RAF squadrons. This could well be because in their high state of excitement in what was their first major action, 242 Squadron's inexperienced pilots simply failed to register them. We know, however, from official records – and in particular personal combat reports from various 11 Group pilots, some of substantial experience, that other Hurricanes and Spitfires successfully engaged. In fact, over fifty RAF fighters were actually engaged, collectively destroying a total of nine enemy aircraft. Given that fifty fighters were actually committed to that battle, Squadron Leader Bader's theory, therefore, that more fighters (than just 242 Squadron) would have executed greater damage was simply incorrect. This action, and Douglas's theory, however, underpinned the remainder of his own personal 'hot' war – and had far-reaching consequences for Fighter Command as a whole.

On that same afternoon of 30 August, the Poles of 303 Squadron were up from Northolt on an affiliation exercise with Blenheim bombers, when the raid came in against Hatfield. In the 1969 film *Battle of Britain*, the events of that day, as befell 303 Squadron, were somewhat embellished – but created an enduring myth concerning this particular action. In the epic movie, 'Blackhawk Leader' (Barry Foster, playing 'Squadron Leader Edwards', the English-speaking cinematic CO of 303 Squadron) gives his pilots a course to steer, away from the trouble, but one, 'Ox' (Andrezej Scibor) sights the enemy, leading to excited Polish chatter over the ether. Unable to contain himself, 'Ox' responds 'Repeat please', feigning receipt, or ignorance, of the order, and peels off to engage the Germans, followed, one by one, by his comrades – while 'Squadron Leader Edwards' flies on, momentarily oblivious, until out of the corner of his eye he catches sight of what is going on and with a cry of 'Oh, Gawd, streuth!' and makes after his errant Poles – by now successfully in action. This is what really happened:

Squadron Leader Ronald Kellett, 303 Squadron's actual CO, recalled that 'On the last training occasion we had twelve Blenheims as "targets" when warned that enemy aircraft were in the vicinity. We were to guard the bombers. I ordered the Squadron to assemble above and behind the bombers and cease "attacking". It was, however, too much for Paskiewicz, who, having seen an enemy aircraft, attacked and shot it down. Fortunately, the Blenheims were not attacked, and I reported to Group Captain Vincent [Northolt's Station Commander] and Air Vice-Marshal Park, that we were ready for combat.

Flying Officer Ludwik Paskiewicz (Green 1) reported:

We took off in two flights, (A and B) for exercises in attacking Blenheims, at 1615 hrs. After climbing to 10,000ft, we flew northward. After a while we noticed ahead a number of aircraft carrying out various evolutions. The centre of the commotion seemed to be about 1,000ft below us, to starboard. I reported it to the CO, Squadron Leader Kellett, by Radio Telephone, and, as he did not seem to reply, I opened up the throttle and went in the direction of the enemy. I saw the rest of the Flight some 300 yards behind me; behind me were the burning suburbs of some town and a Hurricane diving with smoke trailing behind it. Then I noticed, at my own altitude, a bomber with twin rudders – probably a Dornier – turning in my direction. When he noticed me, he dived sharply. I turned over and dived after him. When turning over I noticed the black crosses on the wings. Then I aimed at the fuselage and opened fire. When I drew very close, I pressed down for a new attack and then I saw another Hurricane attacking and a German baling out by parachute. The Dorner went into a steep turn, and then I gave him another burst. He dived and then hit the ground and burst into flames. I then approached the other Hurricane and saw its markings: VC I. I have been firing at an enemy aircraft for the first time in my life.

Paskiewicz was credited with a 'Do 17' destroyed near St Albans, shared with Pilot Officer Bryan Wicks of 56 Squadron. The enemy aircraft concerned was actually an Me 110 of 4/ZG 76, the starboard engine of which was disabled by Paskiewicz before being attacked by Wicks and exploding at Barley Beans Farm, Kimperton.

According to *Destiny Can Wait: The History of the Polish Air Force in Great Britain* (1949): 'Squadron Leader Kellett neither restrained Paskiewicz nor allowed the other pilots to follow him. He continued the exercise, which consisted then of protecting, instead of "attacking", the Blenheims.' In reality, therefore, all but one of Kellett's pilots had obeyed his order, and there was clearly sympathy for Paskiewicz's ill-discipline. What could have happened to the Blenheims, had all the Poles followed Paskiewicz, as in the film, bears no thinking about.

It is not widely appreciated, in fact, that certain aircraft within a squadron at this time were fitted with a navigational device called 'Pip Squeak', which automatically blocked all transmissions for fourteen seconds of every minute while broadcasting a 'fix' on the aircraft's location. It is likely that a squadron commander's aircraft would be fitted with this device, which may explain Squadron Leader Kellett's lack of response to Paskiewicz. Either way, the actual circumstances involving 303 Squadron on 30 August 1940, were rather different to the exaggerated (but more entertaining) version in *Battle of Britain*.

Notwithstanding a certain amount of 'artistic licence' by post-war film-makers, however, after Paskiewicz's victory Squadron Leader Kellett 'reported to Group Captain Vincent [Northolt's Station Commander] and Air Vice-Marshal Park that we were ready for combat'. And so it was that after less than a month, 303 Squadron became operational and entered the fray in earnest. Although initially sceptical owing to the language difficulties, the Poles of 303 Squadron now joined those of the already operational 302 Squadron, and were more than just welcome reinforcements; as Air Chief Marshal Dowding later said 'We needed them. We needed them all.'

Returning to the action over the Thames Estuary, Hurricanes of 111 Squadron were up from Debden, patrolling Manston at 20,000ft when, at 17.10 hrs, AA fire was seen in the vicinity of Hornchurch and a formation of, according to Sergeant William Dymond, 'Thirty Do 215s [*sic*], 100 Me 110s' sighted over the North Foreland. The Hurricanes attacked, Flying Officer Bowring, and Sergeants Craig and Dymond all damaging 110s. Bowring's Hurricane was damaged in the exchange but he returned safely to Manston.

At 16.45 hrs, a section of 253 Squadron Hurricanes comprising Pilot Officers Wlodimierz Samolinski and David Bell-Slater, and Sergeant Allan Dredge, scrambled from Kenley, followed five minutes later by Squadron Leader Tom Gleave, leading 'B' Flight's Blue and Green Sections, comprising three and four Hurricanes respectively. Gleave later reported:

At approx. 1700 hrs we were ordered to patrol base at 1,500ft. Order received just after take-off to proceed SE and climb to 15,000ft. A few miles SE of Tunbridge Wells, Green Section turned East, the leader rocking aircraft and informing me of E/A to the East of us. They proved to be Hurricanes and Green Section turned South. I also turned and opened up to regain position, and shortly afterwards tracer and cannon tracer appeared over Green Section. I turned Blue Section and sighted seven Me 109s coming down from the sun with six more a short distance behind, all in line astern. Scrap developed into fast, circling, melee, all firing ahead. Saw Me 109 on tail of Hurricane, blowing off fabric and wood. Fastened onto E/A and gave him long twelve second burst from 180-200 yards range to less than seventy yards. E/A continued to turn behind Hurricane for a few seconds, then rolled onto back, flew inverted for a while. I kept firing and saw patches of black material coming away from the starboard wing, near the wing root, and from fuselage. A piece of wire or metal dropped away as the E/A turned, still inverted and dropped into dive. Forced to leave E/A as three 109s were fastened on my tail. Dived all out, turning and threw them off and climbed again to scene of fight. No aircraft to be seen, nor sign of damaged Hurricane. Returned to base. Damaged Hurricane safe on tarmac. E/A's destruction confirmed after landing.

On this occasion, 253 Squadron had engaged the Me 109s of JG 26, flying a fighter sweep in support of a raid on Detling. In addition to Tom's claim for an Me 109 destroyed, Sergeant Dredge claimed a probable. Three JG 26 pilots ditched in the Channel after the combat, their machines damaged, and without doubt one of these would have been that claimed by Gleave. As the four 'probables' claimed by Gleave from the morning's engagement were apparently later confirmed by 11 Group and Fighter Command HQs, which overrode the Intelligence Officer's on-the-spot assessment, this further confirmed destroyed enemy fighter made Squadron Leader Gleave a rare 'ace in one day'.

Again, though, after this action, 253 Squadron had two more pilots missing: Sergeant Douglas Cooper was shot down, crashed near Biddenden, and was safe, but Sergeant John Holt 'Dicky' Dickinson, a 21-year-old from Lancashire, was dead – it being widely believed at the time that he had baled out, only to be machine-gunned by an Me 109 pilot while descending by parachute. As Gleave later wrote, 'It may be permissible in war to shoot someone descending by parachute … but only those devoid of all sense of fair fight and chivalry could do it.'

It had been a full first day for 253 Squadron, and despite the losses, Gleave wrote that the CO, Squadron Leader Harold Starr, 'was very bucked, and I was feeling like someone in another world'.

At 17.00 hrs, 'B' Flight of 601 Squadron, scrambled from Debden at 16.30 hrs, also saw the same AA fire and raiders sighted by 253 Squadron. Six miles NNE of North Weald, Flight Lieutenant Willie Rhodes-Moorhouse DFC put Blue Section into line astern and dived on a lone He 111 – a returning Radlett raider – 4,000ft below. As the Hurricanes opened fire the bombers rear-gunner replied but to no avail: the 7/KG 53 machine crashed in flames at near The Rectory, Hunsdon; one crewman was killed, another mortally wounded, two others less so, while only *Leutnant* Eric Fischbach was unscathed; all of the survivors were captured. The victory was shared equally by 'B' Flight.

Detling, though, albeit a Coastal Command airfield, had been bombed: up to fifty bombs had rendered the airfield unserviceable. The station's main spine road had been hit, an oil storage tank set on fire and electricity supply cut off. One airman had been killed and a Blenheim damaged. The survivors would work throughout the night to ensure the aerodrome was operational again by 08.00 hrs the following morning.

It was the turn of RAF Biggin Hill next...

According to Section Officer Felicity Hanbury (later Air Commodore Dame Felicity Peake), 30 August 1940 was when the 'storm broke' for Biggin Hill. As the civilian air raid warning sirens sounded, Hanbury was discussing the day's routine with Flight Sergeant Gartside by the WAAF Guard Room. Nothing developed, so Hanbury made towards her office several hundred yards away. When nearby, the station's alarm sounded, and complying with instructions, Hanbury headed on the double to the nearest trench. There she found a WAAF Cypher Officer, Pam Beecroft, the Padre, and Squadron Leader Mike Crossley, the CO of 32 Squadron who had just landed in his Hurricane and been caught helpless on the ground. In the trench, the tin-hatted occupants were packed together 'like sardines'. The resulting bombs crashing down felt like an 'earthquake'. Then, in a lull, the Padre was urgently summoned by a runner to one of the airmen's trenches on the aerodrome's perimeter – it had taken a direct hit. Climbing out of her trench, Hanbury went to check on the status of her WAAFs. Rubble and debris impeded her progress, and the whole area near the WAAF Guard Room reeked of gas owing to the ruptured mains. At the side of the road lay a female body – the first dead person Hanbury had ever seen, so steeling herself for that unbeknown experience, the Section Officer approached, thinking that she must 'have a good look at her as I may have to get used to this kind of thing'. Finding her reactions 'controllable', Hanbury found the unfortunate casualty to be a civilian, a young girl who sold 'char and wads' (tea and buns) from the NAAFI wagon. There was worse to come. Reaching the WAAF Guard Room, Hanbury discovered that the airwomen's trench adjacent had been hit. Airmen were already frantically digging to locate and free any survivors, eventually clearing the way for survivors to be rescued. Flight Sergeant Gartside emerged on a stretcher with a broken back, her cheerfulness nonetheless having prevented panic taken hold and keeping up the women's morale – for which she would be Mentioned in Despatches. One WAAF, however, was dead: Aircraftwoman 1st Class Edna Lenna Button.

Aircraftwoman Button was the 39-year-old daughter of Edmund and Bertha Button of Scotsdale, Tasmania, Australia. A medical orderly, Lenna had insisted upon evacuating all patients from Station Sick Quarters before heading for shelter herself – the last in, when the entrance was hit and the concrete walls collapsed, the gallant nurse was killed.

After doing all she was able at the airwomen's trench, Section Officer Hanbury hurried off to Station HQ, to see how other sections had fared. Passing by the dead NAAFI girl, Hanbury noticed that 'someone had put a blanket over her, covering her completely. Somehow this had a greater effect on me than when I had seen her the first time. It seemed so final, almost casual.'

The RAF Biggin Hill ORB reported that the raid occurred at 18.00 hrs and was the second of the day:

> A low-level bombing attack was carried out by the enemy on the Station and very serious damage was done to buildings and equipment. The raiders dropped sixteen big HE bombs, estimated 1,000 lbs weight each, of which six fell among the buildings rendering completely useless and unsafe, Workshops, Transport Yard, Stores, Barrack Stores, Armoury, Guardroom, Meteorological Office, and the Station Institute, and shattering by blast part of the Airmen's Married Quarters which was being used as accommodation for WAAF personnel. 'F' Type Hangar in N. Camp was also badly damaged.
>
> One shelter trench received a direct hit and two others near hits. The total casualties were 39 killed and 26 wounded and shocked.
>
> All power, gas and water mains were severed and all telephone lines running north of the camp were severed in three places.

The loss of power and communications meant that control of the sector had to temporarily be passed to Hornchurch.

Among Biggin Hill's fighter squadrons was the Spitfire-equipped 610 'County of Chester' Squadron, the ORB of which matter-of-factly documented: '1255083 AC Burton, 810029 AC Jackson, JJ, & 7589578 Pte. Tarrant, J, killed as the result of enemy action.' All of these men were among those killed in the airmen's trench. So difficult were conditions that work to rescue the living and locate the dead went on throughout the night, RAF teams backed-up by ARP men from nearby Orpington, and even local residents.

AC1 Harold Mead was a Flight Mechanic (Airframes), a rigger, on 610 Squadron and recalled the raid:

We had just entered the Mess when the air raid sirens began their moaning. Immediately I turned and ran out and into the nearest shelter. As I sat down near the door and lit a cigarette it occurred to me that, being so near the Mess, it would soon become crowded and no smoking would be permitted. Also, I realised that I shouldn't be sheltering. My real place should be at dispersal, with the aircraft. So I ran and jumped onto the running board of a passing truck. It was the luckiest day of my life because when the attack subsided and we began taking stock of our surroundings, we saw that our Station was a disaster. Hangars and buildings wrecked, transport and aircraft blazing and exploding, water and gas mains destroyed and the aerodrome itself was a mass of bomb craters and smaller holes with unexploded bombs. But when I approached the air raid shelter I had vacated I literally went into shock: it had sustained a direct hit. Limp, unnaturally posed, mangled bodies of men and women I knew, many friends, were hanging like rag dolls between blocks of concrete and earth. I would have been one of them had I not wanted a smoke. Forever after I smiled wryly at health warnings on packs of cigarettes, because that day smoking saved my life!

Already, WAAF Sergeant Joan Mortimer's courage after the heavy raid on Biggin Hill of 18 August 1940 had shown any sceptical male airmen that frontline women were warriors too. During this latest attack on Biggin Hill, two more WAAFs would demonstrate and later be recognised for their bravery under fire. The Operations Room at Biggin Hill was old and had no reinforced concrete roof; nonetheless when ordered to take shelter, many working within refused to leave their posts. Working alone in a small cubicle, Sergeant Helen Turner remained at her switchboard even after the telephone cables were severed connecting RAF Biggin Hill to the outside world. Instead of then taking cover, Turner steadfastly continued trying to make a connection. Just in time, a male warrant officer pulled her, protesting, to safety – a bomb then smashed through the roof and exploded, sending razor sharp shrapnel slicing through the air – ripping apart the switchboard at which Turner had been sat only seconds before. Corporal Elspeth Henderson was knocked over by the blast but returned to her switchboard post, stubbornly maintaining the only landline in use: the vital direct line to 11 Group HQ at Uxbridge. All three WAAFs would receive the Military Medal for their actions at Biggin Hill – controversial at the time because the MM was considered a man's award. Henderson (who was later commissioned), however, was embarrassed by the award; her son-in-law, John Redfearn, explaining her feelings that 'while she was under the plotting table waiting in case the phonelines were restored, there were engineers outside throughout the raid trying to repair the damage – none of whom received any recognition for their bravery'. That may be so – but no one could deny that Mortimer, Henderson and Turner had set an inspirational example.

Because this raid had swept in fast and low from a direction of the Isle of Sheppey, there was very little warning. Once again, this perfectly executed success was the work of precision bombing unit *Erprobungsgruppe* 210, which attacked from 1,000ft, unmolested by defending fighters – and, despite subsequent Fighter Command claims, returned to Calais-Marck without loss.

Literally minutes before the bombs rained down, 79 Squadron had scrambled from Biggin Hill and while climbing in their first circuit the pilots saw the airfield under attack. The Hurricanes climbed hard but were rapidly hit by Me 109s, a cannon shell shredding Pilot Officer Paul Mayhew's rudder, although fortunately he was unhurt and returned safely to his shattered base. At 18.25 hrs, Flight Lieutenant Geoffrey Haysom, a South African, and Sergeant Henry Bolton both claimed Me 109 'probables' over Tonbridge.

Five minutes later, 222 Squadron – up on its fourth patrol of the day – clashed with Me 109s of JG 54 over Canterbury, one being damaged by Squadron Leader John Hill. Among the 'Grunherz' pilots engaged with 222 Squadron was *Leutnant* Max-Hellmuth Ostermann, of 7/JG 54, who recorded his fourth aerial victory, a Spitfire which was attacking one of his comrades:

At once I flung my machine around and went down after them. Now I was about 200 yards behind the Tommy. Steady does it … wait. The range was much too far. I crept slowly closer until I was only 100 metres away and the Spitfire's wingspan filled my reflector gunsight. Suddenly, the Spitfire opened fire and the Messerschmitt in front of him went into a dive. I too had pressed the firing button, having taken careful aim. I was only in a gentle turn as I did so. The Spit caught fire at once and with a long plume of vertical smoke dived down into the sea.

None of 222's Spitfires crashed into the water, but the squadron had suffered more than the enemy: Sergeant Joseph Johnson was shot down and killed, his Spitfire crashing at Bishopsbourne, near West Malling; Flight Lieutenant Geoffrey Matheson had a lucky escape after being badly shot-up: after crash-landing, wounded, he had only just walked away from the wreck when the aircraft exploded. Pilot Officer Hilary Edridge was hit by a 109 and baled out, burned about the hands and face, landing at Broome Park while his Spitfire crashed near Barham. Sergeant Arthur Spears was also shot down and took to his parachute, coming to earth on the Isle of Sheppey. Indeed, from 222 Squadron's perspective, it was a disastrous end to what had been its first full day at Hornchurch. Typically, new to combat in the south-east, 222 had suffered heavy losses: one pilot had been killed, two wounded, five Spitfires lost and four damaged.

Sergeant Reg Johnson knew the reason why:

We proceeded to go into action in the tight formation we had been trained to use, but consequently our losses were heavy. Eventually we evolved a 'Tail

End Charlie' section which weaved about, above, below and to the rear of the Squadron (which was still in tight formation). It helped. I was made a permanent member of Green Section, with Pilot Officer Laurie Whitbread and one other, and we were given that job to do.

Conversely, over the 12 Group area the day had been a quiet one, with only Pilot Officers John Pickering and Hubert 'Dizzy' Allen, and Sergeant Arthur Smith of Coltishall's 66 Squadron seeing action, sharing the destruction of a Do 17 twenty miles east of Aldeburgh at 16.15 hrs – doubtless either a Do 17 of 3(F)/22 or a 215 of 4/Aufklarungs *Gruppe* of the OKL, both of which failed to return from reconnaissance flights. Pilot Officer Pickering, however, was hit by return fire, baling out and being rescued from the North Sea by a lightship.

On this day, Fighter Command flew more sorties – 1,054 – than on any previous day's fighting. Altogether, twenty-two squadrons and been engaged, most of them twice and some as many as four times. Thirteen Hurricanes had been destroyed and nine damaged, six of their pilots killed and three wounded. Nine precious Spitfires had been lost, six damaged, two pilots killed and two wounded. The greatest contributors to the balance sheet that day were 253 and 222 Squadrons – both new to the battle.

During the day, Coastal Command flew the usual round of patrols, but daylight raids by 2 Group's Blenheims were scrubbed owing to adverse weather conditions – clear skies not being the conditions to send unescorted Blenheims over enemy-occupied Europe. At night, Bomber Command attacked the coastal batteries around Calais and various airfields, and for the third consecutive night Berlin was the primary objective for the Wellington force – which lost an aircraft of 214 Squadron, shot down at 22.43 hrs by *Oberleutnant* Werner Streib of 2/ NJG 1; the 'Whimpey' crew were all killed.

Bomber Command's efforts against the German invasion fleet preparations were starting to have an effect: on this day, the OKM reported that consequently, Operation *Seelöwe* would be unable to sail as originally projected on 15 September 1940. With a proviso of ten days prior warning, D-Day was postponed until 21 September 1940 – meaning that Hitler and the OKW would need to make a decision on 11 September 1940. For both sides, therefore, the period between 31 August – 11 September 1940 would be critical.

Daily Home Intelligence Report:

Air raids in the regions continue to be borne patiently and without panic ...
Fear of invasion appears to be on the wane.

Saturday, 31 August 1940

Up at Acklington in 13 Group, at 07.15 hrs a signal was received ordering the Spitfires of Squadron Leader Anthony Collins' 72 Squadron to Biggin Hill, with thirty-two riggers and fitters. By 12.30 hrs the Spitfires were airborne and en route, landing at the battered sector station at 15.20 hrs to relieve Squadron Leader John Ellis's 610 Squadron – which had fought hard in the Battle of Britain to date, losing eight pilots killed and ten wounded in the process. Casualties had also been suffered among 610 Squadron's groundcrew, the squadron being well-deserved of a rest. Although 72 Squadron was unaware of it upon arrival at the still smouldering Biggin Hill, they were in for a baptism of fire in short order.

Ever-keen, Squadron Leader Tom Gleave of Kenley's recently arrived 253 Squadron was at dispersal before breakfast. The CO, Squadron Leader Harold Starr had agreed to leadership of the squadron to be shared by Gleave and himself on an alternate basis. That morning, Starr had chosen to be at readiness, while Gleave 'spent some time in the portable office clearing those old bits of paperwork – the necessary evils – that plague commanders at all levels'. The day was fine and cloudless, and the enemy was active over the Pas-de-Calais and Channel shortly after 06.00 hrs.

The previous day's heavy fighting and bombing of Biggin Hill provided an indication of the enemy's likely intentions when the morning dawned fine and clear. Indeed, enemy aircraft were active over the Pas-de-Calais and Channel from 06.00 hrs, and by 07.30 hrs there was every indication of an impending attack.

By 07.40 hrs, 1, 253 and 501 Squadrons were all up patrolling the Essex and Kent coastlines. By 07.50 hrs, four enemy formations had assembled between Dunkirk and Cap Gris-Nez, so Flight Lieutenant Kenneth Blair DFC and his 'B' Flight of 151 Squadron were immediately scrambled from Stapleford to patrol Deal and Dover – led by Flight Lieutenant Dick Smith, now commanding 151 after the loss of Squadron Leader Eric King the day before, in his experimental four-cannon Hurricane, V7630. Minutes later Smith led the Hurricanes into an attack on '30 odd' Me 109s over Manston, which were sweeping over east and central Kent. After this initial charge the Hurricanes were separated and pilots operated independently. Smith flew west, then south and back east, climbing to get up-sun of the enemy:

> On passing over Dover at 15,000ft I observed five Me 109s crossing to seaward at 14,000ft, flying silhouetted against the sunlight on the sea. I attacked, getting in a three-second burst on the last of the flight from his starboard beam – he turned over but I was unable to follow him as I was concerned with getting away from the Me 109s as I was by myself. I did this by aileron turning towards Dover, and on my return heard German spoken on the R/T, obviously operational orders from one aircraft to another. I heard 'Achtung! Achtung!' then other orders the whole way back to Stapleford – much more clearly than I could hear other aircraft of my own Squadron.

The 109 was claimed as a probable, and Pilot Officer John Ellacombe damaged another over Manston. No other claims were made and 151 Squadron returned to Stapleford intact. The enemy fighters continued sweeping over Kent, heading up to Ashford before turning east for Sheppey and the Thames Estuary, then another sweep crossed in over Dover, heading north-east towards the Thames. Then a large formation was detected off Dover, which skirted around the coast, heading for Southend. It was now obvious that this was a major attack bound for one or more sector stations north of the Thames; 'Air Raid Warning Yellow' was issued to ARP wardens along the Essex coast, and AA defences were informed. The two enemy forces were thirty Do 17s of III/KG 2 headed for Debden, with more of II/KG 2 bound for Fowlmere in the Duxford Sector, intending to execute a simultaneous attack. The Debden raid was escorted by *Hauptmann* Horst Liensberger's Me 110s of V(Z)LG 1, the Duxford raid's escort provided by *Hauptmann* Hans Schalk's III/ZG 26. At 08.00 hrs the bombers turned west, aiming for landfall between the rivers Crouch and Blackwater on the Essex coast. The coast and approaches were, however, being patrolled at that time by 1 Squadron, which had scrambled from Northolt at 07.40 hrs, and nine Hurricanes of 111 Squadron were scrambled at 08.10 hrs as reinforcements. At that time, 1 Squadron was already going into action against 'Raid 29' over Chelmsford.

Squadron Leader David Pemberton was thwarted in his attempt for 1 Squadron to attack the bombers – 100 of them – by interference from the escorting Me 110s:

In the action which followed Sergeant H.J. Merchant destroyed one Me 110 and damaged another but he himself had to abandon his aircraft and was taken to Halstead Cottage Hospital, suffering from burns. Sergeant A.V. Clowes DFM attacked a formation of fifteen Do 215s [*sic*] and after making a frontal beam attack … saw two E/A leave the formation, one spinning to the ground and the other in a steep turn to the left. He was himself attacked by Me 110s and looping up Sergeant Clowes put the starboard engine of one E/A out of action. He followed the E/A down to ground level but left him after several more bursts which killed the crew and the pilot was seen looking for a place to land. Pilot Officer P.V. Boot DFC attacked several raiders … He 110 … Pilot Officer H. Mann damaged an Me 110.

The Hurricanes were too small a force, however, to impede the advance of so many enemy aircraft, which now split into two formations: one heading for Debden, the other Duxford.

Sensibly, 12 Group support had already been requested – so at 08.10 hrs, Flying Officer Frank Brinsden, a New Zealander, and the four other on-duty members of 19 Squadron's 'A' Flight scrambled from Fowlmere to patrol Duxford and Debden Sectors at 17,000ft. Five minutes later, Flight Lieutenant Wilf Clouston, also a 'Kiwi', scrambled with five members of 'B' Flight.

Sergeant David Cox, 19 Squadron:

> We were caught on the hop! Most of us were still in bed as the Squadron was stood-down! We got a panic message to scramble immediately. I put on my flying boots and jacket over my pyjamas … We took off and climbed South … It was jolly cold up there as the flying jacket only came down to my waist!

To the south, Squadron Leader Starr and two sections of 253 Squadron Hurricanes were up over Kent at 08.25 hrs when Starr was shot down. A note in this officer's Casualty File, however, states: 'Deal area. Shot at and killed when descending by parachute.' The same file note also makes an identical reference to Sergeant Dickinson's fate, killed the previous day, albeit with a rider explaining that 'No witnesses can now be traced but it was generally believed on 253 Squadron that both bodies were riddled with bullets due to attacks by Me 109s while descending by parachute.' In 2019, however, the *Daily Mail* reported on the sale of Squadron Leader Starr's medals, and quoted an eyewitness, a Mr H.G. Bennet, a gardener at Eastry House, near to where the pilot's body fell:

> It was as I returned to work that morning that I saw a parachute coming down over the Hammill Brickworks. As most of the dog-fights took place at some altitude, I didn't hear or see the aircraft, but as the parachute came drifting down, I saw quite a number of enemy aircraft circling. Suddenly, one of the Messerschmitts dived towards the pilot on the parachute, and then the rest also piled in – I could hear the sound of machine-gunning.

Whatever happened, the gallant Starr was dead.

Returning to the battle about to be fought over the 12 Group area, at the same time the Spitfires of 19 Squadron left Fowlmere, 08.10 hrs, nine Hurricanes of 111 Squadron were scrambled from Debden with orders to intercept the approaching 'Raid 29', and at 08.20 hrs, eight 56 Squadron Hurricanes scrambled from Rochford, led by Flight Lieutenant Steve 'Squeak' Weaver, as did seven 222 Squadron Spitfires, all heading for the Essex coast. Somewhat late in the day, inexplicably, at 08.30 hrs, nine 257 Squadron Hurricanes scrambled from Martlesham Heath, and, at the same time, eleven of 601 Squadron hurriedly got airborne from threatened Debden. Also at 08.30 hrs, 1 (RCAF) Squadron scrambled from Northolt with orders to patrol Dover – a precaution in case another raid approached from that direction.

No.111 Squadron, however, first sighted three 'Ju 88s' approaching from the east and 3,000ft, which Flight Lieutenant Herbert Giddings attacked before realising his mistake: these were Blenheim fighters of 25 Squadron returning to Martlesham Heath – fortunately, no harm was done. 'Treble One' was then ordered to Manston; between there and Debden, at 08.30 hrs, the squadron engaged the Me 110s escorting Raid 29. Sergeant William Dymond shot the engine cowling off an Me 110, and over Hildersham, Flying Officer Ben Bowring began a series of four dogfights with individual Me 110s, attacked the first head-on before chasing a 110 to Felixstowe where he left it smoking from both engines, claiming two 110s damaged. No.111 Squadron suffered no loss, just two rounds through the leading edge of Bowring's Hurricane.

As usual, the lethal 109s were way up there, looking down – this time on Flight Lieutenant Weaver's penny-packet force clawing for height over the Thames Estuary. Enjoying the advantage of height and sun, at 08.30 hrs the 109s – elements of *Major* Adolf Galland's JG 26 – bounced 56 Squadron near Colchester, executing a perfect ambush. Within seconds, three Hurricanes were spiralling earthwards, doubtless hit without even having seen their assailants. Pilot Officer Maurice Mounsden was injured, and Sergeant Clifford Whitehead baled out; Flying Officer Innes Westmacott was also shot down, by an Me 110, while attacking a Do 17, and also baled out, wounded. Flight Sergeant Fred 'Taffy' Higginson DFM had led Green Section to attack the bombers in an inconclusive attack:

> I turned and the enemy fighters were just opposite me. I opened fire on a 109 and he climbed steeply, emitting white smoke. I broke away downwards and saw an aircraft diving straight down emitting white smoke and saw it crash and burst into flames in a field West of the road and railway station between Chelmsford and Colchester. I also saw the pilot bale out, and this was later confirmed by the military authorities.

Which 'Me 109' this was, however, is unclear, because no German fighter of that type crashed in the area between Colchester and Chelmsford at this time.

The stalwart Flight Lieutenant 'Squeak' Weaver, however, was missing – but what had happened to him?

A clue is provided by the Essex County Council War Diary entry for 10.09 hrs that day: 'Crashed aircraft report. British Spitfire found West Point, Osea Island. Pilot believed drowned at 0845.'

A further report was made at 11.23 hrs by the Eastern Report Centre: 'Plane now identified as V7373, confirmed pilot drowned.' How though, was this confirmed?

The Situation Report Form, timed 16.55 hrs documents that 'One British plane marked V7373 crashed at Osea Island, River Blackwater, pilot drowned.'

'V7373', however, was not involved (the aircraft was later lost en route to Malta with 261 Squadron) – and nor was this a 'Spitfire'. Flight Lieutenant Weaver, however, was flying Hurricane V737*8*. Further information was received, however, confirming:

Flight Lieutenant Weaver was patrolling over West Mersea at approximately 0830 hrs on 31st August 1940, when his aircraft was seen to dive vertically into the mud banks on the foreshore. There was no trace of the pilot and as he was not seen to abandon his aircraft it is concluded that he is still in the aircraft which is embedded in the mud and completely submerged.

Just hours after Flight Lieutenant Weaver was reported missing, his DFC was announced (gazetted on 1 October 1940): 'This officer has displayed great courage and leadership. He has destroyed six enemy aircraft. His excellent example has contributed materially to the fine standard that exists in the squadron'.

Group Captain Graeme 'Minnie' Manton DSO DFC:

'Squeak' was posted missing the very day I left the Squadron on posting to command RAF Manston, or at least what was left of it! They rang me from North Weald the next day to tell me the news, such was Flight Lieutenant Weaver's standing in the Squadron.

While most eulogies tend to go overboard, my recollections of 'Squeak' Weaver are all clear and sincere. Of all the boisterous, reckless, young men in the Squadron, he stood out. He was universally liked and because of his irrepressible good humour, enthusiasm for life and everything he did, and his fearless attitude to the battle, he became an absolute lynch-pin in the Squadron. His loss was, I know, felt most deeply at a time when we all tried to shrug off such things for obvious reasons.

Returning to the fighting on 31 August 1940: by 08.30 hrs, the Duxford-bound force, Raid 29, had reached its target.

AC1 Fred Roberts, 19 Squadron:

When the first bombs were dropped on Fowlmere we, the ground staff, were queuing for breakfast, our 19 Squadron's Spitfires being airborne. We heard the noise of what transpired to be Do 17s approaching. I dived into the nearest slit-trench and upon looking up could see the sun shining on little dots high in the sky. I could also see the first stick of bombs falling. Fortunately, they were released too late and so only two fell on the airfield, one among the bell tents, making a crater 4ft deep and 5ft across. The earth blown out of the crater collapsed one of the other tents. There were two lads asleep inside who were partially buried, but neither were harmed. The second bomb exploded near the boundary fence, but the rest of that stick fell in the orchards and watercress beds beyond the airfield. Looking back now it makes me smile to think of us crouching in that trench holding enamel plates over our heads with cutlery and mugs in hand! I also recall that Flight Sergeant George 'Grumpy' Unwin's 'A' Flight Spitfire was up on trestles in the blister hangar when the air raid warning came. He came running along with the other pilots, but due to his aircraft being indisposed, was unable to take-off with the others. He was yelling and swearing for his plane, and I reckon that we broke a record for returning a Spitfire to serviceability! George was airborne and after the others just ten minutes later, following a straight take-off from the hangar, across wind and with no engine warm-up. It certainly showed the man's courage and the faith he put in his groundcrew.

Sergeant Bernard 'Jimmy' Jennings, having taken off with Flying Officer Frank Brinsden's Red Section, suffered oxygen system failure so returned to Fowlmere, landing during the immediate aftermath of bombing and the raiders' departure.

Flying Officer James Coward, an Australian, was leading Green Section (Pilot Officer Arthur Vokes and Sergeant David Cox):

We took off from Duxford and were ordered to climb to the East ... intercepted a large raid coming in. I saw them first and called out 'Large formation of bandits straight ahead, slightly higher.' We were still climbing hard and just reached their height in time when our leader, Flight Lieutenant Clouston, ordered the last Section [Flying Officer Brinsden] to carry on climbing and distract the fighter escort. There were, they said, eighty fighters, but I'm unsure – we didn't have time to count them all! There were certainly fifteen Dornier bombers escorted by this large number of Messerschmitts. Three squadrons of 109s, the rest twin-engine 110s.

We did a Fighter Command No 1 Attack in which each section of three goes into line astern and curves in behind three bombers so nine of us went in simultaneously behind the first nine bombers. I was leading the third section and had to take on the bomber on the formation's far side. I was just getting in a nice deflection shot to knock out the rear-gunner – but opened fire and all guns stopped ... I was still pressing the firing button and willing my guns to fire. This was very annoying because a shot came through the side of the cockpit, I think from the leader of the section I was attacking. From the holes in my trouser leg it seemed to have come in from an angle of about 45° ahead. All I felt was a hard kick on the shin. I almost didn't glance down but had a quick shufty to see what it was and was astonished to see my bare foot sitting on the rudder bar. The shoe and sock had just disappeared. It was still held on by some muscles and ligaments but I had only time for a quick look because my aircraft was going out of control. The controls to the elevators had gone and the aircraft was going into a surprisingly steepening dive. I undid my straps and was sucked out of the cockpit at about 450 knots. My parachute got caught on the back of the cockpit and my arms were flung back along the side of it; my gloves were blown off and my foot was thrashing round my knee – which was quite painful.

I was suddenly blown free and found myself falling head over heels, which was also painful. I pulled the ripcord pretty quickly and when my parachute opened I was swinging in a big figure of eight with this wonderful view of Cambridgeshire. I was over 20,000ft and it was a beautiful clear day. I could see about 100 miles in all directions. It was absolutely wonderful and there wasn't the slightest sound of an aeroplane anywhere. I was alone in the sky, everything had gone, quite extraordinary. I suddenly realised something was happening so looked down to see blood spurting from my leg, and also falling in a big figure of eight. I realised I had to do something quickly. I had my helmet on with the radio cord hanging down, so I put that round my thigh, latching it up with a half-hitch and tightening it until I stopped the bleeding. I then found that holding my knee hard back under my shoulder, I could keep the foot wedged under my bottom, which stopped the foot twisting about and was more comfortable. I then floated slowly across the sky.

I went across Duxford at about 12,000ft and on the way one or two Spitfires coming back circled round me, gave me a wave and I waved back. I couldn't see who they were. I nearly got to the farmer's field we had taken off from, about five miles beyond Duxford, when the wind changed. I was drifting backwards so spent some time pulling down on the parachute cords and twisting them about until I was facing the right way. I then came down slowly and the descent seemed to go on forever; I thought I was never going to get down but suddenly, at the last minute, the ground came up and hit me and I was in a stubble field. This was awful, I was pulling the parachute up over my leg to keep it off the dirt.

Then I saw a young lad who was helping to stook corn dashing at me with a pitch fork, obviously thinking I was German. It made me absolutely furious. I had taken all that trouble to get down in one piece and then to have someone trying to stick a pitchfork in me was just too much! I gave a great shout, 'Piss off and get me an ambulance!' He dropped the pitchfork which slithered along the ground and stopped quite a way from me. He turned and went off like a startled hare, opening the gate in the corner of the field. He rushed out into the road and the first car he stopped was an army doctor from the army AA gunners defending Duxford, so I got help pretty quickly.

There was a slight hold up, the doctor sent his driver off to fetch what was necessary, returning ten minutes later with all but morphia on account of the Orderly Corporal having cleared off on leave with the Poison Cupboard's key. This didn't bother me too much, I wasn't in any pain, the whole thing was a bit numb. I was in a certain amount of pain from the petrol, being saturated with the stuff – it stung like anything under my arms and legs, where it couldn't evaporate. An RAF ambulance arrived from Duxford very quickly and I was carted off to Addenbroke Hospital in Cambridge.

Flying Officer Coward had actually been shot down by an Me 110 *Oberleutnant* Hans Barschal, of *Stab* III/ZG 26, landing by parachute adjacent to the Roston-Newmarket road at Pampisford. His Spitfire, the cannon and machine-gun armed X4231, QV-Z, crashed near Little Shelford – the village a few miles North of Duxford where, coincidentally James lived with his wife, Cynthia – who was soon informed that her husband was 'on the seriously ill list suffering from injuries received as the result of air operations' (at 19.20 hrs that evening, 19 Squadron sent a signal to the Air Ministry confirming that the 25-year-old pilot's foot had been amputated).

Sergeant David 'Little Boy' Cox:

I was number three in Blue Section, led by Flying Officer Coward. We were above and behind the bombers but below the 110s. We were put into echelon starboard and dived onto a section of bombers. Before I could open fire, I was attacked by the 110s, so I took evasive action, a very, very sharp left-hand climbing turn, after which I found myself alone and no longer in contact with the Squadron.

I then climbed to about 20,000ft and flew south-east. Over Clacton I saw about twenty to thirty Me 110s milling around in a left-hand circle and about 2,000ft below me. I dived down onto the circle and fired at one 110 that had become detached from the formation. My cannons operated perfectly as I was keeping a straight line with no turning. The 110 turned slightly to port and then dived away steeply with his port engine belching black smoke. I was then attacked by four other 110s and so, being out of ammunition, got the hell out of it!

Flying Officer Frank Brinsden:

We were scrambled before breakfast, myself leading Sub-Lieutenant 'Admiral' Blake and Sergeants Jennings, Roden and Potter, to intercept a large raid heading West at the mouth of the Thames. Our next radio briefing had it turning north-west, towards Debden, which turned us south-east, then easterly in the still rising sun and striving for altitude. During this scrabble for height, Jennings dropped out owing to a technical fault, and the 'Admiral' and Jack Potter lost Roden and me in the glare. Struggling for height and travelling towards the sun put us in the worst possible tactical position. Probably at about 15,000ft, while still climbing and controls therefore still sluggish, I was attacked head-on and from up-sun by a 110 – which I then noticed was part of a large formation. Followed a mighty bang, loss of control – and out. I was lucky not to have caught fire because I reeked of petrol and was violently ill during the parachute descent, possibly because of the parachute's motion. I landed at Starling Green, near Saffron Waldon, and my Spitfire, R6958, at Brent Pelham.

Fortunately, Brinsden was unhurt.

In addition to the 110 destroyed by Sergeant Cox, Flight Lieutenant Wilf Clouston and Pilot Officer Eric Burgoyne shared an Me 110. Tellingly, the 19 Squadron diarist commented that 'The score would most definitely have been higher given eight machine-guns' – clear evidence that the pilots had unsurprisingly lost all confidence in their cannon-armed Spitfires, owing to such frequent jamming.

At some stage in the engagement, 19-year-old Pilot Officer Ray Aeberhardt's Spitfire was damaged. Returning to Fowlmere, his Spitfire was seen to orbit the airfield before landing: 'it is assumed that ... the landing flaps of his machine did not operate, causing the machine to crash, turn over and burn out. When pilot Officer Aeberhardt was reached, he was dead in the cockpit of his burning machine [ORB].'

Meanwhile, at 08.39 hrs, Raid 37, the thirty Do 17s of *Major* Adolf Fuchs' III/KG 2, escorted by the Me 109s of *Oberleutnant* Gerhard Schöpfel's III/JG 26, having flown a confusing dog-leg course, reached Debden unopposed and bombed the airfield from 15,000ft:

> Bombs fell South of aerodrome, straddling the target in a NW direction. About 100 HEs and incendiaries were dropped. The Sick Quarters and a barrack block received direct hits and other buildings were damaged, including a hangar. The operations side of the Station functioned throughout and there was no failure of lighting or communications in the Operations Room [ORB].

A civilian and an airman were killed, the latter being AC2 John Kavanagh, a 24-year-old married man from Beeston.

A minute after bombs began falling on Debden, twelve Hurricanes of 79 Squadron were scrambled from Biggin Hill to patrol base, and while 19 Squadron was fighting high over Colchester, Flight Lieutenant Willie Rhodes-Moorhouse and the Hurricanes of 601 Squadron were also embroiled in the same area. No.601 Squadron had hurriedly left Debden with orders to patrol base at 15,000ft, but while climbing, at 7,000ft, AA fire signposted the enemy approaching from the east. West of Colchester a circle of Me 110s milled about, with Me 109s above. Pilot Officer Thomas Grier:

> I was by myself and attacked an Me 110 which did a stall-turn just in front of me. I gave a short burst and he kept on smoking. He straightened and I got on his tail and gave him another short burst and he went down burning badly. Just as I was breaking away a He 113 [*sic*] fired at me from behind and close on my tail. I took violent evasive action and finally threw him off. Bullets entered my aircraft in many places in the tail. I tried my radio, which was useless. I also tested my hydraulics which were also useless. When nearing base the engine started leaking glycol. I tried the emergency undercarriage release but the wheels wouldn't come down. I decided to land with undercarriage up on unserviceable part of the aerodrome, which I did. Some of the shrapnel from the E/A's bullets hit my right foot, inflicting a slight scratch.

Grier was 601's only casualty in this action. Pilot Officer Humphrey Gilbert shot down an Me 110 of 14(Z)/LG 1 which ditched off Foreness at 09.05 hrs, the pilot, *Leutnant* Karl-Joachim Eichhorn, took to his dinghy and captured by a passing fishing boat, but his *Bordfunker*, *Unteroffizier* Richard Growe was drowned. Another 110 of the same unit was forced down five minutes later, close to the Nore lightship, by Flight Lieutenant Carl Davis, the crew, *Feldwebel* Gottlob Fritz and *Obergefreiter* Karl Döpfer both becoming prisoners of war. The Polish Flying Officer Jerzy Jankiewicz claimed one Me 110 damaged.

Fifty Me 110s, covering the bombers' withdrawal were also attacked, at 08.50 hrs over Clacton, by 257 Squadron, led by Flight Lieutenant Hugh Beresford whose pilots:

> broke up the enemy's defensive circles with a series of head-on attacks and a sharp engagement ensued ... Pilot Officer Henderson brought two Me 110s down and himself baled out of his aircraft in flames. The combat was witnessed by the Captain and other officers of the Brightlingsea Naval Base, who rescued Pilot Officer Henderson and one of the German pilots from the sea. Pilot Officer Henderson was burned on the face and hands and taken to Brightlingsea Naval Hospital [ORB].

Me 110s were later claimed destroyed by Flight Lieutenant Beresford, and Pilot Officers Lancelot Mitchell and the Canadian Arthur Cochrane, while Pilot Officers Kenneth Gundry, and Sergeant Robert Fraser each damaged one. Sadly, though, the squadron had suffered a fatality: Pilot Officer Gerard Hamilton Maffett was shot down and killed by an Me 110, his Hurricane crashing on the foreshore at Walton-on-the-Naze (from where, in 1972, Lieutenant Geoff Rayner RN and friends recovered the aircraft's substantial remains. For many years these formed a memorial centrepiece at the former RAF Battle of Britain Museum, Hendon, sadly now closed and the artefacts are presumably in storage).

As the enemy withdrew, at 08.50 hrs Squadron Leader John Heyworth led 79 Squadron in to attack Me 109s and Do 17s, although as no combat reports appear to have survived, and the ORB is scant in detail, it is difficult to be precise where (indeed, many accounts make no mention of the squadron's involvement at all). According to the ORB, the CO himself claimed a 'Ju 88' [*sic*] probable and Flight Lieutenant Geoffrey Haysom an Me 109 destroyed. Pilot Officer George Nelson-Edwards, however, was shot down, crash-landing at Water Lane, Limpsfield, slightly injured.

To the south-east, enemy fighters remained active, some of which clashed with Spitfires of 603 Squadron off Dover and Dungeness, between 08.55–09.35 hrs. Pilot Officer 'Sheep' Gilroy 'attacked a stray Me 109 in mid-Channel South of Dungeness; he saw it crash in flames into the sea.' Pilot Officer Brian Carbury claimed another 109 in the Canterbury area before the squadron returned to Hornchurch, having suffered no loss. The Hurricanes of 1 (RCAF) Squadron, which were scrambled from Northolt at 08.30 hrs and vectored towards Dover, fared less well when bounced at 09.15 hrs near Cranbrook by Me 109s: three Hurricanes were soon spiralling earthwards. Flight Lieutenant Vaughan Corbett and Flying Officer George Hyde were both shot down in flames and baled out with burns, while Flying Officer William Sprenger baled out unhurt. The damage had been done by *Stab*/JG 51, which had ambushed the Canadians from the sun. The *Kommodore, Major* Werner Mölders, claimed three Hurricanes destroyed, and *Oberleutnant* Georg Claus one.

In Dover, the siren had wailed at 07.59 hrs, and before the German fighters returned to France, the temptation of the Dover balloon barrage was just too great: the first 'gas bag' to ignite and float unceremoniously to earth was that hoisted above Admiralty Pier, another came down on, and set fire to, 189 Folkestone Road, and balloons also descended on the Crabble Athletic Ground, behind Boots and Woolworth's stores in the High Street and on the Isolation Hospital. Civilian casualties were caused by machine-gun and cannon rounds, although astonishingly, at 41 Eldrid Road three people were injured at 10.11 hrs when one of the casualties hit a live cannon round with an axe! So frequent, however, was the assault by enemy pilots on the Dover barrage that one balloon unit chalked on the side of its lorry 'You knock 'em down, we put 'em up.'

Even after the morning's first two major raids had withdrawn, however, the huge map tables in 11 Group's various operations rooms were not free of plots. At the time, Margaret Woolrich was an 18-year-old WAAF 'plotter', who volunteered and was trained at a camouflaged operations room in Harrogate, which 'all seemed very secret and exciting':

> We were trained on a large table with a map worked out in grids, and you were given a grid reference over the telephone. You had little magnetic arrows and a long rod with a magnetic head. You picked up these arrows with this rod and put them down on the correct grid reference. So you had this little trail of arrows, one lot for enemy aircraft and one for friendlies. Looking back it was all very simple but we were terrified of failing this test. You got very nifty with those rods and eventually you could flick your wrist, throw them into the air and then catch them on the rod.

Plotting, however, was no game.

After the morning's first actions, most of the squadrons which had taken part were on the ground being replenished when, at 09.57 hrs, a strong enemy formation was incoming over Folkestone, heading north-west, towards the Thames Estuary. Three minutes later, eight Hurricanes of 151 Squadron scrambled from Stapleford Tawney, and by 10.05 hrs twelve more, of 17 Squadron, were up from Debden. Suddenly, however, the enemy was at low-level, strafing the airfield at Detling before disappearing home. This, however, was simply a diversionary nuisance raid: enemy aircraft remained over the Dover Strait in strength, three formations of which crossing the Kentish coast over Dover at 10.27 hrs. By then, short of fuel, 17 and 601 Squadrons were both returning to Debden, 151 Squadron, with fuel enough for forty-five minutes more patrolling, was over the Thames Estuary, and at 10.30 hrs, a section of 111 Squadron scrambled from Debden, and simultaneously 501 Squadron went up from Gravesend. Ten minutes previously, 151 Squadron were ten miles east of the Thames Estuary and sighted the right-hand of what was the third incoming enemy formation, Pilot Officer John Ellacombe of 'A' Flight reporting 'About thirty bombers and twenty-five fighters':

The Squadron attacked the bombers but I was intercepted by 109s. I got on tail of one and fired a five-second burst at 200 yards. Petrol fumes and white smoke poured from his starboard wing, but I was forced to break off as he outclimbed me and I nearly stalled.

North-east of Eastchurch, Flight Lieutenant Kenneth Blair DFC, the commander of 'A' Flight, claimed a Ju 88 damaged and Pilot Officer Irving Smith, a New Zealander, damaged a Do 17. The Polish Pilot Officer Franciszek Czajowski was shot-up by a 109, however, and crash-landed at Foulness – admitted to Shoeburyness Hospital with a wounded right shoulder, the pilot communicated with his squadron from the war and claimed an Me 109 destroyed. It appears that 151 Squadron had met 9/JG 54 over the Thames Estuary that morning, although the 'Grunherz' pilots' claims were somewhat optimistic on this occasion, considering that Czajowski's was the only Hurricane down: *Oberleutnant* Hans-Ekkehard Bob claiming two destroyed, and one each by *Oberfeldwebel* Adolf Iburg and *Feldwebel* Fritz Dettmer. After 151 Squadron's interception, the raiders continued north-west towards Southend. At 10.30 hrs, the central raid was over Sheppey and bombed Eastchurch airfield, causing little damage; by 10.55 hrs, all three formations had withdrawn and none were engaged by any further squadrons.

By now, civilians living around the Thames Estuary area were becoming almost immune to air raids, such was the frequency. Initially, Betty Martin had been among the children evacuated, but, like many more, when the 'knockout blow' had not materialised, the teenager came home to her family:

When I arrived at Gravesend Station there was an air-raid on, so I went straight to the nearest shelter before going home. During the Battle of Britain I had a wail of a time. My parents kept shouting to me, 'Come down into the shelter!', but we were up there cheering our heads off at the fighting overhead. To me, it was just… fun! We'd get on our bikes and go to where we thought bombs had fallen and search for souvenirs.

Schoolchildren competed fiercely for souvenirs, and those in south-east England had both a ring-side seat and many opportunities. Mick Fitzgerald was a Londoner who spent the summer holidays picking hops in Kent:

One day a fighter came down, trailing smoke. Together with three other young lads I jumped up and crossed the railway line and ran across a couple of fields, towards the plane, which was burning. I picked up a machine-gun. It was hot and covered in oil. The lads said 'Keep it as a souvenir', but I said 'No' and threw it towards the plane. The pilot parachuted down and drifted towards an orchard. The local policeman lived nearby. He was on his bike and asked us where the pilot had come down. I pointed to where I had last seen him and he said 'Let's go and have a look.' We went over some fields and into the orchard and looked through the trees and saw him standing by a tree, which his parachute was caught in. The policeman said 'Come on, lad', and the pilot put his hands up. The policeman took a flare pistol from his prisoner and took him to his police house, from where the military were called. They came and took the German away in an army car.

At RAF Kenley, following the loss of 253 Squadron's CO, Squadron Leader Harold Starr, feelings were running high on the morning of 31 August 1940, 'tempers,' wrote Squadron Leader Tom Gleave, being 'raised to a white heat'. Once more, Squadron Leader Gleave found himself in command.

By lunchtime, it became clear to the defenders that another major threat was developing.

At 12.34 and 12.38 hrs respectively, German formations crossed the Kentish coast near Folkestone and headed towards Biggin Hill and Kenley. Naturally concerned that these important sector stations were once more the enemy's target, 11 Group reacted in strength, scrambling the following bases to protect their bases or go forward and meet the approaching enemy:

1230 hrs: nine Hurricanes of 79 Squadron from Croydon.
1235 hrs: six Hurricanes of 253 Squadron from Kenley.
1235 hrs: six Hurricanes of 17 Squadron from Debden.
1240 hrs: twelve Spitfires of 603 Squadron from Hornchurch.
1245 hrs: eleven Spitfires of 222 Squadron from Rochford to patrol Canterbury.
1248 hrs: ten Spitfires of 616 Squadron from Kenley.
1255 hrs: twelve Hurricanes of 85 Squadron from Croydon.
1255 hrs: seven Hurricanes of 501 Squadron from Gravesend to patrol Colchester.
1255 hrs: twelve Hurricanes of 601 Squadron from Gravesend to patrol Colchester.

Thus, eighty-two 11 Group fighters were committed to defend Air Vice-Marshal Park's airfields against these latest threats. As we have seen, 12 Group perpetuated a myth that Air Vice-Marshal Park failed to ever respond in strength – the actual evidence, however, confirms that he did not hesitate to do so, when the occasion demanded, and this was far from an isolated reaction.

As the 11 Group fighters climbed, another German formation was detected over the Dover Strait, estimated at 50+, another of 20+. The raid that had already crossed inland over Folkestone steadfastly headed for Croydon airfield. Just before the airfield was hit, at 13.00 hrs, the Hurricanes of 79 Squadron intercepted overhead, and in the running battle ensuing Pilot Officer William Millington claimed an Me 109 destroyed, Pilot Officers Leofric Bryant-Fenn and Brian Noble both claiming 'probables', the latter also damaging another.

Only Squadron Leader John Heyworth, however, managed to penetrate the fighter screen to claim a Ju 88 probably destroyed mid-Channel.

Urgently, reinforcements hurried to the scene. At 13.00 hrs, the Czechs of 310 Squadron scrambled from Duxford and headed for north-east London, and concurrently a flight of 1 Squadron's Hurricanes scrambled from Northolt to patrol that sector, and nine Hurricanes of 151 Squadron were ordered up from Stapleford to patrol the Thames Estuary area (fifteen minutes later 242 Squadron were also scrambled from Duxford, to patrol North Weald, but would not sight the enemy).

Bombs were already exploding beyond the eastern boundary of Croydon airport as 85 Squadron's Hurricanes scrambled.

Squadron Leader Peter Townsend DFC, 85 Squadron:

We were scrambled from Croydon and could see smoke rising from the Sector Station at Biggin Hill. Over Tunbridge Wells area we caught up with a circle of Me 110s, but then the 109s came down on us. I hit one in a climbing left-hand turn before singling out a 110. A 109 got in the way, so I attacked it. It disappeared. So focused was I then on a 109 intimately close beneath me that I failed to realise that the 110 ahead with winking nose-guns was firing at me! My Hurricane was hit by 20mm. My left foot was violently kicked off the rudder pedal and petrol splashed into the cockpit. I was so shocked that for a few seconds I lost control and dived steeply. Miraculously, the aircraft did not catch fire but straightened out. I baled out, landing on my backside among some fir trees. My left foot was a mess, so I sat smoking a cigarette while awaiting assistance. The funny thing was that the drive through the Kentish lanes with the local policeman to Hawkhurst Cottage Hospital was the most frightening thing since I took off from Croydon! By 2200 hrs that night, I was on the operating table at Croydon Hospital, where my big toe was amputated. From an operational perspective, that was me out of the Battle of Britain.

The good news was that Hawkhurst Police displayed Townsend's parachute in aid of the local Spitfire Fund, raising £3.00.

Other 85 Squadron pilots had similar successes and lucky escapes in this action:

Pilot Officer Worrall attacked an Me 110 at 25,000ft south-east of Tunbridge Wells … E/A wheeled down and over to the left, apparently out of control, but exact damage could not be seen owing to oiled goggles and windscreen. However, Pilot Officer Worrall had his rudder bar and elevator controls blown away by a cannon shell almost immediately afterwards, landing at Benenden … before baling out a cannon shell hit his aircraft behind the cockpit and did not go through the armour plate … On landing, a member of the Field Ambulance which picked him up confirmed that he had seen the Me 110 go down on fire. Pilot Officer Worrall was slightly wounded in the leg and transferred to Croydon General Hospital.

Flying Officer Gowers fired long bursts into a Do 215 [*sic*] and saw it roll over on its back with black and white smoke coming from it as it fell. End of E/A not seen as pilot had to adopt evasive tactics to get away from Me 109.

Pilot Officer Hemingway fired a burst into an Me 109 and saw much smoke issuing from the E/A.

After the raiders wheeled about, 253 Squadron intercepted the Germans just after 13.00 hrs over Orpington.

Squadron Leader Tom Gleave, 253 Squadron:

Formation turned over base and at a height of 12–15,000ft I glanced up and sighted an extensive formation of Ju 88s, flying in several parallel lines of aircraft in line astern. They were 1,000ft above and closing distance rapidly. When within machine-gun range own formation still forged ahead and I decided to attack before E/A opened fire. Pulled up and fired raking burst at No 5 in line of Ju 88s immediately above. Faked stall-turn at top of climb and dived, repeating process on No 3 of E/A. As I turned over at top of climb, I saw clouds of greyish white smoke pouring from port engine of the No 3 E/A.

Gleave was credited with a Ju 88 damaged – but then, as he wrote in *Eagles of Nemesis*:

at that point something happened which was to cause me inconvenience for many a long day. There was a metallic click above the roar of the Merlin; it seemed to come from the starboard wing and I glanced in that direction, but a sudden burst of heat struck me in the face, and from that moment I started to qualify for what Geoffrey Page, whom I came to know later at the hospital in East Grinstead, rightly described as the 'fried eggs and bacon course'.

I had seen neither tracer nor cannon tracks near my aircraft and I assumed that I had picked up a stray incendiary – and that was the last fully rational thought I was to be capable of while I sat in the centre of that gigantic blow-lamp. Looking down into the cockpit I saw a long spout of flame issuing from the hollow starboard wing-root and curling up along the port side of the cockpit and then across my right shoulder. I had some crazy notion that if I rocked the aircraft and skidded, meantime losing speed, the fire might go out – but it didn't. The blaze became an inferno in a fraction of time and I concluded that baling out was the only solution; a forced-landing was out of the question as I reckoned I was still 7,000–8,000ft up.

I reached down to pull out the R/T jack but the heat was too great. The skin was already rising off my right wrist and hand, and my left hand was starting to blister. My thin gloves were being progressively burned away, but though finally they more or less disappeared and my hands caught the full blast of the flames, I now know that they saved my fingers from the far worse deformities that others have suffered. My shoes and slacks must have been burning all this time but I cannot remember any great pain – that was to come later. Shock is nature's anaesthetic – and if she can be very cruel, she can also be unspeakably kind.

I undid my harness and tried to raise myself but found I had not the strength. I was comforted by another crazy notion – I still had my Colt ready loaded if things came to the worst. With the R/T jack still firmly held in its socket I decided to pull off my helmet, open the cockpit cover, and roll on my back, so that with a sharp dig forward on the control column I would be ejected from the blazing Hurricane. My helmet came off with a determined tug. I pulled hard to get the cockpit cover open and finally succeeded, after using up a lot of my remaining strength. That there was a quick release for the hood passed me by in that strange, drowsy, mood. As the cockpit cover flew back there was a blinding flash. I seemed to be travelling upwards between walls of flame. Then I suddenly found myself turning over and over in the clear air with no sensation of falling – the flames mercifully were no more. Soon I ceased to travel forwards, or so it seemed, and began to fall earthwards, still turning head over heels. My hand instinctively passed over the Sutton Harness release grip and on to the rip-cord handle of my parachute – and I can be thankful that in my semi-coma my hand did not loiter on the way. I pulled hard and felt the Bowden wire being drawn through the strongly woven fabric tubing. Then came a gentle jerk as I was pulled into a vertical position, swinging comfortably and secure in my harness. I looked down at the rip-cord handle buried in the swollen mess that had been my right hand, and then disdainfully threw it as far away from me as I could. It was a gesture of temper at having been shot down. I did not remind myself of earlier days when the punishment for failing to bring back the rip-cord handle after baling out was a fine of half-a-crown, or so ran the story!

An interminable length of time seemed to have elapsed while struggling to escape from that inferno. From the time the incendiary struck to the time my parachute opened was, in fact, less than a minute. Like most pilots, I had always wanted to make a parachute descent, but now I could raise no enthusiasm for it as I floated down. I was feeling distinctly browned off.

That Gleave's Hurricane, P3115, had exploded and thrown him clear in the process, was a blessing – but as the grievously burned pilot came closer to earth, the ground rushed up at him:

I then stood in this field … thought I should see a doctor, so called out 'Anybody about?' Out of a cowshed nearby came a very stalwart man who insisted on putting me onto his back, and he carried me up to a house belonging to a Mrs Wilson. I regret, to my shame, that I kept saying 'How much longer?'

Mrs Wilson's son, Alec, recalled that 'Tom was in a terrible state, but all he was worried about was making a mess on Mum's nice clean bed, because of his injuries.'

Tom wrote that 'When I look back, I feel ashamed of myself for all the trouble I must have given her. No one could have done more for me than she did, and I shall always be grateful to her.'

More help than that administered by the kindly Mrs Wilson, however, was needed. In due course the local Air Raid Warden arrived with an airman on leave, and the pair managed to make the wounded Squadron Leader comfortable on the back seat of the car before 'we pushed off for a nearby war hospital'. It was during that journey that Tom began feeling terrible pain, prompting the repeated question 'How much further?' Although the journey seemed like hours to the grievously wounded pilot, just fifteen minutes later the open-top car arrived at Orpington Hospital, and Tom was immediately treated 'for shock and secondary burns'. A shot of morphia sent merciful oblivion, and as Tom later wrote,

> From that moment I started accumulating a debt that mounted daily ... Every time I see a nurse or doctor now I feel a hidden sense of humility, prompted not only by the ceaseless care and attention I received ... but also what I saw them do for others far worse than myself, all but dead casualties who have become living miracles.

Squadron Leader Gleave, however, was fortunately 253's only casualty in this engagement, during which the Polish Pilot Officer Tadeusz Nowak claimed a He 111 destroyed; Pilot Officer John Greenwood claimed a Dornier 'probable', and Pilot Officer John Clifton a Ju 88 damaged.

During the raid, Croydon's Redwing Aircraft hangar was hit again, in addition to the adjacent shelters, although both had already been abandoned owing to previous damage. A bomb exploded in Purley Way, opposite the airport's main gates, and thirteen more fell harmlessly on open land to the east. A Royal Artilleryman was injured and a lorry destroyed, but overall the damage had been surprisingly light. Yet again the Germans responsible were actually the Me 110 fighter-bomber crews of *Erprobungsgruppe* 210 – which had suffered grievous losses attacking the same target on 15 August 1940. On this occasion, just one Me 110 was lost, the Me 110 of 2nd *Staffel's Unteroffizier* Ernst Glaeske's being badly damaged; with a mortally wounded *Bordfunker*, Obergefreiter Konrad Schweda, the pilot forced-landed at Wrotham, Stansted – too late to save Schweda. Two other Me 110s of 2nd *Staffel* returned to Calais-Marck damaged.

So far, the day was going in the Luftwaffe's favour: Fowlmere, Debden, Biggin Hill, Eastchurch and Croydon had all been successfully bombed with varying degrees of damage – and the escorting German fighters had done a good job of protecting their charges, with only two III/KG 2 Do 17s returning damaged to Cambrai, only 5/KG 2 suffering an aircraft destroyed. Considering the depth of penetration – so far as 12 Group's Duxford Sector and Biggin Hill, south-east of London, this is remarkable. The morning's foray to Duxford also proved that the Me 110 was still effective as a long-range escort fighter in the right circumstances – Fighter Command opposition to that raid, which had achieved surprise, having been comparatively light. Conversely, Fighter Command had not, so far, fared well: already, seventeen Hurricanes had been destroyed and another damaged, with three of their pilots killed and twelve wounded; four Spitfires had been lost, a pilot killed and three wounded – in other words a combined total of twenty-one aircraft destroyed and one damaged, four pilots killed and fifteen wounded – and the day's fighting was far from over. Replacing lost aircraft, thanks to the sterling efforts of Lord Beaverbrook and MAP, was not an issue: but replacement pilots were.

Earlier on this day, for example, 603 Squadron at Hornchurch had received three replacement pilots: Flying Officer Brian MacNamara and Pilot Officers James MacPhail and WPH 'Robin' Rafter – all of whom were former Army Cooperation pilots fresh to 11 Group at the height of battle after just one week converting to Spitfires at Hawarden, near Chester. Quite how these postings were decided remains a mystery, however. All three were not just inexperienced on Spitfires, but comparatively so as pilots generally. The threesome had trained, however, with much more experienced pilots, such as Flying Officer Ian Hallam, another, older, former Army Cooperation pilot, more arguably suited to an 11 Group posting than being sent north to 610 Squadron, resting at Acklington (where, in relative safety, he was able to accumulate a further 21.05 flying hours on Spitfires before eventually going south, to 222 Squadron, on 1 October 1940). Before going south, in fact, 603 had already received three OTU-fresh RAFVR NCO replacement pilots, among whom was Sergeant Jack Stokoe:

> During my Spitfire training at 5 OTU, Aston Down, I logged between 10–15 flying hours. Fortunately I then went North, to 603 Squadron in Scotland, which meant that I was able to further get to grips with the Spitfire. When we arrived at Hornchurch I was therefore fortunate to have a total of around 70 hours on Spits. Had I gone straight from Aston Down to Hornchurch I would not have rated my chances of survival very highly.

Just a few days after arriving at Hornchurch, Stokoe was already a combat veteran.

It was not just RAF fighter squadrons receiving inexperienced replacements, however. Across the 'Kanal', on 25 August 1940, *Hauptmann* Johannes Jank had led the Me 109s of his I/JG 77 from Aalborg to Mardyck, Dunkirk, where the *Gruppe* came under the orders of Jafü 2. Less than a year after starting flying training, 22-year-old *Leutnant* Bruno Petrenko, reported for duty there shortly afterwards, yet to make an operational flight. On the morning of 31 August 1940, I/JG 77 prepared to fly a bomber escort mission:

> I was not supposed to be on the flight since I was a beginner and they did not want to take me as the mission would be over England. But another pilot who was supposed to be on the flight suddenly developed stomach pains and

had to rush to the toilet. Everybody awaited his return but he didn't come back, and so they said 'Well, you had better take his place'. So, I was on that mission by chance.

So far, Hornchurch aerodrome, on the north bank of the Thames and at the extremity of the escorting Me 109s' range, had escaped serious damage; it was now that sector station's turn to experience a major raid.

This raid was being mounted by Do 17s of KG 3, escorted by Me 109s of JG 51 and JG 77, with other fighters, of LG 2 and JG 2, ready to cover the raid's withdrawal. As the raid crossed the Channel, 1 Squadron was already airborne, patrolling Northolt, and 151 Squadron remained over North Weald. At 12.40 hrs, twelve 603 Squadron Spitfires scrambled from Hornchurch to patrol Biggin Hill; five minutes later ten Spitfires of 222 Squadron scrambled from Rochford to patrol base; at 12.55 hrs, Flight Lieutenant Willie Rhodes-Moorhouse led a flight of 601 Squadron Hurricanes up from Debden, heading for the Thames Estuary, and at 12.59 hrs, the Hurricanes of 501 Squadron left Gravesend. A minute later, as this enemy force crossed in over Dover, simultaneously with *Erprobungsgruppe* 210's attack on Croydon, 310 Squadron had scrambled from Duxford, heading south, towards the Thames and North Weald.

The first RAF fighters to intercept the raid was 310 Squadron, which had been diverted from North Weald to patrol Hornchurch at 10,000ft, being led on this occasion by Flight Lieutenant Gordon Sinclair DFC, commander of 'A' Flight:

I almost at once saw twenty Do 215s [*sic*] proceeding North in two-line astern formations, being fired at by AA. The E/As turned East [over Tilbury], apparently on sighting us [not the case, the bombers had deliberately turned towards their target] so I climbed to about 2,000ft higher and ordered 'B' Flight [being led by Flight Lieutenant Jerrard Jeffries] to go to port of E/A and I led 'A' Flight to starboard. We then formed line astern to attack from the quarter. I picked on one 215 at the rear of the formation and did four attacks on him, the first two with my Section behind me, two above. The E/A fire ceased on the third attack, and on the fourth he went into a dive with the port engine stopped. I saw him dive into the mouth of the Thames. I was then attacked by three Me 109s, so I dived away and came home.

The Do 17 belonged to 5/KG 3; one of the crew was killed, the others captured. Anither was claimed destroyed by the Czech Green Leader, Pilot Officer Emil Fechtner, but his Hurricane was peppered by return fire in the wings and left tyre, so being unable to continue his attack, the pilot returned to Duxford. Flight Lieutenant Jeffries also claimed a Do 17 destroyed, 'in flames [ORB]'.

Squadron Leader Sacha Hess, the Czech leader of the squadron in the 'double-banking' system, claimed an Me 109 destroyed, then, at 13.25 hrs:

attacked a Do 215 [*sic*] over outskirts of London ... I gave one burst from rear and he dived steeply with me in pursuit. At 1,000ft he straightened out and I gave him the balance of my ammo from rear and side. He fell to ground near Canewden on river Crouch. Three jumped out and put hands up. A second Hurricane (UF-B) came up and circled; I landed at Honnington with him and then returned. Pilot of UF-B confirmed he saw my Do 215 fall.

This was a Do 17 of 4/KG 3 which crash-landed at Eastwick Farm, Burnham-on-Crouch, the crew were captured, two of which were wounded, one so badly that he died a week later. The other Hurricane involved was flown by Flying Officer William Clyde of 601 Squadron, with whom the victory was shared.

Me 109s, however, had pounced on 310 Squadron; Pilot Officer Jaroslav Sterbacek was shot down – the first Czechoslovak pilot to be killed during the Battle of Britain – whose Hurricane crashed and burned out near Romford (although, curiously, this pilot remains missing); Pilot Officer Miroslav Kredba was also shot down, baling out safely over the Thames Estuary, and, like Fechtner, Pilot Officer Jaroslav Maly returned his damaged machine to Duxford.

Wing Commander Alfred 'Woody' Woodhall, Station Commander, Duxford:

I met the Czechs on their return to the airfield and spoke with Squadron Leader Sacha Hess; he had disabled a Do 17 over Epping Forest which made a wheels-up forced landing in a field. He followed it down with the intention of making certain that no one got out of it alive. He saw three Germans climb out, who, when they realised Sacha was diving on them, held up their hands. To quote his own words: 'I hesitate, then it was too late, so I go round again to make sure I kill them – they wave something white – again I do not shoot – then (disgustedly) I think it is no use – I am become too bloody British!'

Hess had good reason to desire revenge that day: he had recently received notification that his wife and daughter had been killed by the Germans.

Hornchurch, however, had been bombed at 13.15 hrs:

although our squadrons engaged, they were unable to break the enemy bomber formation, and so about 30 Dorniers dropped some 100 bombs across the airfield. Damage, however, was slight, although a bomb fell on the new Airmen's Mess, which had almost been completed. The only vital damage, however, was to a power cable, which was cut. The emergency power equipment was brought into operation until repair was effected. Three men were killed and 11 wounded. 54 Squadron attempted to take off during the attack and ran through the bombs. Three aircraft were destroyed, one being blown from the middle of the landing field to outside the boundary, but all three pilots miraculously escaped with only slight injuries [ORB].

No.54 Squadron:

A large formation of enemy bombers – a most impressive sight in vic formation at 15,000ft – reached the aerodromes and dropped their bombs (probably sixty in all) in a line from our original dispersal pens to the petrol dump and beyond into Elm Park. Perimeter track, dispersal pens and barrack block windows suffered but no other damage to buildings was caused, and the aerodrome, in spite of its ploughed condition, remained serviceable. The Squadron was ordered off just as the first bombs were beginning to fall and eight of our machines safely cleared the ground; the remaining section, however, just became airborne as the bombs exploded. All three machines were wholly wrecked in the air, and the survival of the pilots is a complete miracle. Sergeant Davis, taking off towards the hangars was thrown back across the River Ingrebourne two fields away, scrambling out of his machine unharmed. Flight Lieutenant Deere had one wing and his prop torn off; climbing to about 100ft, he turned over and, coming down, slid along the aerodrome for a hundred yards upside down. He was rescued from this unenviable position by Pilot Officer Edsall, the third member of the Section, who had suffered a similar fate except that he had landed the right way up. Dashing across the aerodrome with bombs still dropping, he extricated Deere from his machine. All three pilots were ready again for battle by the next morning [ORB].

The indomitable Al Deere had just used up another of his nine lives.

The Spitfires of 603 Squadron had been patrolling at 30,000ft over Biggin Hill when ordered to do so over Hornchurch. At 13.15 hrs, Flight Lieutenant Harold MacDonald was:

approaching base from South and saw considerable aircraft and AA fire over base at about 20,000ft. I put Squadron into line astern and gave the order to attack. I selected a He 113 [sic] which was coming straight in my direction but below me. Owing to the speed at which we approached I had difficulty in getting my sights onto him before he disappeared below me. I got a momentary burst in from almost vertically above but was unable to allow enough deflection. I then pulled out and did a steep climbing turn and came again above and behind him to the South. He broke away from the rest of the battle and turned SE at about 20,000ft. I followed and after a bit gradually overhauled him, keeping slightly above and to the South of him. As I approached very close behind he suddenly made a very steep turn to the right. I gave him a full deflection burst of about two to three seconds and he immediately emitted a long trail of white 'smoke' and went into a steep spiral dive. I watched him to see him crash, but at about 4000ft he pulled gradually out and proceeded SE, flying low. I drew down from 20,000ft and again overtook him, flying about 1,000ft and 350 mph. As I approached again he went into a gradual left-hand turn and I gave him another burst of about two seconds from immediately behind, having to pull up very suddenly to avoid him. He then flew down into a field and rolled over and over. He came down approximately five miles South or SE of Maidstone.

This was *Feldwebel* Evers of 1/JG 77, whose Me 109 cartwheeled during what was an emergency high-speed crash-landing at Court Farm, Hunton Lane, Chainhurst. Evers was rescued from the wreckage but died of his injuries later the same day.

Me 109s were also claimed destroyed by Pilot Officers Richard Hillary and Brian Carbury, the latter claiming two, and a Do 17 was claimed by Pilot Officer James Morton – all for no loss.

No.151 Squadron, again led in the air by Flight Lieutenant Kenneth Blair, was at 6,000ft east of Hornchurch when the raiders had approached, 4,000ft above. By the time Blair climbed, as he later reported, to intercept the enemy 'they had unloaded their bombs'. Attacking from astern and below, Blair went on to claim a 'Do 215' [*sic*] destroyed and another damaged in the ensuing combat. Pilot Officers Irving Blair and William Patullo also claimed bombers destroyed, but Pilot Officer John Ellacombe, in what was his third action of the day, was shot-up by a Dornier's return fire, baling out just as the Hurricane's gravity tank exploded. Coming down near Southend, Ellacombe was admitted to the General Hospital there suffering from burns.

Also in action were 54 and 601 Squadrons, which engaged the retreating enemy over the Thames Estuary. The latter's Pilot Officer Howard Mayers, an Australian, and Flying Officer William Clyde both claimed Do 17s destroyed, and the latter also one damaged. Flight Lieutenant Marcus Lister Robinson, commander of 'A' Flight, reported having approached the bombers from 'astern and to one side', when he noticed:

an Me 109 below and to my left. I dived down and the Me 109 pulled up and we carried out head-on attack at each other. The Me 109 broke away at last moment and I turned and got on his tail. He was smoking from below his engine and after a short burst he rolled over and dived inverted for the ground. At this time I saw a second Me 109 and got a short burst in from the quarter. He also emitted smoke and white vapour and dived vertically ... I then ran out of ammunition but saw a third Me 109 dive past me. I followed him down to ground level and chased him southwards. He never rose above 100ft until well South of Maidstone, and then throttled back.

I overtook and formated on him, pointing downwards for him to land. He turned away so I carried out a dummy quarter attack, breaking away very close to him. After this he landed his Me 109 in a field at about 140 mph (twenty-five miles SE of Maidstone, approx.). The pilot got out, apparently unhurt, and put his hands up above his head. I circled around and waved to him and as he waved back I returned and threw a packet of twenty 'Players' at him. He picked up his cigarettes.

Clearly, at least in the air, was not yet dead. The German pilot was *Oberleutnant* Hans-Joachim Ehrig, *Staffelkapitän* of 1/JG 77, who was taken prisoner at Gates Farm, High Halden, near Tenterden.

Sergeant Norman Taylor of 601 Squadron also claimed a 109 destroyed, and Flight Lieutenant Rhodes-Moorhouse claimed two Me 109 probables – but these successes were unfortunately offset against substantial casualties (most likely inflicted by JG 51 and JG 77). Sergeant Taylor, in fact, was in turn hit, baling out over Gravesend; Sergeant Arthur Woolley baled out and was admitted to hospital suffering from burns; Pilot Officer Humphrey Gilbert also took to his parachute, landing unhurt, but Pilot Officer Michael Duke Doulton was missing (and would remain so until recovered by amateur aviation archaeology enthusiasts in 1984; the pilots remains were then cremated and interred at Salehurst churchyard).

In the same action over north-east Kent, the Spitfire pilots of 54 Squadron were eager to avenge the bombing of their airfield. Also up in that highly volatile scenario was *Leutnant* Petrenko, flying his first combat mission – and it was his Me 109 which Flight Lieutenant George Gribble DFC and Sergeant John Norwell caught and at 7,000ft near Hornchurch at 13.10 hrs. The Spitfires opened fire – hitting the protective armour plate behind the pilot's back and head.

Leutnant Bruno Petrenko:

It was a kind of 'ticky, tick, tick'. I decided to evade my assailants by nose-diving. When I thought I had shaken them off I climbed, thinking 'Well, that wasn't so bad, and the armour protected me' – but then, as I was still climbing, I was again attacked from behind. It happened so fast that I couldn't avoid it, at least I, a beginner, couldn't. The Spitfire was just suddenly there – and down I went again, thinking 'Well, what do I do now?' Some pilots advised that in such a case you drop to tree-top height and hedge-hop home, but I thought 'That sounds too easy', so I climbed again – a big mistake an experienced jagdflieger would never have made.

As I was climbing I was attacked again, from below and on the right-hand side. Someone more at home playing these games attacked me where there was no protective armour – a real problem. The glass from the cockpit was splintering, the instrument panel shattered, and now I was really hit, many times – at which point I blacked out.

I came to in a vertical dive and became aware of lots of noise, a kind of fluid leaking from the side of my aircraft, and what struck me was the ground approaching very fast. I realised that I had to regain control immediately and recover from the dive. In so doing the blood rushed from my head and I blacked out again. When I came to I found I was at tree-top height with little power – the machine could still fly, but not for long. I was now very, very low and looked for somewhere to land.

I looked around I saw two Spitfires behind me, still shooting occasionally, but that wasn't easy for them as I was flying so slow and erratically. I don't

know whether they didn't shoot me because I was in a difficult situation ...
I just saw English park-like landscape, some bushes and trees. There was a
group of trees ahead, so I flew directly at them before pulling up, over them,
and blacking out again.

Sergeant John Clancy was stationed nearby with his searchlight unit, and hearing
that a German aircraft had been shot down locally:

[I] jumped into my van with a couple of men ... We soon located the aircraft
near Brook Farm house, on its back... nose broken away and burning 90
yards away ... tail cocked up in the air with plane at a 45° angle. The airscrew
had torn off and bounced two or three hundred yards away. The wings had
broken off ... the pilot was hanging upside down in his cockpit, unconscious
and bleeding badly. The cockpit hood was shattered.

I had set out with my rifle, breathing fire and slaughter, but when I saw this
poor gory head hanging there the rifle went down on the ground and I started
wriggling under the plane to get the pilot out, which I finally did, and with
the aid of water from the van tried to bring him round and clean up his face.

The pilot seemed to have head injuries. He said 'Spitfire?'

I said 'Yes'.

He then said, which stumped me, 'Why are you being so good to me?'

I came back with a father fatuous reply: 'I don't know, you might have been
one of our boys, mightn't you?'

Then he looked at me and said 'How far to the sea?'

'Too far!' I replied.

Having come down at Navestock, near Romford, Petrenko, now a PoW like
his *Staffelkapitän*, was admitted to Epping Hospital where he would remain
for ten days before being taken to the infamous 'London Cage' at Cockfosters
for interrogation.

In this action, 54 Squadron's Pilot Officer Des MacMullen shared a 'Do 215'
probably destroyed with a Hurricane of another squadron; the Spitfires landed
without loss, the only casualties being Flight Lieutenant Deere's section of three,
caught taking off in a shower of exploding bombs and earth.

Over Gravesend, 501 Squadron also engaged the withdrawing enemy fighter
escort, the Polish Pilot Officer Stanislaw Skalski and Sergeant Anton Glowacki,
and Sergeant James 'Ginger' Lacey all claiming Me 109 destroyed. Glowacki,
however, was himself shot down, baling out slightly injured.

Diverted from their patrol of Rochford to intercept the raid near Gravesend,
Squadron Leader John Hill's 222 Squadron found two circles of Me 109s at
26,000ft over the Maidstone area, attacking them at 13.30 hrs. Pilot Officer
Laurie Whitbread:

I encountered an Me 109 at 16,000ft over Sittingbourne. I manoeuvred till
it appeared in my sights, the Me climbing slowly away, not having seen me.

I fired from about 400 yards and rapidly closed to within 50 yards, when I could see the bullets entering the fuselage from tail to cockpit. The Me half-rolled onto its back and remained in that attitude, flying quite slowly with a little white smoke issuing from it. It eventually nosed down slowly when I was obliged to lose sight of it having noticed an aircraft approaching my tail, which turned out to be a Spitfire.

Flight Lieutenant Andrew Robinson reported having:

fired a short burst into one Me 109 which turned on its back with smoke pouring from it. I followed it down until it crashed on the south bank of the Thames about five miles east of Gravesend. The pilot was rescued from the blazing aircraft by soldiers who were nearby.

This was *Feldwebel* Kramer of 1/JG 77, whose aircraft burned out after his forced-landing near Shornemead Fort.

Pilot Officer Tim Vigors also claimed a 109 destroyed 'in flames, and probably destroyed another [ORB]'. No.222 returned to Rochford having suffered no loss.

New to the battle over England, like squadrons arriving in 11 Group, I/JG 77 had suffered at the hands of the defenders. During the day's first operation, *Oberleutnant* Priebe, Kapitän of 2/JG 77 had been shot down and baled out over Elham, becoming a PoW. On the second, *Oberleutnant* Ehrig, Kapitän of 1/JG 77, was among the four pilots of his *Staffel* made PoWs, and 1 *Staffel* also lost a pilot killed. A pilot of 3/JG 77 ditched in the Channel but was rescued by the ever-watchful (and brave) *Seenotdienst*, and another crash-landed his damaged 109 back at Mardyck. In total, seven I/JG 77 Me 109s had been destroyed, and one damaged. Whether the pilot suffering from 'Channel sickness', whose place was taken by the rookie *Leutnant* Bruno Petrenko, remained in the lavatory when the battered remnants of 1/JG 77 returned to base is unknown.

As RAF fighter squadrons feverishly rearmed and refuelled, various German reconnaissance aircraft flew over southern England. At 14.00 hrs, Flight Lieutenant Ken Gillies led Red Section, Pilot Officer Crelin 'Bogle' Bodie and Sergeant Douggie Hunt, up from Coltishall in 12 Group to intercept one of these snoopers. At 15.43 hrs the Spitfires were orbiting Cromer when a Do 215 of 4/*Aufklärungsgruppe* was sighted 12,000ft above. Seeing the danger, the German pilot climbed hard to 30,000ft and turned south-west before beginning a shallow dive, picking up speed. The Spitfires climbed hard, all three pilots attacking out of the sun. The Dornier was losing height when approaching Felixstowe, then flew south-east over the sea at 50ft – still harassed by the Spitfires. Minutes later it was all over, the Spitfire's quarry crashing into the sea; *Unteroffizier* Vogel and *Feldwebel* Maurer were later found dead, but *Unteroffiziers* Goebbels and Kamolz remain missing.

According to the 79 Squadron ORB, at 16.30 hrs 'Six aircraft took off [from Croydon] to return to Biggin Hill. Sergeant Bolton missing, later learned that he was killed near Kenley' – Sergeant Henry Bolton was killed when crash-landing after combat at Haliloo Farm, Warlingham.

Apart from the foregoing isolated incidents, all otherwise remained ominously quiet. By 17.00 hrs, however, RDF screens were indicating more enemy formations assembling inland of and off Calais. This would be the day's fourth major raid – and there would now be respite for Biggin Hill or Hornchurch.

Around 17.00 hrs (BST) *Major* Adolf Galland led all three *gruppen* of JG 26 from their various bases in the Pas-de-Calais to rendezvous with Do 17s of KG 76, the *Kommodore's Stabsschwarm* and *Hauptmann* Gerhard Schöpfel's III/JG 26 flying a supporting *freie hunt* while close escort was provided by I and II/JG 26: target Hornchurch.

Only a flight of 79 Squadron's Hurricanes was airborne at the time, in transit between Biggin Hill and Croydon, so these Hurricanes were directed towards the 'trade' incoming over the Dover Strait. In terms of reinforcements, the 11 Group Controller's response was immediate:

1704 hrs: nine Spitfires of 54 Squadron scrambled from Hornchurch to patrol Manston.
1710 hrs: ten Hurricanes of 85 Squadron sent from Croydon to patrol Hawkinge.
1725 hrs: eleven Spitfires of 222 Squadron ordered up from Rochford to patrol Canterbury.

RDF had detected at least four German formations, the total number of enemy aircraft approaching exceeding 100. As 222 Squadron scrambled, the Hornchurch raid – thirty Do 17s of KG 26 and at least 100 Me 109s of JG 26 and Me 110s of ZG 26 – crossed the south-east coast between Dungeness and Dover, then droned steadily on towards Maidstone.

Five minutes later, at 17.30 hrs, another enemy formation, flying at high-altitude, attacked Biggin Hill:

A high-level bombing attack was made on the Station and further extensive damage was caused to buildings, Hangars in the South Camp were badly damaged. In the North Camp, the Triple Bay Hangar was damaged, the operations Block received a direct hit and was burnt, the Officers Married Quarters were all severely damaged by blast and rendered unsafe. The Officers Mess was also damaged. The temporary lash up of telephone lines and power cables which had been made after the previous evening's raid was completely destroyed [ORB].

It was estimated that 100 bombs were dropped on Biggin Hill during this raid, which caused extensive damage; the efficiency of the Sector Operations Room was seriously compromised.

Air Vice-Marshal Keith Park: 'Only one squadron could operate from there, and the remaining two squadrons had to be placed under the control of adjacent sectors for over a week.'

It was another successful attack on an important sector station, leaving many personnel dead. Sadly, the fatalities included 30-year-old AC1 William Wright of Birkenhead, whose 610 'County of Chester' Squadron was in the process of moving to Acklington for rest and refitting.

This raid had reached Biggin Hill without being intercepted.

Having scrambled to patrol Hawkinge at 17.10 hrs, 85 Squadron was ordered to intercept the raid that had crossed the coast at 17.25 hrs and was heading towards the Thames Estuary:

> About thirty Do 215s [sic] were sighted at 1740 hrs flying at 16,000–17,000ft, accompanied by approximately 100 mixed Me 109 and Me 110, and attack was opened about twenty miles South of Purfleet. The Squadron effectively broke up enemy formation and separated bombers from fighters by diving in sections in line astern in the box. Pilot Officer Hodgson did a head-on attack on a Do 215 and saw pieces fall off nose and starboard wing. Then engaged Me 109 with long burst, followed by a short burst at 200 yards, and E/A rolled over and went down with engine on fire near Thames Haven oil storage tanks. At this juncture Pilot Officer Hodgson's machine was hit by cannon shell which blew up his oil lines and glycol tank, and set fire to his engine. He prepared to bale out and was actually half way out of his aircraft when he realised that he was over a thickly populated area and also still close to the oil tanks. Fully appreciating the danger he decided to remain with his aircraft and endeavour to forced-land and thus avoid the serious consequences of a flaming Hurricane crashing in the area mentioned. By skilful side-slipping he managed to keep the fire under control and finally succeeded in making a wheels-up landing in a field near Shotgate, Essex, narrowly missing wires and other obstacles erected with a view to preventing the landing of hostile aircraft [ORB].

Pilot Officer William Hodgson, a New Zealander, was clearly made of the 'right stuff', and his heroic deed was marked near the site of his crash-landing by a street named in his honour (sadly, he would be killed, along with Pilot Officer Sammy Allard DFM in a flying accident on 13 March 1941).

> Pilot Officer Marshall was hit in the rudder and had to break away downwards. Flying Officer Woods-Scawen gave a five-second burst into Me 109 from dead astern and it pulled up and span out of the fight. He then did a quarter attack on another Me 109, followed by a long burst from dead astern and the E/A caught fire and dived down with a trail of black smoke pouring from it.
> Pilot Officer Allard on opening quarter attack from the sun saw a Do 215 wheel over and go out of sight. He then attacked another Do 215 and from 200 yards closed until he nearly hit the E/A. Pieces of metal flew off and one engine burst into flames as E/A went down.
> Sergeant Goodman fired long burst into Do 215 and saw tracers entering centre of fuselage. Had to break off combat as Me 109 was on his tail but

definitely damaged E/A as his windscreen was covered with oil from the Dornier. Sergeant Booth attacked Me 110 from astern and fired a long burst. E/A dived for about 5,000ft and then continued to dive inverted. Sergeant Booth followed it to this point but broke away when his ASI sowed 400 mph and the fabric seams on the wings were coming apart. Position: a few miles West of Sittingbourne. Sergeant Evans, during head-on attack on Do 215 put port engine of E/A on fire but was unable to see further result.

Fortunately, at 17.20 hrs, 54 Squadron had taken-off from Hornchurch, and at 17.51 hrs, thirteen Spitfires of 603 Squadron were hurriedly scrambled – it was just in time. With the enemy approaching London, however, their intention remained unclear; as a precaution, Air Vice-Marshal Park – who had already scrambled 1, 1 (RCAF), 17, 72, 79, 253, 501 and 616 Squadrons between 17.33–17.50 hrs, in addition to requesting that 242 and 611 Squadrons of 12 Group come down from Duxford to the North Weald and Hornchurch sectors – at around 18.00 hrs, scrambled 257 Squadron to patrol their Martlesham base, 602 Squadron from Westhampnett to patrol the Biggin Hill–Gravesend Line, and the Poles of 303 Squadron from Northolt to Biggin Hill. However, although assistance was requested from 10 and 12 Groups, it was not until 17.50 hrs that 242 Squadron, which was operating at Duxford, scrambled a flight with orders to patrol North Weald and another to cover Hornchurch, and 611 Squadron, also from Duxford, with orders to proceed to Hornchurch, over fifty miles to the south. Similarly, assistance was provided by 10 Group, but 'A' Flight of 609 Squadron did scramble from Middle Wallop with orders to patrol over Windsor, until 18.00 hrs. Given the distances 12 and 10 Group squadrons had to cover, and time to climb en route, to comply with those orders, the assistance request had been left too late – suggesting that this was a precautionary measure only by Air Vice-Marshal Park, confident that 11 Group's squadrons were able to repel the current assault. As already evidenced though, there can be no credibility attached to the notion that Air Vice-Marshal Park was averse to a response in strength when necessary.

With only 85 Squadron having intercepted the raid so far, it was the turn of Hornchurch:

The fourth attack of the day was also directed at Hornchurch, and, once again, despite strong fighter opposition and AA fire, the bombers penetrated our defences. This time, however, their aim was most inaccurate, and the line of bombs fell from then towards the edge of the aerodrome. Two Spitfires parked near the edge of the aerodrome were written off, and one airman was killed. Otherwise, apart from the damage to dispersal pens, the perimeter track and the aerodrome surface, the raid was abortive and the aerodrome remained serviceable [ORB].

It is fair to say that had Duxford's squadrons been scrambled at, say 17.45 hrs even, a flight of 242 and the whole of 611 Squadron may well have intercepted immediately before and disrupted the bombing. But … this narrative is not about 'ifs' – but what actually happened. And the fact is that 12 Group was requested too late (not so much regarding 10 Group, because Windsor was clearly a precautionary measure, with the previous day's raids in mind).

At 17.30 hrs the Hurricanes of 1 (RCAF) Squadron had scrambled from Northolt and engaged the retiring Hornchurch raiders over Gravesend. Unfortunately the squadron was hampered by AA fire, but nonetheless, Pilot Officer Beverley Christmas claimed two Me 109s destroyed, one of which being *Unteroffizier* Horst Liebeck of 7/JG 26, whose Me 109 broke up over Stansted; the enemy pilot took to his parachute and was captured. Flying Officer Ross Smither also claimed a 109 destroyed, and Flying Officer John Kerwin claimed a 'Do 215' [*sic*] destroyed and Flying Officer Dal Russell damaged another. Flying Officer Jean-Paul Desloges, however, was shot-up by a 109 and baled out 'with quite severe burns about the face, hands and legs [ORB]'.

As the Hornchurch raiders fought their way back to the coast, more 11 Group squadrons intercepted, the first of which was 54 Squadron, at 18.00 hrs.

Pilot Officer Colin Gray DFC:

> I was on patrol over Maidstone at 28,000ft when I sighted some fighters behind and below me. I then saw approximately thirty enemy bombers in vics of three going West at 15,000ft. I followed Red Section and attacked bombers from front and above, firing a good burst at the leading section. I then pulled up to 20,000ft and engaged an Me 109, giving it various bursts with deflection at short range. I observed a stream of glycol and followed E/A down, firing as I went. The E/A forced-landed two miles North of Headcorn, which is ten–twelve miles SE of Maidstone.
>
> E/A was not camouflaged but a pale silvery blue colour all over, nor had it a yellow nose, wing tips etc … Before landing the pilot opened the hood over the cockpit. The evasive tactics of the pilot were extremely clever considering the small reserve of engine.

Gray had shot down *Oberleutnant* Willi Fronhöfer of 9/JG 26, who forced-landed at Jubilee Hall Farm, Ulcombe.

Sergeant Dudley Gibbins attacked a 109 South of Dartford, which 'rose slightly and then fell in a very slow spiral as though the pilot was killed'. Gibbins, however, was 'subsequently shot down by an unknown aircraft'. The Spitfire pilot baled out and landed unhurt at Tinley Lodge, Shipbourne.

At the same time, 222 Squadron went into action near Canterbury (although the detail recorded in the ORB concerning Flight Lieutenant Robinson's victories are incorrect, as these actually refer to the lunchtime action). Pilot Officer John Broadhurst was leading Green Section which, as the squadron dived to attack the bombers, took on the Me 109s. Broadhurst fired and hit one at close range, which dived, 'obviously damaged', then 'dived on a larger bomber formation with a fighter escort. I gave an Me 109 (yellow nose) a long burst and he went down with flames and smoke coming from his engine.' 'Probable' Me 109s were claimed by Pilot Officers John 'Chips' Carpenter and John Cutts, and 109s 'damaged' by Flying Officer Brian van Mentz, a South African, and Pilot Officer Laurie Whitbread and Sergeant Iain Hutchinson. Flight Lieutenant Robinson's Spitfire was hit by cannon-fire in the exchange, and he returned to Hornchurch slightly wounded; Pilot Officer Graham Davies was shot down over Ashford and baled out badly burned – reconstructive surgery would be required at East Grinstead, the pilot not returning to duty until December 1940.

Details of 79 Squadron's engagement at 18.10 hrs are scant, the personal combat reports of pilots involved not appearing to have survived, but this is believed to have occurred over the Dungeness area. According to the ORB, the following claims were made: 'Pilot Officer Tracey one Do 17 or 215 destroyed ... Pilot Officer Stones DFC got one Do 17 destroyed and one probable. He landed at Hawkinge.' Pilot Officer William Millington, an Australian, was shot-up over Romney, crash-landing in flames at Conghurst Farm, Hawkhurst, suffering from burns and a wounded thigh. Pilot Officer Edward Morris, a South African, was attacking a Do 17 when his Hurricane was damaged by a 109, forcing him to crash-land back at Biggin Hill, wounded.

At 18.20 hrs, the Hurricanes of 17 Squadron were in action against 'a large formation of bombers protected by thirty–fifty Me 109s over Maidstone. There was a general dogfight in which Pilot Officer Bird-Wilson got one Me 109 destroyed and one probable, and Flight Lieutenant Bayne got one Me 109 destroyed [ORB].' Sergeant George Steward was shot down and made a successful forced-landing at Yalding, from which he walked away unhurt.

For 72 Squadron, having only arrived at Biggin Hill three hours before, the chaotic skies over Kent at 18.20 hrs were the squadron's entrée to combat over 11 Group. Flight Lieutenant Ted Graham, commander of 'B' Flight, was 'Tennis Leader':

Ordered to patrol base at Angels 10. Squadron took off with leading section of four aircraft, another of four and a rearguard of four aircraft in two pairs. About thirty Do 17s were sighted protected by many 109s were encountered ten miles South of Maidstone at 15,000ft. A head-on attack was attempted on the Do 17s but I was compelled to break off the attack on account of swarms of 109s coming down on our tails. A dogfight ensued from which I broke away with Blue 3. Blue 3 and myself (Blue 1) then encountered about thirty Do 215s [sic] protected by many Me 109s over Dungeness. I made a beam attack on the Do 215s, raking the leading aeroplanes – my bullets entered the fuselages of at least two E/A. I was then attacked by many Me 109s and after a dogfight broke away and returned to base. Return fire from 215s very concentrated indeed.

Flight Sergeant Jack Steere (younger brother of 19 Squadron's Flight Sergeant Harry Steere) and Sergeant Maurice Pocock also claimed damaged bombers. Pilot Officer Edgar Wilcox, though, was shot down and killed, his Spitfire crashing at Chickenden Farm, Staplehurst. The commander of 'A' Flight, Flight Lieutenant Forgrave Smith, a Canadian, was also shot down, baling out badly burned over New Romney. Both men were experienced pilots who had previously seen action, Wilcox being a veteran of the Dunkirk fighting.

At 18.25 hrs, east of Biggin Hill, Squadron Leader Ronald Kellett was leading the Poles of 303 Squadron in line astern and up-sun of the Do 17s and Me 109s withdrawing eastwards. Immediately the Hurricanes were sighted three Me 109s curved towards the RAF fighters. Kellett ordered Red Section to attack, opening fire himself on a 109 which 'swerved from side-to-side, and pulled up his nose in a steep climb endeavouring to escape but I saw my ammunition going into the E/A which finally burst into flames and, turning over, fell perpendicularly.'

Flying Officer Zdzislaw Henneberg:

> I was Yellow 1. I saw Red Section attacking three Me 109s and Squadron Leader Kellett's Me 109 in flames. I went up and my Section did not follow me. I attacked four Me 109s which were in search formation going SE. One E/A separated from its fellows and descended a little. I followed it, keeping an eye on the others. I started firing at 300 yards and E/A began smoking. I gave him two more bursts. He went into a vertical dive trailing thick black smoke. He fell into the sea six miles South of Newhaven.

Pilot Officer Miroslaw Feric:

> I was Yellow 2 ... Yellow Section met three Me 109s which did not see us as we had the sun behind us. The surprise was complete. Each of us took one E/A. A higher section of Me 109s tried to descend on us. I gave a short burst at my Me 109 from seventy yards at fuselage and engine. The engine caught fire. The pilot baled out and E/A crashed in flames.

Miraculously, Feric had brought the 109 down with just twenty rounds from each of his eight machine-guns. The 109 belonged to 3/LG 2, which crashed at Chathill Park Farm, Crowhurst. *Oberleutnant* von Perthes landed in telephone wires, grievously wounded – the allegation being made that the Poles had deliberately fired upon him while descending by parachute. The Poles' hatred of the Germans, who were occupying their homeland, was no secret, but in his diary Sergeant Kazimierz Wunsche, who also claimed a 109 destroyed in this action, wrote that the Poles circled the enemy pilot because 'They were protecting him, so nothing bad happened to him in the air' – which does seem rather unlikely. Whatever the truth of the matter, von Pertes died of his wounds a fortnight later.

Sergeants Stanislaw Karubin and Eugeniusz Szaposzinikow also claimed Me 109s destroyed, 303 Squadron landing back at Northolt without loss. There, the Poles would received the following signal from Air Vice-Marshal Park: 'Group Commander sends congratulations to 303 Squadron on their excellent fighting this afternoon when they destroyed four enemy aircraft without casualties to their own pilots or aircraft, which demonstrates good team-work and straight shooting'.

For 303 Squadron, it was just the start.

No.602 Squadron had come up from Westhampnett to patrol between Biggin Hill and Gravesend, intercepting '28 Ju 88s [*sic*] escorted by 60 Me 109s' at 18.25 hrs over Westerham. 'When attacked, the bombers turned South and crossed the coast between Beachy Head and Dungeness [ORB]'. Sergeant Jack Proctor subsequently claimed a 'Ju 88' destroyed, and Sergeant Douglas Elcome a 109, while Flying Officer Hugh Coverley and Pilot Officer Henry Moody each claimed 109s 'probably destroyed'. Elcome's Spitfire was hit by return fire over Dungeness, forcing the pilot to land at nearby Ford, fortunately unhurt.

As the one enemy force retired eastwards, the Spitfires of 603 Squadron, which had scrambled from Hornchurch just before it was bombed, also went into action at 18.25 hrs, over the Thames Estuary.

Pilot Officer 'Raz' Berry:

> As I had no oxygen, I had to leave the Squadron at 22,000ft and waited below in the sun for straggling enemy aircraft. After patrolling for thirty minutes I saw an Me 109 proceeding very fast. To overhaul him I had to press emergency boost – indicated speed 345. I caught the E/A off Shoeburyness. I opened fire at close range and fired all my ammunition until the E/A streamed with smoke and pancaked on the mud at Shoeburyness.

This Me 109 belonged to 3/JG 3, the pilot of which, *Oberleutnant* H. Rau, being captured.

Flying Officer Brian Carbury and Pilot Officer Basil Stapleton attacked another Me 109, also of 3/JG 3, which crashed and burned out near the Whalebone Lane Gunsite, Chadwell Heath; the pilot, *Oberleutnant* J. Loidolt, baled out but was reputedly attacked by members of the LDV upon landing. Carbury's Spitfire was shot-up in the action, the pilot returning safely to base.

Sergeant Jack Stokoe:

> as I was rather late, the formation took off without me. I took off alone, climbed into the sun and rejoined the formation which was circling at about 28,000ft. I observed two Me 109s above, and climbed after them in full fine pitch.
>
> The Me's kept close together in a steep spiral dive towards the sun. I pumped several bursts at the outside one from about 200 yards with little effect. I

closed to about fifty yards and fired two long bursts. Black smoke poured from his engine which appeared to catch fire, and eight or nine huge pieces of his fuselage were shot away. He spun steeply away and crashed inside the balloon barrage. I continued climbing after the other Me 109, and fired two long bursts from about 150 yards. White smoke came from his aircraft and he spiralled gently downwards. I broke away as I was out of ammunition and failed to see what happened to him.

The Me 109 Stokoe definitely shot down was another 3/JG 3 machine, in which *Oberleutnant* W. Binder was killed when the fighter crashed between Ann Street and Robert Street, Plumstead.

The reports of Berry and Stokoe are of particular interest, the former referring to the advantage of being able to use emergency boost in order to temporarily increase speed sufficiently to catch a 109, and the latter refers to being able to select 'full fine pitch', owing to the more efficient Constant Speed propeller.

Pilot Officer George 'Sheep' Gilroy, however, was shot down in flames; he baled out and the Spitfire crashed onto 14 Hereford Road, Wanstead, causing substantial damage to the dwelling but fortunately killing only a dog. Apparently, when Gilroy landed by parachute he was 'badly treated by Home Guard (lynching threatened) [ORB]', and later admitted to King George Hospital, Ilford.

Sadly, Flying Officer Robin Waterston, an auxiliary member of 603 Squadron, was shot down and killed in this combat; his Spitfire was seen by eyewitness in a spin over Woolwich, from which it went into a dive, crashing at Woolwich Common, near Repository Road. Both *Leutnant* Heinz Schnabel and *Oberleutnant* Lothar Kellar of 1/JG 3 claimed Spitfires destroyed – but who was responsible for which 603 Squadron casualty is impossible to say.

No.603 Squadron's pilots were not the only casualties suffered by the unit on this day: during the bombing of Hornchurch, 603 also lost LACs Baldie and Dickson, and AC1s Dickinson and Worthington all killed, and Sergeants Gillies and MacKenzie and AC1s Forrest, Adams and Ritchie were all wounded.

With the bombers' withdrawal things quietened down – and both 242 and 611 Squadrons returned to their 12 Group bases frustrated further still and having not found and engaged the enemy on account of having been called for too late. This, especially considering how eager Squadron Leader Bader was for action following 242's successful combat the previous day, did nothing to improve 12 Group's resentment of 11 Group – which was fast becoming a festering sore. Similarly, 10 Group's 609 Squadron, patrolling over Windsor, was not engaged.

The raids had been successful, but at Hornchurch, as the diary of the 'Fighting Fifty-Fourth' recorded: 'The unremitting efforts of the whole Station were rewarded when it could be announced that there would be "night flying as usual" [There were, in fact, five Blenheim sorties]. This spirit – and the determination which has "opened" Manston again – is going a long way towards deciding this war'.

Throughout the day, the German fighters had done an excellent job protecting the bombers, only four of which, three of II/KG 3 and one of 2/KG 76, were lost on the various raids on Biggin Hill and Hornchurch. This was primarily because while certain units provided close protection, others were able to roam, seeking out the RAF fighters and bringing them to battle. Indeed, even after the bombers retired, German fighters continued sweeping the Channel and south-east Kent. Consequently, several squadrons continued patrolling, including nine Hurricanes of 85 Squadron, which left Croydon at 19.17 hrs to patrol Hawkinge. While en route, the squadron was ordered to intercept Raid 18, AA fire over Dover drawing the defenders' attention to the presence of nine Me 109s. As the enemy aircraft passed the Hurricanes on the left, 85 Squadron continued out to sea, as if unawares – then suddenly turned about and surprised them. Individual combats ensued over the Kentish coast, Pilot Officer Allard DFM claiming a 109 destroyed which 'crashed near Folkestone, either on land or just in the sea'. Flying Officer Woods-Scawen attacked a 109 from astern, which 'went down on fire with wing tank burning'. Pilot Officer Lewis fired at another which went down in a steep dive billowing black smoke. Flying Officer Gowers blew a large section of wing off another 109, which streamed petrol and last seen diving, 'in flames'.

After this action, 85 Squadron returned to Croydon having suffered no loss.

That evening saw another fiery spectacle when Me 109s destroyed fourteen of Dover's eighteen 'Blimps', bringing the day-fighting to a close.

The point has previously been emphasised that replacement aircraft were not an issue (and on this day Fighter Command lost forty fighters either destroyed or damaged) – but pilots were. Nonetheless, 54 Squadron reported having been strengthened throughout August by the arrival of 'sixteen new pilots'. Now these pilots, like 603 Squadron's 'new boys', may have lacked combat experience – but they were trained fighter pilots, and with luck would survive long enough to learn. The fighting, however, was increasingly fierce, so the odds of survival were far from even.

Generalfeldmarschall Kesselring had resumed heavy attacks on 24 August 1940, and excepting raids of Southampton and Portsmouth on that day and the 26th, and Luton four days later, all other raids between 24–31 August 1940 were firmly directed at RAF airfields. Eleven out of fifteen such attacks had been mounted against airfields in 11 Group – and the strategy was working. Manston remained a mess, and Kenley and Biggin Hill sector stations were both operating at reduced capacity. On this last day of August 1940, the pilots of nine single-engine RAF fighters had been killed – the largest number in a single day since 18 August 1940 (ten). The month had certainly seen some big numbers: seventeen killed on the 15th, twenty-five on 11th – the highest number on any day throughout the entire battle – and fourteen on the 8th. In total, throughout the month, Fighter Command had lost 108 pilots of single-engine fighters.

No.85 Squadron's CO, Squadron Leader Peter Townsend, wounded and in hospital having been shot down earlier in the day, commented: 'By the end of August 1940, the Luftwaffe, by sheer weight of numbers – four to one in their favour – was wearing us down: we were weary beyond caring, our nerves tautened to breaking point.'

As for the Luftwaffe, 116 RAF fighters had been claimed destroyed on this day, a somewhat exaggerated figure, against only 39 Luftwaffe aircraft lost (of which 38 were fighters). Although RAF pilots claimed ninety-four German aircraft destroyed, the fact was that both sides had lost virtually the same number – although all of the RAF's forty destroyed or damaged aircraft were fighters. As we have seen, Fighter Command lost nine pilots killed on 31 August 1940 – whereas twenty-two Luftwaffe fighter pilots had either been killed, reported missing or captured. Fighter Command, therefore, was actually doing well, despite how it may have felt at the time. Indeed, in what was becoming a battle of attrition, the Luftwaffe fighter force was falling behind. In August 1940, 230 Me 109s had been lost but the German aircraft factories only produced 173 new machines – an unsustainable ratio. Conversely, Fighter Command had lost 499 aircraft, and Lord Beaverbrook's factories delivered 476 – a nearly equal ratio.

At his Wissant HQ, *Generalmajor* 'Onkel' Theo Osterkamp, an ace of both world wars and the *Jagdfliegerführer*, was under no illusion as to how the Battle of Britain was really going – in spite of Luftwaffe Air Intelligence's optimistic reports. According the British writer Len Deighton (see Bibliography), concerned that the current rate of aircrew casualties was unsustainable, this remarkable airman and fighter leader reported accordingly to *Generalfeldmarschall* Erhard Milch, the Luftwaffe's Inspector General, who was currently flying himself around in his personal Fieseler Storch communications aircraft and visiting *Luftflotte* 2 units in the Pas-de-Calais. Osterkamp's report, Deighton claimed, was unavoidably critical of Göring – a risky strategy indeed – and Milch's reaction was to discipline the 'Alte Adler', reduce him in rank and threaten him with court-martial in the event of any repetition of such defeatist views. While no actual evidence appears to support this claim, Osterkamp, who had already drawn fire for questioning Göring's strategy in person, was undoubtedly fully aware that the Luftwaffe was unable to sustain the current rate of attrition.

At Hornchurch, however, 54 Squadron was certainly upbeat on this last day of the month:

After Dunkirk with its traumas and losses, it was suggested that a new 54 Squadron – Squadron in the real sense of the word – would arise before long to compare at least favourably with the old 'Fighting Fifty-Fourth'. The last days of August have seen the realisation of this and although most of the faces are new, 54 is a Squadron once again.

By night Bomber Command kept up the pressure on Berlin, Wellingtons raiding the Henschel aircraft factory, a gas works and marshalling yards, although bad weather prevented Hampdens bombing the BMW works and Templehof airfield, so an oil refinery at Magdeburg was hit instead. Whitleys successfully bombed an oil facility at Köln and a chemical factory at Leverkusen. Meanwhile, Blenheims targeted the heavy gun batteries around Cap Gris-Nez, Emden docks and the enemy airfields at Ypenburg and Bremerhaven. Coastal Command's 53 Squadron raided fuel tanks at Vlaadingen, losing one aircraft, and a Swordfish of 812 Squadron failed to return from attacking invasion barges congregated at Amsterdam; a 59 Squadron Blenheim disappeared during a raid on Cherbourg's oil depot.

Across the Channel, however, the Luftwaffe was hell bent upon giving the defenders no respite.

Sunday, 1 September 1940

During the night, just as Bomber Command had taken the war to Germany, *Luftflotte* 3 continued targeting the great west port of Liverpool. Indeed, bombers of LG 1, KG 27, KG 40, KG 51, KG 55, KGr 100, KGr 606 and KGr 806 attacked Liverpool and Birkenhead that night, the strategy being to compromise the dock's efficiency in unloading supplies received from overseas. Thanks to cloud obscuring the target, damage caused was slight. The pathfinding KGr 100's six He 111s were using the X-Verfahren radio-guided navigational aid, which the British still did not yet fully understand as the 'Battle of the Beams' continued.

The day itself dawned fine and sunny with the Luftwaffe flying extensive reconnaissance sorties over the British Isles. Shortly after 10.00 hrs, RDF screens began showing the build-up of enemy aircraft and in anticipation of an impending attack, at 10.23 hrs, eleven 222 Squadron Spitfires scrambled from Rochford to patrol Manston; at 10.28 hrs ten of 616 left Hawkinge, from which forward airfield it was operating, to patrol base; at 1040 hrs, eight of 54 Squadron also left Rochford and prepared to intercept any raiders over northern Kent, and at 10.45 hrs, nine Hurricanes of 1 Squadron took-off to patrol between base and Maidstone. At the same time, two enemy formations estimated at '50+' each crossed the south-east Kent coast, one over Dover, the other slightly further north, over Deal. Nine minutes later, fifteen Spitfires of the freshly arrived 72 Squadron scrambled from Croydon, from where the unit was operating owing to Biggin Hill being badly damaged, 'to search for a number of bandits over Tunbridge Wells [ORB]'.

As the raiders had approached, at 10.37 hrs 616 Squadron, patrolling behind Dover at 15,000ft, were ordered to intercept 'Raid 14', this being the southernmost enemy force, but only seven of Squadron Leader Marcus Robinson's Spitfires remained together, three having somehow lost the squadron.

Climbing to 23,000ft, five miles west of Hawkinge, the handful of Spitfires attacked and broke up a formation of thirty I/JG 52 Me 109s. Squadron Leader Robinson and Pilot Officer John Brewster both claimed an Me 109 destroyed, and the latter also damaged two more. Flight Sergeant Fred Burnard claimed a probable and a damaged, Pilot Officer Ken Holden two damaged, and Flight Lieutenant Denys Gillam and Pilot Officer 'Buck' Casson probables. Only one Me 109, however, was actually lost during this skirmish, *Oberfeldwebel* P. Gerber being killed when his aircraft exploded and crashed at Burnt Oaks, Capel Farm, Orlestone. The Spitfires, though, were unable to attack the bombers because they were already too far inland, but 'When the enemy bombers saw their fighter formation broken up they returned to France [ORB]'.

The more northerly German force had proceeded towards the Thames Estuary, and at 11.00 hrs, before any bombs had fallen, the Spitfires of 222 Squadron were engaged by Me 109s over Manston; Pilot Officer John 'Chips' Carpenter:

> failed to engage one but while returning to base I came out of cloud in the middle of enemy fighters. Using cloud as cover I engaged one 109 fighter at 100 yards range. Immediately I opened fire the 109 burst into flames – I continued firing until my guns stopped due to a separated case. I then dived out of the engagement to a lower height from which position I noticed a plume of white smoke descending to the ground which I took to be the 109 … The engagement took place round Gravesend.

The squadron CO, Squadron Leader John Hill, 'was flying alone at about 17,000ft when I sighted two Me 109s making for France. I dived down behind the right-hand one and put a long burst into it from 100 yards … It burst into flames and I saw it diving towards the ground.' Pilot Officer Tim Vigors also claimed a 109 destroyed in the action, during which 222 Squadron suffered no loss.

The bombers, however, pressed on, attacking the docks at Tilbury, where the Harland and Wolff shipyard, railway station and various buildings were damaged. Hornchurch was also bombed, but the damage was slight, possibly, according to 54 Squadron, having been 'diverted by intense AA fire'. The Spitfires were to have 'little contact with the enemy', although Pilot Officer Colin Gray, another ace from New Zealand, 'intercepted two vics of three Heinkel bombers with an escort of Me 109s. These were at a height of 15,000ft returning home in the vicinity of Maidstone.' Gray subsequently claimed a He 111 destroyed, which, when last seen, had 'both engines on fire and black smoke'. Like 222, 54 Squadron suffered no loss and returned to Hornchurch at 11.55 hrs.

Over Tunbridge Wells, 72 Squadron sighted the retiring enemy, a 'stern chase' developing between Maidstone and Beachy Head. Pilot Officer Douglas 'Snowy' Winter subsequently claimed a 'He 113' [*sic*] destroyed, Sergeant Basil Douthwaite a 109, and, over Gatwick at 11.05 hrs, Pilot Officer John 'Pancho'

Villa claimed a probable. Flying Officer Ronald Thomson, a New Zealander, was shot-up and very badly wounded. With no power, the pilot glided away from the action and prepared to crash-land near Leeds Castle. Too late, he realised that the field was strewn with anti-invasion obstacles, steel hawsers stretched tight across it. Unable to pull up or go round again, Thomson flew beneath the hawsers at 120 mph and eventually crashed into trees. Lucky to survive, Thomson was admitted to the military hospital at Leeds Castle. Less fortunate, though, was Pilot Officer Oswald St John Pigg, who was shot down and killed over Pluckley.

At 11.10 hrs, 'East of Tunbridge, South of Gravesend', 1 Squadron sighted a formation of fifteen German bombers flying south, in a wide formation. As Flight Lieutenant Harry Hillcoat led the Hurricanes to engage, Me 109s came down from high above and attacked in a high-speed diving pass – Flight Sergeant Fred Berry's Hurricane was hit, forcing the pilot to abandon the aircraft. Unfortunately, Berry's parachute failed to open and his body was found 'some distance', according to his Casualty File, away from the wreck of his fighter, which crashed at Stone Cross, south of Ashford. Flight Lieutenant Hillcoat, however, shot down *Leutnant* H. Strasser of 7/JG 53, who baled out over Winchelsea and was captured. Pilot Officer Peter Boot chased an Me 109 'out to sea and got in a long burst … it plunged into the sea about twelve miles from the French coast', and Me 109s destroyed were also claimed by Pilot Officers Colin Birch and Charles Chetham.

Among the escorting Me 109s were all of JG 53, II and III *Gruppen* engaging RAF fighters. On the way out, pilots of 7/JG 53 once more set fire to Dover's balloons, *Unteroffizier* Poschenrieder claiming two destroyed. At 11.30 hrs, this spectacular performance was spotted by Pilot Officer Sammy Allard, who was leading 85 Squadron, which had left Croydon at 11.05 hrs with initial orders to patrol base before being sent to intercept Raid 23 in the Hawkinge area. Allard climbed, attacking from the sun, damaging a 109 himself which he sent plunging into the sea ten miles off Cap Gris-Nez. Sergeant George Goodman's starboard guns jammed but using port guns only he shot pieces off a 109 which 'immediately started to fall over and over sideways after a sharp pull upwards [ORB]'. Goodman was forced to break away, however, as his own aircraft was hit by another 109, but he returned his damaged aircraft to Croydon and was unhurt.

Suddenly, as was so often the case, the sky was clear of aircraft – with little having been achieved by way of bombing. Afterwards, various Luftwaffe reconnaissance sorties were made of the Thames Estuary area, and, in anticipation of another raid, at 12.50 hrs 72 Squadron scrambled from Croydon to patrol Hawkinge at 15,000ft. By 13.30 hrs there were signs of a further raid assembling, so 253 Squadron was scrambled from Kenley at that time and also ordered to Dungeness. The Controller's instinct was correct: at 13.40 hrs the enemy, estimated at just '12+', came in over Dungeness, heading north-west, towards

Tunbridge Wells. Concurrently, 54 Squadron was sent from Hornchurch to cover Canterbury, and 85 Squadron left Croydon to intercept over Tunbridge Wells. The raid was substantially larger, however, than RDF predicted: over Dungeness, 72 Squadron sighted 'a large formation of bombers ... escorted by Me 109s and Me 110s [ORB]'.

The Spitfires attacked, but were unable to reach the bombers, which doggedly continued towards their objective. A running battle ensued between the opposing fighters, during which Flying Officer Thomas Elsdon engaged a circle of Me 110s ten miles south-east of Croydon but was in turn attacked by two Me 109s and became separated from his section. Having evaded the 109s, Elsdon resumed his attack on the 110s, firing a long burst at and flying through the circle: 'two of them just dropped out of formation and went down. An eyewitness on the ground [Sergeant Rolls] saw the machines falling and crash into the ground and confirmed they were from a circle of aircraft very high up and to the south-east of Croydon.' Certainly one Me 110 came down at the material time and place, a machine of 15/LG 1 which exploded with such violence at Hosey Wood, Brasted, that formal identification of the two crewmen, *Feldwebel* Martin Jäckel and *Flieger* Heinz Rösler, was impossible. Me 109 'probables' were claimed by Pilot Officer Robert Deacon Elliot and Flight Sergeant Jack Steere, one damaged by Flying Officer 'Pancho' Villa and two by Flight Lieutenant Ted Graham. The latter's Spitfire, however, was shot up by a 109 over Lympne, returning to Hornchurch with a damaged oil system, and the tail of Sergeant Norman Norfolk's Spitfire was damaged in combat with 109s off Dungeness, although he too returned safely to base.

At 13.55 hrs, five minutes after scrambling from Croydon, the hard-pressed and now leaderless Hurricane pilots of 85 Squadron sighted the Germans, estimated as '150–200 aircraft', 'approaching the Tunbridge Wells/Kenley area' at 15,000ft. No.85 Squadron, however, was at a great tactical disadvantage, being 5,000ft below the enemy and still climbing. The hapless Hurricanes' presence had not gone unnoticed by the fighter escort, which immediately pounced on the British fighters, attacking them, according to the squadron's combat report, 'continually'. Pilot Officer Sammy Allard managed to get through to attack a straggling Do 17, hitting both engines and setting one ablaze, the bomber, of 9/KG 76, also attacked by Sergeant Harold Howes, eventually crash-landed at Lydd while attempting to return home; three of the crew baled out and were captured, but the wireless operator was killed. Pilot Officer Charles English claimed a 'Do 215' [*sic*] destroyed, which 'dived, then circled down, finally pancaking in a field South of a canal running between Ham Street and Hythe, about midway between Ashford and Lydd. Two of the crew were seen to emerge' – this was, in fact, an Me 110 of 13/LG 1 which forced-landed at Bilsington, near Ham Street. Sergeant Walter Evans hit an Me 109, which issued white glycol vapour and dived away, but was unable to press home with that or a subsequent attack on an Me 110 because of counter-attacks by Me 109s. These successes, however, were not without loss.

Flying Officer Arthur Gowers was shot down by an Me 109 and baled out badly burnt, landing at Oxted. Sergeant Glendon Booth also fell victim to a 109 and baled out – but his parachute was alight; already suffering from burns, Booth was badly injured in a heavy landing (and lingered in hospital until eventually finding peace on 7 February 1941). Pilot Officer Albert Lewis DFC, a South African, was also shot-up over Kenley; unhurt, he returned safely to Croydon. Two pilots, however, were missing.

Flying Officer Patrick Woods-Scawen DFC, the elder of two brothers from Farnborough serving with Fighter Command, a veteran of the Fall of France, was shot down over Kenley and baled out. Although the crash-site of his Hurricane was located, there was no news of the pilot until his body was discovered, his parachute unopened, in the grounds of The Ivies, Kenley Lane, on 6 September 1940. Such was the chaos of the time, however, that Sergeant John Ellis, also shot down by an Me 109, was buried as an unknown airman at St Mary Cray – but in 1992, when his Hurricane was recovered from its crash-site at Chelsfield, near Sevenoaks, and more human remains were found, these were irrefutably identified as being those of Sergeant Ellis and appropriately buried at Brookwood Military Cemetery (this pilot, therefore, has two graves, and it was his family's wish that the original grave was not disturbed).

These were sad losses indeed, which effectively reduced 85 Squadron as a frontline unit: since 10 July 1940, the squadron had lost six pilots killed and five more wounded, including the CO, Squadron Leader Peter Townsend, and Sergeant Glendon Booth who would later die of wounds. In this particular combat, it was *Major* Adolf Galland and his JG 26, escorting elements of KG 76 to Kenley, which had hit 85 Squadron, claiming five Hurricanes destroyed. JG 26 would also claim four Spitfires during what proved to be an exceptionally successful afternoon, during which only one of Galland's men failed to return: *Oberleutnant* Josef 'Jupp' Bürschgens of 7/JG 26, who was apparently shot down by an Me 110 rear-gunner in a not uncommon instance of 'Friendly Fire'; the German pilot forced-landed near Rye and was captured.

At 14.00 hrs, 54 Squadron's Spitfires arrived over the Biggin Hill area but were kept away from the bombers by Me 109s; Pilot Officer Stanley Baker:

> I pulled up from the bombers at 28,000ft and saw an Me 109 over fifty yards away, below, to the left. I turned over on my back and, with a steep diving turn fired through roof of E/A as I turned. E/A dropped and I think the pilot was hit. This Me 109 had yellow wing tips.

Baker was credited with a 'probable', and Pilot Officer Colin Gray claimed one destroyed.

Another raid, confirmed as 100+ by the Observer Corps, had crossed the coast over Hythe at 13.50 hrs. On this occasion, the 11 Group Controller reacted remarkably slowly, especially considering that the airfields south of London were clearly threatened. At 14.00 hrs, 1 (RCAF) Squadron was scrambled from Northolt to intercept the first raid, which was about to bomb Biggin Hill, and concurrently, just in time, 79 Squadron hurriedly took-off from Biggin Hill, and 616 left Kenley to patrol base. At 14.05 hrs, 303 Squadron was ordered from Northolt to patrol base, and 501 Squadron scrambled from Gravesend to patrol between there and Maidstone.

RAF Station Biggin Hill ORB:

> A high-level bombing attack was carried out on the aerodrome. Bombs fell among the Camp buildings without doing much further damage, but shaking buildings and making them unsafe.
>
> One aircraft was destroyed, but the aerodrome remained serviceable. It was decided to disperse Sections in the vicinity of Keston at the cross-roads, between Croydon Road and Westerham Road, chiefly because of the damaged buildings which made it necessary to salvage all equipment and transfer it elsewhere. Practically no buildings were left in a safe condition after the series of raids, and the road running through the Camp was blocked by three large craters caused by 1,000 lb or 1,500 lb bombs. All main services and communications were destroyed.
>
> The AA Command School, Biggin Hill, being evacuated by the Army, this was taken over to accommodate squadron personnel and the Station Defence and Administrative personnel of Station HQ.

Minutes after taking off from Northolt, the Hurricanes of 1 (RCAF) Squadron intercepted Raid 29 over Biggin Hill at 14.15 hrs, initially attempting a head-on attack against the bombers, which did not work because the Hurricanes were still climbing, and so the Canadians acted largely independently. Flight Lieutenant Gordon McGregor claimed a 'Do 215' [sic] destroyed and another damaged, and Flying Officers Otto Peterson (an American volunteer), Beverly Christmas, and John Kerwin also claimed to have damaged bombers. Regarding the latter, Yellow 3, the squadron's Intelligence Patrol Report recorded:

> It has been reported by an independent eyewitness on the ground that he observed with his glasses Yellow 3 engage and shoot down an Me 110 in flames before being shot down himself, and baling out. This witness picked up Flying Officer Kerwin who was burned on the legs, arms and face';

Kerwin's Hurricane crashed at Shipbourne. Flying Officer Art Yuile's Hurricane was hit by the bombers' return fire and baled out, unhurt, over West Malling. Pilot Officer Eric Beardmore was also shot-up, but managed to land his badly damaged Hurricane safely at Northolt.

At 14.15 hrs, 253 Squadron, which had already lost two commanding officers the previous day, one killed, the other badly wounded, encountered 'some fifty Do 215s [*sic*] and He 111s escorted by 100 Me 110s, Me 109s and possibly He 113s [*sic*]' in the Maidstone area. Attacking from the sun, Flight Lieutenant William Cambridge, who, being the senior flight commander had assumed command of 253 Squadron, damaged an Me 110, and both Flight Lieutenant Jefferson Wedgwood and Pilot Officer John Greenwood damaged bombers. Pilot Officer John Clifton, however, was shot down and killed, his Hurricane crashing at Grave Lane, Staplehurst.

Having been scrambled from Kenley too late, at 14.00 hrs, the five Spitfires of 616 Squadron concentrated on climbing so that they could at least intercept the retiring enemy. At about 14.20 hrs, having led the small formation of fighters up-sun and 1,000ft higher than the enemy, Flight Lieutenant Denys Gillam led the attack on the withdrawing Biggin Hill raiders near Maidstone. Gillam and Sergeant James Hopewell successfully attacked the Dorniers, as did Pilot Officer 'Buck' Casson, whose Spitfire was 'hit by a cannon shell'. Somewhat optimistically, for no loss, 616 Squadron would be accredited with four 'Do 215s' destroyed.

Over East Grinstead, also at 14.20 hrs, Biggin Hill's 79 Squadron entered the fray, as the South African Flight Lieutenant Geoffrey Haysom reported:

Patrolled base 12–15,000ft – before reaching this height wave of bombers passed over from West to East about 4,000ft above. Bombs dropped West of base. E/A travelled East to Ashford, turned round and did another cut on base. Attempted quarter attack on extreme E/A (bomber) broke off owing to attack by 110. Evaded E/A. Bomber formation turned South almost devoid of fighter escort – attacked E/A on extreme right – fired one long burst from dead astern – no return fire observed – attacked from rear by 109 – broke off attack – result of attack not observed. Aircraft collapsed on landing. Aircraft shot-up from the rear.

Haysom was credited with two damaged bombers. Pilot Officer Paul Mayhew claimed a Dornier destroyed, and Pilot Officers Donald 'Dimsie' Stones DFC and George Peters both damaged bombers; Pilot Officer Douglas Clift claimed an Me 110 'probable'. Two of 79 Squadron's pilots were shot down: Pilot Officer Leofric Bryant-Fenn baled out, wounded in a leg, landing at Dunton Green, and similarly Pilot Officer Brian Noble also abandoned his Hurricane, landing by parachute at Marley Lake, Riverhead; such were his wounds that reconstructive plastic surgery was required by the 'Maestro', Sir Archibald McIndoe, at East Grinstead's unorthodox Burns Unit.

At 14.30 hrs, Kenley airfield was hit:

1430 hours: <u>duration</u>: One minute. About eight bombers escorted by fifty enemy fighters attacked Kenley with high and dive-bombing. Extent of damage, only one bomb exploded on RAF property North of 'T' Block causing damage to temporary huts. Two bombs fell in immediate vicinity of main gates; one bomb exploded east of temporary sick quarters, breaking windows and felling ceilings. Three bombs fell in Buxton Lane causing serious damage to temporary RAF living quarters.

Casualties: One army personnel dead; one RAF airman slightly wounded [ORB].

The final defending squadron to see action during this series of raids was 501 Squadron, engaging 'twenty-seven Me 110s over Tunbridge Wells. One Me 110 was damaged [ORB]'.

Only Biggin Hill had been substantially damaged, and although Kenley had been hit, bombs fell randomly at various locations in Kent unconnected with any actual targets. The withdrawal of these raids, although the defenders were not to know it, concluded *Luftflotte* 2's major operations on this day. Nonetheless, in order to maintain pressure, German fighters swept over the Dover Strait, so 11 Group remained alert.

Enemy fighter-bombers attacked the RDF Station at Dunkirk, near the North Foreland, and, at 16.00 hrs, the Coastal Command aerodrome at Detling:

Attacked by fifteen Me 109s and three bombers. Two bombs fell at the back of the Operations Room, damaging the Teleprinter Room. One wireless mast was brought down, and the Guardroom was machine-gunned. Flying operations were not affected. Casualties: one fatal, four injured.

Having taken-off from Hornchurch at 15.45 hrs to patrol Manston with 603 Squadron, at around 17.00 hrs, Sergeant Jack Stokoe was over Canterbury at 3,000ft 'and attacked a single Me 109'. A low-level tail-chase ensued across Kent until Stokoe shot down *Oberleutnant* Oskar Bauer of 9/JG 53, who was killed when his aircraft hit the ground, cartwheeled, and burst into flames at Chilham. Stokoe was the only member of 603 to sight and engage the enemy. III/JG 53 made their exit over Dover – where *Unteroffizier* Poschenrieder could not rest the temptation of the Dover balloon barrage and shot down two more.

Later, Detling was hit again:

Incendiaries and HEs dropped by E/A. Fires were started at the Officers' Mess and Dispersal Point, but were soon put out. An MT shed was hit. There were no casualties. Group [16 Group, Coastal Command] was informed that Detling would be unserviceable until 0600 hrs on the 2nd, when the aerodrome would be inspected.

This, however, was wasted effort on the Luftwaffe's part, like the earlier raid on Tilbury, which would have better been directed at RAF Honchurch.

During the day, 151 Squadron had flown several uneventful patrols from North Weald's satellite airfield of Stapleford Tawny and took-off at 17.55 hrs to rest and re-form at Digby in 12 Group – having lost seven pilots killed and eight more wounded in the fighting to date. Indeed, 151 Squadron had lost its CO, Squadron Leader Eric King, and was reduced to ten Hurricanes and twelve pilots. At 10.00 hrs, 46 Squadron had left Digby and flown to North Weald, to relieve 151 Squadron. 'A' Flight of 46 Squadron had been operating from Ternhill in Shropshire, the personnel of which were transported to Stapleford, while those of 'B' Flight arrived at Stapleford by road where they were joined by the squadron's Hurricanes, which flew in from North Weald. Conditions at Stapleford were found to be basic:

> The aerodrome was found to have a pronounced slope down towards the hangars, there were several ridges running across the 'drome and the surface was extremely rough. Aircraft were dispersed around a wood, which ran along one edge of the landing field, crews and equipment were housed in Hurricane and Bell tents, and marquees. There were two corrugated iron huts and several trenches for protection from blast. A small stream running through the wood was used by airmen for washing purposes [ORB].

There was relief too for 56 Squadron, which had so far lost five pilots killed and seven wounded, when 249 Squadron flew in from Boscombe Down early afternoon. In the case of both 46 and 249 Squadrons, it was necessary to exchange aircraft with 151 and 56 Squadrons respectively because the former squadrons' Hurricanes were fitted with HF radios while the latter used the newer VHF sets. No.249 Squadron's ground personnel, however, remained at Boscombe Down, to work with 56 Squadron's pilots and aircraft, while 249 Squadron's Hurricanes would be maintained at North Weald by the groundcrews of 56 Squadron.

> On arrival at North Weald the Squadron was met by the Station Commander [Wing Commander Victor Beamish DSO AFC] and Squadron Leader Cherry, the Sector Operations Officer [who] gave a short lecture to all pilots on code words etc in use in the Sector, and on the use of VHF radios ... the rest of the day was spent getting to know the groundcrews and NCOs [ORB].

In short order, both 46 and 249 Squadrons would be hotly engaged.

If the pre-war air power strategists, taking their lead from the Italian General Douhet, still believed that the bombing of a civilian population could turn the people against their own government and into an angry mob, they clearly needed to think again. Already the evidence confirmed that, notwithstanding the terror of bombing generated by the fates of Guernica, Warsaw and Rotterdam, British civilians could take it. Indeed, the novelist and playwright J.B. Priestley, paid tribute to the public in his 'Postscript' radio broadcast of this particular evening:

The true heroes and heroines of this war, whose courage, patience and good humour stand like a rock above the dark morass of treachery, cowardice and panic, are the ordinary British folk. Talk about giving courage and confidence … not only courage and confidence in the outcome of this war, but also faith in what we can all achieve after this war. Not only for ourselves but for all decent men and women throughout the world, who all await the hour when the dragons will fade from the sky.

Monday, 2 September 1940

With the weather fine, the 'dragons' of the Pas-de-Calais rose early and prepared to do battle once more over south-east England.

At 07.15 hrs, RDF stations indicated a heavy raid assembling. Fifteen minutes later two formations were milling about the Dover Straits and another was off the North Foreland. None of these formations made any effort to cross the coast. Although aware of the enemy, the 11 Group Operations Room had no idea at this point of these formations' composition, or what their objectives were – which is why, once the enemy were within visual range of the coast, the Observer Corps' reports were so important. Nonetheless, in anticipation of yet another airfield attack, at 06.50 hrs 249 Squadron had scrambled from North Weald to patrol Rochford; at 07.15 hrs, No.253 went up from Kenley to cover Hawkinge; at 07.28 hrs 603 Squadron left Hornchurch to patrol the Thames Estuary, and at 07.30 hrs 501 took-off from Gravesend and headed to Dungeness. No.54 Squadron scrambled from Rochford to patrol Chatham – just as the Germans eventually crossed the coast. Had the enemy done so immediately after assembling, instead of wasting time over the Channel, their targets may well have been reached before they were intercepted – but on this occasion the Germans' delay had enabled Air Vice-Marshal Park and his senior controller, Wing Commander Lord Willoughby de Broke, to prepare a pre-emptive strike. Five minutes after the Germans crossed the coast, 72 Squadron was scrambled from Croydon with orders to patrol Maidstone, and a few minutes later assistance was requested from 12 Group, Flight Lieutenant Wilf Clouston, a New Zealander and commander of 'B' Flight, leading 19 Squadron off from Fowlmere at 08.00 hrs to patrol Debden; again, however, the assistance had been called for too late. Two of the enemy formations came in over Dover and Folkestone, the other to the north, and all headed from the Thames Estuary. Unfortunately the cloudless dawn had turned hazy, with broken cloud at 3,000ft, rendering the Observer Corps impotent.

The German formation comprised Do 17s of *Hauptmann* Erich Rathmann's III/KG 3, escorted by Me 110s of *Hauptmann* Wilhelm Makrocki's I/ZG 26, and *Hauptmann* Ralph von Rettberg's IInd *Gruppe*, and Me 109s of I/JG 51 and I/JG 53, commanded by *Major* Albert Blumensaat. The raiders were crossing the coast in strength before separating into sub-formations, often difficult to track, and bound for multiple targets, a tactic that had caused confusion the previous day.

For Squadron Leader John Gandy's 249 Squadron, which had returned to North Weald the day before following its sojourn at Boscombe Down, the incoming raid was bigger than anything encountered by the squadron previously:

Squadron ordered to patrol Rochester at 15,000ft at 0650 hrs and, for the first time in its history, led by the Squadron Commander, intercepted a large enemy formation of twenty-thirty Do 215s [*sic*] escorted by approximately 100 Me 109s and Me 110s, approaching London from the SE. A beam attack was carried out on the bombers after which the Squadron was split up and a general each-man-for-himself fight ensued [ORB].

The interception was made at 08.00 hrs over the Thames Estuary and continued to Rochford. Flight Lieutenant Robert Barton, a Canadian, and Pilot Officer James Meaker of Blue Section managed to attack a Do 17 from astern which had broken formation. Barton reported:

a lot of return fire, some of which hit my aircraft. Pieces flew off the E/A and I noted what appeared to be a weight on a piece of wire ejected from the E/A, but this did not hit me. The E/A gradually lost height ... it crash-landed on Rochford aerodrome having first caught fire. An occupant baled out at 100ft but his parachute failed to open.

The dead man was *Unteroffizier* Karl Hilbrecht; the remainder of the crew, from 9/KG 3, were captured. So effective, however, were the German fighter escorts that 249 Squadron was unable to press home its attack on the bombers. In addition to Barton's Hurricane being hit by return fire from a bomber, three Hurricanes were shot down by fighters: Pilot Officer Richard Wynn crash-landed near Chartham with a bullet in his neck, and Pilot Officer Percival Burton, a South African, forced-landed at Meopham, unhurt; Pilot Officer Hugh Beazley, however, was shot down in flames, baling out over Gillingham, landing at Boxleywood, also unhurt. His victor's triumph was short-lived, though: *Oberfeldwebel* Kurt Rochel and his *Bordfunker*, *Unteroffizier* Willy Schöffler, of 5/ZG 26 was in due course badly shot up (probably by Sergeant Rolls of 72 Squadron, see subsequent combat) and ditched off The Nore – both enemy airmen were captured.

Also at 08.00 hrs, 54 Squadron was over Sheppey at 20,000ft when the enemy, which were being subjected to 'intense AA' fire, was sighted over Chatham. Squadron Leader 'Prof' Leathart astutely climbed 5,000ft higher and attacked a *Schwarm* of five Me 109s over the Chatham area but without result: 'I dived away and pulled up vertically under a second formation of five Me 109s, firing at the flank one with full deflection. He dropped vertically and exploded on hitting the ground South of Chatham.'

This was *Leutnant* Helmut Thörl of 1/JG 51 who baled out and was captured unhurt, his Me 109 crashing in flames near Leeds Castle.

Flying Officer Des McMullen claimed a 109 probably destroyed, which he left streaming 'glycol and oil smoke', and Pilot Officer Colin Gray hit another which 'burst into flames'; Flight Lieutenant George Gribble hit one which leaked glycol and was last seen 'spinning down'. 1/JG 51 also lost *Leutnant* Günther Ruttkowski in this clash, who was killed when his aircraft crashed at Womenswold, east of Barham – but which Spitfire pilot was responsible is impossible to say. Again, the fighter escorts had well protected their charges, with only Sergeant Robert Robbins managing to penetrate their protective screen to fire at a 'Do 215' [*sic*], shooting a piece of an engine cowling away. No.54 Squadron suffered no loss in this sharp action.

For all the good the German fighter screen had done, at 08.10 hrs this force dropped some fifty bombs around Rochester, which only caused damage to domestic property.

Around 08.00 hrs, 253 Squadron was at 20,000ft over Hawkinge, ordered to intercept Raid 49, when twenty-thirty bombers and twenty escorting Me 109s were sighted incoming 'ten miles South of Manston'. For once, the Hurricanes were 3,000ft higher than the enemy, so started a shallow dive towards the bombs before being attacked from above by unseen, high-flying, Me 109s. Sergeant James Metham was immediately shot down, by either *Hauptmann* Wolfgang Lippert or *Oberfeldwebel* Erich Kuhlmann, both of 3/JG 53; the Hurricane pilot baled out over Thanet, 'slightly wounded'. Pilot Officer Alec Trueman, however, dived to 6,000ft and 'turned towards Rochester aerodrome when he encountered and attacked an Me109 from the ear … and observed pieces breaking away from the tailplane and fuselage'; this was 253 Squadron's only combat claim throughout this interception.

To the west, over Maidstone, also at 08.00 hrs, 72 Squadron's Spitfires went into action against the other incoming formation; Sergeant William Rolls, Green 1:

> We saw the enemy approaching from ESE and Blue Section led the attack on the bombers while I followed above them. I saw Blue Section break away and the enemy was then turning to South as I approached. I saw one Me 110 leave the formation and dive onto the tail of a Spitfire and as no other Spitfire was near enough, I dived after it and came in at the Me 110 [probably Oberfeldwebel Kurt Rochel of 5/ZG 26, who had shot down Pilot Officer Hugh Beazley of 249 Squadron, see foregoing combat] from 15° above and astern from port. I opened fire at the 110's port engine and put about 640 rounds into it. It caught fire and appeared to fall away with part of the wing, and the machine went over on its back and then went down with flames from the port wing. I had opened fire from 200 yards but did not see any return fire. I dived down to the starboard side of it and saw seventeen Do 17s below me at about 12,000ft. I had one in my sights and fired all my rounds at it. The fuselage blew to pieces and then the engine caught fire … I went into a spin to avoid the Me 109s behind … I pulled out … Above

me I saw three parachutes drifting down and to my starboard I saw the Do 17 coming down in flames and crash into a wood NE of Maidstone. I went up to investigate the parachutes. I saw that one was empty, another appeared to be a sergeant-pilot with Mae West [Sergeant James Metham, 249 Squadron], and the other had no Mae West and I circled round him and he landed near a factory at Chatham.

Sergeant Rolls was mistaken; the second aircraft he had destroyed was actually another 2/ZG 26 Me 110 which crashed at White Horse Wood, Birling; the pilot, *Feldwebel* Karl Schütz was killed in the crash while his *Bordfunker*, *Unteroffizier* Herbert Stüwe (probably the German Rolls saw descending by parachute) was captured, wounded.

For no loss, 72 Squadron's pilots claimed 'three Do 17s and one Me 110 destroyed, and one Do 17 and one Me 110 damaged [ORB]'. As 72 Squadron attacked, the bombers had actually wheeled about, scattering bombs randomly around the rural areas of Maidstone and Canterbury. No.501 Squadron, however, reported bombs falling on the edge of Gravesend airfield at 07.50 hrs, causing 'no material damage', but 'three soldiers slightly injured'. The squadron's Hurricanes, fortunately, were already airborne but intercepted the enemy too late to prevent 'a few 40lb bombs being dropped across the lower part of the aerodrome [ORB]'. Sergeant James 'Ginger' Lacey DFM an Me 109 which crash-landed on the Hythe Ranges, the pilot, *Unteroffizier* Werner Karl being captured unhurt. Me 109s were also claimed destroyed by the Polish Pilot Officers Stanislaw Skalski (two) and Pilot Officer Hugh Adams; Flying Officer Stefan Witorzenc, another Pole, claimed a Do 17 destroyed; Sergeant Lacey also damaged a 'Do 215' [*sic*] and Sergeant Paul Farnes a 'He 113' [*sic*]. Both *Leutnant* Hans Riegel and *Oberfeldwebel* Kühlman of 3/JG 53 both failed to return from this mission – one of whom was undoubtedly the pilot of the 109 which crashed at Bridge Farm Field, Bilsington, but buried as an 'Unknown German Airman at Aylesford Cemetery. No.501 Squadron, however, did not escape unscathed: Sergeant William Henn was shot-up and wounded but made it safely back to Gravesend, and Pilot Officer Skalski was likewise shot down, suffering slight injuries when he forced-landed at Longport.

As the enemy withdrew, the Spitfires of 603 Squadron were patrolling at 25,000ft over the Channel off Dover, when the approaching Germans were sighted; Sergeant Jack Stokoe:

I became separated from my Squadron. Not contacting any E/A I heard Control say 'Gate to homebase at 15,000ft' [use emergency boost to return to Hornchurch at high speed]. I climbed to 17,000ft and observed a mass of enemy bombers flying South towards me at about 15,000ft. They were flying in irregular vics but packed very close. There must have been at least fifty Me 110 and Dorniers. I dived on the right of the formation, putting in two short bursts at about 100 yards range. I did not observe what happened then as my windscreen was hit and Perspex was scattered into my cockpit. I slid away under the formation and glanced at my instruments to see if the engine was alright. It seemed normal, so I climbed and attacked another Me 110 on the left of the formation, closing from 200 to 175 yards and firing several long bursts until my ammunition ran out. White smoke appeared from the port engine of the Me 110 and it was losing height towards the coast. I spiralled down to 1,000ft and headed for home base.

Many years later, Squadron Leader Jack Stokoe DFC recalled that: 'During the morning patrol my own aircraft was damaged by a cannon shell in the windscreen, and my hand was slightly cut by splinters.' On this occasion Stokoe was credited with damaging an Me 110 – it would turn out a busy and memorable day for him.

Flying Officer Brian Carbury and Pilot Officer 'Raz' Berry shared the destruction of an Me 109, and further claims for 109s destroyed were filed by Pilot Officer Richard Hillary and John Haig. No.603 Squadron suffered no loss.

Squadron Leader George Denholm:

603 Squadron had to learn quickly. We rapidly determined not to allow ourselves to be bounced. I therefore decided to fly on a reciprocal of the course provided by the ground controller, until at 15,000ft when the Squadron would turn about, climbing all the time. Flying in this way meant that we usually saw the enemy striking inland beneath us and were therefore better positioned to attack. We also ensured that pilots always flew in pairs, for mutual protection. After an action, though, the Squadron would come home individually, or in ones and twos at intervals of about two minutes. In addition to leading the Squadron in the air, my duties also included checking who was missing after each action, which I generally did an hour after the end of each patrol. In that time a call would often come in from a pilot who had baled out or landed elsewhere.

Shortly after 08.30 hrs, a retiring formation of German bombers dropped thirty bombs on the coastal airfield of Lympne, causing a few craters in the landing ground, but this was of no significance to Fighter Command. And so the enemy withdrew back across the Channel, having achieved comparatively little in terms of bomb damage. Again, the reinforcing 12 Group squadron, 19, had seen no action patrolling Debden.

For the next three hours, all was ominously quiet – until just before midday, when RDF once more indicated the assembly of another major raid over the French coast. From 12.05 hrs onwards, 11 Group began scrambling squadrons, which continued until 12.30 hrs, by which time six were patrolling airfields north of the Thames Estuary, including 12 Group's 19 Squadron, led by Squadron

Leader Phillip Pinkham AFC, which took-off at 12.25 hrs to patrol Duxford and Debden (as had Duxford's 310 Squadron, uneventfully, between 10.47 and 11.44 hrs). Five minutes previously a raid of 30 or 40+ had crossed the coast over Hythe, heading towards Ashford before steering for Chatham, and at 12.30 hrs 100+ flew over Dover and also set course for Chatham. Concurrently, 40+ more enemy aircraft appeared over the Thames Estuary and North Foreland, making for the Essex coast. This was clearly a huge attack aimed at overwhelming the defences, the bombers provided a substantial fighter escort of Me 110s from I and II/ZG 2, and Me 109s of II and III/JG 2, and III/JG 54.

Five of the airborne defending squadrons were sent forward to the Maidstone-Chatham-Rochford line, with, interestingly, 46 and 111 Squadrons ordered to co-join over Rochford and patrol in strength – and that was very much at the forefront of Air Vice-Marshal Park's mind: with the enemy approaching the Isle of Sheppey, six more squadrons were scrambled, to cover their bases while 43 flew from Tangmere to reinforce squadrons over Maidstone, as did 501 from Gravesend. Still, however, apart from an educated guess that the Germans' targets were airfields around the Thames Estuary, the enemy's precise intentions remained unknown.

At 12.20 hrs, ten Spitfires of 72 Squadron had scrambled from Croydon to patrol Hawkinge. At 12.50 hrs, according to Flight Lieutenant Ted Graham (Blue 1), 100+ 'Do 17s, Me 110 and Me 109' were sighted at 19,000ft over Deal:

> Red Section attacked from above and quarter, and I tried to follow but was intercepted by the Me 110s. One Me 110 overshot me and in taking evasive action he turned on his belly right into my sights. I gave him two bursts and he seemed to go away and down in a spiral turn. After a dogfight with twenty or thirty Me 110s, during which I was unable to draw a bead, I dived out of the battle and below me saw an E/A twin-engine aircraft spinning down. It crashed and burst into little pieces ten miles North of Dover. When I landed to rearm, Flight Sergeant Steere informed me that he had shot this aircraft down.

Graham was credited with a damaged Me 110.

Flight Sergeant Jack Steere, who was part of 'Tennis Squadron's' rearguard, reported having pursued an Me 110 that broke away to the left: 'I followed him down, firing and saw him crash and blow up, position between Dover and Canterbury, near Knowlton Station.' This aircraft, of 6/ZG 2, exploded at Venson's Farm, Eastry, killing *Feldwebel* Lorenz Beil and *Obergefreiter* Hans Oehl.

Flying Officer John 'Pancho' Villa also claimed an Me 110 probable, which he last saw 'going down fairly steeply with smoke pouring from one engine and the other stopped'. This was *Leutnant* Georg Schipper of 2/ZG 2, whose *Bordfunker*, *Gefreiter* Theo Schockenhoff, baled out unhurt and was captured at Alkham; the pilot remained with his aircraft and crash-landed at Hougham where he set fire to the 110 before his capture.

'Tennis Leader', Squadron Leader Anthony Collins, 72's CO, was shot-up, returning to Croydon slightly wounded, as was Pilot Officer Basil Douthwaite, who landed back at base unhurt. Sergeant Norman Norfolk was shot down, and crashed at Garrington Farm near Bekesebourne, where his Spitfire burned out, although the pilot survived unscathed.

As the Germans proceeded to their target, Squadron Leader 'Uncle' George Denholm had climbed 603 Squadron to 22,000ft below cloud and at about 12.50 hrs, five miles east of the Isle of Sheppey, the Spitfires were ordered into line astern and climbed to engage a *Schwarm* of Me 109s sighted 1,000ft above. Denholm hit a 109 which:

> dived and thick black smoke came from the engine in intermittent puffs. I left the E/A thirty or forty feet above the water, about ten miles from the French coast. We then passed a FW seaplane which was apparently scouting for pilots in the sea and the Me 109 then pulled up steeply and turned back over the seaplane. In the meantime I had broken off and made an attack on the seaplane, but found I had no more ammunition and returned home.

After 603's initial charge, the squadron became split up, pilots acting independently. Pilot Officer James Morton pursued a 109, opening fire from below at 300 yards, the German pilot immediately taking evasive action by turning steeply to the left before diving vertically. Morton 'got in a long burst and observed much white smoke … Pilot Officer Berry, who was in my vicinity reports having seen the aircraft dive vertically into the ground'. This 109 crashed at Mountain Street, Chilham, and there the pilot, *Oberleutnant* Ekkehard Schelcher of *Stab* III/JG 54, would remain, buried with the wreckage of his fighter, until 1977 when recovered by a Territorial Army unit.

Pilot Officer Richard Hillary claimed an Me 109 destroyed and another damaged, but only Flight Lieutenant Fred 'Rusty' Rushmer, the commander of 'B' Flight, managed to get through and attack the Do 17s. On breaking away and climbing, Rushmer 'immediately saw a Do 17 on fire, diving into the Thames Estuary'. As no record exists of a Do 17 perishing in such circumstances during this combat, however, it is more likely that Rushmer had actually witnessed the demise of 4/ZG 2's *Unteroffiziers* Hermann Deuker and Ewald Knapp, who failed to return from this mission and were presumed to have been shot down into the Thames Estuary.

No.603 Squadron's only casualty in this action was Pilot Officer John Haig, who was shot-up, causing his undercarriage to collapse on landing back at Hornchurch – the pilot was unhurt.

As the German force crossing in over Hythe flew west over the Thames Estuary, at 12.50 hrs the enemy was sighted by 111 Squadron, which identified the bombers as 'Twenty He 111s with fighter escort.' Flight Lieutenant Herbert Giddings led his section into a head-on attack on one big formation, and Flying

Officer Bowring, after which various individual combats occurred. The squadron shared in the destruction of a He 111 (although no such loss appears in German records), which Flight Lieutenant David Bruce reported seeing 'crash into the sea', and the pilots also claimed a shared probable; Sergeant Cyril Hampshire claimed an Me 110 probable, and Flight Lieutenant Bruce and Flying Officer Ben Bowring each a damaged one; Pilot Officers John Simpson and Vic Ekins claimed damaged He 111s, while Sergeant Ron Brown damaged an Me 109. While attacking a He 111, however, Pilot Officer Simpson was hit by a 109, damaging his sliding cockpit canopy and fuselage, and Flight Lieutenant Giddings was hit by return fire, landing his damaged Hurricane at Detling, and similarly Pilot Officer James Ritchie was shot-up and landed his damaged machine at Rochford – both pilots were unhurt. Sergeant William Dymond DFM, an ace of the Battles of France, Operation *Dynamo* and the Battle of Britain, failed to return and was never seen again – an experienced pilot whose loss Fighter Command could ill-afford.

By 13.05 hrs, 111 Squadron had disengaged, and both enemy formations were now able to attack their intended targets unhindered. Five minutes later, the first raid bombed Eastchurch airfield – causing great damage: a bomb dump storing 350 x 250lb bombs was hit and exploded when a delayed-action device went off. E1 Hangar was damaged by a blaze, administrative buildings and the station hospital were 'partially wrecked. The NAAFI was destroyed by fire and water mains cut and sewerage system broken. Most roads were hit. The teleprinter service was put out of action and most of the telephone communications cut. Five aircraft were damaged beyond repair [ORB].' Surprisingly, casualties were three killed and eight wounded – it could have been much worse.

After leading 111 Squadron's initial head-on attack, Flight Lieutenant Giddings had broken away and forced-landed his Hurricane, damaged by return fire, at Detling aerodrome. At 13.15 hrs, the airfield was hit by the second German force, Giddings being 'subjected to machine-gunning and bombing from the air after landing'. The pilot escaped injury but the 'C' Flight hangar was severely damaged, the Station Commander subsequently reporting the aerodrome as unserviceable until 16.30 hrs.

As the enemy formations wheeled about and headed home, the Hurricanes of 43 Squadron, up from Tangmere, sighted and engaged Me 109s over Maidstone at 13.10 hrs. The recently appointed South African CO, Squadron Leader Caesar Hull, led Green, Red and Yellow Sections down to attack the JG 2 fighters, which were several thousands of feet below; Sergeant George Jeffereys shot down *Unteroffizier* Glomb of 4/JG 2, whose aircraft crashed at Cale Hill Park, Little Chart, where the German was captured, and Flight Lieutenant Richard 'Dick' Reynell, an Australian, pursued *Unteroffizier* von Stein, of the same unit, out to sea, attacking him relentlessly and forcing the German to turn about and crash-land, severely wounded, West Hythe.

Meanwhile, Yellow 2 and Blue Section of 43 Squadron, which had joined up with the rest of 43 Squadron, sighted fifty Me 109s approaching the south-east from the Thames Estuary. Again, Squadron Leader Hull led the charge and the fighters clashed in a dogfight in which the Hurricanes were well outnumbered. Hull 'got in two bursts at two 109s', but made no claim, and Sergeant Charles Hurry fired a long burst at one which 'emitted a lot of black smoke'. Sergeant Jeffereys hit another which he saw 'stagger and fall over', considering it to be 'severely damaged'. Flying Officer Malcolm Carswell, a New Zealander, was shot down in the melee over Ashford, baling out so badly burned and wounded by cannon-shell shrapnel that he would never fly operationally again. Pilot Officer Reginald 'Du Viv' Du Vivier was shot up and crash-landed at Bell Corner, Old Romney, with leg wounds. No Hurricanes were claimed as destroyed by the Me 109 pilots, although *Oberleutnant* Oto Bertram, and *Oberfeldwebel* Werner Machold (2), both of 1/JG 2, all claimed 'Spitfires [*sic*]' at the material time in the area of 'New Romney'. Their claims were for 43 Squadron's Hurricanes, and were accurate: there was a third tragic casualty: Pilot Officer Charles 'Tony' Woods-Scawen was killed when his Hurricane crashed at Ivychurch. This was a grievous blow to the Woods-Scawen family, because the elder of the two brothers, Flying Officer Patrick Woods-Scawen of 85 Squadron, had been killed in action only the previous day (but still officially missing because his body had yet to be discovered near Kenley). In due course, the tragic brothers' father, Mr Phillip Woods-Scawen, received his sons' DFCs from a grateful King, but these putty medals were little comfort for two young lives so nobly given.

Before the enemy retired, 253 Squadron was bounced by Me 109s over Rye. The Hurricanes, up from Kenley, made no combat claims but lost a single Hurricane over Rye, to the west of Dungeness and just over the East Sussex border. Pilot Officer David Bell-Salter was surprised and shot down. He had been flying without gloves so his hands were numb and he struggled to pull the release pin of his restraining Sutton harness. Eventually the pin was pulled and at 1,500ft he baled out but was battered by his damaged Hurricane's propwash and passed out. Having fortunately already deployed the parachute, the pilot recovered his senses just 100ft above the ground, horrified to discover that he was hanging upside down, tangled in his parachute's rigging lines; the life-saving silk canopy was badly torn and he had fallen out of his parachute harness. Hitting the ground fast, the pilot was fortunate indeed to survive the fall, albeit with both shoulders dislocated, crushed vertebrae, a broken knee and a smashed right heel.

The enemy withdrew back to France, by way of the Thames Estuary and Dungeness, and things went quiet again – for a while. Again, with the action further south than Duxford and Debden, 12 Group's 19 Squadron saw no action. Successful though these two raids were, though, both of which were carefully planned and perfectly executed, with no bombers being recorded lost, the effort and outcome remains questionable: both Eastchurch and Detling belonged not to Fighter Command but to 16 Group Coastal Command. Nonetheless, if the dual intention was to destroy 11 Group in the air and on the ground, the German fighters were getting results through sheer weight of numbers.

For both sides, there was little respite: by 15.45 hrs, RDF screens were busily indicating the build up of another heavy attack. Ten minutes later, 249 Squadron scrambled from North Weald to patrol Rochford, and 72 from Hawkinge to patrol Dungeness. At 16.00 hrs, 222 Squadron left Hornchurch to patrol Canterbury, and four minutes later 603 Squadron from the same aerodrome to patrol base; at 16.15 hrs, from Kenley, 253 Squadron was sent forward to patrol Maidstone, and concurrently 616 Squadron scrambled to patrol base. Assistance must also have been requested from 12 Group, with attacks on aerodromes north of the Thames in mind, and at 16.15 hrs, 242 Squadron scrambled from Duxford, having flown there from Coltishall that morning so as to be closer to the action, took off to 'Patrol London area' (at 16.50 hrs, 19 Squadron would scramble from nearby Fowlmere to once more patrol Duxford and Debden).

At 16.15 hrs, three German formations crossed the Kentish coast between Dungeness and the North Foreland. The southernmost was bound for Hornchurch; the middle, which came in over Deal, headed towards Rochester, and the northernmost made for Eastchurch.

As the Hornchurch raid approached Dungeness, the Spitfires of 72 Squadron, having been ordered to patrol too low at Angels 10, sighted the incoming raid, comprising Do 17s of KG 76, the Me 110s ZG 26 in *Geschwader* strength, and Me 109s. The Spitfires engaged the escorting Me 110s from astern and the beam, claiming four of the *Zerstörers* damaged, but the CO, Squadron Leader Ron Lees, an Australian attached to 72 as supernumerary, was shot-up and crash-landed back at Hawkinge, wounded.

Information regarding 501 Squadron's involvement in this action, as the raid headed inland, is scant, and, indeed, contradictory. According to the ORB (Form 541) the squadron took-off from Gravesend at 16.30 hrs on an 'Active ops patrol'; the Form 540 states that 'PM. A further engagement took place in the vicinity of Ashford. Most pilots engaged superior forces of the enemy' – but where, or at what time, is unrecorded. Those pilots which scrambled at 16.30 hrs returned to base between 17.00 hrs and 17.10 hrs, and the five who took-off at 16.40 hrs were back between 17.50 and 18.00 hrs. According to certain secondary sources, the squadron went into action at 16.30 hrs over Dungeness, which is inconsistent with both Forms 540 and 541. According to the Form 541, Sergeant Hugh Adams 'Destroyed E/A', but no other details are given, while the 540 states that the squadron recorded four confirmed victories after the engagement, but no details of the pilots involved are provided. According to a secondary source (Foreman, see bibliography) the successful pilots were Pilot Officer Gibson, Flight Sergeant Morfill and Sergeants Lacey and Farnes (no mention of Adams), but no combat reports survive.

The Form 541 also records that 'Pilot Officer Price', who had scrambled at 16.30 hrs, was 'Missing, E/A'. This refers to Pilot Officer Arthur Rose-Price (the brother of actor Dennis Price, who in 1940 was serving in the RA, and son of Brigadier-General Thomas Price), a former flying instructor, recently converted to Hurricanes, who had only joined 501 Squadron that morning, making his first operational patrol, in company with Sergeant Paul Farnes, between 13.15 and 13.50 hrs the same day. Following the late afternoon's action, Rose-Price was never heard of again, so is assumed to have been shot down over the Channel – suggesting that the combats involving 501 took place between Ashford and Dungeness. Sergeant Adams is also believed to have been shot down in the action, coming down south of Ashford, fortunately unhurt. (All of this, of course, perfectly illustrates the difficulties of forensically reconstructing certain air battles given conflicting information – even in official records.)

In 1989, Air Vice-Marshal Harry Hogan, 501 Squadron's CO throughout the Battle of Britain, recalled that:

> Operational training had to be cut significantly to provide a flow of replacement pilots from the OTUs. Some had very few flying hours on single-engine fighters, usually around ten. We were committed with operations and so it was difficult or impossible for us to offer them extra training before sending them up. Some replacements didn't last long. Rose-Price I particularly recall because, having arrived to join us at Gravesend on the day he was reported missing, his suitcase remained in his car – no time even to unpack.

At 16.30 hrs, Flight Lieutenant Andrew Robinson was leading 222 Squadron towards Maidstone when, as he reported, the Spitfires were:

> broken up by friendly fighters. Sergeant Ramshaw and I climbed to 25,000ft and saw the E/A below us. I dived on the tail of a stray 109 and after a short burst the aircraft caught fire. We were now almost over Hornchurch and I engaged a 110. I fired a long burst in a deflection attack and stopped the rear gun. At this moment I was myself attacked by an unseen aircraft which punctured my petrol tank and stopped my engine. I was shot in the leg and forced-landed at Hornchurch.

Sergeant Sidney Baxter claimed an Me 110 probable and another damaged, and a Do 17 damaged in this action which occurred between Maidstone and Gravesend. (In addition to Robinson being shot-up, two other 222 Squadron Spitfires were damaged but no details survive.)

Between 16.20 and 16.25 hrs, 1 Squadron took off from Northolt to patrol base, led by Flight Lieutenant Bryan Hillcoat, and (reportedly at 16.45 hrs, although in reality probably a few minutes later) noted AA fire bursting over London at 18,000ft. The enemy was heading south-east, so the Hurricanes followed, still climbing. Shortly before reaching the coast, Hillcoat saw a 'bomber formation well over the sea', covered by 'many fighter formations'. Hillcoat climbed to 20,000ft and attacked a formation of Me 109s 1,000ft lower, firing at one enemy fighter which poured glycol from a radiator: 'It went down in a shallow dive about ten miles north of Dungeness, near Ashford. About a dozen Me 109s were manoeuvring to get on my tail, so I dived to ground-level and made my way back home.' The 109 shot down by Hillcoat belonged to 8/JG 54, the pilot, *Unteroffizier* H. Ebers crash-landing, crossing a field, smashing through a hedge and ending up nose-down in a ditch; the pilot was captured unhurt.

Pilot Officer Charles Chetham of 1 Squadron claimed an Me 109 damaged in the exchange.

At Kenley, a local Tannoy failure led to neither Flight Lieutenant Denys Gillam or Sergeant James Hopewell of 616 Squadron hearing the order to patrol base, so this pair of Spitfires climbed, failed to locate the other four Spitfires involved but sighted enemy aircraft in the vicinity of Gravesend. Investigating, they found 'sixty to seventy Me 110s. There were a few Me 109s above, but they did not attack our fighters who went into line-astern to attack five Me 110s at the side of the formation.' These *Zerstörers* were from 7/ZG 26, and Gillam attacked the aircraft of *Feldwebel* Hermann Dibowski, whose *Bordfunker*, *Obergefreiter* Karl-Heinz Boock, returned fire. *Leutnant* Kanopka, however, went to assist, getting on Gillam's tail and hitting his engine. The Spitfire broke downwards, descending to 4,000ft when the Merlin burst into flame, forcing Gillam to bale out safely over Tonbridge. Sergeant Hopewell, who had already set a 110's starboard engine alight, 'emptied his ammunition' at Kanopka, but without 'definite' results. Meanwhile, the squadron's other four Spitfires patrolled Kenley uneventfully.

The Germans continued on their way, turning south when five miles south of North Weald, steered for and bombed RAF Hornchurch: 'Accurate AA fire, coupled with the attacks by our fighters, succeeded in disturbing the formation to such an extent that, of 100 bombs dropped, only six fell in the landing field, and no essential damage was caused [ORB].'

After the enemy had bombed, 54 Squadron engaged, at 17.00 hrs, near Hornchurch; Pilot Officer Eric Edsall:

Yellow Section took off at climbed to 18,000ft. We arrived slightly behind the enemy formation which was going back home North of Thameshaven. There was a straggling Do 215 [*sic*] with quite a number of Me 110s milling around it. Yellow Section dived on E/A and I myself attacked ... gave it a burst of about five seconds, and it did evasive action. I followed it, gave it another short burst, and E/A flew straight and level, full throttle, home. I followed it and gave it the rest of my ammunition at 75 yards range. The rear gunner was blown right away. Huge pieces of the E/A fell in all directions. It was badly damaged and heading for the ground over Chatham. I was then attacked by a 110 and took evasive action, having no more ammunition.

Squadron Leader James 'Prof' Leathart DSO made no actual claim, but was clearly a brave man indeed:

> I was caught at a disadvantage about 4/5,000ft below two squadrons of Me 109s. I decided that the best thing would be to act as a decoy. I harassed them and weaved among them and ended up by getting them about twenty miles away from the aerodrome, North of Rochford.

Sergeant Robert Robbins claimed a Do 17 damaged, and an Me 109 destroyed, while Pilot Officer Desmond McMullen claimed a Do 17, although none appear to have actually crashed.

No.603 Squadron was also up over their Hornchurch base, having climbed to 23,000ft, and saw 'a large solid triangle of about fifty bombers and at least fifty fighters, loose and in vic, stepped up to 20,000ft. The squadron dived to attack and a dogfight ensued.' Pilot Officer Richard Hillary subsequently claimed an Me 109 probable, and Pilot Officer Dudley Stewart-Clarke a 110 probable. Sergeant Jack Stokoe, however, was shot down:

> On 2 September 1940, I was involved with two more interceptions, during the course of one of which I damaged two enemy aircraft but was myself shot down in flames – fortunately baling out. On that occasion, as I was attacking an enemy aircraft, I remember machine-gun bullets, or maybe cannon shells, hitting my Spitfire, followed by flames in the cockpit as the petrol tank exploded. I thought 'Christ! I've got to get out of here and *quick!*' I undid the straps and opened the hood, but this turned the flames into a blowtorch. I was not wearing gloves, as during our hasty scramble I had forgotten them, but had to put my hands back in the fire to invert the Spitfire so that I could drop out (no ejector seats in those days!). I remember seeing sheets of skin peeling off the backs of my hands before I fell out of the aeroplane. I was then concerned whether the parachute would function or whether it had been damaged by fire, but I pulled the ripcord and fortunately it opened perfectly.
>
> I landed in a field, but the Home Guard queried whether I was an enemy agent! A few choice words in English soon convinced them I was genuine, and thereafter I was rushed into the emergency hospital at Leeds Castle, suffering from shock and severe burns to my hands, neck and face.
>
> At the time, 603 Squadron was suffering casualties and the administration got pretty chaotic. For four days after baling out, although safe in hospital, I was officially posted Missing in Action! I was in hospital for six weeks before returning to operational duties on 22 October 1940.

Some of the Hornchurch raiders made their exit over the Essex coast and Thames Estuary, while most left via the south-east coast. As the Germans retired, bombs fell on Maidstone and around Ashford, possibly dropped by aircraft having not found their intended targets. The force which had crossed the coast over

Deal approached and attacked Rochester unmolested, at 16.50 hrs, damaging the drawing office at the Short Brothers' aircraft factory. The more northerly force had approached via the Thames Estuary, unmolested, and subjected Eastchurch to another devastating attack: 'by twelve enemy aircraft in waves of three, escorted by fighters. Eight large craters in landing ground, E3 Hangar completely wrecked. Further damage to roads [ORB].'

Such was the damage, in fact, that the Station HQ and Accounts Section were forced to abandon the airfield and move into alternative accommodation at Wymswold Warden, and Station Sick Quarters relocated to Eastchurch village. There was one man killed and four wounded. Again, however, successful though the attack was, and although Eastchurch was a base from which anti-invasion operations were being flown by Coastal Command, the enemy's effort would have been better directed against Hornchurch or North Weald, once more demonstrating a failure of Luftwaffe air intelligence.

As the Eastchurch raiders withdrew, they were engaged by 249 Squadron; Flight Lieutenant Denis Parnall, Red 2, the commander of 'A' Flight (and son of George Parnall, founder of the Bristol-based Parnall Aircraft Ltd) reported his combat occurring at 'about 1650 hrs', at '17,000ft' 'five miles South of Billericay':

> After Red 1 attacked the bombers, I saw two Me 110 1,000ft above and heading South … I immediately climbed and turned into the rear Me 110 and gave him a steady burst from ¾ below of about 5 seconds. He immediately turned to the right, through 180° and went into a vertical dive. At 1,000ft something in the machine blew up and Me 110 then span slowly into ground where it burst into flames by a wood near Billericay – I followed flight of aircraft to 200ft.

This Me 10, of *Stab* II/ZG 76, crashed at Frith Farm, Laindon Road, Billericay, killing Karl Wrede, the *Gruppe* Technical Officer and acting *Gruppe* Adjutant, and his *Bordfunker*, *Unteroffizier* Richard Kukawka (the latter having been wounded on 15 August 1940 and recently returned to operational flying).

Pilot Officer James Meaker and Sergeant Henry Davidson also claimed an Me 110 destroyed, and Pilot Officer George Barclay one damaged in the engagement; none were actually shot down, but two Me 110s of 4/ZG 76 and one of 5/ZG 76 returned to base damaged. No.249 Squadron suffered no loss in the action, which 'ended the Squadron's first day's experience of fighting against the intense German air offensive directed against the capital [ORB]'.

As these raids retired, another threat loomed large.

No.46 Squadron, having arrived at Stapleford from Digby and Ternhill the previous day, had patrolled uneventfully on the morning of 2 September 1940, and as this latest raid approached was patrolling between North Weald and the Thames Estuary. At 17.06 hrs, eight Spitfires took-off from Hawkinge with orders to patrol base – the squadrons second scramble in just over one hour. At 17.20 hrs, the Poles of 303 Squadron were ordered from Northolt to intercept the raid approaching Chatham, and simultaneously 257 Squadron left Martlesham to patrol East Mersea.

By this time, RDF indicated 20+ making for the North Foreland, and, acting as a diversion, various smaller plots appeared to-ing and fro-ing over the south-east coastline, one of which, at 17.35 hrs, bombed Folkestone Harbour. This was a lone aircraft which dropped an oil bomb on the harbour and a HE bomb near the Royal Pavilion Hotel.

No.72 Squadron climbed to 22,000ft and was searching for these south-easterly intruders when, at 17.30 hrs, AA fire was seen bursting south of Chatham. The Spitfires investigated and sighted the enemy. Sergeant Basil Douthwaite:

> we approached in a right-hand sweep on their up-sun side. We were ordered into line-astern. We approached the bombers from above and astern. As we dived down I saw at least five Me 109s in my mirror preparing to attack us. We carried out evasive tactics on approaching the bombers, and during one turn I saw one Me 109 chasing a Spitfire. I attacked him while turning from port and starboard, and saw black smoke pour from the region of his port radiator. He immediately turned South and I followed and attacked from dead-astern … I saw red flashes from the starboard side of his fuselage. I had very few rounds left and on expending these I broke off the attack and returned to Hawkinge. One bullet had entered the leading edge of my tail fin from in front, my sliding hood was shattered. These bullets were presumably fired by the 109 as I was not attacked by any other aircraft.

As 72 Squadron had climbed to attack the forty Me 109s sighted travelling east, the enemy fighters moved into a circular formation.

Pilot Officer Ernest Males:

> I … climbed into the sun and came down on a 109 from 2,000ft above. He dived away for the coast and I had difficulty in keeping up with him from 15,000ft to sea-level. I fired several bursts and used all my ammunition while we were flying South at fifty feet above the sea. White smoke came from underneath the engine and three large pieces fell off and after five minutes he dived into the sea about three miles from the French coast. There was no sign of the pilot or wreckage. The aircraft was travelling at about 200 mph when he went in. The Me 109 was painted in a green and grey mottled camouflage. I returned to forward base, flying due North to Dover.

These were 72 Squadron's only claims in this action, in which Squadron Leader Anthony Collins, the CO, was shot-up and wounded for the second time this day, returning his damaged Spitfire to Hawkinge.

At the same time as 72 Squadron engaged, 17.30 hrs, 46 Squadron sighted the enemy formation, comprising Do 17s, Me 110s and Me 109s, flying north-west in the 'vicinity of Eastchurch'. Pilot Officer Charles Ambrose:

engaged a 109 which dived towards ground. Some tracer was fired at me from astern but was avoided. On second burst glycol was seen to pour from the enemy's radiator. He slowed up, fire was continued until his speed dropped to approx. 100 mph when he glided through HT cables, tearing off hood, and was taken into custody on a ploughed field apparently uninjured, south-east of Herne Bay.

The German pilot was *Feldwebel* H. Verlings of 1/JG 52, who came down at Tile Lodge Farm, Hoath, near Westbere, Canterbury.

Sergeant Ernest Bloor also claimed a 109 destroyed over Eastchurch, and Flight Sergeant Eric Williams a damaged Do 17. Flight Lieutenant Alexander Rabagliati, commander of 'A' Flight, was shot-up, forced-landing near Sittingbourne, unhurt; sadly, 20-year-old former Cambridge scholar Pilot Officer John Bailey was shot down in what was the first engagement, dying of his wounds at RAF Detling.

The efforts of 72 and 46 Squadron were not enough to prevent Eastchurch being bombed yet again – although no record of the exact time or damage caused has survived.

At 17.45 hrs, 257 Squadron was patrolling off Ramsgate at 17,000ft when twelve Me 109s approached, one of which made to attack the Hurricanes.

Sergeant Reg Nutter:

> 257 Squadron was patrolling off North Foreland and I managed to get some good burst at an Me 109 which had swung in front of me while attempting to attack us from the rear. He immediately dived, streaming coolant, but I lost sight of him in the thick haze.

Having scrambled from Northolt, led on this occasion by the Canadian Flight Lieutenant Johnny Kent, at 17.50 hrs the Polish 303 Squadron was patrolling Ashford at 19,000ft with Sergeants Jan Rogowski, Green 1, and Josef Frantisek, a Czechoslovak, Green 2, flying as 'Tail End Charlies', weaving behind the squadron. Suddenly, Rogowski spotted nine Me 109s diving on the Hurricanes, out of the sun from 22,000ft, and immediately shouted a warning over the R/T while pulling up to meet the enemy head-on, and Frantisek engaged the two 109s closest to him. This frustrated the enemy's surprise attack, the 109s scattering and diving for the French coast. Being too far distant, Red and Blue Sections were unable to engage, but the leading sections of Green and Yellow Sections gave chase.

Ten miles from the French coast, Sergeant Rogowski attacked a 109 which he set on fire and watched crash into the sea (possibly *Leutnant* Rohwer of I/JG 3, although the circumstances of the crash are inconsistent with this pilot being rescued by the *Seenotdienst*, which he apparently was). Sergeant Frantisek chased a 109 which latched onto the tail of Pilot Officer Zdzislaw Henneberg but failed to hit the Hurricane. Frantisek – a real 'killer fighter' – soon sent Henneberg's assailant nose-first into the Channel. Oblivious, Henneberg was himself pursuing a 109 – perhaps too enthusiastically, given that he was now eight miles inland of the French coast – leaving his target belching flame and smoke at 3,000ft, before being forced to break off and climb owing to heavy ground fire.

Pilot Officer Miroslaw Feric was also engaged over the French coast, hitting a 109 which turned onto its back and dived vertically. Feric continued the chase but his windscreen became covered in oil, so, blind, he pulled out of the dive at 10,000ft and upon opening his canopy hood discovered smoke pouring from his engine, which was running rough. Switching off, he began gliding towards England, escorted by Sergeant Rogowski. Making landfall near Dover, Feric successfully forced-landed near Eythorne:

> I selected a field and landed with undercarriage down, but it was too small and I ran into bushes. The undercarriage collapsed and the airscrew and left wing were smashed … Engine was still smoking. I took my papers and parachute out of the plane. Soldiers came up, after hesitation was convinced I was RAF. I was taken to a RA Mess, given supper and driven back to Northolt at midnight.

Given that Henneberg was wearing Polish Air Force, not RAF, uniform, and possessed very little English, the LDV's 'hesitation' was understandable.

Back at Northolt, the Poles claimed two Me 109s confirmed and two not so; apart from *Leutnant* Rohwer down in the sea, a 5/JG 3 Me 109 crashed at Marquise, damaged, as did one of 6/JG 3 at Sangatte.

This chase and action over France concluded the day's fighting. Despite well-planned attacks, the only airfield heavily damaged was Eastchurch, which was unconnected with Fighter Command, and, in truth, the enemy's apparent fixation with this target is somewhat difficult to understand. It is difficult to be exact regarding how many aircraft were lost or damaged on a given day, because despite what appears to have been an almost irrebuttable presumption that that Luftwaffe loss records are complete, that is, in fact, questionable. Substantially so – probably; complete – no. Nonetheless, from the records available there can be no doubt that the escorting German fighters did sterling work in protecting their charges, only one Do 17 being brought down over England and two returning home damaged. The fighters, in achieving this result, had suffered losses, however: fifteen Me 109s had been destroyed and six damaged, with three pilots killed and six wounded; six Me 110s had been destroyed, six more damaged, with seven crewmen killed, five wounded and five captured.

No.11 Group's Hurricane and Spitfire squadrons had lost thirteen aircraft destroyed and eighteen damaged, with four pilots killed and eleven wounded, one of them twice. Considering what the bombing had achieved, the balance was in Fighter Command's favour. Nonetheless, resources remained limited, requiring careful shepherding, and hence this signal from Air Vice-Marshal Park that evening to the exuberant and brave Poles of 303 Squadron at Northolt: 'The Group Commander appreciates the fine offensive spirit that carried two Polish pilots over the French coast in pursuit of the enemy today. This practice is not economical or sound now that there is such good shooting within sight of London.'

The AOC had a very fair point: fighting over water had already cost the lives of far too many pilots either missing or killed, and at least two were so far prisoners, having pursued the enemy to France.

Throughout the day, 19 and 242 Squadron had patrolled over Duxford and Debden, the former four times, which, frustrating though that was for the keen pilots of both squadrons, was exactly how the System was intended to work – 12 Group covering 11 Group's airfields north of the Thames while Air Vice-Marshal Park's squadrons were engaged further forward, and which still provided for 12 Group meeting its own defensive responsibilities to the Midlands and industrial North. The only action on this day occurring involving 12 Group fighters, in fact, was at 16.36 hrs when Red Section of 66 Squadron, up from Coltishall, intercepted and destroyed a 'He 111' over the North Sea, some six miles north-east of Smith's Knoll (although no He 111 is documented as lost in German records, a Do 18 failed to return from operations over the North Sea). For 66 'Clickety-Click' Squadron, however, the following day would bring great excitement – and action.

Elsewhere in 12 Group, at Fowlmere – the Duxford satellite (codename 'G1') – there was 'Great displeasure' when 19 Squadron was 'told that it was probable Squadron would be moved to Digby due to faulty functioning of cannon'. How Squadron Leader Phillip Pinkham and his exasperated pilots felt at this news was described by a certain Pilot Officer James Edgar Johnson – known universally as 'Johnnie' – who had joined 19 Squadron that day with Flying Officer Terence Forshaw and Sergeant Rufus Ward, all replacement pilots fresh from 7 OTU at Hawarden:

> a bunch of Spitfires arrived overhead in a loose but neat formation ... The pilots left their aircraft and were soon grouped around the tall figure of their Squadron Leader ... Already the two flight commanders were chalking the names of pilots for the next flight on a large blackboard. A wingless officer joined the group and said that Fighter Command had been on the blower. The pilots fell silent and listened intently. The speaker went on to say that the Squadron would probably be withdrawn from the battle until the faulty cannon were put right. They would move to an airfield further North and be replaced at Fowlmere by an eight-gun Squadron.
>
> The angry pilots loudly exclaimed their displeasure. Why couldn't they have their eight-gun fighters back? There were eight-gun fighters at Hawarden for training pupils? The young flying officer turned to me for confirmation and I nodded my head vigorously – glad to contribute something to this

bitter discourse. All right, send the blasted cannon Spitfires to Hawarden and exchange them for training Spitfires. Now the Squadron Leader, who had remained silent, stepped into the breach and soothed them with a promise that he would get onto the Station Commander at Duxford that very afternoon. Meanwhile, chaps, where was the tea?

Squadron Leader Pinkham, true to his word, reported to Wing Commander Woodhall:

In all of the engagements so far occurring it is considered that had the unit been equipped with eight-gun fighters it would have inflicted far more severe losses on the enemy. Furthermore, Captain Adams from the Ministry of Aircraft Production, who recently visited the unit to report on the guns, has stated that the guns would never function satisfactorily until they are mounted up-right, or possibly with a modification to the existing wing. It would take some months before this modification could be completed and it is considered most unfair that pilots should be expected to attack enemy formations of the size encountered at present with unreliable armament. It is most strongly urged that until the stoppages at present experienced have been eliminated this Squadron should re-equip with Browning-gun Spitfires. It is suggested that a way of doing this would be to allot the present cannon armed Spitfires to an OTU, and withdraw Browning-gun Spitfires from there for use in this Squadron.

Wing Commander Woodhall endorsed his subordinate's view, emphasising to 12 Group HQ that 19 Squadron's 'pilots have no confidence in their weapons' owing to 'frequency of stoppages' and because 'no tracer ammunition is used with cannon ... and pilots have no indication as to where their rounds are going, as they do with eight-gun Spitfires'.

The prospect of moving to an even quieter sector was a crushing blow to 19 Squadron.

For Coastal Command things continued with the usual round of operations, striking enemy shipping, reconnaissance and anti-submarine and convoy protection patrols. By day, adverse weather conditions led to a cancellation of a proposed North Sea operation by 2 Group's Blenheims. By night, Hampdens attacked oil installations and factories in Germany in addition to the U-boat bunkers at Lorient, on Brittany's Atlantic coast; one of 144 Squadron Hampden failed to return from Ludwigshaven, shot down by *Feldwebel* Paul Gildner of 3/NJG 1 over Maastricht. A 40 Squadron Blenheim crashed into the North Sea during either the outward bound flight to a target in north-west Germany or return trip, its crew all missing; two Whitleys ditched off the East Coast returning from attacking the Genoa power station, one crew taking to their dinghy and paddling ashore to Margate, the other being rescued off Harwich by HMS *Pintail*. The Wellington force attacked military supply depots hidden in the Black Forest, suffering no casualties.

Daily Home Intelligence Report:

Despite the activities of German raiders, all reports confirm the steadiness and fortitude of the population.

Tuesday, 3 September 1940

That this day was the first anniversary of Britain and France declaring war on Germany must undoubtedly have been on the minds of many people – a tumultuous year indeed. Poland, Norway, Denmark, the Netherlands, Belgium, Luxembourg and even that old empire and military power France had all fallen; Czechoslovakia had been under the Nazi yoke since the Munich Crisis on September 1938, and further afield Abyssinia had been annexed by fascist Italy since 1936. Italy had sided with Germany, as had Japan, which was making advances in the Far East, forming the Axis alliance. Stalin had signed a Non-Aggression Pact with Hitler, and America, Britain's only potential ally and great hope in the Western world, steadfastly clung to its insular policy of Isolationism from events in Europe. Only Britain held out, as Churchill wrote 'Alone'. Many historians have since argued that this was untrue, because Britain stood on the shoulders of the Empire and Commonwealth, and enjoyed the benefit of those countries' collective vast human, natural and military resources. Indeed that was so, in theory, but it was Britain alone that was being bombed by Germany and enduring the very real prospect of invasion. In that sense, then, Britain really was 'alone' – and yet the people did not falter or fail. This is not to say, though, that the British people were uncritical of the government or aspects of how war was being waged.

Daily Home Intelligence Report:

There are still reports in certain towns which have been vigorously bombed that there is no evidence of searchlight, AA, or fighter activity.
    In Luton, after a severe first raid, bombs fell before the warning, which has caused criticism of the Local Authorities...

Interestingly, considering the 'Bomber Barons' belief that the bombing of a civilian population would cause an uprising against their own leaders, the first evidence was beginning to appear in the reports that the reverse was actually point of fact:

there is the strongest feeling of satisfaction with the work of the RAF and AA defence, and for the first time reports indicate that really strong feelings against the raiders are appearing.

[In Swansea], although their defences and the siren system are the subject of criticism, morale remains high.

In Bradford people ask 'Why have we no Spitfires?'

[In Reading] Enthusiasm for the numerous Spitfire funds shows the temper of the people, in spite of the rise in cost of living, shortages of various commodities, and the ever present threat of air attacks.

Nationally it was summarised that, 'People today are more cheerful than any day since air-raid warnings became so frequent.'

And there was reason to be 'cheerful', thanks to Britain's combined defences and more offensive operations of Coastal and Bomber Commands: Britain, alone, was holding out.

By now, though, certain 11 Group squadrons were substantially depleted, requiring relief.

Since 10 July 1940, 54 Squadron had lost fifteen Spitfires destroyed and four damaged, five pilots killed and at least seven wounded, so on this day was relieved at Hornchurch by 41 Squadron, whose place at quieter Catterick was taken by 54. At the Debden satellite of Castle Camps, 85 Squadron could only muster one flight of six Hurricanes for operations, having lost fifteen Hurricanes, five pilots killed and five more wounded, one of whom would later die of his injuries. No.111 Squadron, which had operated from Debden since 24 August 1940, took 85's place in the line. In the fifteen days that 616 Squadron had operated from Kenley, eleven Spitfires had been destroyed and three damaged. Five pilots had been killed, six wounded and another captured. In response, the squadron had claimed ten enemy aircraft destroyed, three probably destroyed and six damaged; of that squadron 'bag', seven destroyed, two probables and three damaged were claimed by Flight Lieutenant Denys Gillam, who also deserves credit for really holding the battered squadron together and received a well-earned DFC for this outstanding effort. Such losses of both men and machines, however, meant that 616 Squadron too had ceased to exist as an effective fighting unit and was also withdrawn, changing places with 66 Squadron at Coltishall. No.616 Squadron's exhausted CO, Squadron Leader Marcus Robinson, was relieved of his command by the newly promoted Squadron Leader Howard 'Billy' Burton, formerly a flight commander on 66. Burton – the Cranwell Sword of Honour Winner in 1936 and a veteran of the Dunkirk fighting – was an exceptional young officer who now remained at Coltishall to rebuild his new command into a frontline squadron.

AC1 Bob Morris was an 18-year-old engine fitter on 66 Squadron:

When we of arrived at Kenley it was a shambles: there was hardly a building left standing. As we drove around the aerodrome to our assembly point, I saw a car park full of vehicles – but there was not one which hadn't been riddled by gunfire or shrapnel. There were shelters destroyed, buildings flattened. We knew we would be in for a hard time.

Margaret Woolrich had recently joined the WAAF, aged 18, completing her 'square bashing' in Harrogate before training as a plotter in a secret underground operation room at Leighton Buzzard, which all seemed 'very secret and exciting'. Having successfully completed the various exercises and tests involved. ACW2 Woolrich was also posted to Kenley:

I didn't know it then but we plotters were a very privileged group. Because we did shifts and our work was very secret, we were excused most parades and came in at odd times for meals – so we weren't terribly popular with the rest of the WAAF. Also, quite a lot of aristocratic people found themselves plotting. The unpopularity of the trade was pointed out fairly forcibly on my first night at Kenley.

I arrived in a raid during September 1940 and found a whole group of people under the table in the Mess Hall. Someone grabbed me and pulled me under the table where we all huddled. Eventually, one of them said 'What's your trade, luv?'

I said 'I'm a plotter.'

They said 'A *plotter*! Well, if you are one of them toffee-nosed tarts, you can get out of here!', and pushed me out to take my chances.

When I got there, the Ops Room had been bombed out recently and they were operating in a butcher's shop in Caterham. We would be bussed there. I don't know who it deceived because a whole group of people in uniform walking into a butcher's shop must have looked a bit suspicious. This was just an emergency ops room and after a few months we were moved into a much smarter one in an old rectory and that's where I spent the war.

It had been pointed out in our training that you only had to put an arrow in the wrong place and that could mean someone's life. So you did feel very bowed down by all this. One-person manned headphones connected to radar stations on the South Coast, which gave you plots coming in over the sea. That's where you picked up most of the enemy raids. The Observer Corps posts gave you plots from seeing or hearing enemy planes coming over. We wore earphones and when we heard the pilots we placed our arrows in the appropriate positions. It was terribly exciting. You felt you were at the hub of everything. The people you dealt with were in the newspapers every day. The pilots had the sort of status pop stars do today. You would get the list of pilots going off on an operation so you would know if you had a friend flying, but you wouldn't know until they'd all come back and been de-briefed whether anyone was missing, and then you'd find out who it was.

At RAF Hornchurch, Pilot Officer Richard Hillary had a problem. Six days previously he had been shot-up and crash-landed his Spitfire, L1021, XT-M, nicknamed 'Sredni Vashtar' after the murderous ferret in Hector Hugh Munro's famous short story, this aircraft since replaced with X4277. This replacement aircraft, however, had been damaged in a raid on the aerodrome, requiring a new cockpit canopy. The problem was that this would not slide freely – meaning that in a emergency, the pilot could be trapped within. Consequently, Hillary, with the help of several 'Erks', set-to with a file and oil 'in a fury of haste'. By the time dawn's early morning mist had evaporated, the offending hood was still stuck half-way. Hillary continued filing – and hoping that the Germans would be later than usual.

Apart from the odd enemy reconnaissance flight from 09.00 hrs, on 3 September 1940, the RDF screens and plotting tables in 11 Group were clear until 09.45 hrs – when various German formations over the Dover Straits and French coast indicated another threat. By 10.00 hrs, two German formations of fifty plus were headed for the Essex coast. Another was flying north over Le Touquet, while a fourth – doubtless fighter cover – was flying up and down, half way across the Straits. In anticipation of the sector stations north of the Thames being the enemy's intended targets, 11 Group had already scrambled seven squadrons: 222 was positioned between Hornchurch and Eastchurch; 46 was covering Rochford, 501 Detling; 603 Manston, and both 17 and 257 were up over the Essex coast, between the Crouch and Blackwater rivers. At 09.40 hrs, 12 Group having been requested, Flight Lieutenant Jerrard Jefferies led 310 (Czech) Squadron from Duxford to patrol North Weald at 20,000ft. At 10.15 hrs, while the raid was still off but approaching the Essex coast, 12 Group's 19 Squadron, led by Squadron Leader Pinkham AFC, scrambled from Fowlmere to patrol between Duxford and Debden, while 11 Group sent 1 Squadron to intercept over Maidstone and 54 to cover its Hornchurch base. This was a strong response (although arguably 19 Squadron would have benefited from scrambling earlier, with 310 Squadron).

The inbound raid was headed to North Weald, thirty Do 17s of II/KG 2 escorted by *Major* Adolf Galland's JG 26, which had been given a break from the previous day's operations, and Me 110s of ZG 2 and ZG 26.

First of the defenders to intercept was 603 Squadron, shortly after 10.00 hrs, off Manston and Margate: 'At 22,000ft … six Do 17s in vic at the same height and about twelve Me 109s; above this formation was a further formation of Me 109s.'

Pilot Officer Richard Hillary:

At about 12,000ft we came up through the clouds; I looked down and saw them spread out below me like layers of whipped cream. The sun was brilliant and made it difficult to see the next plane when turning. I was peering anxiously

ahead, for the Controller had warned us that at least fifty enemy fighters were
approaching very high. When we sighted them, nobody shouted, as I think
we all saw them at the same moment. They must have been 500–1,000ft
above and coming straight on like a swarm of locusts. I remember cursing
and going automatically into line astern; the next moment we were in among
them and it was every man for himself. As soon as they saw us they spread
out and dived, and the next ten minutes was a blur of twisting machines and
tracer bullets. One Me 109 went down in a sheet of flame on my right, and
a Spitfire hurtled past in a half roll; I was weaving and turning in a desperate
attempt to gain height, with the machine literally hanging on the airscrew.
Then, just below me and to my left, I saw what I had been praying for: a 109
climbing and away from the sun. I closed in to 200 yards and from slightly
one side gave him a two second burst. Fabric ripped off the wing and black
smoke poured from the engine, but he did not go down. Like a fool, I did not
break away, but put in a three-second burst. Red flames shot upwards and he
spiralled out of sight.

No.603 Squadron had been hit by II/JG 26, and now Hillary's Spitfire filled
the Revi gunsight of *Hauptmann* Erich Bode, the *Gruppe Kommandeur*. The
German thumbed the cannon button on his joystick, simultaneously squeezing
the machine-gun trigger – the Spitfire instantly erupted into flames, becoming
Bode's first aerial victory.

Pilot Officer Richard Hillary:

I felt a terrific explosion which knocked the control column from my hand,
and the whole machine quivered like a stricken animal. In a second, the
cockpit was a mass of flames; instinctively I reached up to open the hood. It
would not move. I tore off my straps and managed to force it back; but this
took time, and when I dropped back in the seat and reached for the stick in
an effort to turn the plane on its back, the heat was so intense that I could
feel myself going. I remember a second of sharp agony, thinking 'So this is it!'
and putting both hands to my eyes. Then I passed out.

Miraculously, considering his problematic sliding hood, Hillary was thrown
clear of his blazing Spitfire. In spite of horrendous burns, he managed to deploy
his parachute, drifting down into the Channel where he was fortunate to be
rescued by the Margate lifeboat.

Next, Bode shot down Pilot Officer Dudley Stewart-Clark, who was
also wounded, baling out over Creeksea Church, Burnham and admitted
to Chelmsford Hospital. Pilot Officers Peter Pease and James Caister both
claimed Me 109s destroyed in the engagement. Once more, the German fighters
were doing a good job of protecting the bombers, so it is surprising that the
603 Squadron Form 'F' (Fighter Command Combat Report) states that 'The

Squadron attacked the fighters, which they considered to be inferior to any they had encountered before.'

At 10.20 hrs, the Hurricanes of 257 Squadron reported the enemy over the sea, flying west towards the Thames Estuary – fifty bombers at 15,000ft with a hundred fighters above at 20,000ft. While Squadron Leader Hill Harkness was making his dispositions for an attack, the Hurricanes were attacked from astern by Me 110s of 8/ZG 26. Immediately, Sergeant Robert Fraser saw 'Yellow 3 go down in flames' and attacked and damaged an Me 110, 'a straggler from a formation of twenty', before receiving the attention of four other *Zerstörers*, forcing him to break away. Pilot Officer Kenneth Gundry claimed an Me 109 probably destroyed, but Hurricanes suffered badly: the Canadian Pilot Officer Camille Robespierre Bonseigneur was shot down and baled out but was killed when his parachute failed; it was Pilot Officer David Hunt seen in flames by Sergeant Fraser, who baled out over Margretting and was admitted to Chelmsford Hospital with severe burns. Pilot Officer Gundry's port tailplane was shot off by a burst of 20mm cannon fire, the pilot landing unhurt at Martlesham [ORB].

At 10.30 hrs, 17 Squadron was at 18,000ft over the Thames Estuary, and also saw the enemy approaching, flying west, the 100 fighters reportedly South of Colchester:

> Green Section, flying out of the sun, attacked a straggling Do 215 [*sic*] which had broken away from the formation, and was heading North towards Ipswich. Two stern and quarter attacks were made from the starboard side, Green 1 [Pilot Officer Harold Bird-Wilson] and Green 2 [Pilot Officer Ross] experiencing return fire. On the second attack No 2 did not fire, and as Green 3 [Sergeant Sewell] broke away from his second attack, the E/A was seen to go down in a vertical dive and one parachutist was seen to leave the machine. E/A crashed in the mud flats East of the reservoir North of Colchester, and exploded.

This was a 5/KG 2 Do 17Z-2, which actually crashed at Pyefleet Creek, Lagenhoe, killing three of the crew, while the 'parachutist', *Feldwebel* M. Kriegl, was captured.

In the ensuing fight, Flying Officer Count Manfred Czernin destroyed an Me 110 of 3/ZG 2, which was also attacked by Flight Lieutenant David Bayne and Pilot Officer Denis Wissler, crashing near Rayleigh. The two crewmen, *Obergefreiter* G. Winkler and *Gefreiter* O. Weiler, abandoned their aircraft and were captured. No.17 Squadron would claim a total of 'two Me 110s, two Do 215s [*sic*] destroyed and two Me 110 probable [ORB]'. The squadron suffered casualties, however.

Sergeant Desmond Fopp was shot down in flames, baling out badly burned near Brentwood and being admitted to the hospital there. Flying Officer David Hanson was 'seen to shoot down a Do 17 into the river Crouch [more likely a I/ZG 2 Me 110 reportedly abandoned off Herne Bay, as the only Do 17 lost during the whole raid was that claimed by Green Section], after which his aircraft crashed on Foulness Island. An observer reports that he 'tried to bale out [ORB]'; Hanson was 'missing, later reported killed'. The CO, Squadron Leader Anthony Miller, was shot-up by a 110 and forced-landed, unhurt, near North Weald, and Pilot Officer Wissler's Hurricane sustained a damaged radiator, forcing him to land, also unharmed, at Castle Camps.

Flight Lieutenant Jerrard Jefferies of 310 Squadron was leading his 'B' Flight and slightly ahead of the four Hurricanes of Flight Lieutenant Gordon Sinclair DFC's 'A' Flight when these pilots sighted the enemy approaching North Weald from the south-east. 'B' Flight attacked the bombers from astern while 'A' Flight, satisfied that no 109s lurked above and unseen, attacked the Me 110 escorts from out of the sun. According to the squadron's after-action report, 'afterwards a general dogfight ensued as the sky was black with enemy aircraft'. Sinclair set an Me 110 alight before attacking and setting a bomber on fire. Nonetheless, North Weald was hit, after which the raiders turned east. Jefferies then pursued and opened fire on an Me 110 which dived and exploded at Harlow. Pilot Officer Jaroslav Maly attacked another which reportedly crashed; Sergeant Bohumir Furst sent another down in flames which crashed 'south of Chelmsford', and Pilot Officer Emil Fechtner shot one down which crashed 'south of North Weald' (probably the same aircraft also claimed by Jefferies); Sergeant Josef Koukal hit a 110 which 'crashed immediately'. The squadron's only combat casualty was Sergeant Josef Kopriva who was shot-up and baled out, landing with burns to his hands (although according to the ORB, suffering only from shock).

Sergeant Reg Nutter of 257 Squadron was also over North Weald:

> While intercepting some bombers attacking North Weald, I foolishly allowed myself to watch the fall of their bombs on the aerodrome, instead of watching my tail. I was promptly pounced upon by an Me 110. Although my Hurricane had been quite badly shot up and leaked petrol all over me, and despite having received shrapnel wounds to my right side, I managed to make it back to Martlesham Heath.

RAF North Weald:

> The aerodrome was bombed by twenty-five to thirty Do 215's or 17, escorted about fifty Me 110s. 249 took off to intercept this raid, but was unable to gain sufficient height to engage the enemy as they had just landed, and were refuelling. Hangars 151 and 25 were set on fire: two Hurricanes were set on fire on the ground and one Blenheim fired in the hanger. The MT Section yard was badly damaged, several lorries were set on fire. There was some damage to living quarters; the old Operations Room housing The Intelligence Office was hit and partly destroyed. The Tannoy system panel was destroyed, and the

loud speaker warning system was rendered unserviceable. The new Operation Room received a direct hit on the roof but stood up to it, and no damage was done. However communication with the Observer Corps was severed, with the exception of Watford. HF relay system between receiver and transmitter was severed. The Main Stores was severely damaged. The aerodrome was not rendered unserviceable for day operations although there was many craters and delayed action bomb on south and south-western corners. One airman, and one civilian were killed; seven seriously wounded, and thirty received minor injuries [ORB].

At 10.20 hrs, 46 Squadron encountered the enemy formation, flying west two miles west of Southend. Leading the squadron was Flight Lieutenant Alexander Rabagliati, commander of 'A' Flight, who ordered his leading section to attack the bombers while the remainder of the squadron occupied the escorts. Attacking from the sun, Rabagliati damaged a 'Ju 88' [*sic*] but was forced to break off a second attack owing to the unwelcome attention of three Me 110s. Sub-Lieutenant John Carpenter had to break away from attacking a bomber and shake a 109 off his tail; the FAA pilot then saw and fired at an Me 110 flying east, which dived away, pursued by the Hurricane:

> He lost height and speed, I overshot him and turning saw the E/A land in a field with his undercarriage up and go half way through a hedge. I circled around, saw the crew get out, and as one appeared to be dragged out presumed he was wounded. A farm hand approached the crew and then ran across a field to a farm house. When I went down again to investigate two members of the crew waved and as I saw that they had offered no resistance to the farm hand I climbed up and identified the position as four of five miles South of Maldon, Essex.

Carpenter was unclear, however, regarding the type he had shot down, describing it as 'either a Do 215 [*sic*] or Me 110'. It was, in fact, one of the latter, of 6/ZG 26, the pilot being *Leutnant* Walther Manhart and whose *Bordfunker*, *Unteroffizier* Werner Drews, was seriously wounded.

Flying Officer Peter Lefevre claimed a 'Ju 88' [*sic*] destroyed, although his aircraft was badly damaged in the process, and 46 Squadron claimed six enemy aircraft damaged – but the action had not gone in the Hurricane pilots' favour. Sergeant Gerald Edworthy was shot down, his aircraft crashing and exploding at Redwood Creek; no trace of the pilot was ever found. Flying Officer Hugh Morgan-Gray was hit by a Dornier's return fire and baled out, wounded, over Canewden; Sergeant Ernest Bloor was also shot down and baled out slightly burned, his Hurricane crashing into the sea wall at Fambridge, and Flight Sergeant Eric Williams was shot-up and wounded, landing at Debden.

At 10.30 hrs, 12 Group's 19 Squadron went into action, as detailed by the squadron's Intelligence Report:

Eight aircraft of 19 Squadron were ordered to patrol between Duxford and Debden at 20,000ft. They were operating in pairs, two aircraft to each section. All aircraft were fitted with two cannon, except Green Leader's which had eight machine-guns. The weather was brilliantly fine, with excellent visibility. While climbing towards the patrol line, the Squadron Commander, who was flying as Blue Leader, was warned by the Sector Controller that enemy aircraft were approaching from the south-east; later he was told that they were over North Weald. On reaching 20,000ft he saw explosions and clouds of smoke from North Weald; two isolated bursts of AA fire indicated the position of the enemy aircraft. These were heading East at 20,000ft when sighted, and consisted of fifty to sixty enemy bombers in three groups and close box formation, starting directly astern of the bombers and stretching upwards and backwards through about 5,000ft were about 100 fighters, mainly Me 110s, all flying singly and turning, searching and weaving. Ahead of and above of the whole formation was a single fighter.

Our Squadron continued climbing on a course which would bring them up with this single aircraft and planned to attack it first. On approach, however, other fighters left the main group and Blue Leader led the Squadron into the attack on two of these, which turned towards them. He fired at the left hand one which went passed him and then turned to pursue it; having lost it he turned back and attacked another almost head-on. He then discovered that his guns had jammed; he had fired only ten rounds from each.

Blue 2 attacked the right-hand aircraft of the two and his starboard gun jammed. He was then attacked by two others but shook them off and fired at another until his port gun also stopped. He fired forty rounds from port and sixteen from starboard with gravity stoppages in each gun.

Green Leader (Flying Officer Haines), with the eight-gun aircraft attacked the leading fighter which dived towards the bombers for protection, so he turned and attacked two other fighters below him on his right. One of these dived away, and he opened fire on the other at about 250 yards range, giving it a very long burst. During this attack the enemy aircraft employed violent evasive action ending in a vertical dive. Green Leader followed it down towards the Thames but it eventually flattened out and flew towards Whitstable at a height of about 50ft, still taking evasive action. On nearing Whitstable, enemy aircraft turned towards the mouth of the Thames and flew straight and level. Green Leader, who had been following, now closed in again and fired the rest of his ammunition from 100 yards range. A piece of fabric came off the tail and the enemy aircraft dived into the water. Rounds fired 2,194. Green 2 stayed with Green Leader and prepared to attack the same enemy aircraft; when he saw it destroyed he returned to base without firing.

… Red Two [Sergeant H.A.C. Roden] fired at several enemy aircraft without result. He considers he was using too much deflection.

Yellow Leader [Sub-Lieutenant Blake] carried out a quarter attack from above on an enemy aircraft on the port side of the formation. He experienced no return fire and his attack ended as the enemy aircraft turned violently downwards. He could not follow it down as he had to take evasive action to avoid two Me 110s which attacked him. He fired thirty-three rounds from the port drum with a gravity stoppage and fourteen rounds from starboard with a deflector plate stoppage.

Yellow 2 [Pilot Officer W. Cunningham] attacked the same aircraft as Yellow Leader, but his guns jammed with gravity stoppages after firing only nine rounds from port and four from starboard. He saw this enemy aircraft go down with smoke issuing from it after Yellow Leader's attack ... There was return fire from some of the enemy aircraft but no hits were sustained by our fighters.

Flight Sergeant George 'Grumpy' Unwin was Red Leader:

we formed line astern and climbed into the sun in front of the bombers, intending to take on the fighters. My CO turned to attack and I then saw an Me 110 turn towards him. This machine was two–three miles ahead of the other enemy aircraft, apparently a look-out. Upon sighting me he turned away and I gave a very short deflection burst but missed. However, he then flew straight and I closed to 100ft and blew his port engine out. He still flew, so as there was no return fire I closed right in and gave him the rest of my port gun, as my starboard had stopped. His starboard engine fell out and the pilot baled out. Aircraft crashed North of Malden, I think near Battlesbridge. In any case, he crashed at the inland point of one of the rivers.

The Me 110 George destroyed was a machine of *Stab* I/ZG 2,, which crashed at Stowmaries; the pilot, *Oberleutnant* Messner, the *Gruppe* Technical Officer, and *Unteroffizier* Santoni, were both captured.

Although it suffered no casualties, for 19 Squadron the morning's action, which saw six of eight pilots suffer cannon stoppages, had been exasperating – and brought the vexing matter to a head.

Wing Commander Woodhall (who had personally flown cannon-armed Spitfire R6687 on 7 July 1940):

This further failure of 19 Squadron's cannons was unacceptable, so I got on the phone to 'LM' and urgently requested that the Squadron should have its eight-gun Spitfires back. The following afternoon the AOC-in-C, Air Chief Marshal 'Stuffy' Dowding himself, landed at Duxford without warning. I greeted him and he gruffly said 'I want to talk to the pilots of 19 Squadron', so I drove him over to Fowlmere. There he met Lane and the other pilots. He listened to their complaints almost in silence. Then I drove him back to his aircraft, which he was piloting personally. As he climbed into the aeroplane, he merely said 'You'll get your eight-gun Spitfires back.' 'Stuffy' was a man of few words, but he had listened to us all, asked a few pertinent questions then made his decision.

Air Chief Marshal Dowding is often said to have been a remote figure, largely remaining at his Bentley Priory HQ. The evidence, however, is contrary to this, because Dowding actually visited his squadrons when the need arose. In this case, his visit was warranted because overcoming the cannon problems was an important issue, to give the Spitfire parity with the Me 109's hard-hitting armament, and clearly that was irresolvable by 19 Squadron, which was consequently unable to operate at maximum efficiency. Replacing the troublesome Mk IBs with machine-gun-armed Mk IAs was the right decision in the heat of battle – and kept 19 Squadron at Duxford, potentially closer to the action that Digby: 'Squadron very pleased to hear from C-in-C that they were to be re-equipped with eight-gun machines in a day. No.611 Squadron from Digby came to Fowlmere and stood-by for 19 Squadron for the changeover [ORB].' For the rest of the day, Squadron Leader Pinkham's pilots collected their replacement Spitfires, which had been delivered to Duxford from various OTUs.

AC1 Fred Roberts:

These second-hand and well-worn Spitfires were delivered to Duxford by the first female pilots I had ever seen, members of the Air Transport Auxiliary (ATA). We armourers had been unable to resolve the cannon problems on the Squadron, and had taken a lot of stick over it, unfairly. We were glad to have machine-guns back!

Returning to the action over North Weald, 501 Squadron was patrolling Detling but only Sergeant Paul Farnes brought his guns to bear, damaging an Me 110 over North Weald at 10.35 hrs in what was considered 'a minor engagement [ORB]'.

At 10.15 hrs, when unclear whether the enemy's target was North Weald or Hornchurch, 54 Squadron had scrambled from the latter, and thirty minutes later the Spitfires were at 18,000ft above the aerodrome. Pilot Officers Colin Gray and Stanley Baker went for a 'mass of Me 110s', attacking one from above which, the latter reported, 'dived at the ground with glycol coming from one engine'; the 'probable' was equally shared between the two pilots. Only Pilot Officer Basil Stapleton managed to attack the Do 17s, one of which he claimed destroyed (although no such loss appears in German records). 54 suffered no loss in the exchange – it would be their last combat of this deployment to 11 Group: in the afternoon, the squadron left for Catterick.

With Hornchurch's Spitfire squadrons airborne, Blenheims of 25 Squadron had also hurried into the air – but became overtaken by tragedy. As has been shown on countless occasions, in the heat of battle aircraft identification was often poor. The Blenheim, however, with its glazed nose, was not dissimilar to the Ju 88 – and as none of that type were involved in this North Weald raid, it is likely that the 'Ju 88s' claimed by 46 Squadron were, sadly, Blenheims of 25 Squadron. The CO, Squadron Leader Wilfred Loxton, was attacked and damaged by a Hurricane but returned safely to base; Pilot Officer Ernest Cassidy also fell victim to a Hurricane, crash-landing at Hatfield, unhurt – but Pilot Officer Douglas Hogg was killed: 'Sergeant Powell, who was Pilot Officer

Hogg's rear-gunner, was instructed to jump by the pilot before he died. Powell crawled to the front, the pilot dead over his controls, returned aft and jumped. The machine crashed about a mile away from North Weald.'

Which Hurricanes were responsible is difficult to say – but not all of the 'Me 110s' reported crashed by 310 Squadron – which was in action over North Weald at the material time, can be verified with German aircraft on the ground.

As the enemy withdrew eastwards, the Spitfires of 222 Squadron were waiting over the Rochford area. Although Sergeant Ernest Scott claimed a 'Do 17' destroyed, this was actually the Me 110 of 1/ZG 2's *Staffelführer*, *Oberleutnant* Siegfried Gottschalt, which crashed into the sea off Reculver; the pilot and his *Bordfunker*, *Unteroffizier* Max Hoffman, both baled out and were rescued from the sea to become prisoners. The rest of 222 Squadron also engaged the fighter escorts, the South African Flying Officer Brian van Mentz, and Pilot Officer 'Chips' Carpenter and Tim Vigors all claiming Me 110s destroyed, while Squadron Leader John Hill and Sergeant Sidney Baxter claimed probables. Pilot Officer John Cutts, however, shot down an Me 109:

> I was climbing to regain the formation from about 4,000ft when at about 16,000ft I saw a number of Me 109s below me, heading East at about 12,000ft. I was about to attack these aircraft when I noticed an Me 109 straight ahead at a distance of fifty yards. As I noticed him he turned slightly to starboard and I gave him a short burst, after which his starboard wing broke away. I saw nothing further as I had been caught in his slipstream and was temporarily out of control. I then dived down and returned to base. This aircraft must have crashed in the mouth of the Estuary or just out at sea.

Cutts was right: this was the II/JG 26 *Gruppe* Adjutant, *Leutnant* Eckhardt Roch, who was reported missing.

The Hurricanes of 1 Squadron were also embroiled in the action over Kent, dealing with a diversionary fighter incursion south of the Thames.

Flying Officer Colin Birch:

> I was flying as the third member of Flight Lieutenant Hillcoat's Section. We were bounced by Me 109s with yellow-painted spiral motifs on their airscrew spinners. I stalled in a hefty 'g' turn, coming to at 8–10,000ft with no other aircraft in sight. I never saw either Flight Lieutenant Hillcoat or Pilot Officer Shaw ever again.

Pilot Officer Pat Hancock:

> After so long, all I can say is that at the time I was convinced that I saw Robert Shaw in his parachute, drifting seawards, land in the sea and float in his Mae West. I thought that he must have succumbed to the cold water quickly.

The squadron lost two pilots, both of whom were reported missing: Pilot Officer Robert Shaw and Flight Lieutenant Bryan Hillcoat. On 29 September 1940, PC 265 Whyman of the Kent County Constabulary would join civilian contractors of AV Nicholls to investigate the crash site of a British fighter at Park House, Chart Sutton. The aircraft wreckage, however, had been recovered by an RAF squad three days previously and identified as Hurricane P3782 – Pilot Officer Shaw's aircraft. Although there is no evidence confirming that the missing pilot remained buried at the site, local people marked it with a cross and planted a memorial garden (at which a commemorative service was held annually for many years).

No.1 Squadron made no combat claims in this engagement.

The Poles of 303 Squadron, having left Northolt at 10.28 hrs, were also patrolling over Kent. At 11.20 hrs the Hurricanes were bounced by Me 109s over Dungeness, resulting in a 'momentary contact [ORB]'. Sergeant Stefan Wojtowicz was shot-up and crash-landed, slightly wounded, near Tenterden, and Flying Officer Zdzislaw Henneberg's tail and wings were holed by machine-gun fire, although he was unhurt and returned safely to Northolt. It was a fleeting attack, lasting seconds, the remainder of the squadron having no contact and no combat claims were made.

Throughout this operation, visibility had been excellent and all RAF squadrons scrambled, intercepted. The problem was that half did so after North Weald had been bombed, and all involved acted independently, so the huge German fighter escort was at ease fending off these comparatively small individual squadron attacks – and, again, the German fighters had done an excellent job of protecting the bombers. Fifteen RAF fighters had been destroyed and thirteen pilots were either dead, missing or wounded; only one Do 17 was destroyed and the wreckage of just five German fighters littered the fields of Kent and Essex.

The North Weald raid represented the day's only major Luftwaffe effort, the afternoon seeing an unusual mix of fighter sweeps and feints, including over 100 enemy aircraft which crossed the Kentish coast between Dungeness and North Foreland. This raid, which appeared to be another attack on the sector stations north of the Thames, about-turned at Tilbury however, and according to the AHB narrative only West Malling was 'lightly bombed'. Twelve defending squadrons were scrambled but only two contacted the enemy.

At 14.15 hrs, nine Hurricanes of 303 Squadron left Northolt to patrol Maidstone and Dover, and:

> met many friendly fighters. Sergeant Frantiszek, Green 2, rearguard, descended from 22,000ft to investigate aircraft at 8,000ft, above cloud, and found Spitfires, and then below cloud saw a solitary He 113 [*sic*] over sea. He dived and closed to 100 yards firing two seconds into cockpit. E/A dived slowly and disappeared into sea mid-Channel from Dover [ORB].

Up at Rochford, Sergeant Ernest Scott of 222 Squadron was ordered to fly a damaged Spitfire to Hornchurch for repair. Having taken-off, Scott saw the rest of the squadron doing likewise and so climbed above the clouds to await and join them. Sighting the Spitfires in the distance, Scott caught them up:

> just in time to see one Me 109 about to make an attack on one of our aircraft, the height of which was approximately 8,000ft. I immediately made a steep turn and got on his tail, giving chase. He climbed to about 15,000ft. I climbed with engine full out and kept 500ft below him, but did not get any nearer than 600 yards. I decided to try a long shot. This appeared to have effect, because the machine dived very steeply towards sea-level. I followed him down and was able to close in from 600 yards to ten yards and expend all my ammunition. I found I had gathered too much speed and overshot him, so I did a steep turn to port and was able to see the Me 109 hit the water with a big splash. I did not stay to make any further investigation because I saw two or three black dots coming towards me which I imagined to be enemy aircraft, so I went full out and hedge-hopped to Maidstone, where I tried to get refuelled.

Both Sergeants Frantiszek and Scott are clear that the enemy aircraft they destroyed crashed into the sea – and yet no record of these losses appears in German records. Yet again, this supposedly irrebuttable presumption that German loss records are both complete and accurate has to be questioned.

Suffice it to say that the afternoon's operations, while not another major raid, still put a strain on the defenders – so much so that the previous day's heavy raids saw Fighter Command respond by flying 568 sorties, and yet this comparatively quieter day still saw 404 flown. Nonetheless, the Luftwaffe had failed in its objective of destroying Fighter Command in four days, and was no closer to achieving aerial supremacy by mid-September.

Since 20 August 1940 daylight operations had been the responsibility of *Luftflotte* 2, the determined offensive against 11 Group's airfields beginning four days later. Throughout this time, *Reichsmarschall* Göring's directive that RAF fighters must be brought to battle and annihilated had been rigorously pursued. At a conference held by Göring at The Hague in early September 1940, there appeared confusion as to how RAF fighters were deployed. It had apparently been noted that although RAF squadrons comprised twelve aircraft, they appeared to be intercepting in smaller formations of up to six – leading *Generalfeldmarschall* Kesselring to conclude that Fighter Command was finished. Again, faulty air intelligence was the problem: squadrons were sub-divided into two flights, and often one went for the fighters while the other attacked bombers. Luftwaffe Air Intelligence reported that Fighter Command possessed just 100 fighters at the end of August, that figure having already risen to 350. *Generalfeldmarschall* Sperrle of *Luftflotte* 3, though, argued that 1,000 was closer to the mark. Neither were right: on 23 August 1940 Fighter Command's strength was 672 fighters. One fact was becoming clear, however: the aerial supremacy required for Operation *Seelöwe* was not going to be achieved through pursuance of the Luftwaffe's current strategy.

On 2 September 1940, Hitler, frustrated at the Luftwaffe's lack of progress and having lost face owing to the bombing of Berlin, ordered the revenge bombing of London. Previously, the Poles and Dutch had surrendered after the bombing of their capital cities, and the Danes had capitulated at just the threat of it, so it was now hoped that a similar bombardment of London would have the same effect. Hitler's new orders, therefore, were that the civilian populations of large cities should be targeted. Göring remained optimistic that Fighter Command could still be exhausted and that a change in fortunes could still provide the victory and result Hitler required. Thus, therefore, another change of tack was literally in the air.

Matters of high strategy, however, were far from the minds of newly wedded Sergeant Bernard Jennings of 19 Squadron, who was able to snatch some well-earned leave; Mrs Madeleine Jennings:

> During September we spent a few days, a belated honeymoon, at a cross between a country club and a holiday camp in Surrey. There we played tennis, went for long walks and danced the evening away. All too soon the respite was at an end and Bernard returned to the fray. How he had ever managed to snatch those few days in the first place I have never been able to understand. According to the propaganda at the time, and certainly publicity since, positively every pilot was needed and all leave cancelled.
>
> The countryside itself was peaceful, yet there were many vicious dogfights going on overhead ... Arriving at the office one morning ... I found all that remained of it was a heap of rubble.

Wednesday, 4 September 1940

Reducing British cities to 'a heap of rubble' was very much on the *Führer*'s mind when on this day he addressed the opening of the *Kriegswinterhilfswerk* (Winter Relief Campaign) at Berlin's Sportpalast:

> It is truly magnificent to see our Volk at war and its total discipline. We realise this all the more in a time when Mr Churchill is demonstrating to us the use of his invention: the nightly air raid. He does not do this because air raids at night are particularly effective, but because his Air Force cannot penetrate German airspace during the day. While the German pilots, the German planes, fly over English land day by day, no Englishman has yet managed to as much as cross the North Sea by daylight. That is why they come at night and drop their bombs – you know it well – indiscriminately and without plan on civilian residential centres, on farmsteads, and villages.
>
> Wherever they see a light, they drop a bomb.

I did not answer for three months because I was of the opinion that they would ultimately stop this nonsense. Mr Churchill perceived this as a sign of our weakness. You will surely understand that now we are giving our answers night after night, and this at an increasing rate.

And should the Royal Air Force drop two thousand, or three thousand, or four thousand kilograms of bombs, then we will now drop 150,000; 180,000; 230,000; 300,000; 400,000; yes, one million kilograms in a single night. And should they declare they will greatly increase their attacks on our cities, then we will erase their cities! We will put these night-time pirates out of business, God help us! The hour will come that one of us will crack, and it will not be National Socialist Germany!

The question was whether this new strategy would work. As *Generalfeldmarschall* Kesselring wrote, 'To accomplish our purpose, for all our zeal and ability, we needed luck.' As Luftwaffe staff officers busied themselves preparing for this new phase of operations, however, the battle of the airfields continued.

At dawn, the Hurricanes of 111 Squadron flew from Croydon to operate from Hawkinge, from where it was scrambled at 08.45 hrs to patrol Folkestone, RDF having indicated 20+ assembling over Cap Gris-Nez. Freshly arrived from Coltishall the previous day, 66 Squadron had been sent from Kenley to operate from Hawkinge, and took-off at 09.05 hrs to reinforce 111 Squadron and patrol the same area. Another German formation was then detected near Calais, and a third over Crecy. Ever wary of raids on the sector stations north of the Thames, the Controller also scrambled 222 Squadron from Rochford to patrol Canterbury, and 46 Squadron then went forward from North Weald to cover that forward base.

At 09.00 hrs, 111 Squadron was five miles east of Folkestone and sighted the Me 109s of JG 2 and JG 54, stepped up all the way to 30,000ft in several large but loose and flexible formations. Flight Lieutenant Herbert Giddings led the charge, making a head-on attack at 21,000ft, shooting a 109 down in flames. In turn, Giddings was attacked from behind and broke away, forced-landing at Staplecross with a damaged oil system. Sergeant Thomas Wallace also got a 109, and watched its pilot bale out over the Channel. Flying Officer Ben Bowring fired at several 109s but had a round explode in his cockpit, but was unhurt and returned safely to base. Pilot Officer Peter Simpson claimed a 109 destroyed which 'was seen to dive into the sea with smoke pouring from the engine [ORB]'. Two Hurricane pilots, however, were missing. The Polish Pilot Officer Janusz Macinski was shot down and baled out over the sea, 'and was shot at by enemy fighters, although both Flying Officer Bowring and Sergeant Wallace attempted to protect him as he came down [ORB]'. Also missing was Flying Officer David Bruce – neither pilot was ever seen again.

Flight Lieutenant George Christie DFC of 66 Squadron intercepted a lone Me 109 west of Folkestone at 09.15 hrs:

As soon as I approached he barrel-rolled and dived for the sea at 450 mph. I followed and my first burst, coming from straight in behind, missed. The second burst, also astern, pierced his petrol tank from which petrol poured out but did not catch fire. By then he had reached sea-level and flew straight towards France at about 50ft. I carried out a series of quarter attacks and after the last the propeller practically stopped, and the pilot jumped over the left side just before the plane hit the water. The machine exploded and the petrol ignited. I was then within five miles of the French coast and two more Me 109s came out from the coast and attacked me. As I was low on ammunition I kept turning underneath them, working my way back to our coast. They broke off the attack about half way across the Channel.

Sergeant Arthur Smith was shot down over Mersham, near Ashford, baling out so seriously wounded that he would succumb to his injuries two days later. By this time, two German formations had crossed in near Dungeness and were heading north, towards the Thames Estuary. No.66 Squadron gave chase, but were unable to penetrate the fighter screen to attack the twenty Do 17s in the enemy formation. At 09.20 hrs, between Ramsgate and Deal, Pilot Officer Peter King claimed a 109 probably destroyed, but the battle over the Thames went against the Spitfires: Flight Lieutenant Felix Dunworth was shot-up and forced-landed near Billericay, slightly wounded, and Pilot Officer Alexander Appleford baled out, also with slight wounds, over Purleigh.

By now, various squadrons had been scrambled by the 11 Group Controller, all of which were ordered to patrol their bases because the Germans' intended target was still unclear. Indeed, various German formations were over Kent and Essex, some constantly changing course, making interpretation of movements and intentions impossible. Eventually the aerodrome at Bradwell on the Essex coast was hit by the raiders intercepted by 66 Squadron, although this was a pointless exercise given that the station was not even operational. Afterwards, bombs fell at random locations across Kent as the raiders withdrew, but of the thirteen defending squadrons airborne only 66 and 111 Squadrons engaged, owing to the need to cover the all-important sector stations.

No.253 Squadron had scrambled from Kenley at 09.30 hrs to patrol base and was not engaged by the enemy – but Pilot Officer Alec Trueman, a Canadian, fell out of formation over Kenley, probably due to oxygen system failure, and was killed when his Hurricane crashed at Banstead.

Again, 12 Group had contributed to the defence of aerodromes north of the Thames, 19 Squadron having patrolled Debden uneventfully, and similarly 73 Squadron, which had flown down to Duxford from Church Fenton, patrolled North Weald.

At 12.30 hrs, RDF screens were busy again as more German formations assembled over Calais. Squadron Leader Rupert 'Lucky' Leigh scrambled with his 66 Squadron from Hawkinge at 12.30 hrs, to patrol base, and 222 Squadron was soon sent up from Rochford to the Canterbury line, and 602 Squadron flew east from Westhampnett to patrol Beachy Head. By 12.50 hrs RDF was indicating one raid of 100+ and another of 50+ crossing the Channel. No.1 (RCAF) Squadron was scrambled from Northolt to patrol base – which was timely considering a visit from the Canadian press was in progress – and 72 Squadron took-off from Croydon, also to patrol base. No.10 Group having had a quieter time since *Luftflotte* 3 switched to night operations, a flight of 234 Squadron Spitfires scrambled from Middle Wallop to cover Tangmere (on previous days the squadron had reinforced 11 Group, protecting airfields, but had not engaged). Tangmere's 43 Squadron was sent forward to intercept the raid over the Channel, 249 Squadron went up from North Weald to patrol base, and 12 Group sent 19 Squadron to patrol Debden, and 73 Squadron to Eastchurch. But, given the morning's incoherent incursions, what were the Germans up to?

Inevitably, the Germans were heading for multiple targets. Fourteen Me 110 fighter-bombers of *Hauptmann* Hans von Boltenstern's *Erprobungsgruppe* 210, escorted by Me 110 fighters of V(Z)/LG 1 and III/ZG 76, were headed for the Vickers-Armstrong factory at Brooklands, which was producing Wellington bombers and Hurricane fighters. A formation of He 111s was bound for Gravesend airfield; another raid was to attack Eastchurch, and a fourth was to bomb the Pobjoy's aircraft factory at Rochester. An infinite number of Me 109s also provided escort to all four raids.

At 13.10 hrs, 602 Squadron was at 15,000ft over Beachy Head and sighted forty Do 17s escorted by fifteen to twenty Me 110s flying south-east, down-Channel fifteen miles south of Beachy Head. The Me 110s were leading and circled to attack the Spitfires. Combat ensued, with the Spitfire pilots claiming an Me 110, two Do 17s and an Me 109 destroyed, a Do 17 and Me 110 probably destroyed and a 110 damaged. One Spitfire was 'destroyed [ORB]', but the details are unknown and no pilot was either killed or wounded. *Erprobungsgruppe* 210, however, lost its *Kommandeur*, *Hauptmann* Hans von Boltenstern – not to a Spitfire, but pilot error. Having sighted the danger, Boltenstern dived, intending to pull up at sea-level, but left the pull-up too late and crashed into the sea; both he and his *Bordfunker*, *Feldwebel* Fritz Schneider, were killed. Height in an air battle is everything, a golden rule, so what von Boltenstern was trying to achieve by dropping to zero feet is difficult to imagine – and so *Erprobungsgruppe* 210 lost its second *Kommandeur* in less than a month.

At 13.15 hrs, six Hurricanes of Biggin Hill's 79 Squadron were also in action against the Me 110s over Beachy Head; Pilot Officer Donald 'Dimsie' Stones DFC was leading a section made up of Sergeant John Wright and himself – and ordered an attack. Stones fired two long bursts at a 110, the port engine of which belched smoke and the aircraft fell away in a steep dive. Another Hurricane then attacked a 110 that was firing at Stones from fifty yards astern, enabling Stones to break away. Although hampered by a 602 Squadron Spitfire getting in his way, Pilot Officer George Peters claimed a 110 destroyed, and Pilot Officer

Thomas Parker damaged two. Sergeant Wright, however, was shot up and forced-landed at Surbiton, sadly dying from his fatal wounds the following day.

The Brooklands raiders, having flown down-Channel, turned inland over Worthing and flew north, where the Me 110s were intercepted by 43 Squadron – which had a height advantage of 1,000ft. Squadron Leader Caesar Hull put sections into line astern and attacked from the sun. In that initial assault, Hull claimed a probable.

Flight Lieutenant Thomas Dalton-Morgan:

> I climbed above five Me 110s endeavouring to form a defensive circle. I selected one Me 110 and dived to engage. As it turned towards me I gave it a long burst and broke away, climbing to the left. I noticed the nose break up and black smoke coming from one engine. As I climbed and turned I saw it diving vertically and flames starting from the nose. I did not see it crash as I engaged another Me 110, but it was seen to crash behind Worthing by Pilot Officer Upton.

This was a machine of 7/ZG 76 which crashed at High Salvington; the crew, *Oberleutnant* Walter Schiller, the *Staffelführer*, and *Feldwebel* Helmut Winkler both baled out and were captured.

After this action 43 Squadron was ordered west, to patrol Tangmere at 17,000ft.

Next to harry the Me 110 force heading for Brooklands, at 13.20 hrs, was 234 Squadron, being led by the popular and able Australian Flight Lieutenant Pat Hughes:

> As Cressy Leader was patrolling Tangmere, Angels 15. Saw about fifty Me 110s approaching coast with about fifteen 110s circling South of Haslemere. Red, Yellow and Green Sections engaged the rear formation and Blue Section engaged the fifteen. These aircraft immediately formed a circle and in a head-on attack I fired two short bursts and the leading aircraft pulled up and I fired one short burst into the fuselage. This aircraft caught fire and crashed just North of Brighton.

This 110, of 9/ZG 76, crashed at Wisborough Green, killing the crew, *Oberleutnant* Kurt Raetsch and *Obergefreiter* Werner Hempel.

Hughes was then attacked himself by three Me 110s; counter-attacking, the Australian then pursued and attacked a 110 that broke away from the formation. Off the coast, both engines caught fire and the German pilot turned back towards land – also attacked by a Hurricane – but crashed into the water.

Pilot Officer Bob Doe, flying Red 2 to Hughes, also attacked a circle of Me 110s, hitting one which 'crashed straight down into sea'. On his way home, the Spitfire pilot saw another 110 at 500ft, off Littlehampton and also being chased by a Hurricane (601 Squadron, this very likely also being the second

110 claimed by Hughes). Doe opened fire and the enemy aircraft crashed into the sea close to a 'cargo boat'. This was most likely a 5/ZG 76 machine which came down seven miles off Pevensey Bay; the crew, *Oberleutnant* Ernst-Hartman Freiherr von Schlotheim and *Unteroffizier* Georg Hommel, were captured.

No.234 Squadron actually enjoyed what could only be described as a 'Turkey Shoot', claiming a total of fourteen Me 110s and a Do 17 destroyed, and four 110s damaged, all for no loss. Although these claims were somewhat optimistic, the fact remains that at least seven Me 110s can be confirmed and accredited to 234 Squadron – although some of these were undoubtedly attacked by, and also claimed by, pilots from other squadrons. Nonetheless, it was an excellent result for this 10 Group squadron.

As the depleted Brookland raid forged inland, at approximately 13.20 hrs the Hurricanes of 1 (RCAF) Squadron fell on Me 110s prowling around over East Grinstead. Flying Officer Deane Nesbitt promptly shot down the *Gruppenadjutant* of *Stab* II/ZG 76, *Oberleutnant* Hermann Weeber, who forced-landed near Wadhurst and was captured with his *Bordfunker*, *Unteroffizier* Max Michael. Flying Officer Blair Russell chased a section of 110s to Dungeness, attacking one and seeing smoke emit from its port engine before a Spitfire took up the attack; Russell did not see the outcome but last saw the enemy machine diving towards the sea a mile offshore. Flying Officer Julian Smithers claimed a 110 destroyed which 'fell out of formation in flames and crashed'. The squadron also claimed five Me 110s damaged (and Russell also claimed a 'Ju 88' [*sic*] damaged), all for no loss.

At 13.30 hrs, the nine Hurricanes of 253 Squadron sighted the Me 110s of *Erprobungsgruppe* 210 about to attack Brooklands. Flight Lieutenant William Cambridge, the senior flight commander, had assumed command after the squadron lost two COs in a single day, and now led the Hurricanes from 12,000ft to attack out of the sun. Again, the Hurricanes had the height advantage, the 110s being at 6,000ft; Cambridge expended all his ammunition in a single burst on a 110 of 14/LG 1, and watched his target 'crash in flames in a field about fifty yards north of a farm about six miles from Brooklands' – the *Bordfunker*, *Unteroffizier* Joachim Jäckel baled out wounded and was captured, but *Feldwebel* Karl Röhring was killed in the crash. Sergeant Allan Dredge hit another 110, setting both engines and the cockpit alight, this aircraft, also an escorting fighter of 14/LG 1, crashing near Dorking, killing the crew, *Oberleutant* Michel Junge, the *Staffelkapitän*, and *Unteroffizier* Karl Bremser. The Polish Pilot Officer Tadeusz Nowak claimed a 110 destroyed, which he reportedly saw 'dive and crash', and Flight Lieutenant Jefferson Wedgwood similarly reported that his target 'caught fire' and was 'seen to crash into a wood'. Other pilots filed claims, and in total the squadron claimed a 'bag' of six Me 110s destroyed and one damaged, all for no loss. This was good shooting, and a boost to the morale of this squadron, which had taken a battering upon arrival at Kenley – but, again, some of this claims were duplicates.

While the action was happening above, Brooklands was bombed; some aircraft of *Erprobungsgruppe* 210 approached the Vickers factory from Byfleet, out of the sun, while others swept in from the east. The attack lasted three minutes and was the most devastating raid on a British aircraft factory to date: much of the Vickers Machine Shop, Wing Shop, Repair Hangar and various other buildings were destroyed, bringing production to a standstill for several days. Daily Home Intelligence Reports frequently include criticisms of late air raid warnings being given, and such was the case here: the alarm sounded almost simultaneously with the attack, not giving workers time to shelter or the local defences time to react; eighty-three workers were killed and 419 injured. Apart from von Boltenstern, lost to pilot error, *Erprobungsgruppe* 210 suffered no other casualties, but four escorting V/LG 1 fighters were lost, so the raid was certainly a success from the enemy's perspective.

As these raids began dispersing over Surrey and East Sussex, 43 Squadron had been ordered back to patrol Tangmere, and at 13.30 hrs were en route when a formation of seventy Me 110s was sighted between Ford and Worthing, withdrawing south. Again, Squadron Leader Hull led his Hurricanes into the attack, damaging a 110 himself over the sea; although, according to the squadron's after-action report, he did not watch it crash, 'he has no doubt that the machine must have come down in the sea as it was obviously out of control, the wheels being down and smoke pouring from the engines and fuselage'. Flight Lieutenant Dalton-Morgan recorded his second victory that day when he shot down another Me 110, this one of *Stab* III/ZG 76 which exploded at Pulborough, killing the crew, *Oberleutnant* Florenz and *Gefreiter* Herbert (indeed, such was the violence of the crash and explosion that no trace of these airmen was ever found). Pilot Officers Hamilton Upton and the Belgian Albert van den Hove d'Ertsenrijck both claimed 110s destroyed off Worthing, but the latter, 43 Squadron's only casualty, landed at Ford, his engine, fuselage and wings damaged by cannon and machine-gun fire.

At 13.30 hrs, the Hurricanes of 601 Squadron also engaged the enemy over Worthing, the American Flight Lieutenant Carl Davis and Pilot Officer Humphrey Gilbert claiming Me 110s destroyed, and probables by Pilot Officer Howard Mayers and Flight Lieutenant Michael Robinson (shared), and the Polish Flying Officer Jerzy Jankiewicz, who was himself shot-up and forced-landed at Goring, slightly wounded. Off Worthing, Flying Officer Hugh Riddle shared the destruction of a Do 17 with a Spitfire from an unknown squadron (although more likely this was the Me 110 claimed by 234 Squadron's Pilot Officer Bob Doe, who reported it also attacked by a Hurricane), another was claimed destroyed by Flight Lieutenant Willie Rhodes-Moorhouse, and Mayers also claimed a 'Do 215' [*sic*].

As the raiders hurried back to France, Yellow Section of 10 Group's 152 Squadron, up over Bognor Regis from Warmwell, and 'saw a Do 17 1,000ft below. They followed the E/A and attacked it at 5,000ft [ORB].' The combat, which may have been with a reconnaissance aircraft, if, indeed, it was a Do 17 and not actually an Me 110, was apparently inconclusive – but Sergeant John Barker was hit by return fire, baling out over the Channel, never to be seen alive again.

Further east, the raids bound for Gravesend, Rochester and Eastchurch were also being engaged.

At about 13.15 hrs, 66 Squadron sighted 'Raid 8' at 17,000ft over Maidstone: twelve He 111s and up to fifty escorting Me 109s above, all flying north-west. Squadron Leader Rupert Leigh led the Spitfires to attack from up-sun when there was a warning shout over the R/T: 'Lots of enemy fighters coming down from above!' Leigh made a head-on attack at an approaching Me 109, passing over the enemy fighter before taking evasive action owing to enemy fighters on his tail. Flight Lieutenant George Christie also made a head-on attack, damaging a 109 before – as he prepared to attack the bombers – his wing was hit so he broke away. Pilot Officer Peter King had taken over the lead of 'A' Flight after Flight Lieutenant Ken Gillies had to drop out owing to technical trouble, and he now led 'A' Flight against the 109s. King hit a 109 which streamed white vapour and petrol, noticing 'a tongue of flame' (although King did not see the 109 crash, the Duty Pilot at Hawkinge received confirmation from 'Major Sergeant of the Marine AA Battery at Warren Lodge that an Me 109 was shot down into the sea 7,000 yards out ... at the approximate time and place Pilot Officer King broke off). King heard a:

> sharp crack behind him, and, looking in his mirror, saw an Me 109 on his tail. By a series of turns he managed to reverse the position and used up the rest of his ammunition ... The E/A was seen to judder but not crash. He landed at Hawkinge at 1325 hrs to rearm and refuel but found his machine had been damaged by machine-gun fire.

Pilot Officer Crellin 'Bogle' Bodie was also engaged by Me 109s, one of which he fired at and last saw going 'vertically downwards, towards a wood'. The German fighters, however, were once more doing a good job of protecting the bombers, Bodie being fended off from attacking the He 111s three times. Similarly, Pilot Officer Charles Coke damaged a 109 but after his third attack:

> he was himself hit by cannon fire from behind, the shells passing his left leg and exploding the petrol tanks. He immediately abandoned the aircraft at a height of 20,000ft, sustaining burns on his face and wrist, and one small piece of shrapnel in his left leg. He landed in the top of a tree near Capel Farm, due North of Ham Street.

Five minutes after 66 Squadron engaged, the Spitfires of 222 Squadron went into action against the Me 109 escorts over the Ashford area, the enemy 'approaching

Canterbury from the South'. From German combat claims it seems that over this area of Kent, the 109s were from various units, including JG 2, JG 3, JG 54, and JG 77 all of which made combat claims this afternoon.

Pilot Officer John Broadhurst:

> I saw an Me 109 diving after being attacked by two Hurricanes. I followed it down and gave it a burst from astern but slightly above. Smoke appeared from the E/A's engine and the angle of dive increased. When I last saw it, it was diving vertically with smoke and flames coming from the engine.

Pilot Officer William Assheton:

> I saw one Me 109 about 200ft below me and 500 yards away. I dived to attack, firing short bursts which appeared to hit him. He went into a steep left-hand turn. I closed rapidly. At a range of about twenty yards I saw a large white flash from the rear of the cockpit and the E/A disappeared in a vertical dive.
>
> I saw another Me 109 on the tail of a Spitfire. I fired one burst and the E/A broke and headed for France. Climbing, I fired several bursts at 250 yards range. The machine did a right-hand turn and my last burst appeared to hit him. He flicked over on his back and went down in a vertical dive.

Pilot Officer John 'Chips' Carpenter 'shot a 109 down in flames and while diving away his aircraft was hit by an AA shell which blew him out of the cockpit. He landed successfully by parachute [ORB].'

Sergeant Douglas Chipping claimed a probable Me 109 but was himself attacked and 'hit in the rudder bias, elevator and flap'; he was unhurt and returned safely to base.

Two 222 Squadron pilots were missing, however.

Sergeant John Ramshaw, who had only joined the unit straight from OTU just five days before, was shot down over West Malling and crashed at Yalding – rescued from the wreckage of his Spitfire, the 24-year-old pilot died of his injuries before reaching West Kent Hospital. Of Pilot Officer John Cutts, who was posted missing, there was apparently no trace. Later, though, the remains of a pilot were recovered from a Spitfire crash site at Amberfield Farm, Chart Sutton, Kent, and buried as 'unknown' at Bell Road Cemetery, Sittingbourne; in 1998, these remains were proven to be those of Pilot Officer John Wintringham Cutts and the headstone was consequently named accordingly.

The formation engaged by 222 Squadron proceeded north-west to its target but was not intercepted again before bombing the airfield at Gravesend. Fortunately, 501 Squadron had scrambled immediately beforehand so escaped unscathed, and no bombs hit the airfield. The Hurricanes, however, were too late to intercept and so the enemy withdrew in good order.

At 13.15 hrs, the Hurricanes of 46 Squadron, up from Stapleford, were bounced by Me 109s over Rochford, 'which then escaped into the clouds'. It was a perfect ambush and 'A' Flight suffered accordingly: Flying Officer Richard Plummer baled out, landing at Stanbridge suffering from severe burns (he would die of these injuries at Rochford Hospital on 14 September 1940); Pilot Officer Charles Ambrose also baled out, landing unhurt. Pilot Officer Robert Barber was shot-up, suffering a broken neck and lower jawbone in a heavy forced-landing at Malden, and Flying Officer Frederick Austin luckily escaped injury after being shot-up when his Hurricane overturned on landing at Rochford.

The Rochester-bound force was intercepted in the Tenterden-Tunbridge Wells area by 72 Squadron at 13.20 hrs and reportedly comprised 'Ju 86 [*sic*] and Me 110 at 15,000ft [ORB]'.

The Spitfires were 1,000ft higher and went into line-astern to attack the circle of Me 110s. Sergeant John Gilders, No.3 of the rear-guard section, hit a 110 from astern in the fuselage and wings, setting the starboard wing and engine alight. The German dived steeply:

> I had a final burst as he died and had the satisfaction of seeing brownish-black smoke coming back from it. It went down near Ashford and nobody left the machine. I had only a small bullet hole in my machine. Two Germans were descending near Ashford from another machine.

Flight Lieutenant Thomas Elsdon, Flying Officer John 'Pancho' Villa and Pilot Officer Dennis 'Dutch' Holland also claimed 110s destroyed, the latter and Villa also damaging one each. Sergeant William Rolls claimed two 'Ju 86 [*sic*]' destroyed. Holland's Spitfire was damaged but he was unhurt and returned to Croydon, but Pilot Officer Ernest Males was shot down by a 110 and baled out over Tenterden, fortunately not wounded.

Like the Gravesend raid, this force also pressed on northwards, without being further harassed, and bombed Chatham and Rochester, where minor damage was reported to Pobjoy's. The raiders then made their exit over the Essex coast. At 13.45 hrs, the raid that had crossed the coast over Dover bombed Eastchurch, seriously damaging two huts, the Ration Store and two Fairey Battles, and leaving six craters in the runway. This force escaped the defenders' attentions while in and outbound. The Brooklands raid was the most successful of the day, but the German tactics of simultaneous multiple raids had overwhelmed the System, which was unable to deal with more than six enemy formations at a time. Indeed, Air Chief Marshal Dowding later acknowledged that by 13.10 hrs, the plotting tables were saturated.

There was no further daylight action, as both sides counted the cost. Fighter Command had suffered the loss of fourteen Spitfires and Hurricanes, with at least the same number damaged; six pilots had been killed and ten wounded –

two of whom would later die of their injuries. The enemy fighter pilots claimed fifty-one Spitfires and Hurricanes destroyed.

Owing to a combination of tactics and efforts of escorting fighters, not one German bomber had been lost to the defending fighters – although this was at some cost to the enemy fighter force. Six Me 109s had been destroyed and two damaged, with three pilots killed and two wounded. The Me 110s, however, had suffered badly: seventeen had been destroyed and at least two damaged; nineteen crewmen had been killed, one returned wounded and fourteen were PoWs. It is evident that the Me 109s simply did not suffer the same volume of casualties. During the earlier phase of fighting over Portland, the Me 110s had fared better – but were now being intercepted by more defending fighters over the 11 Group area. Inevitably, Fighter Command had substantially overclaimed, claiming the destruction of nine Me 109s, nine probables and six damaged, and thirty-five Me 110s destroyed, eight probables and nineteen damaged. It is impossible to say exactly how many of these claims were confirmed, but the fact remains that both sides thought they were doing better than they actually were in terms of inflicting losses upon the enemy. One thing Air Chief Marshal Dowding and Air Vice-Marshal Park knew full-well however: too many pilots were being lost.

Fortunately, RAF pilots wounded in action over England, unlike the enemy aircrews, if they recovered sufficiently, were able to return to duty – which helped. One such was Pilot Officer Alexander Osmand, shot-up and wounded in the eyes by glass splinters on 18 August 1940, who was freshly returned to 213 Squadron at Exeter. On this day, the young pilot made his first operational flight since reporting back several days previously: 'Patrol base at 25,000ft for photographic Me 109 – but too late for it'.

Daily Home Intelligence Report:

There are further signs that the feeling of bitterness against the enemy is becoming more directly associated with Nazi airmen, although this is not always as apparent as might be expected in areas that have suffered the worst raid damage.

Thursday, 5 September 1940

As the day dawned fine, at RAF Hornchurch 19-year-old Pilot Officer William Pearce Houghton Rafter, known as 'Robin' to his family and friends, anxiously awaited the call to scramble for the first time. From Harborne in Birmingham, Robin was the younger son of the late Sir Charles Rafter, a former Chief Constable, and his elder brother, Pilot Officer Charles Rafter, was flying Wellingtons with 214 Squadron at Stradishall. The younger Rafter had been given a SSC, straight from Cheltenham College, on 26 June 1939; his flying training complete, on 7 May 1940, Pilot Officer Rafter joined 225 Squadron, an army cooperation squadron flying the Westland Lysander communications aircraft, at Odiham. In August, however, Pilot Officer Rafter and Flying Officer Ian Hallam answered Fighter Command's call for volunteers, leaving Odiham on 22 August 1940, bound for 7 OTU at Hawarden, where they converted to Spitfires. Hallam was an experienced airman, with over 500 flying hours on single-engine types already, including six on Spitfires. At Hawarden the student pilots recorded just fifteen hours flying on Spitfires. Upon conclusion of the course, the young and inexperienced Pilot Officer Rafter was posted to 603 Squadron at Hornchurch, while the infinitely more experienced Hallam was sent north, away from the combat zone, to fly Spitfires with 610 Squadron. Indeed, before Hallam too was posted to 222 Squadron at Hornchurch on 1 October 1940, he would have a further 21.05 Spitfire hours in his log book. Surely, however, from 7 OTU it would have made more sense to send Rafter to 610 Squadron, where he could gain more essential experience? Clearly, none of this was a consideration, just the luck of the draw. For Pilot Officer Robin Rafter, 5 September 1940 would be a significant day indeed.

Two heavy raids were made by *Luftflotte* 2 this day, the first following the pattern of sub-diving into various formations, spreading out and heading for different targets, thereby intending to confuse and overwhelm the defences. As we have seen, the tactic had worked, with various raids reaching and bombing their targets unmolested by Fighter Command. The downside for the enemy was that target selection often remained questionable.

At 09.34 hrs, 603 Squadron was scrambled from Hornchurch, Pilot Officer Rafter making his first operational flight since having joined the squadron five days previously. Ten minutes later, a large formation of enemy aircraft crossed the coast at Dungeness, heading for various airfields in Kent. Over Maidstone the enemy separated into numerous smaller formations, the coherent progress of which the Observer Corps found difficult to track.

According to the South African Pilot Officer Gerald 'Stapme' Stapleton of 603 Squadron, at 09.50 hrs fifteen Me 109s were sighted at 20,000ft over Biggin Hill, part of the escort to another large raiding force. For Pilot Officer Robin Rafter, the sight must have been bewildering; indeed, the young pilot later described his experience in a letter to his mother, Lady Rafter:

Well I was over Kent at a little over 25,000ft ... when I sighted a huge formation of Jerries. I very nearly shot a Spitfire down by mistake, but then saw on my starboard side, underneath me, an Me 109. I got all fixed and started my dive on the 109 and was nearing it when I saw in my mirror a couple of 109s on my tail. Well, I took what evasive action I could, but found two a bit of a problem. I started to get away from them when my tail must have been damaged as all movement on the control column was to no avail, thus putting my machine out of control. By this time I had a little piece of shrapnel in my leg, and probably owe my life to the fact that my machine was out of control as the Jerries evidently found difficulty in getting their sights on me as my machine was going all over the place. Luckily, I was very high up and it then occurred to me to bale out. My oxygen tube had already become detached, but I had great difficulty in undoing the pin of my harness to loosen myself out of my seat. I eventually got the pin out, but could not get out of the aircraft. By this time the Jerries had ceased firing at me, but I had no idea where I was over. The next part of my experience was rather a miracle. The machine's nose dropped violently, thus having the effect of throwing me forward, the force so great that I went through the canopy, thus injuring my head. You can't imagine my surprise! I was then at about 15,000ft and floating about in the air rather like a cork. You will understand why when I explain that instead of diving at 400 mph, I had rapidly slowed down to about 180 mph as the human body never falls faster, that being the terminal velocity. I then felt so light that I had to look to ensure that I was wearing a parachute. Luckily I had given it an inspection that morning. I pulled the cord and the 'chute opened up and I breathed once more.

Now the most terrifying experience happened. I floated down, right through the aerial battle that was taking place. I came through it without a scratch, but then I noticed a 109 coming towards me, and you have no idea what a damned fool you feel suspended in mid-air with an enemy fighter buzzing around you.

Well he never fired at me, as a Spitfire came along and drove him off; whether he would have done or not cannot be said. Next worry was where I was going to land as there were a lot of trees near. I avoided them and landed in a nice field. My Spitfire, which was new, crashed into a ploughed field some way away. The LDV accosted me with a shotgun as I was wearing my RAF battledress which must have confused them a bit. I was treated by a local first aid post and then taken to hospital.

The Me 109 'buzzing' the defenceless Pilot Officer Rafter had been seen off by Pilot Officer Stapleton:

I was diving to attack the bombers when I was engaged by two Me 109s. When I fired at the first one I noticed glycol coming from his radiator. I did a No 2 attack and as I fired was hit by bullets from another 109. I broke off downwards and continued my dive. At 6,000ft I saw a single-engine machine diving vertically with no tail unit [Rafter's Spitfire]. I looked up and saw a parachutist coming down circled by an Me 109. I attacked him [the 109] from the low quarter; he dived vertically for the ground then flattened out at ground level. I then did a series of beam attacks from both sides, and the enemy aircraft turned into my attacks. He finally forced landed. He tried to set his radio on fire by taking off his jacket and setting fire to it and putting it into the cockpit. He was prevented by the LDV.

The Me 109 pilot concerned was *Oberleutnant* Franz von Werra, the *Gruppenadjutant* of II/JG 3, who was captured at Loves Farm, Winchett Hill,

Marden. A flamboyant character, von Werra had recently appeared in the German press posing with his pet lion cub, 'Simba'. He later achieved notoriety as the only German prisoner to escape from Allied custody; returning to combat flying thereafter, he scored further successes over Russia and commanded I/JG 53. On 25 October 1941, however, he was routinely patrolling off the Dutch coast and went to a watery grave in the North Sea following an engine failure.

Pilot Officer James Morton also damaged a 109 – but there was a most experienced and valuable pilot missing: Flight Lieutenant Fred 'Rusty' Rushmer, one of 603's original auxiliaries. Of the former engineering draughtsman, the youngest of eleven children, there was no news. Eventually his death was officially presumed and, in due course, this gallant officer's name was included on the Runnymede Memorial. In 1970, however, a Spitfire crash-site was excavated by enthusiasts at Smarden, documented as having crashed on the day in question, both a process of elimination and certain personal effects, including a pocket watch stopped at 10.10 hrs, suggesting that this was in fact Rushmer's aircraft, X4261. The pilot of this aircraft was known to have been buried at the time as 'Known unto God' at All Saints, Staplehurst – and eventually, in 1998, the authorities accepted that this was actually Flight Lieutenant Rushmer; his headstone was changed and named accordingly.

At 10.00 hrs, RAF Biggin Hill was bombed again: 'A further high-level bombing attack was made. Damage was done to some Dispersal Points and the aerodrome surface, but most of the bombs overshot the aerodrome and fell on the Westerham Road and again destroyed telephone lines [ORB].'

Like 603 Squadron, 41 Squadron's Spitfires, which had arrived at Hornchurch from Catterick two days previously, had scrambled at 09.15 hrs to patrol Manston when the raiders crossed the coast. According to Flight Lieutenant Norman Ryder DFC, commanding 'A' Flight, at 10.10 hrs, south of Gravesend, 41 Squadron – led by Squadron Leader Hilary 'Robin' Hood, Red 1 – also sighted a 'large escorted bomber formation', comprising 'He 111s, Ju 88s and Me 109s'. Squadron Leader Hood ordered Blue and Green Sections to attack the ponderous bombers, while his own Red Section – comprising just Pilot Officer George Bennions, Red 2, and himself – and Ryder's Yellow Section went into line-astern to protect them from Me 109s. Pilot Officer George 'Ben' Bennions shouted a warning that two Me 109s were diving to attack Red 1. The two Spitfires broke into a steep right-hand turn, behind the 109s, and Bennions noticed another 109 800 yards astern and to his left. The 109 followed but was out-turned by the Spitfire and stalled after the second turn, falling away. Bennions pursued the diving enemy fighter, opening fire and noting glycol issuing from the 109, which was so close 'I was then almost colliding with him'. The stricken 109 was last seen throttled back, descending 'in a series of steep gliding turns', and – apparently finished – was left by the Spitfire pilot 'at 6,000ft eight miles South of Maidstone'.

Flight Lieutenant Ryder attacked and damaged a 109, but had to break away upon being attacked himself; having shaken off his assailants, Ryder investigated 'stray aircraft, which turned out to be Spitfires (XT)', of 603 Squadron. Flying Officer John Boyle caught a 109 attacking two Spitfires and promptly set the enemy machine on fire, while Flight Lieutenant Terry Webster, commanding 'B' Flight, hit two other 109s – one in the engine and another that burst into flames, although neither were seen to crash; Webster then hit another 109 which rolled over and went in near Maidstone. Squadron Leader Hood and Pilot Officer Ron Wallens managed to penetrate the escorts and damage Do 17s. Sergeant Robert Carr-Lewty also claimed a 109 destroyed, but was shot-up himself, forced-landing at Stanford-le-Hope.

Also at 10.10 hrs, Squadron Leader Harry Hogan's 501 Squadron, up from Gravesend and patrolling between Canterbury and the coast, reported thirty Do 17s escorted by seventy Me 109s, the latter attacking Hogan's Hurricanes at 10.10 hrs. The Polish Pilot Officer Stanislaw Skalski was shot down; he baled out and, slightly wounded, was admitted to Herne Bay Hospital – most likely by *Leutnant* Hans Berthel of *Stab* 1/JG 52, who claimed a Hurricane at 10.05 hrs (BST). In response, Pilot Officer Peter 'Hairy' Hairs claimed an Me 109 destroyed.

While Air Vice-Marshal Park's fighters were engaged further forward, 12 Group was again called upon to protect the sector stations north of the Thames. At 09.47 hrs, 19 Squadron was scrambled, Squadron Leader Phillip 'Tommy' Pinkham AFC and twelve Spitfires ordered to patrol Hornchurch at Angels 15. Over the patrol line, at 10.10 hrs, Sergeant Bernard Jennings sighted forty Do 215s [*sic*] at 15,000ft and forty Me 109s above, heading east over the Thames Estuary – probably being the formation which attacked Biggin Hill but failed to hit its target. According to the 19 Squadron Combat Report, Jennings, having the enemy in sight, led the squadron towards the raiders. Squadron Leader Pinkham's voice then came over the pilots' radios, ordering 'B' Flight to attack the bombers while 'A' Flight, led on this sortie by New Zealander Flying Officer Frank Brinsden, climbed to engage the enemy fighter screen. 'B' Flight, led into the attack by the CO, was flying in pairs, but his wingman, Blue 2, Pilot Officer Eric Burgoyne, lost sight of his leader in the sun and attacked independently, closing from 400 to 150 yards. Burgoyne attacked the rearmost section of three bombers, braving return fire from the rear-gunner, watching bits fly off his target, but his Spitfire was suddenly hit, hard, from behind by an unseen Me 109's 20mm cannon – 'causing serious damage to empennage, elevator and rudder; auxiliary controls being unserviceable'. Blue 2 broke away, struggling to return his damaged Spitfire to base.

Flying Officer Jack Lawson and the Czech Pilot Officer Frantisek 'Dolly' Dolezal, Black 1 and 2, then attacked the same bombers from astern. The former later reported that:

I followed with Black Section and got in a two second burst from astern, which caused enemy aircraft to lurch to the right, drop starboard wing and dive away downwards, apparently out of control and with every appearance of crashing … I was then fired at from the rear and my port mainplane was hit, so I broke quickly away and dived – so I was unable to see what happened to the Do 215. As I was diving down I found myself on the tail of a 109, at which I fired a short burst at about 300 yards, causing him to get in a vertical dive. I was again fired at from astern so did another steep diving turn to the right, and could not see what happened to the Me 109. My tailplane and port wing were damaged so I returned and landed at base.

'B' Flight had been well and truly bounced by the fighter escort, it having proved impossible for the handful of 'A' Flight Spitfires to gain sufficient height in time to fend them off. Pilot Officer Dolezal fired a few bursts at a 109 without effect, but broke away when a *schwarm* of four more 109s attacked him.

Flying Officer Leonard Haines, Green 1, and another Czech, Sergeant Stanislav Plzak, Green 2, were approaching the bombers when also attacked from above by the high-flying Me 109s. Flying Officer Haines reported:

I was attacked by two Me 109 fighters. I did a steep turn and as they dived past me opened up my engine and chased the second one. I waited until I was at 200 yards range and opened fire. After a five-second burst the enemy aircraft's engine began issuing 'puffs' of smoke and the pilot began hedge-hopping. I kept in range and let him have the rest of my ammunition, when I noticed a burst of flame from the engine, which issued a continuous stream of black smoke. He was then over the fields and approaching Maidstone. On reaching more or less the centre of the town he climbed his aircraft 800ft and baled out. The enemy aircraft crashed in flames in the garden of a house, and the pilot landed safely. The enemy aircraft was camouflaged in the usual way, and the pilot tried various weaving tactics in an endeavour to shake me off his tail. There was no cloud and the sun was mostly behind me.

The German pilot was *Unteroffizier* F. Hotzelmann of 1/JG 54, who broke both legs when he landed heavily on the roof of 41 John Street, Maidstone, his parachute having only partially opened at 400ft, according to an eye-witness, Mrs Mavis Seager. Hotzelmann's 109 crashed onto 6 Hardy Street, Maidstone, tearing off the gable of one room and exploding on the lawn – fortunately the occupants, Mrs Gladys Hatterseley and her 3-month-old son, were safely sheltering in the cellar.

Sergeant Plzak:

singled out an enemy aircraft diving to escape attack by another squadron and got in two bursts from rear and above at the belly of the enemy aircraft, which had turned upside down. He saw black smoke emerge but had to break away on being attacked by two other enemy aircraft which he escaped by diving and doing an Immelmann turn, subsequently returning to base.

Flight Lieutenant Brian Lane DFC had ordered 'A' Flight into line astern, climbing hard in a wide circle towards the 109s, sitting at 20,000ft and 5,000ft above 'B' Flight, which they were preparing to attack. Climbing into the sun, 'A' Flight lost sight of the enemy and failed to find them again in spite of a fifteen-minute long search over eastern Kent.

Flying Officer Walter 'Farmer' Lawson and Pilot Officer Eric Burgoyne both returned their badly damaged Spitfires safely to Fowlmere – but there was a pilot missing: Squadron Leader Pinkham, who had been shot down by the bombers' withering cross-fire and killed after baling out too low, probably due to difficulty abandoning the aircraft owing to wounds. Squadron Leader Pinkham's Spitfire, P9422, crashed at Birling in Kent and, according to the casualty report, was 'completely burnt out'; at 'approx. 1015 hrs' the pilot fell at nearby Snodland'. Although Squadron Leader Pinkham had no combat experience when he took command of 19 Squadron, he was a most experienced pilot with a number of hours on the Hurricane, gained while an instructor. Although heavily burdened by the troublesome cannon issue and urgent need to identify an effective tactical formation, Squadron Leader Pinkham could not have tried harder to see action: between 10 July 1940 and his death in action on 5 September 1940, he had, perhaps appropriately, led his Squadron on nineteen operational patrols.

Eight Hurricanes of 111 Squadron had left Croydon at 09.50 hrs and were ordered to intercept a raid heading west towards Biggin Hill. At 10.15 hrs, Flying Officer Ben Bowring, Red 1, led 'Treble One' in to attack two formations of Do 17s 'in two blocks of twenty-four aircraft, each flying level three abreast, with one section of three aircraft flying in vic formation on each side, their height 16,000ft … fighter escort was about sixty aircraft flying all around and above to 25,000ft [ORB].' When the Hurricanes attacked, the whole enemy 'formation swept south-east'; Bowring was followed by Red Section but the remaining sections failed to engage on account of Blue Leader's oxygen system failing, forcing him to dive, followed by Blue, Green and Yellow Sections:

Red 1 had his machine damaged by machine-gun and cannon shells, but after diving out of control from 15,000–1,500ft he chased an Me 109 out to sea and destroyed it ten miles SSW of Dungeness. He twice caught up with the Me 109 and beckoned the pilot to land, as he was obviously in a bad way, but each time the enemy pilot shook his fist, throttled back and opened fire. Flying Officer Bowring had previously destroyed one Me 109 probable and damaged a Dornier bomber. Red 3, Sergeant Ekins, destroyed one Me 109 probable which was seen diving out of control East of Dungeness. Pilot Officer Ritchie and Sergeant Silk, who forced-landed at Lullington Castle with wound in his forearm, engaged but were unable to see result of the fire [ORB].

The final combats of these operations were fought by 79 Squadron, six Hurricanes of which had rushed into the air from Biggin Hill as the airfield was actually being attacked, at 10.00 hrs over the Orpington area: 'At 1045 hrs, Pilot Officer Tracey landed to refuel, he claims one Do 215 [*sic*] probable, took off again at once. Flight Lieutenant Haysom landed at 1040 hrs with his port aileron badly shot up. He took off again in another aircraft at once [ORB].'

No.79 Squadron's pilots had certainly demonstrated true grit, and all were safely back at Biggin Hill by 11.10 hrs.

During the morning's raids, bombs had also fallen, apparently randomly, at various locations around Kent, and the Charing Cross line was severed by one salvo at Chislehurst. Considering that some sixty bombers were involved, and that Biggin Hill was undamaged, it is impossible to fathom what the Germans were trying to achieve. Following Hitler's decree that London was to be attacked in force, the sting had undoubtedly gone out of the airfield attacks, as Luftwaffe planners were preoccupied with organising this next phase of operations, one possible explanation for the lack of bombing by these large formations being that this was more a reconnaissance in strength of London's approaches and defences, but that seems rather elaborate. Nonetheless, the Me 109s had well protected the bombers once again, none of which were lost. Seven Me 109s had been destroyed, however, one pilot killed, another missing over the sea, and four were captured. Conversely, three Spitfires had been destroyed, one damaged, with two pilots killed and two wounded; no Hurricanes or pilots had been lost, just seven aircraft damaged and two pilots wounded.

At Fowlmere, having lost its CO, 19 Squadron's mood was depressed; Pilot Officer Johnnie Johnson:

> Later that morning the Squadron Adjutant sent for us. 'You chaps are to report to 616 Squadron at Coltishall at once. They've just been pulled out of the front line and will have time to train new pilots. It's probably the best thing. You can see what the form is here. We must have experienced pilots who can take their place in the Squadron.' The phone rang and the Adjutant listened for a few moments before he slowly replaced the receiver.
> 'They've found the CO. Probably dead when he crashed.'
> For a moment he brooded.
> 'Well, good luck with 616.'

Johnnie and his two companions, who had got nowhere near a Spitfire cockpit during their brief time at Fowlmere, had nonetheless received an early initiation into life and death on a fighter squadron. (Johnson went on to survive the war as the RAF's official top-scoring fighter ace.)

At 13.20 hrs, seven Spitfires of 72 Squadron flew from Croydon to Hawkinge, where they refuelled before patrolling overhead at 25,000ft. Very soon after 14.00 hrs RDF indicated enemy activity over the Dover Strait, Pilot Officer Dennis 'Dutch' Holland later reporting that at 14.25 hrs:

I was flying as rear-guard for the Squadron when I saw about nine or more Me 109s starting to attack us from above. I shouted 'Me 109s coming down on us!' over the R/T and turned to attack the centre aircraft head-on as they were diving down. I fired a short burst of two seconds at him. I could see my tracer going into him when he broke away. After my attack the formation of E/A split up. I then attacked one of the E/A as they were trying to form up again. I did a quarter attack on E/A, developing into astern. I gave E/A about twelve second burst, I saw white smoke pouring from him. He then dived slowly down and seemed to be out of control. I think that I hit the pilot of E/A. I followed him down to about 8,000ft when I was attacked myself by an Me 109. I turned over on my back and dived down. He did not follow me. The last I saw of the E/A I attacked, the machine was smoking furiously. I am convinced that this machine was destroyed.

These were 72 Squadron's only combat claims; however, three Spitfires were shot down. Pilot Officer Douglas 'Snowy' Winter baled out too low and was killed, his Spitfire crashing near Elham; Sergeant Malcolm Gray was killed when his Spitfire also crashed at Elham, and Flight Lieutenant Des Sheen DFC, the Australian commander of 'A' Flight, baled out over Bladbean and was admitted to Queen Mary's Hospital, Sidcup, suffering from burns.

No.222 Squadron had gone forward from Hornchurch to Rochford, and was refuelling there shortly after landing when scrambled at 14.20 hrs to patrol Maidstone. Because refuelling was in progress, however, the pilots could not go off as a cohesive unit but raced into the air as and when able. Sergeant Ernest Scott's section was still in transit to Rochford when the scramble order came, so climbed to 29,000ft over Maidstone. At 15.00 hrs, five Me 110s and two Me 109s were seen some distance away. Scott stalked the enemy and attacked one of the 110s over Thameshaven, presuming it to have been destroyed as 'blazing wreckage was seen from the air afterwards'. (No Me 110s were lost over England this day, however.) Scott was then engaged by a 109, which he 'counter-attacked' north of Rochford and damaged. Much further south, Sergeant Douglas Chipping claimed a 109 probably destroyed over Dover – but was himself shot down and wounded, baling out over Pineham.

At 14.59 hrs, twelve Spitfires of 41 Squadron scrambled from Hornchurch and patrolled the area of Thameshaven and Gravesend. Minutes later an enemy formation approached from the east, over Rochford, comprising, the squadron's Form 'F' recorded, 'about thirty Ju 88 [sic] in very close vics with He 111 in the leading section ... escorted by Me 109'. The CO, Squadron Leader 'Robin' Hood, ordered sections into line astern, and leaving Red and Green Sections to cover their tails, led Blue and Green Sections to attack the bombers head-on. At this point the enemy 'turned North about', down came the 109s and a 'general dogfight ensued'. Pilot Officer Eric 'Sawn Off' Lock, and pilots from various other squadrons, brought down a 7/KG 53 He 111 west of Margate, the crew of which were all killed, and Pilot Officer George Bennions claimed a Ju 88 probable and another damaged (although no record exists of the type having been involved). Me 109s were claimed destroyed by Flight Lieutenant Norman Ryder, and Pilot Officers Ronald Wallens, Oliver Morrogh-Ryan, and Eric Lock, the latter being shot-up and slightly wounded; Pilot Officer Roy Ford claimed a 109 damaged – but the squadron had suffered grievous losses.

Pilot Officer 'Wally' Wallens:

As usual, I was flying No 2 on 'Robin' Hood, leading 'B' Flight, and being unable to gain height advantage in time he put us into line-astern and open echelon port and attacked head-on – a desperate manoeuvre that could age one very prematurely. Within seconds, all hell broke loose, and as the action developed, 'B' Flight was overwhelmingly attacked by the 109s.

Wallens was shot-up and wounded, forced-landing near Orsett, and Pilot Officer Tony Lovell was shot down and baled out of his Spitfire over South Benfleet.

For many years it was widely accepted that Flight Lieutenant Terry Webster DFC and Squadron Leader Hood collided while attacking the bombers, the former baling out but found dead at Laindon, while the latter remains missing – but this now appears unlikely. At 14.55 hrs, the Hurricanes of 73 Squadron had scrambled from Castle Camps to patrol north of Gravesend, at 15.10 hrs sighting the same enemy formation engaged by 41 Squadron, 1 mile to the south and being engaged by AA fire. According to the squadron's Intelligence Report:

'A' Flight, led by Flight Lieutenant Reginald Lovett DFC, attacked the rearmost formation. Leader commenced quarter attack, but as E/A travelling very fast it developed into astern attack at 350 yards. Leader experienced considerable crossfire and was hit by MG fire on the port side. Closed to 300 yards, but hit on starboard leading edge by cannon shell, and in breaking away a Spitfire came up almost vertically and they collided. Leader baled out and landed near Rochford, uninjured after a delayed drop.

It is more likely, therefore, that Squadron Leader Hood collided not with Flight Lieutenant Webster, but with Flight Lieutenant Lovett of 73 Squadron. What became of either Squadron Leader Hood or his Spitfire has never been satisfactorily explained, however, and he remains missing to this day (see research by Philip Harvey published in this author's *Missing in Action: Resting in Peace* (see Bibliography).

No.73 Squadron had actually moved on this day from Church Fenton to the Debden Sector, in fact by the time ground personnel arrived there this action had already been fought by the squadron's pilots. After the Fall of France, 73 Squadron had been returned to full-strength, but many of its pilots were replacements with little or no combat experience beyond the 'Junkers Party' of

15 August 1940, and none of fighting the Me 109. Consequently and as so often happened, 73 Squadron, fresh to the visceral battle over the 11 Group area, was hacked to pieces by the lethal 109s in this first engagement.

In addition to Flight Lieutenant Lovett baling out after the Spitfire collision, Pilot Officer Robert Rutter was shot down and took to his parachute, landing near West Hanningfield with a bullet in an ankle. From Billericay Hospital, he wrote to his CO, Squadron Leader Maurice Robinson:

> Although only slightly damaged, it appears that I shall be out of the show for some little time, and I am very sorry that this should have happened on our first time up.
>
> I followed you into the first attack, and went into echelon and tackled the bombers to your right, 'a la No 5 Attack!' Smoke poured from his starboard engine and as I broke away the engine was well ablaze. Turning for an attempt at a second one, I noticed several 109s just below. Next there was a sharp cracking as several bullets came through the floor from underneath and in front, presumably fired by the bomber. I dived steeply out of trouble, as oil came spurting from the engine and covered the dashboard. The engine seemed to be running fairly well, so having wiped some of the oil from my eyes and the altimeter, I noticed that I was down to 5,000ft and looked round for a suitable forced-landing field.
>
> The next minute there was a load explosion from the engine, followed by smoke, and as I couldn't by then see much, baling out seemed the best course. The machine crashed in a field and I landed down in a beet field, reached the road and was picked up by an ARP Warden who took me to his house. An Army Major and MO soon arrived and applied field dressings while I knocked back a treble brandy, afterwards driving me here. After an X-Ray and a shot of 'gas' I awoke to find a foot swathed in bandages and splints, and the 'verdict': one bullet was extracted, another went in and came out again, and a bone was splintered. The wounds ought to heal in a fortnight, after which the foot goes into plaster for a month or so, so that's that!

Squadron Leader Robinson had also been shot-up in the engagement, crash-landing at Wallasea Yacht Club, but was unhurt. Sergeants Geoffrey Garton and Alfred Marshall both returned damaged Hurricanes safely to base, but one of their peers was missing: Sergeant Alexander Logan McNay.

That afternoon, Jack Friedlein was working near his cattle sheds at Whitehouse Farm, North Fambridge, while his wife, Winnie, his parents and two other farm-workers took shelter. Jack himself 'rarely went to the shelter during air raids as they were becoming so commonplace the disruption was too frequent to be practical'. Having watched a formation of twin-engine bombers flying up the Thames towards London:

> I heard a mighty explosion, and looked up to see a huge ball of flame next to my chicken sheds, the flames quickly spreading to the adjacent pig sheds ...

The aircraft must have gone in at an extremely shallow angle from the East for me not to have seen it. It clipped the tops of some trees and piled in. An RAF salvage team arrived later and over a period of a week various items of wreckage were recovered. The crater was guarded by Scottish soldiers who told me that the pilot had been shot on his way down but had not burned. No trace of him was recovered, so I presumed that he had been blown to pieces.

Jack Friedlein may well have been right; in 1979, enthusiasts excavated the crash-site, recovering substantial aircraft remains confirming its identity of Sergeant McNay's Hurricane: P3224. According to John Tickner, who was present, only 'a few pieces of lifejacket were discovered, nothing else connected with the pilot' – and so Glaswegian Sergeant Alexander Logan McNay remains missing to this day.

In that first, fateful, engagement, 'Squadron Leader Robinson and Sergeant Brimble got probable He 111 each [ORB].'

After 14.40 hrs there were at least four German formations over Kent, estimated by RDF at 190 aircraft. No.17 Squadron was sent south from Debden to patrol Hornchurch; 249 and 46 Squadrons from North Weald to cover Rochford, while 501 was up from Gravesend patrolling Maidstone; 66 Squadron covered its Kenley base when 253 was sent from there to the Maidstone line, and 43 Squadron was ordered from Tangmere to patrol Biggin Hill. Assistance was also requested from 10 Group, 234 Squadron scrambling from Middle Wallop at 14.45 hrs to patrol the Kenley area.

At 14.53 hrs, Squadron Leader Ronald Kellett led the Poles of 303 Squadron up from Northolt, and at 15.05 hrs:

> After various vectors, Squadron Leader Kellett, Red 1, at 22,000ft, near Gillingham, saw AA across the Estuary and led Squadron to attack. Red Section attacked Me 109s circling round thirty-five Ju 88s, and about a dozen enemy fighters in addition came in to attack from above. Yellow Section apparently mistook enemy's direction owing to circling fighters, and after taking avoiding action, lost the enemy. Blue Section went in under Red and attacked the bombers. Squadron became scattered and returned independently [ORB].

Squadron Leader Kellett claimed an Me 109 destroyed and a probable, Flying Officer Waclaw Lapkowski a Ju 88, Sergeant Kazimierz Wunsche an Me 109, and the Czech Sergeant Josef Frantisek an Me 109 and a Ju 88 destroyed. Frantisek's Hurricane was damaged by enemy fire, although the pilot was unhurt and he regained base safely. Lapkowski was shot down, baling out suffering from burns and a broken leg, he landed at Rectory Road, Hawkwell.

No.303 Squadron had intercepted the raid heading for Thameshaven, He 111s of KGs 26 and 53, escorted by Me 109s of JG 53 and 54, which had been successfully fighting off the RAF fighters.

At 15.10 hrs, 17 Squadron sighted the same raid over Chatham and Gravesend, but had to attack into the sun: Flight Lieutenant Alfred Bayne's Blue Section, comprised of two Polish pilots, Pilot Officers Pawel Niemiec and Tadeusz Kumiega, and himself, went into line astern to tackle the Me 109s, and a general melee immediately developed. Bayne sent a 109 down streaming smoke – seen by Sergeant George Steward to crash near South Benfleet. Flying Officer Harold Bird-Wilson DFC – whose award had been announced earlier this very day – led Green Section to attack the bombers but without recording any noticeable results. The CO, Squadron Leader Anthony Miller, and his Red Section, attacked the leading bombers, badly damaging at least one, while Flying Officer Count Manfred Czernin's Yellow Section went for the rearmost vic of He 111s. After the initial charge, during which two Heinkels were left with engines ablaze, Czernin, Yellow 1, attacked another He 111 from abeam, watching the bomber's undercarriage drop and starboard engine stop; Yellow 3, Sergeant Clifford Chew, pressed home his attack on the same aircraft, which burst into flames. Two of the crew were seen to bale out, but only one parachute opened, and the bomber broke up in mid-air – this was the He 111 of 7/KG 53 also attacked by Pilot Officer Lock of 41 Squadron, and Squadron Leader Robinson of 73, which crashed off Margate. Czernin then out-manoeuvred a 109 which attacked him – this being 9/JG 54's *Feldwebel* Heinrich Dettmar, who was killed owing to parachute failure; his 109 crashed near Pitsea.

Surprisingly, considering its unfavourable tactical position of having to attack into the sun, 17 Squadron's only casualty was damage to Sergeant Leonard Bartlett's Hurricane, caused first by a He 111 nose-gunner who shot away his rudder and aileron controls, then by a 109 which sent a cannon shell into his port wing, damaging the main spar. Luckily, Bartlett was unhurt, and no doubt with some skill, returned his damaged but sturdy mount to base.

At 15.20 hrs, the Hurricanes of 46 Squadron engaged Me 109s five miles south of Sheppey; Flight Lieutenant Alexander Rabagliati was flying a Hurricane (V7360) armed with four 20mm cannon and managed a quick burst at a fleeting 109, which two other pilots pursued to sea-level. Rabagliati then climbed to 12,000ft 'and spotted an Me 109 on the tail of a Spitfire. Gave the E/A a three-second burst and he blew up in the air. He took no evasive action and did not appear to see me.'

Clearly, the cannon, when it worked, was a devastating weapon – although an Me 110 subsequently attacked was more fortunate, escaping by taking violent evasive action and diving for the sea. Rabagliati noted that these combats occurred 'over the middle of Kent and the marshes just South of the Isle of Sheppey'. The 109 which exploded was a machine of *Stab* III/JG 54, flown by the *Gruppenkommandeur*, *Hauptmann* F. Ultsch, who was killed, his fighter crashing near Pitsea. Pilot Officer Alan Johnson and FAA pilot Sub-Lieutenant Jack Carpenter also claimed 109s destroyed in the combat, in which 46 Squadron suffered no loss.

No.501 Squadron joined up with an unspecified squadron, also going in to action over the Isle of Sheppey, at 15.30 hrs; Sergeant James 'Ginger' Lacey claiming two Me 109s destroyed and Sergeant Raymond Gent a probable.

No.249 Squadron saw the enemy approaching Gravesend, Sergeant Richard Smithson reporting 'Fifteen Do 215s [sic] and countless Me 109s'. In the ensuing interception, Smithson claimed one Dornier probably destroyed and another damaged; Pilot Officer Hugh Beazley and Sergeant Henry Davidson both damaged 109s, and Sergeant William Davis a Do 17 damaged. The Canadian Flight Lieutenant Robert Barton was shot down, however, and baled out, unhurt, over Shellhaven.

Patrolling over Kenley at Angels 20, 234 Squadron saw AA fire bursting over the Thames Estuary and investigated, arriving over Gravesend at 15.45 hrs, Blue Section were attacked out of the sun by three Me 109s. Turning into the attack, the Australian Flight Lieutenant Pat Hughes, Blue 1, saw twelve more 109s approaching so dived, followed by two Hurricanes. Over Eastchurch, the squadron's Intelligence Report recorded that 'a dogfight ensued ... Blue 1 fired a full deflection shot at one 109 and hit his ammunition tanks. The E/A blew up and spun down' – this being the same machine attacked by Flight Lieutenant Rabagliati. Hughes then pursued another 109, shooting away the enemy fighter's oil tank, the contents of which covered his Spitfire. 'The Me 109 finally forced-landed in a field fifteen miles from Manston' – this being *Hauptmann* W. Mayerweissflog of *Stab* JG 53, who was captured unhurt. Blue 2, the Polish Pilot Officer Janusz Zurakowski duelled with a 109, which, after a short burst:

> rolled and dived and flew low, due South. Blue 2 stayed on his tail; fired a short burst at 120 yards, and closed in to spend the rest of his ammunition. The E/A crossed the coast near Hastings and landed on the sea. The pilot got out and two minutes later the aircraft sank.

Feldwebel A. Ochsenkühn, of 9/JG 53, was picked up by the Hastings lifeboat and captured. Blue 3, Sergeant Michael Boddington, engaged a 109 travelling south-east over Sheppey, and 'chased him all the way to Ramsgate, caught him up, climbed to twenty feet above him and fired in a shallow dive over his nose. The E/A went straight into the sea from 2,000ft.' Red 2, Pilot Officer Bob Doe, saw seven Me 109s attacking a squadron of Hurricanes:

> I dived down and fired at the leading enemy aircraft, but my bullets went behind him. I saw them enter the second 109 and then the third burst into flames and blew up. I went right between the rest.
>
> I was then attacked by the remainder who left the Hurricanes. I did tight turns with three shooting at me and three above me who came down in their turn. I half-rolled down, round the edge of the balloons, went through a pall of smoke above the burning oil tanks at full boost and at nought feet, weaving up a river.

Short of fuel, Pilot Officer Doe landed at Kenley. The Me 109 he had destroyed was a machine belonging to 7/JG 53, which had also been shot-up by Flight Lieutenant Hughes, among others.

No.66 Squadron, however, fared badly in this swirling mass of aeroplanes over the Thames Estuary and Essex coast; 19-year-old Pilot Officer Peter King was shot down by Me 109s over the Medway – he baled out but was killed due to parachute failure. Flight Lieutenant George Christie DFC, commanding 'A' Flight, was shot down, forced-landed near Canterbury and admitted to the RN Hospital at Gillingham suffering from shrapnel in his left arm and right leg. Pilot Officer John Mather was similarly shot-up and forced-landed, and Pilot Officer Hubert 'Dizzy' Allen returned to Kenley unhurt but with a damaged Spitfire. No.66 Squadron was unable to register any combat claims after this action.

As the enemy withdrew back to their bases in France, eight oil tanks were ablaze at Thameshaven, where an oil refinery plant was also hit and a wharf badly damaged, the thirty-strong He 111 force being responsible. Protected by over 100 Me 109s, again the escorts had done their job through sheer weight of numbers alone, which seems to have compensated for their limited time over England owing to limited fuel: just two He 111 were lost to RAF fighters. All other losses and claims were between the opposing fighter units. During the afternoon action, ten Spitfires were destroyed and three damaged, five of their pilots killed and five wounded; five Hurricanes were destroyed and five damaged, with one pilot killed and two wounded.

At 16.00 hrs, the airfield at Detling was hit by Me 109 fighter-bombers, which then flew WNW over Maidstone. No.43 Squadron, which was patrolling Biggin Hill at 20,000ft. Blue 1 (identity unknown) was forced to descend owing to oxygen system issues, followed by the rest of Blue Section and all of Green. Blue 2 and 3, however, lost their leader in the haze, and when at 18,000ft, sighted up to forty Me 109s near Maidstone. The 109s were in the process of wheeling about after the attack, and turned south. Blue 3, Sergeant Charles Hurry, had a hasty deflection shot at the rearmost formation, one of which half-rolled away – pursued by Hurry. At 6,000ft the 109 pulled out of the dive, heading south-east, still chased by Hurry who engaged it a second time and watched the German fighter crash in flames near Appledore. Hurry's victim was *Leutnant* Helmut Strobl of 5/JG 27 – killed on his twenty-fifth birthday. The enemy pilot, however, would remain missing, entombed with the wreckage of his 109 near Appledore Railway Station, until recovered by aviation archaeologists and identified on the forty-sixth anniversary of the crash in 1986. At the request of the family, Helmut Strobl's remains were interred in the family grave at Kolbnitz. Some time later, *Leutnant* Strobl's sister wrote to Charles Hurry: 'The letter caused me to do some soul-searching. It was a courteous letter, and I responded accordingly. I was glad she didn't ask how her brother died. I was shot down thirteen days later and would not wish the experience on anyone.'

So closed the day fighting. In total, thirteen Spitfires had been lost and six damaged, seven pilots killed and six wounded; six Hurricanes had been destroyed and nine damaged, a pilot killed and two wounded. As previously mentioned, just two He 111s were lost; losses among the Me 109s amounted to fifteen destroyed and five damaged; eight pilots had been killed, at least one wounded, and six were PoWs.

Oberleutnant Ulrich Steinhilper of 3/JG 52: 'we began to openly discuss the subject of *Kanalkrankheit* – 'Channel Sickness' ... some court-martials had been instituted for pilots who had returned too frequently with mechanical faults which could not be found by the ground-crews.'

AC1 Bob Morris:

From a ground viewpoint we had to learn very quickly about air raids which were coming in thick and fast. Once I looked up and saw five parachutes descending. We of 66 Squadron were now dispersed around the edge of the aerodrome at Kenley, with plenty of space to work between the aircraft. We could not put the aircraft either in a hangar or in a group for fear of them being wiped out together. This meant that we had to work on them out in the open, often without any cover when a raid came in. They had built some blast pens at Kenley, but nowhere near enough, so you could be quarter of a mile from a shelter. It is perhaps surprising but you got used to it, almost blasé about it, in fact. We used to carry on working after the siren had gone, right up until the Germans were practically overhead. If you then left your aircraft and lay down on the ground some distance away from it, the chances of being killed by a bomb were remote. Strafing was a bit more hazardous, but the greatest problem was bomb-blast, i.e. what it actually threw into the air. If it exploded near a road, building or runway then huge slabs and chunks of concrete and masonry could come falling down on you. You therefore tended to lie there and keep your fingers crossed that when all the rubbish thrown up came down, it didn't hit you.

During the day, Beauforts of Coastal Command's 22 Squadron bombed German shipping in Boulogne Harbour, but clear weather conditions saw operations scrubbed for 2 Group's Blenheims, excepting an uneventful North Sea sweep. By night Bomber Command was busy: the battleship *Tirpitz* was attacked by a lone aircraft at Wilhelmshaven, and Boulogne's E-Boats and the guns around Cap Gris-Nez were also bombed. Wellingtons attacked military, industrial and communications targets in Germany, and Whitleys bombed oil installations at Regensburg and the Fiat aircraft factory at Turin – a long flight – reporting an explosion and smoke rising 6,000ft. Oil facilities were also successfully targeted by Hampdens. And so it went on, day after day, night after night.

Daily Home Intelligence Report:

> Hitler's speech is generally regarded as 'encouraging'. The public read into it that the work of the RAF and blockade are taking effect ... Demands for, and satisfaction at, reprisals continue.

North-western (Manchester): '...if any "cities are to be razed" we shall do likewise'.

Friday, 6 September 1940

On this day, Air Vice-Marshal Leigh-Mallory, the AOC 12 Group, following consultation with Squadron Leader Douglas Bader, commanding 242 Squadron, ordered that in future 19, 242 and 310 Squadrons would operate from Duxford as a wing. This was, however, a purely parochial arrangement without consultation with HQ Fighter Command. As we have seen, training had revolved around the flight of six aircraft, not even a squadron of twelve as a whole, which was the largest tactical formation Air Chief Marshal Dowding considered practical. Over Dunkirk, Air Vice-Marshal Park had his squadrons travel together in convoy across the sea to patrol the French coast – but these were not 'wings' in the true sense of the word, this was simply a case of arriving over the French coast in strength. Once battle was joined, owing to the TR9D radio's limitations, inter-squadron communication was impossible, and so an airborne leader was unable to command and control any formation larger than a single squadron.

Wing Commander Gordon Sinclair was a flight commander with 310 Squadron at Duxford:

> There was never any possibility of three or more squadrons taking off from Duxford together and receiving battle orders from a wing leader while airborne. Our R/T sets, TR9s, were not up to it, but in any case, such a situation never arose or was even contemplated. Each squadron acted on its own, down to flight or section level, and we received information regarding the whereabouts of enemy aircraft from the Duxford Operations Room, based upon advice they had received from the relevant RDF station.

Indeed, Group Captain Sir Douglas Bader, as he became, elaborated on the impossibility of communicating with the wing when airborne:

> Only the squadron commanders were on the same frequency. We had four buttons on the VHF in those days, which we had received just before the Battle of Britain. It was ridiculous, anyway, trying to tune this thing with someone shooting up your backside! Anyway, the other pilots each had their own squadron frequency. The Controller would talk to me on my frequency, but to talk to the chaps I would have to keep changing frequency from squadron to squadron. Later, of course, we got it so that we were all on the same frequency.

When we were above the enemy I would say 'Diving, diving now, attacking now', and my Section of three would go down – followed by everyone else. As soon as we had made once pass, though, our formation was broken up. My objective was to get the wing into the right position, then say 'Attacking now', after which it was up to them. They awaited my order, every man knew what he had to do, but the wing was impossible for me to control after that point.

Not all Fighter Command aircraft had VHF, however, that was the problem. Squadron Leader Ronald Kellett was commanding the Polish 303 Squadron at Northolt, in 11 Group:

The squadron leader's role was to bring his pilots into contact with the enemy in such a way that his formation maintained cohesion until the firing commenced – after which it was every man for himself. Thereafter it was virtually impossible to reform and make renewed concerted attacks – partly [in the case of 303 Squadron] due to language problems but also because of the distance travelled in a few seconds and the large number of aircraft in the sky … The problem, was of course, to see the enemy formation in plenty of time and sum up the various components. Sometimes you could see the enemy over France from 10,000ft over London.

Air Vice-Marshal Park's 'problem' was how to preserve limited resources while inflicting maximum losses on the enemy. Nonetheless, the AOC 11 Group had decided it sometimes appropriate to use his precious Spitfire squadrons in pairs, as a high-altitude umbrella, protecting the Hurricanes which were better-suited to operating lower down, against bombers. Indeed, he reported:

As the enemy penetrated further inland, we adopted the tactics of meeting enemy formations in pairs of squadrons, while calling on 10 and 12 Groups to provide close cover for our aerodromes near London and for suburban aircraft factories West of London. This arrangement enabled us to meet the enemy further forward in greater strength while giving a measure of close protection against enemy raids which might elude us at various heights. On some occasions it therefore became practicable to detail a wing of two Spitfire squadrons to engage escorting enemy fighter while a wing of Hurricanes engaged the bombers.

In this context, clearly a 'wing' is a pair of squadrons, representing flexible thinking on Park's part and again confirming that he was not averse to using larger formations than a flight or squadron when the tactical circumstances required the enemy to be met in greater strength. Although those squadrons were unable to talk to each other in the air, they could speak to pilots in their own squadrons and the controller – and passing information efficiently to two squadrons presented no difficulty for him. As for the matter of meeting the enemy in strength, although 11 Group squadrons were acting independently, Air Vice-Marshal Park was doing exactly that, scrambling multiple squadrons and, indeed, bring 12 Group squadrons down from Duxford to cover airfields north of the Thames, and 10 Group to patrol Surrey, defending Kenley sector station and the aircraft factory at Weybridge.

Pilot Officer Michael Appleby, 609 Squadron, 10 Group:

> Throughout August and early September, we of 609 Squadron, operating from Warmwell in the Middle Wallop Sector of 10 Group, were usually patrolling Brooklands, Guildford and other areas West of London in support of 11 Group. We generally harried the stragglers who had dropped their bombs and were on the way home. Things do happen fast at 20,000ft in the air, collision speeds at well over 600 mph, so it is not surprising that with all that space around you it was not always possible to locate the enemy. Even if you did, they might be so far away that by the time you caught them up something else had happened in between. Nonetheless, if we did catch them we attacked, and the Squadron had quite a lot of success.

Air Vice-Marshal Park, therefore, was faultlessly working to his Commander-in-Chief's wishes and the System. Conversely, the 12 Group three squadron wing was a maverick scenario. This arose from Squadron Leader Bader's belief that the action fought by 242 Squadron on 30 August 1940 was much more successful than it actually was, and that his Hurricanes alone had inflicted the damage – leading Bader to conclude and argue that had more 12 Group squadrons been in the air, the execution would have been greater still. No.242 Squadron, however, had *substantially* overclaimed, in fact, and 11 Group squadrons *were* also engaged. Nonetheless, in this idea, both the ambitious Leigh-Mallory and swashbuckling Bader, who so craved to be at the forefront of the action and limelight, found a means of 12 Group, and, of course, Bader in particular, playing a prominent role in the fighting.

At the time, Squadron Leader Douglas Blackwood was commanding the Czech 310 Squadron at Duxford:

> The 'Big Wing' thing was all started by Douglas Bader who, of course, had a Cranwell background, and so he naturally became leader. He also had the support of the Duxford Sector Controller and Station Commander, Wing Commander 'Woody' Woodhall. Douglas Bader was an extremely brave and inspirational chap; we are, of course, talking about a man without legs who flew fighters, played squash and had a very low golf handicap! His pilots of 242 Squadron would have followed him anywhere. At Duxford in 1940, we never did any practice sorties as a Wing, we just went off on an operational patrol one day with Douglas leading.

Group Captain Bader explained the theory behind the 'Big Wing' concept:

'Woody' would ring me up and say that the Germans were building up over the Pas-de-Calais, and I remember saying 'Well why the hell don't we go off now and get the buggers while they're forming up?' You see the bombers would come from their bases in France and orbit the Pas-de-Calais, that area around Calais and Boulogne, and the fighters would then take off from their airfields within that area, such as Wissant and St Omer. Of course the fighters have very short range, not more than forty-five minutes. They would climb up and join the bombers and then the whole armada would set course over the Channel. If our Duxford Wing had got off when they were building up, we'd have got about seventy miles south of base, probably down to the Canterbury area, and we had got them there, on the way in. We would have been at the right height and therefore have controlled the battle.

The issue here is that the System required 12 Group to cover 11 Group airfields while Air Vice-Marshal Park's squadrons were engaged further forward, and maintain sufficient strength to discharge its own defensive responsibilities to the industrial Midlands and the North. The attack on north-east England by *Luftflotte* 5 on 15 August 1940 had already confirmed the fact that such mass raids north of the Thames could not be discounted, and that Dowding had deployed his Command in such a way as to defeat *Luftflotte* 5 in a single day was described by Churchill as 'genius'. Again conversely, Air Chief Marshal Dowding had found it necessary, on 1 October 1939, to write to Leigh-Mallory, in detail, on the subject of 'lateral reinforcement', in which letter [reproduced in full in *Bader's Big Wing Controversy: Duxford 1940*] he made clear that:

I have delegated tactical control almost completely to groups and sectors, but I have not delegated strategic control, and the threat to the line must be regarded as a whole and not parochially. The units at Debden and Duxford may be urgently required at short notice for the defence of London and, although they have been put under you to balance the number of stations in groups, this function of theirs must not be overlooked. (You will remember there is an emergency order 'Concentrate on London', which involved action by these two stations.)

The Commander-in-Chief's wishes, therefore, were plain – but, going forward, 12 Group would bludgeon its way into battle regardless.

By 08.15 hrs, RDF along the South Coast was indicating enemy formations assembling over Calais, the first raid arising from which crossing in over Hythe at 08.36 hrs, followed by another, minutes later, also over Hythe, while others came in over Ramsgate, Sandwich, Dover and New Romney. The latter, *Major* Adolf Galland and the Me 109s of JG 26 escorting Do 17s, turned west, towards Hailsham, and was en route to attack Farnborough; the rest flew towards Maidstone, where, typically, they would separate to strike different targets: the first formation to reach and turn on Maidstone was the Me 110s of *Erprobungsgruppe* 210, escorted by Me 110s of V/LG 1, returning to Hawker's factory at Weybridge; the rest headed north-west, possibly intending to attack Biggin Hill or Kenley.

In total, seventeen RAF fighter squadrons were scrambled to meet these raids – a response in strength by individually operating units. At 08.37 hrs, 10 Group's 234 Squadron had scrambled from Middle Wallop and ordered top patrol Brooklands. At 08.50 hrs, Flight Lieutenant Brian Lane DFC (who was promoted to command the squadron that day) led 19 Squadron off from Fowlmere to rendezvous with the slower Duxford Hurricanes of 242 and 310 Squadron on the 12 Group Wing's first sortie, a patrol of North Weald and Hornchurch at Angels 20.

Frequently, times recorded on combat reports are approximations, and this is certainly the case with 234 Squadron's pilots recording theirs on this morning at 09.30 hrs. The fact is that the squadron actually went into action shortly after 09.00 hrs, this being confirmed by both German timings and those of RAF casualty files. Squadron Leader 'Spike' O'Brien DFC had climbed the Spitfires to 24,000ft, and when north of Beachy Head sighted the Farnborough-bound raid below. The Spitfires, which had the height advantage, attacked the escorting German fighters in sections line astern.

Flight Lieutenant Pat Hughes, Blue 1: 'fired a long burst into one Me 109 which crashed on landing approx. five miles West of Littlestone'. What is known is that this Me 109 belonged to *Oberleutnant* Joachim Müncheberg's 7/JG 26 – but not which of the unit's two pilots reported missing after this operation. During the pilot's crash-landing at Old Romney, the enemy fighter caught fire; soldiers on the scene were unable to save him from the inferno – so shot him, thereby preventing further suffering. The remains, however, defied identification, and were buried as unknown at Hawkinge Cemetery. Whether this was *Gefreiter* Karl Biecker or *Gefreiter* Peter Holzapfel cannot be ascertained.

Hughes continued: 'I climbed back to 10,000ft and intercepted five Me 109s escorting an Me 110 across Dover. This 110 had one engine on fire and just after passing Dover the crew baled out and the 110 crashed into the sea.' The blaze had actually been caused by an electrical fault, not enemy action, the aircraft, of *Stab* ZG 26, being abandoned off Dover; *Oberleutnant* Friedrich Viertel was captured but his *Bordfunker*, *Unteroffizier* Rudolf Roth, was killed.

Hughes then attacked the rearmost Me 109 which had escorted the burning Me 110, hitting the fighter's oil tank, the viscous black fluid covering the closely pursuing Spitfire. Hughes broke away, being attacked by three other 109s, and last saw his opponent 'losing height and smoking badly'.

The same Me 109 brought down by Hughes was also attacked by the Polish Pilot Officer Janusz Zurakowski, Blue 2:

Saw formation of Do 17 with Me 109s. Attacked an Me 109 in front of bombers from front and abeam. He holed my wing. He went over on his back, dived and I followed him. He climbed and went on his back again. Fired a second burst, and third burst, and he crashed. Three Me 109s attacked me at 3,000ft … returned to base and my machine overturned on landing.

Fortunately Zurakowski was unhurt.

Sergeant Michael Boddington, Blue 3, attacked an Me 109 from astern, a chase ensued during which the fighters descended to 500ft: 'Enemy finally crash-landed nine miles NNE of Ashford, near Wye. Pilot vacated machine and set on fire, I believe by pulling an incendiary mechanism, although there were a number of civilians and soldiers near who could perhaps confirm this.'

This was another of Müncheberg's men, *Oberleutnant* Hans Christenecke, who forced-landed at Hothfield and was captured.

Pilot Officer Bob Doe was Red 2, flying wingman to Squadron Leader O'Brien, who was attacked from behind by two Me 109s. Doe reported that he engaged 'the rear one and eventually shot it down, just north of Dover, and it crashed on land'. What aircraft this was, however, cannot be ascertained. Doe then found fourteen Do 17s and attacked the rearmost vic of three, damaging them all before going home 'at full boost'.

Squadron Leader O'Brien claimed two Me 109s destroyed, as did Sergeant Alan Harker, although only three JG 26 machines were actually destroyed. *Hauptmann* Erich Bode's II/JG 26 *Stabschwarm*, however, destroyed two of the Spitfires, one by the *Gruppenkommadeur*, the other by *Oberleutnant* Kurt Ebersberger. Pilot Officer William Gordon was killed, his Spitfire crashing at Hadlow Down, and Sergeant William Hornby baled out with facial injuries, his Spitfire exploding over Northam.

Farnborough, however, was not bombed, and nor were any bombs dropped attributed to this raid, making it impossible to fathom why.

The Spitfires of 41 Squadron were patrolling their Hornchurch base at 20,000ft when Pilot Officer Eric Lock became unconscious, doubtless due to an oxygen system failure. Coming to at 8,000ft, Lock:

climbed up again hoping to find my Squadron but without success. I sighted a Ju 88 at 18,000ft, which I attacked. I opened fire over the Channel, when it started to dive. I fired more bursts as we crossed the French coast. I saw it crash about twenty miles inland.

Lock was credited with a Ju 88 destroyed at 09.00 hrs (no such loss is apparent in German records). The rest of 41 Squadron 'saw nothing [ORB].'

At 08.50 hrs, Flight Lieutenant Willie Rhodes-Moorhouse DFC had led 601 Squadron up from Tangmere with orders to patrol Mayfield at 15,000ft. Sensibly, the Hurricanes climbed higher, to 17,000ft, and at 09.30 hrs sighted fifty Me 109s 3,000ft above, which 601 Squadron climbed to engage. Having the all-important height advantage, the 109s pounced, one of which, attacking the Hurricanes from the rear, over-shot and presented Pilot Officer Thomas Grier with a perfect target – the 109 was given a 'good burst and it immediately exploded and went down, a twisted, smoking, mess'. Grier then chased and destroyed a second 109 over Ramsgate. Flight Lieutenant Michael Robinson blew the cockpit canopy, rudder and fin off another enemy machine. Sergeant Norman Taylor found and damaged a Do 17 over the sea, and the Polish Pilot Officer Juliusz Topolnicki claimed two 109s destroyed before being shot down himself and baling out slightly wounded. Flying Officer Humphrey Gilbert also baled out, and he too was safe. Two pre-war 'Legionnaires', however, were missing. It was soon confirmed that the American Flight Lieutenant Carl Davis – brother-in-law of 601's CO, Squadron Leader Sir Archibald Hope – was dead, having crashed, inverted, in the back garden of Canterbury Cottage, Brenchley, near Tunbridge Wells. Of Flight Lieutenant Rhodes-Moorhouse, however, there was no news. No.601 Squadron reported that he had been 'seen to attack a Dornier, which he disabled, and immediately after that his plane was seen to come down vertically. It straightened out and flew for a few seconds at 3,000ft, and then went vertically into the ground.'

No.601 Squadron had been engaged by *Major* Adolf Galland's *Geschwaderstabschwarm*, and 2/JG 26. Galland, and both *Unteroffizier* Bernhard Adam and *Leutnant* Horst Ulenberg all claimed Hurricanes destroyed – their claims exactly matching 601's losses, although who shot down who is impossible to know – as is so often the case.

It was to Flight Lieutenant The Hon Max Aitken DFC, the son of Lord Beaverbrook, a close friend of Willie Rhodes-Moorhouse, that the sad duty fell to deliver the news to his wife, Amalia – whose brother, Flying Officer Richard Demetriadi, also of 601 Squadron, had been reported missing on 11 August 1940. Sir Stephen Demetriadi then set off from East Sussex, with Amalia and her mother-in-law, Linda Rhodes-Moorhouse, to ascertain his son-in-law's fate. Touring Kentish hospitals proved fruitless, but then it was discovered that a Hurricane had crashed at High Broom on the right date. Further investigation on site revealed that the machine had completely buried itself, but among wreckage on the surface was a plate bearing the numbers '88'. The missing 601 Squadron Hurricane was P8818. Sir Stephen then arranged for civilian contractors to excavate the site and recover the pilot's remains, which grim task was eventually accomplished.

The 'mercurial' Flight Lieutenant Willie Rhodes-Moorhouse, the 'Flying Etonian' and first ever air VC, was cremated, his ashes buried on top of the hill at the family seat, Parnham, with his father. 'Willie's life,' his mother wrote, 'had been vivid and, like a meteor, had ended before it dimmed'; he was 26 years old. The loss of this charismatic, hugely popular, highly competent and natural leader hit 601 Squadron hard. The following day the unit was withdrawn to the quieter sector of Exeter – and would lose no more pilots during the Battle of Britain.

Flight Lieutenant Mark 'Hilly' Brown DFC, a Canadian, was leading 1 Squadron up from Northolt with orders to patrol Kenley at 20,000ft with the Northolt-based Poles of 303 Squadron, although the two squadrons failed to contact each other in the air. Pilot Officer Roland 'Roly' Dibnah, another Canadian, was forced to leave the formation owing to technical issues with his propeller. En route back to Northolt, the lone Hurricane pilot found *Erprobungsgruppe* 210 bombing the Hawker factory at Weybridge, which the enemy had approached without being intercepted. On this occasion, fortunately, most of the bombs missed the factory and little damage was caused. The Germans turned about, heading south-east, beating their retreat, pursued by Dibnah, who gave chase, engaging an Me 110 from abeam which was attacking two Hurricanes. The 110 executed a stall-turn in an attempt to evade, but Dibnah then attacked head-on, after which the enemy aircraft 'did a wavering turn and one of the crew baled out. The aircraft did a spiral dive into the ground and burst into flames. The member of the crew was captured by members of a service unit.' This was *Erprobungsgruppe* 210's only loss during the operation, which crashed at Crowhurst, near Oxted; the pilot, *Unteroffizier* Gerhard Rüger, was killed in the crash, his *Bordfunker*, *Gefreiter* Edmund Ernst, having taken to his parachute and was the man captured.

At 08.55 hrs, Flying Officer Ben Bowring, Red 1, of 111 Squadron was patrolling Croydon with four other Hurricanes, but although he could communicate with his fellow pilots, R/T messages from 'Runic' (Biggin Hill Sector Control) were distorted. Consequently, Bowring ordered Blue 1 to lead, but had dropped behind. Carrying on, the enemy formation heading for Kenley was sighted, approaching Kenley from the Maidstone direction. Without hesitation, Bowring, followed by Red 2, Sergeant Leslie Tweed, made a diving head-on attack against 'forty Ju 88s [ORB].' No results were noted from this initial attack, but Bowring espied a straggling Ju 88 which 'was shot down with both engines on fire, and crashed between Kenley and Biggin Hill [ORB]'. This aircraft, of 6/KG 76, was actually attacked by various other pilots from as many squadrons, and forced-landed and burned out at Tanyards Farm, Tonbridge; the four crewmen, one of whom had baled out, were captured. During the combat, Bowring's windscreen was smashed by return fire, forcing him to disengage and land, and Sergeant Tweed was shot down and injured in a crash-landing. Meanwhile, Pilot Officer John Simpson, leading Blue Section, had climbed to 20,000ft, engaging ten Me 110s, one of which Simpson damaged.

Having reached their patrol line and heading east, the rest of 1 Squadron, minus Pilot Officer Dibnah, also engaged this third German formation, at 09.05 hrs, between Kenley and Tunbridge Wells. German fighters were seen above and on the squadron's right, and, Flight Lieutenant Brown reported, the Hurricane pilots were then surprised to see:

a very large formation of E/A at 20,000ft, stepped up vertically and backwards, going West. It consisted of Ju 88s and Me 110s. We had not been informed of the presence of this enemy formation. I put the Squadron into line astern and turned left in an attempt to gain a position to attack the bombers. A favourable position was not gained. I saw a Ju 88 crossing underneath me and attacked him. I gave him one burst of five seconds as I closed in until I had to break away to avoid collision. I silenced the rear-gunner and his starboard engine was streaming a white trail. After breaking away I could not see him any longer. The E/A was last seen going SE, towards Tunbridge Wells.

Pilot Officer George Goodman, Blue 3, was attacked by a *Rotte* of Me 109s which he evaded by executing a steep, climbing, turn before sighting a twin-engine aircraft flying south. Goodman attacked, setting the starboard engine on fire, then:

got in closer to finish him off, and was continually fired at by the rear-gunner, who seemed to have more than one gun in the turret. I got in fairly close and broke away to the right and downward, and was hit while below in my oil tank. The windscreen and cockpit were filled with oil and the machine was smoking. I was going down in a spin, levelled off, and abandoned my aircraft. While floating down I could see the E/A well below with the engine on fire and his crash two to three miles South of Penshurst.

Goodman was unsure as to the enemy aircraft's identity, suspecting it to be an Me 110 – it was, in fact, the Ju 88 which crashed at Tanyard's Farm.

Also at 09.00 hrs, 303 Squadron was patrolling over western Kent 'and saw very large formations of enemy aircraft moving up from the coast, to the East of them and above'. Given the Hurricanes' lack of height, Squadron Leader Ronald Kellett desperately climbed the squadron – but with the numbers of enemy fighters present, the result was inevitable – as Kellett later recalled:

all surprise was gone and we were going headlong into the fighters. I decided to attack the centre of the bomber formation, which the Squadron did. The Controller had made an error of judgment, as we should never have been placed on a collision course but bought round from a flank.

It is not possible for me to say how each pilot fared. I can only describe my own experience. I picked my bomber, a Heinkel [Squadron Leader Kellett claimed a Do 17 destroyed, but was more likely the Me 110 of Erprobungsgruppe 210, which, having also been attacked by Hurricanes of 1 Squadron, exploded at Foyle Farm, Crowhurst], and opened fire at about 200 yards. I could see the gunner trying to get a bead on me, so I kicked the right rudder and his cupola and gun disappeared. I continued firing at the left engine, but no flames. I was being hit by the bomber behind me and finally the ammunition in each wing exploded and my guns stopped firing. At the same time, the Heinkel's left engine caught fire. I received a blow on my left knee and the cockpit was covered with smoke and a red liquid. I yelled 'I'm getting the hell out of here!', put the Hurricane into a spin and thought I would get out at 8,000ft. I took it out of the spin and found I could control it, stick hard back and over to the left and a speed of 150 mph. I then found the canopy would not move, nor could I move the emergency jettison device.

Biggin Hill appeared just below me and I started a long approach, but the Heinkel I had just shot down came down with me and kept getting in the way. However, it crashed near Biggin Hill and I landed at 150 mph. It took the whole of the long runway. I did not use the flaps as the Hurricane was nose-heavy, one tyre was punctured and so the aircraft ran with the left wing low. However, the brakes were working so I swung it right before going through the boundary onto the road.

Airmen came out of the dugout and axed off the canopy, and I was bundled into said shelter as bombs were still exploding on the runway I had just used. I reported to the Operations Room, relocated above a small shop near the airfield, owing to bomb damage, and asked them to inform Northolt that I was safe. It had been a near thing. The aircraft had virtually no rudder or elevators left, a hole in each wing large enough for a man to jump through, but, even worse, the incendiary rounds used by the Germans had burnt holes in my parachute and ruined my helmet, goggles and uniform.

In his post-action personal combat report, Squadron Leader Kellett wrote: 'After diving I realised that it was very difficult to control the aircraft as there was a big hole in the starboard wing and the aircraft was very right wing low. There was no elevator control and not much rudder control.' Safely landing that Hurricane, therefore, represented an astonishing feat of airmanship, especially as it was possibly the most badly damaged RAF fighter to return to base during the Battle of Britain.

After the combat, Squadron Leader Kellett claimed a 'Do 215 [*sic*] [ORB]' destroyed. The Poles were also credited with five Me 109s destroyed – but one of these was the same 3/JG 52 machine attacked by various pilots, including Flying Officer Urbanowicz, Pilot Officer Feric and Sergeant Frantisek, which was abandoned over Seal, near Sevenoaks, by *Oberleutnant* H. Waller, who was captured unhurt. A 'He 111 [*sic*]' was also claimed destroyed, and two further Me 109s were claimed as probables. No.303 Squadron, owing to its unenviable tactical position, suffered accordingly, however; Squadron Leader Zdzislaw Krasnodebski was shot down and baled out, horrendously burned, and required reconstructive surgery at East Grinstead; Sergeant Stanislaw Karubin and Flight Lieutenant Athol Forbes were both shot-up and forced-landed, wounded; Flying Officer Wojciech Januszewicz was shot-up and wounded, also making a forced-landing, and Flight Lieutenant Johnny Kent, a Canadian, crash-landed back at Northolt but was also unhurt. Sergeant Josef Frantisek returned his damaged Hurricane to Northolt and was unhurt. As Squadron Leader Kellett later wrote, from 303 Squadron's perspective it had been 'a bad battle' – but nonetheless, the German formation had wheeled about without bombing Kenley or Biggin Hill.

The same enemy formation was also sighted, at 09.00 hrs, over Redhill by the six Hurricanes of 79 Squadron, which had scrambled from Biggin Hill at 08.40 hrs, who witnessed the Germans turning about. Squadron Leader John Heyworth had climbed the small formation to 22,000ft and ordered his pilots to patrol in pairs when the enemy was sighted approaching from the south-east and 2,000ft below; Pilot Officer Herbert Laycock:

> My partner, Flight Lieutenant Clerke, dived to attack and I was about to follow when I observed nine Me 110s above and in the sun. I did not dive but turned to port and positioned myself behind them. Before I was in range, however, they wheeled to port and dived slightly. The main enemy formation had turned to port and were now heading South. It was at this stage I saw a lone machine behind and above and as I came nearer I steeply turned to port, as he came nearer I steeply turned to port and after three quick aileron turns I straightened out and again pulled back, the Me 109 passing under my starboard mainplane. I turned onto it and opened fire well within range. The Me 109 climbed and I then opened fire with a second burst. Just before my ammunition was exhausted I observed trails of black smoke from port mainplane. The Me 109 turned slowly to starboard and went down in a shallow dive, heading South.

The 109 was claimed as a probable. After the action, Squadron Leader Heyworth and Pilot Officer George Nelson-Edwards both claimed Ju 88s damaged, and Flight Lieutenant Rupert Clerke claimed a probable Ju 88, although this was actually destroyed, being the bomber down at Tanyards Farm, Tonbridge, also attacked by pilots of 1 and 303 Squadrons. No.79 Squadron suffered no loss in the action.

Eleven Hurricanes of 501 Squadron had first flown to Dymchurch, near Lympne, and sighted 100+ Me 109s at 20,000ft and upwards incoming over Rye.

At 09.00 hrs, Me 109s of 2(J)LG 2 and JG 2 were sweeping over Ashford and pounced on the Hurricanes of 501 Squadron. In short order, *Oberleutnant* Hans 'Asi' Hahn, *Staffelkapitän* of 4/JG 2, and *Leutnant* Julius Meimberg, also of 4/JG 2, both claimed two Hurricanes each, destroyed. Three were actually shot down: 19-year-old reservist and a former aero fitter Sergeant Oliver Houghton was killed when his aircraft crashed at Charing, and Pilot Officer Hugh Adams, also a reservist, was killed at Claveryte, near Elham when his parachute failed. Sergeant Geoffrey Pearson, yet another reservist, however, was missing – or was he?

Certain members of 501 Squadron remembered those days:

Flight Sergeant Peter Morfill: 'those days were busy times. We used to start ops at about 0600 hrs and it was usually still busy at 1600.'

Sergeant Tony Pickering: 'We NCOs used to play a card game together, to while away the time spent at readiness, but I put a stop to it as I was taking too much money off Geoffrey Pearson and I'm no gambler!'

Pilot Officer Peter 'Hairy' Hairs:

> I was certainly very busy. We used to fly up to eight patrols and scrambles a day. On this particular day I recall seeing a pilot falling through the air trailing an unopened parachute and have always assumed this to have been Adams. There was certainly much activity during this combat with aircraft all over the place and a large number of parachutes.

The following day, 49 MU would investigate the crash-site of an aircraft at Cowleas Farm, Hothfield, north-west of Ashford, confirming it to be Sergeant Pearson's Hurricane, P3516. The pilot's remains had already been recovered – but somehow in the chaos of the times, positive identification was overlooked, leading to the airman being buried at St Stephen's, Lympne as 'Known unto God'. (So the case would remain until 1982, when research by Sergeant Pearson's brother-in-law, Richard Griffiths, himself a former fighter pilot, confirmed that this was he and a named headstone was erected accordingly.)

For 73 Squadron, at the Debden satellite Castle Camps, which had received its baptism of fire the previous day, the squadron diarist recorded that 'Weather continues to be marvellous and it is so peaceful that up here at "Freddie 1" [satellite aerodrome] it is difficult, apart for the occasional hum of Jerry aircraft to believe that war and London are so close to us [ORB].' 'Close' however, the war was: at 08.50 hrs, Flight Lieutenant Reginald Lovett DFC, commander of 'A' Flight, led three sections up to patrol Gravesend (codename 'Monkey') at 15,000ft – the squadron being unable to 'muster any more aircraft as the previous day had reduced us considerably. All left the Mess in cheery mood, Pilot Officers Eliot and Marchand in particular, and the Station Intelligence Officer waved them off with wishes for good luck [ORB].'

Red and Green Sections sighted a large number of Me 109s, but made no contact, while Flight Lieutenant Michael Beytagh, commanding 'B' Flight, led Blue Section to attack up to 100 Me 109s over the Thames Estuary and northern Kent. Beytagh attacked a 109, claiming it as a probable – but the manner of awarding such categories on 73 Squadron is puzzling, the ORB recording that Beytagh's probable was 'nowadays … almost as good as destroyed', and:

> Pilot Officer Marchand destroyed a 109 ten miles north-east of Maidstone, thus opening the squadron's score in that category. He landed at Penshurst, having run short of petrol and rather lost his way. He got back in the evening, his smiles even as large as if his wife had walked suddenly into Freddie 1. It was a tonic to see him but when he came to make out his individual combat

report the IO noticed that he had only claimed a 'probable'. Even more pleased was he when told it obviously came into the 'destroyed' class and he was first to get a definite kill for 73 Squadron [ORB].

According to 73 Squadron's Intelligence Patrol Report, Pilot Officer Marchand, Blue 2:

followed an Me 109 and attacked at 22,000ft, ten miles north-east of Maidstone, firing two bursts of three seconds each. E/A poured black smoke out and Blue 2 followed him down to 10,000ft, by which time flames were coming from the engine, but the E/A's fuselage was actually on fire at this time. Blue 2 had to break away owing to the presence of E/A.

Nobody saw this Me 109 crash, however, and none down in Kent that morning correspond to this claim, which doesn't mean that it was not an enemy fighter that went into the sea and did not make it back to France. Nonetheless, it is difficult to see how this could be considered a confirmed victory under the circumstances – but easy to see how claims and figures can be misleading.

Nineteen-year-old Pilot Officer Eliot, however, was shot down by an Me 109 over the Thames Estuary and baled out wounded: 'We waited anxiously for Eliot and were delighted to get news that he had baled out and was in Twickenham Hospital – even if he was wounded. We cannot afford to lose "Chubby" Eliot, one of our best and the youngest pilot officer [ORB].'

Also patrolling 'Monkey' was 249 Squadron, up from North Weald, led by Squadron Leader John Grandy. East of Maidstone, at 09.30 hrs, the Hurricanes encountered the withdrawing Germans and attacked the Ju 88s from abeam before the squadron broke up. Afterwards, Squadron Leader Grandy climbed to rejoin the fight but was set on fire by 109s and baled out over Maidstone with cannon splinters in his legs: 'Unfortunately, he had some trouble with his parachute and his right leg was badly strained [ORB].' No other 249 Squadron Hurricanes were lost, however, and Grandy was safe, although wounded, the unit claiming the destruction of a Ju 88, an Me 110 and four Me 109s, and others probably destroyed or damaged (although, again, none correlate to actual enemy wreckage on the ground).

As the enemy finally withdrew back towards the south-eastern Kent coast, Tangmere's 43 Squadron, having first patrolled over Brooklands, were vectored towards Tenterden and sighted the raiders retiring, ten–twelve miles north of Dungeness. Having already been engaged many times, the enemy was not in any particular formation, although the Me 109s still had the height advantage: 'A' Flight of 43 was at 20,000ft, 'B' at 22,000ft – but the top cover 109s were at 24,000ft. No.43 Squadron did, however, have the advantage of attacking rom the sun, which the Hurricane pilots wasted no time in so doing. The three members of Blue Section, Flight Lieutenant Tom Dalton-Morgan, Pilot Officer David Gorrie, and Sergeant Charles Hurry out manoeuvred three Me 109s flying in line astern and which tried to attack the Tangmere fighters, each of the Hurricane pilots claiming a 109 destroyed. The South African CO, Squadron Leader Caesar Hull, Red 1, and Flight Lieutenant Richard 'Dick' Reynell, Yellow 1, an Australian and former Hawker test pilot currently serving with 43 Squadron to gain current combat experience, attacked a straggling Ju 88, silencing the rear-gunner, and last seen out to sea in a shallow dive with both engines smoking. Flight Lieutenant John 'Iggy' Kilmartin attacked a lone Me 110 which was heading for the coast, which Squadron Leader Hull confirmed having seen crash into the Channel – this was an escorting fighter of 7/ZG 26, the crew of which, *Feldwebel* Leonhard Kauffmann and *Gefreiter* Gerhard Schumann, were both killed.

It had been a hard-fought contest but if success was measurable in bombs dropped and damage arising, the attack, from the German perspective, was a definite failure.

The next raid, although including up to twenty bombers, was largely another great offensive sweep by Me 109s. At 12.43 hrs, the first of four enemy formations crossed the Kentish coast over Hythe, all of which again headed for Maidstone. Two minutes later, the Duxford Wing was scrambled to patrol north of the Thames; although the sortie would prove uneventful for 12 Group, 19 Squadron considered the presence of so many friendly fighters 'a most comforting feeling indeed [ORB]'.

At 12.30 hrs, as RDF had begun warning of the enemy's assembly, the six Spitfires of 66 Squadron's 'A' Flight had already scrambled from Kenley and ordered to Maidstone. Reaching 22,000ft, the enemy, reported as nine He 111s, escorted by thirty Me 109s, was sighted at 12.50 hrs approaching from the south. Flight Lieutenant Ken Gillies led 'Clickety-Click' to attack six Me 109s in line astern, 2,000ft below. After the dive, Red and Yellow sections became separated, and, after becoming detached from the rest of the Flight, only Pilot Officer Crellin 'Bogle' Bodie successfully engaged, claiming one Me 109 probably destroyed and two damaged. Gilles then led his Red Section, Pilot Officer Bob 'Oxo' Oxspring and Sergeant Matthew Cameron, made a fleeting attack on two He 111s before losing the enemy. Having been unable to climb high enough to reach aircraft circling high above them, the Spitfires turned for home.

More Me 109s crossed the coast over Hythe, fanning out over Kent, while the bombers proceeded to Rochester, bombing Pobjoy's aircraft factory and Rochford airfield, slightly damaging the works, and in the south, a small number of bombs fell near Dymchurch.

Just four Spitfires of 72 Squadron had scrambled from Croydon, which engaged the Germans over Maidstone at 13.15 hrs, Pilot Officer Robert Deacon Elliott, leading Yellow Section, reporting 'Do 17s and Me 109s' south-west of Marden. The squadron was ordered to join up with 66 Squadron near Kenley, and provide a rearguard to the four 'Clickety-Click' Spitfires. As 66 Squadron went into the attack, an Me 109 singled out Elliott:

and a battle commenced. A head-on attack, each of us firing until each passed the other and both of us turned round and made a similar attack. I could see his shell and machine-gun fire hitting me and likewise mine hitting him. On his second attack as he closed towards clouds, smoke burst from his cowlings and he spiralled earthwards out of control, coming to earth SW [of] Marden. I continued to spiral down in an effort to evade further attacks and at 2,000ft proceeded to flatten out and continue home, but at 100ft my machine (which I could tell was badly wounded) suddenly burst into flame and at this point I vacated aircraft. The incident was witnessed by members of the army staff at Luce Barracks, Staplehurst, who came and collected me. No injury either to myself or to anyone on the ground.

This was 72's only claim and loss.

Twelve Spitfires of Westhampnett's 602 Squadron were also up, having scrambled at 13.02 hrs to patrol Mayfield at Angels 20. When on a northerly course at 13.30 hrs over Hailsham, 'A' Flight sighted the withdrawing bombers and 100 Me 109 escorts flying south. The Spitfires were at 20,000ft, as ordered – but as nearly always was the case, the 109s were at 25,000ft, in two formations, one each side of the bombers. 'A' Flight set off in pursuit and reached mid-Channel without managing to engage, but Me 109s fell upon and surprised 'B' Flight. Only Sergeant Jack Proctor managed to reply, claiming a 109 destroyed and attacking several others without apparent effect. Sergeant George Whipps was shot down, however, baling out unhurt over Peasmarsh, and Pilot Officer Thomas Ritchie was shot-up, returning his damaged Spitfire to base with leg wounds requiring admission to Chichester Hospital. Pilot Officers Henry Moody and Peter Ferguson also returned their damaged aircraft to Westhampnett, landing safely, unhurt.

The Hurricanes of 1 Squadron, scrambled from Northolt at 13.02 hrs, to patrol Maidstone were ordered from there to intercept 'Raid 43c' over Dungeness. Pilot Officer Michael Stavert was Blue 3:

While on patrol at 27,000ft near Dover I saw E/A diving out of the sun from about 3,000ft above us. There were six Me 109s and He 113s [sic]. Two opened fire on the formation as they went screaming past. The fire was very wide. I turned and followed one who did not know I was there, because he throttled back and lost speed. At 10,000ft I caught up with him and fired four long bursts of four seconds each and saw a lot of black smoke come from his engine. I followed him as he continued his steep dive towards the sea but was attacked in turn by an Me 109. I evaded him with a steep turn to the right and he carried straight on. The original E/A was last seen diving towards the sea in a steep dive with smoke pouring out.

Stavert claimed a 'He 113 [*sic*] damaged'. As 1 Squadron scattered after the 'bounce', there were no other claims, but nor were any Hurricanes lost.

The final fighting during these lunchtime raids occurred over the Thames Estuary and Manston areas, again, given the type's abundance, with Me 109s. No.43 Squadron's Hurricanes had left Tangmere at 12.40 hrs and vectored to Chatham, where some minutes later Flight Lieutenant Dick Reynell claimed a 109 probable over the Thames Estuary, but little else of the circumstances is known. Hornchurch's 603 Squadron was also up, patrolling Manston at 30,000ft when at 13.50 hrs the Spitfires dived to attack six Me 109s sighted below. Only one claim arose, by Flight Lieutenant Harold MacDonald also claiming a probable. Pilot Officer James Caistor, a married man of just a week, pursued the enemy out to sea and was shot-up, forcing the pilot to land in France, thereby presenting his Spitfire, X4260, to the Germans, this being the third Spitfire and pilot so captured during the Battle of Britain to date. Reported missing, on 22 September 1940 welcome news was received that Caister was a prisoner – who had yet to learn of his DFM award, gazetted nine days previously.

While bomb damage achieved by these lunchtime raids was slight, the pressure was maintained on the defenders. With the move of Me 109s to the Pas-de-Calais and switch to night-bombing by *Luftflotte* 3, by daytime things had been quiet for a few days over the 10 Group area. At 13.45 hrs on this day, however, Pilot Officer Patrick Horton, a New Zealander, of 234 Squadron engaged a Ju 88 reconnaissance machine off Portland but fell victim to return fire, baling out over the sea; fortunately the Spitfire pilot was 'rescued comparatively unhurt by a navy launch from Weymouth [ORB]'.

Further trouble loomed at tea-time. At 17.15 hrs RDF indicated the enemy assembling yet again, and at 17.30 hrs over 100 high-flying German aircraft crossed in over Dungeness, heading towards Maidstone. These were Me 109s providing a diversionary raid for I/KG 53 He 111s which, at 17.40 hrs, approached over the Thames Estuary and at 18.00 hrs bombed the oil facilities at Thameshaven – 46 and 249 Squadrons, up as a pair from North Weald, having arrived too late to prevent this happening. Thameshaven was badly damaged, the Shell Mex refinery burnt out and serious fires started at the three other oil wharves – which would burn all night and into the following day. Having not been intercepted while incoming, the bombers similarly withdrew unmolested by RAF fighters. No.249 Squadron ORB reported that 'A flight of seven Ju 87s made a low-diving attack on Shellhaven. These were not seen by the squadron from 20,000ft but Wing Commander Beamish, who had taken off later and was climbing up to join us saw them and destroyed two on his own.'

Beamish, of course, was a legendary airman and fighter ace, but there were no *Stuka*s involved with these operations, having been withdrawn from the daylight battle the previous month, so this must be a mistake – and no combat report appears to survive.

Nos. 41 and 222 Squadrons were also sent up, both of which engaged Me 109s over the Thames Estuary.

Pilot Officer George 'Ben' Bennions of 41 Squadron's 'A' Flight reported action at 17.55 hrs east of Eastchurch. Sighting forty Me 109s below, Red and Yellow Sections descended to attack while Bennions and Sergeant Frank 'ITMA' Usmar remained above, performing 'S' turns, acting as top cover. Bennions saw two sections of five Me 109s each turn to attack Red and Yellow sections – and opened fire on the rearmost aircraft of the second *Schwarm* from 150 yards:

> The aircraft burst into flames and the hood came back towards my aircraft, the remainder of the E/A went down in flames with black smoke pouring from it. I turned about to starboard and attacked No 5 of another formation of Me 109s. I closed to 150 yards, again slightly left and astern. I fired another short burst … and the Me 109 burst into flames. Again, the hood of the machine came back towards me and I saw the pilot make a parachute jump out of the left-hand side of his aircraft. The aircraft went down in flames.

Although the pilot of this 109, of 8/JG 53, *Feldwebel* E. Hempel, baled out, he was killed, his fighter exploding and crashing onto the Kingsnorth Marshes.

Flight Lieutenant Norman Ryder also destroyed a 109, which exploded in the sea near the Shoeburyness firing range buoy at Pig's Bay – the pilot was captured and was a significant loss: *Hauptmann* Joachim Schlichting, *Gruppenkommandeur* of III/JG 27.

Pilot Officer John MacKenzie, a New Zealander from Otago, also claimed an Me 109 destroyed and a probable, and Flying Officer William Scott and Sergeant Edward Darling also claimed probables.

No.222 Squadron had taken-off from Rochford at 17.30 hrs, and at 18.00 hrs sighted the enemy force withdrawing from Thameshaven. Sergeant Iain Hutchinson reported that north of Maidstone the Spitfires were engaged by a 'superior force of Me 109s at 23,000ft', one of which the young Scot 'pursued to the Thames Estuary, opening fire at 300 yards and closing to fifty. Smoke came from this machine and I could see it was on fire … When I last saw the Me 109 it was diving steeply towards the sea at 100ft.' Although Hutchinson claimed the 109 as 'damaged', it was credited as destroyed. East of Southend, the Spitfires contacted the escorting Me 109s, Pilot Officer Tim Vigors attacking a 109 in the lower of two formations, noting that 'Bits fell off the starboard wing', but was then forced to break away when attacked himself. There were no other claims and all of 222 Squadron's pilots returned safely to their actual base at Hornchurch.

After the enemy's withdrawal following this Thameshaven raid and diversionary sweeps, although the odd plot showed up on RDF screens, there were no more interceptions.

During the day's operations, German losses amounted to thirteen Me 109s destroyed, four damaged, five of their pilots killed, four wounded, and eight captured; four Me 110s were destroyed, five of their aircrew killed, one wounded and three captured. The fighters, however, through overwhelming numbers and the advantage of height, had again protected the bombers well: only two Ju 88s were lost, one damaged, four aircrew killed, and four captured. In total, nineteen aircraft of all types had been destroyed, five damaged, fourteen aircrew killed, five wounded and fifteen captured.

Fighter Command's fighters fared worse than the enemy: thirteen Hurricanes were destroyed, nine damaged, six pilots killed and twelve wounded. Six Spitfires were destroyed, five damaged, one of their pilots killed, three wounded and one captured. In total: nineteen fighters had been destroyed, fourteen damaged, seven pilots killed, fifteen wounded and one captured. In terms of personnel, as we will in due course explore, this was unsustainable: the situation was becoming critical.

It must not be forgotten, however, that while the day-fighting over England was visible and thereby in the public eye, the aircrews of Coastal Command continued to fly dangerous reconnaissance, anti-submarine and invasion, patrols, often far out to sea, and this day was no exception: forty-eight anti-invasion sorties were made by eighty-three crews, and twenty convoys were also escorted. A Hudson of 206 Squadron forced a He 115 down in the North Sea, and after dark Beauforts and Swordfish aircraft successfully attacked barges at Ostend, and Blenheims likewise hit Boulogne Harbour, noting explosions in the harbour area and adjacent railway network. The weather during the day, however, had proved unsuitable for 2 Group's Blenheims to operate – alone and unescorted – over enemy occupied territory, and excepting an uneventful patrol over the sea by a single flight, all such operations were scrubbed.

Daily Home Intelligence Report (London):

> Woolwich observer notes great excitement and satisfaction at hearing guns in action during day battle and disappointment that they did not fire in the night; also, people who have lost everything are cheerful and willing to put up with any discomfort provided Germany is getting her fair share of raids.

Bomber Command was certainly doing its best to oblige the British public. That night, the brave crews of Bomber Command continued taking the war across the sea: gun emplacements around Cap Gris-Nez were bombed by Blenheims; Wellingtons attacked west Berlin's power station and targets in the Black Forest, and the Whitley force also attacked Berlin, starting large fires at an oil facility and scoring at least one direct hit on Spandau's marshalling yards. Bad weather over the Ruhr industrial area – otherwise known to RAF crews as 'Happy Valley' – led to just three Hampdens attacking oil works in Dortmund. Unfortunately, these sorties were not without loss: a Hampden of Waddington's 44 Squadron was hit by flak and crashed near Munster, killing the crew, and a Whitley of Leeming's 10 Squadron and its crew simply disappeared over the North Sea.

That evening, according to the Station ORB, RAF Hornchurch personnel enjoyed:

> An ENSA concert party in the Workshops at 2000 hrs, [which] ended a little hurriedly when flares were dropped over the aerodrome and the 4.5 battery opened fire and shrapnel pattered down on top of the glass roof. Although the lights went out, the show (then) went on to the end.

What the defenders did not know, though, was that the Battle of the Airfields was over.

Reflections

The popular Battle of Britain narrative tells us that by 6 September 1940, 11 Group's airfields were battered by bombing and, if this continued, would soon be non-operational. Often, though, the facts are at odds with the myth: certainly, the phase 19 August 1940 – 6 September 1940 was critical for Fighter Command and the defence of Britain – but not because the airfields were on their knees. The real reason this phase was critical for Fighter Command had nothing to do with airfields – but everything to do with a shortage of pilots.

Some 300 RAF fighter pilots had been sacrificed on the altar of France, a battle lost before it even began, and by 1 August 1940 Fighter Command was short of over 100. By the end of that month, the deficit was 181. The length of operational training was substantially reduced to alleviate the situation, but replacement pilots were not combat ready – and that was the problem. RAF pilots shot down over England, of course, and who survived the experience could be back in the air later the same day. Conversely, German pilots downed over England were captured. Were that scenario reversed, the shortage of RAF pilots would have been even more acute.

The combat claims of both sides, however, were exaggerated – partially because of the confused and fast nature of air fighting, but also because both sides were comforted by believing greater losses were being inflicted upon the enemy. Luftwaffe combat claims were consistently more accurate than Fighter Command's, and subject to rigorous scrutiny before a kill was awarded, but, nonetheless, the Luftwaffe still believed it was shooting down far more RAF fighters than was really the case. Indeed, Luftwaffe intelligence chiefs reported that by the beginning of September 1940 Fighter Command had no more than 300 fighters left. Given that Fighter Command remained an effective fighting force though, doubts were arising in Luftwaffe circles as to its actual strength. At the conference of senior Luftwaffe commanders and their staff held at The Hague in early September 1940, *Generalfeldmarschall* Kesselring, chief of *Luftflotte* 2, supported the view that Fighter Command was finished – but *Generalfeldmarschall* Sperrle, commander of *Luftflotte* 3, disagreed, suggesting that 1,000 aircraft were still available. This, however, completely missed the point: it was the number of pilots, not aircraft, that was the crucial tipping point.

Because the whole of the British Isles was within range of German bombers, Air Chief Marshal Dowding's strategy was to disperse his strength around the whole Command – the wisdom of which had paid dividends on 15 August 1940, when *Luftflotte* 5 attacked north-east England and was effectively defeated in a single day. Nonetheless, by necessity a large number of squadrons had to be concentrated in 11 Group, and these had to be maintained at a state of frontline efficiency. The policy, therefore, was to rotate depleted squadrons to quieter areas, enabling them to rebuild and re-fit, absorbing and training replacements, their place in the line taken by rested squadrons, thus maintaining the strength of 11 Group. If the current rate of attrition continued – nearly 100 casualties per week in 11 Group (pilots killed, missing and wounded) this would prove unsustainable. Dowding was under no misapprehension: Fighter Command was 'going downhill' and a solution had to be found; he hoped that would arise from the conference he was convening at Bentley Priory on 7 September 1940, which would be attended by the DCAS, Air Marshal Sir Sholto Douglas, Air Vice-Marshals Keith Park and Strath Evill, the latter an Australian and Dowding's SASO. This, Dowding knew, was a crucial meeting and solutions had to be found (as will be explored in Volume V).

As repeatedly emphasised in this new narrative and perspective, Luftwaffe air intelligence was demonstrably poor, leading to inappropriate target selection and wasted effort attacking airfields inconsequential to Fighter Command. When significant damage was achieved, such as at Kenley and Biggin Hill, instead of following this up with further attacks on those targets – which may well have rendered these all-important sector stations non-operational – the focus shifted elsewhere, thereby dissipating effort and wasting opportunities to severely hurt 11 Group. Indeed, the only airfield put out of action for any length of time was the vulnerable coastal station of Manston – which was a Hornchurch satellite and not a sector station. Target selection was also dictated by the range of escorting fighters, the Me 109 only having twenty minutes flying time over England, even when operating from the Pas-de-Calais – meaning that many important targets could not be attacked in strength by day – and the defeat of *Luftflotte* 5 on 15 August 1940 provided a grim reminder of what happened to bomber formations over England without Me 109 protection. Furthermore, the enemy's approach of attacking multiple targets simultaneously, which had confused and overwhelmed the defences on occasion, certainly puzzled Air Chief Marshal Dowding, who was unable to understand why the Germans did not instead mount a single, massive, raid per day on a target of maximum importance.

Throughout August 1940, Bomber Command had attacked, night after night, German oil refineries, airfields, factories and naval installations, and even sent Whitley bombers to Italian factories in Turin and Milan, and by day the Blenheims of 2 Group attacked airfields in north-west France and the Netherlands. Like the Luftwaffe, however, Bomber Command was ill-equipped at this point to mount a successful strategic bombing campaign, the aircraft involved having limited bombloads. Nonetheless, these raids were crucially important for multifarious reasons, not least to show the British public that the lion still had teeth. Neither side, however, had so far unleashed terror attacks on civilian populations. Indeed, Hitler had forbidden raids on London and was incensed by the accidental bombing of the British capital on the night of 24/25 August 1940. To Churchill, however, this navigational error was a Godsend: immediately ordering a reprisal raid on Berlin the following night, the Prime Minister correctly guessed that Hitler's penchant for revenge would divert the Luftwaffe from bombing airfields and instead attack London. That being so, the Germans would have longer flights over England to reach their targets, providing more opportunities for interceptions, and the Me 109s would be operating at the extremity of their limited range, meaning that heavier losses could be inflicted on the enemy bomber force. Hitler took the bait.

Although Bomber Command's Berlin objectives on the night of 25/26 August 1940 were both specific and legitimate, owing to poor weather conditions these were not hit, and nor were they on the next few nights. That made no difference: the moral and psychological effect on the German *Volk* was immense. The American journalist and Third Reich observer William Shirer wrote that Berliners were 'stunned. They did not think it could ever happen. Göring assured them that it couldn't.' But it had. On 31 August 1940, the OKL ordered *Luftflotten* 2 and 3 to prepare for reprisal attacks on London. Hitler had vented his spleen and made his intentions clear in his speech of 4 September 1940, that the Luftwaffe was to 'erase' British cities – and the following day ordered round-the-clock attacks on London. The plan involved daylight bombing by *Luftflotte* 2, with fighter escorts, and nocturnal raids by *Luftflotte* 3, which was already engaged on a night-bombing campaign against Liverpool and other targets. Still, however, Hitler forbade indiscriminate bombing, although the service chiefs agreed that generating chaos in the capital prior to the proposed invasion was helpful, and Hitler, of course, was mindful that the Poles and Dutch had surrendered when their capital cities were bombed – and the Danes ran up a white flag at the very threat of it. London was also considered to be the one target Dowding would throw everything at defending – meaning that his fighters could still be destroyed in the air, en masse.

At the 1946 Nuremberg International Military Tribunal, *Reichsmarschall* Göring gave the court his view on Hitler's change of aerial strategy, claiming that he personally was sure that sustained attacks on RAF airfields and British aircraft factories would have achieved the required decision, but had to obey Hitler's orders to change tack and bomb London instead. According to Göring, he put to Hitler that destruction of the sector stations around London was a prerequisite for attacking London, but the *Führer*:

> insisted he wanted to have London itself attacked for political reasons, and also for retribution. I considered the attacks on London useless, and I told the Führer again and again that inasmuch as I knew the English people as well as I did my own people, I could never force them to their knees by attacking

London. We might be able to subdue the Dutch people by such measures –
but not the British.

In the event, the *Reichsmarschall* would be proved correct. The following day
would bring death to Londoners but relief to Fighter Command – even if not
quite so dramatic or decisive as the popular myth would have it.

Generalfeldmarschall Kesselring was under no illusion: 'From the new nature
of our missions, those who could read the signs knew that sentence had been
passed on Operation *Seelöwe*, and with it the opportunity missed to exploit a
unique chance.'

Delays caused by Hitler's initial indecision and bad weather were also factors in
why that 'unique chance' had passed by – but the main reason was that the RAF
remained an efficient and effective fighting force in both defence and offence.

Although Air Chief Marshal Dowding and Air Vice-Marshal Park did
not know it, the crisis they were about to meet and discuss at Bentley Priory
had passed.

Acknowledgements

This unique series of books has arisen from over forty years of research and study of the subject, throughout which time I had a privileged relationship with survivors, and the relatives of casualties – too many to thank individually, but all have my appreciation.

In relation to this special project, I must thank Charles Hewitt, Martin Mace and Matthew Potts of Pen & Sword, and the production and marketing teams, who are always a pleasure to work with and collectively do a first-class job. Martin, of course, deserves a special mention for his sterling work on my behalf at The National Archives, and for being a very good friend and kindred spirit.

Suffice it to say, it has been an absolute privilege to produce this work for the Battle of Britain Memorial Trust and National Memorial to The Few, and I must thank our Chairman, Richard Hunting CBE, Honorary Secretary, Group Captain Patrick Tootal OBE DL RAF, Trustee Wing Commander Andrew Simpson RAFVR(T), Major (Ret'd) Jules Gomez, Site Manager, National Memorial to The Few, and both Malcolm Triggs and Becca Collier-Cook for their help in promoting 'Battle of Britain: The People's Project', and Sarah Halil for assisting with research.

As ever, my old friend Andy Long was ever-helpful, and I would also acknowledge kind assistance from Nevin Williams and Arfon Owen; Glenn Gelder; Martin Hayes; Heather Redfearn; Katie Edwards, Director, Biggin Hill Memorial Museum; Stuart Hadaway, RAF Air Historical Branch; Philip Harvey; Edward McManus; Tony and Trish Osmand; Stephen Clark; Martin Chisholm of The Classic Motor Hub at the former Bibury airfield; Brock Kirby.

Finally, I must reserve a special thanks to my wife, Sue, for everything.

Bibliography

The National Archives
The National Archives at Kew is the main repository for primary source documents; the following documents were consulted during the course of research for this book.

Operations Record Books

AIR27/2018:	'A' Flight, 1 Photographic Reconnaissance Unit	AIR27/712:	87 Squadron
		AIR27/776:	97 Squadron
		AIR27/801:	101 Squadron
AIR27/2015:	'B' Flight, 1 Photographic Reconnaissance Unit	AIR27/807:	102 Squadron
		AIR27/813:	103 Squadron
		AIR27/841:	107 Squadron
AIR27/589:	1 Squadron	AIR27/857:	110 Squadron
AIR27/528:	1 (RCAF) Squadron (Listed as 401 Squadron by TNA)	AIR27/866:	111 Squadron
		AIR27/882:	114 Squadron
		AIR27/969:	141 Squadron
AIR27/32:	3 Squadron	AIR27/984:	145 Squadron
AIR27/164:	12 Squadron	AIR27/1025:	152 Squadron
AIR27/202:	15 Squadron	AIR27/1298:	210 Squadron
AIR27/252:	19 Squadron	AIR27/1315:	213 Squadron
AIR27/287:	23 Squadron	AIR27/1340:	217 Squadron
AIR27: 305:	25 Squadron	AIR27/1360:	219 Squadron
AIR27/317:	26 Squadron	AIR27/1365:	220 Squadron
AIR27/341:	29 Squadron	AIR27/1371:	222 Squadron
AIR27/360:	32 Squadron	AIR27/1385:	224 Squadron
AIR27/441:	43 Squadron	AIR27/1428:	232 Squadron
AIR27/447:	44 Squadron	AIR27/1442:	235 Squadron
AIR27/460:	46 Squadron	AIR27/1445:	236 Squadron
AIR27/554:	50 Squadron	AIR27/1453:	238 Squadron
AIR27/503:	53 Squadron	AIR27/1471:	242 Squadron
AIR27/511:	54 Squadron	AIR27/1495:	248 Squadron
AIR27/528:	56 Squadron	AIR27/1498:	249 Squadron
AIR27/554:	59 Squadron	AIR27/1511:	253 Squadron
AIR27/598:	66 Squadron	AIR27/1526:	257 Squadron
AIR27/624:	72 Squadron	AIR27/1553:	264 Squadron
AIR27/629:	73 Squadron	AIR27/1558:	266 Squadron
AIR27/640:	74 Squadron	AIR27/1661:	302 Squadron
AIR27/655:	77 Squadron	AIR27/1663:	303 Squadron
AIR27/664:	79 Squadron	AIR27/1680:	310 Squadron
AIR27/681:	82 Squadron	AIR27/1941:	500 Squadron

AIR27/1949:	501 Squadron	AIR27/2102:	609 Squadron
AIR27/1964:	504 Squadron	AIR27/2106:	610 Squadron
AIR27/2059:	600 Squadron	AIR27/2112:	612 Squadron
AIR27/2068:	601 Squadron	AIR27/2123:	615 Squadron
AIR27/2028:	604 Squadron	AIR27/2126:	616 Squadron
AIR27/2088:	605 Squadron	AIR27/2263:	928 Squadron
AIR27/2093:	607 Squadron		

Pilots' Combat Reports

AIR50/1:	1 Squadron	AIR50/64:	152 Squadron
AIR50/4:	3 Squadron	AIR50/83:	213 Squadron
AIR50/9:	17 Squadron	AIR50/84:	219 Squadron
AIR50/10:	19 Squadron	AIR50/85:	222 Squadron
AIR50:	29 Squadron	AIR50/88:	232 Squadron
AIR50/16:	32 Squadron	AIR50/89:	234 Squadron
AIR50/18:	41 Squadron	AIR50/91:	238 Squadron
AIR50/19:	43 Squadron	AIR50/92:	242 Squadron
AIR50/20:	46 Squadron	AIR50/96:	249 Squadron
AIR50/21:	54 Squadron	AIR50/100:	257 Squadron
AIR50/22:	56 Squadron	AIR50/104:	264 Squadron
AIR50/24:	64 Squadron	AIR50/105:	266 Squadron
AIR50/25:	65 Squadron	AIR50/116:	302 Squadron
AIR50/26:	66 Squadron	AIR50/177:	303 Squadron
AIR50/31:	73 Squadron	AIR50/122:	310 Squadron
AIR50/32:	74 Squadron	AIR50/165:	601 Squadron
AIR50/33:	79 Squadron	AIR50/166:	602 Squadron
AIR50/36:	85 Squadron	AIR50/167:	603 Squadron
AIR50/37:	87 Squadron	AIR50/171:	609 Squadron
AIR50/40:	92 Squadron	AIR50/173:	611 Squadron
AIR50/43:	111 Squadron	AIR50/172:	610 Squadron
AIR50/62:	145 Squadron	AIR50/175:	615 Squadron
AIR50/63:	151 Squadron	AIR50/176:	616 Squadron

Casualty Files

AIR81/2688:	AC2 A. Jones, 92 Squadron
AIR81/2924:	AC2 J. Kavanagh, RAF Debden
AIR81/2889:	Sergeant J.H. Dickinson, 253 Squadron
AIR81/2692:	Pilot Officer J.A.P. Studd, 66 Squadron
AIR81/2921:	Pilot Officer R. Aeberhardt, 19 Squadron
AIR81/2896:	Pilot Officer D.N.O. Jenkins, 253 Squadron
AIR81/2927:	Pilot Officer J. Sterbacek, 310 Squadron
AIR81/2922:	Flying Officer J.B. Coward, 19 Squadron
AIR81/2721:	Sergeant G.R. Collett, 54 Squadron
AIR81/2730:	Sergeant M. Keymer, 65 Squadron
AIR81/2775:	Pilot Officer K.R. Gillman, 32 Squadron
AIR81/2934:	Flight Lieutenant P.S. Weaver, 56 Squadron
AIR81/2766:	Squadron Leader P.A. Hunter DSO and Sergeant F.H. King DFM, 264 Squadron

AIR81/2957:   Squadron Leader G.D. Garvin and Flight Lieutenant R.C.V. Ash,
                 264 Squadron
AIR81/2910:   Squadron Leader H.M. Starr, 253 Squadron
AIR81/2929:   Squadron Leader T.P. Gleave, 253 Squadron
AIR81/3078:   Squadron Leader P.C. Pinkham, 19 Squadron
AIR81/2922:   Flying Officer J.B. Coward, 19 Squadron
AIR81/2962:   Flight Sergeant F.G. Berry, 1 Squadron
AIR81/2840:   Multiple casualties, RAF Manston, 24 August 1940
AIR81/3035:   Pilot Officer D.W. Hogg, 25 Squadron
AIR81/3071:   Pilot Officer J.W. Cutts, 222 Squadron

Miscellaneous
AIR22/296:   Personnel: Casualties, Strength and Establishment of the RAF.
AIR16/142:   Report by Squadron Leader P.C. Pinkham regarding cannon Spitfires.

RAF Station Operations Record Books
AIR28/64:   RAF Biggin Hill
AIR28/178:   RAF Croydon
AIR28/345:   RAF Hawkinge
AIR28/384:   RAF Hornchurch
AIR28/512:   RAF Manston
AIR28/526:   RAF Martlesham Heath
AIR28/419:   RAF Kenley
AIR28/509:   RAF Lympne
AIR28/601:   RAF Northolt
AIR28/815:   RAF Tangmere
AIR28/907:   RAF West Malling
AIR28/603:   RAF North Weald

Pilot's Flying Log Books (ranks as at time consulted)
Air Vice-Marshal Sir Keith Park (courtesy RNZAF Museum)
Squadron Leader D.R.S. Bader, 242 Squadron (courtesy RAF Museum)
Squadron Leader R.G. Kellett, 303 Squadron
Flight Lieutenant H.C. Burton, 66 and 616 Squadron
Squadron Leader P.C. Pinkham, 19 Squadron
Flight Lieutenant B.J.E. Lane DFC, 19 Squadron (AIR4/58)
Flying Officer J.B. Coward, 19 Squadron
Pilot Officer D. Crowley-Milling, 242 Squadron
Pilot Officer H.S.L. Dundas, 616 Squadron
Pilot Officer W.L.B. Walker, 616 Squadron
Pilot Officer D.M.C. Crook DFC, 609 Squadron (AIR4/21)
Pilot Officer R.L. Jones, 19 and 64 Squadron
Pilot Officer A.G. Osmand, 213 Squadron
Flight Sergeant G.C. Unwin, 19 Squadron
Sergeant W. Green, 501 Squadron
Sergeant B.J. Jennings, 19 Squadron

German Documents

OKW Directives for Invasion of the UK, Operation *Seelöwe*, summer and autumn 1940, Bundesarchiv

Luftflotte 2 and 3 records, available via Digital History Archive (see website detailed below)

German fighter combat claims can be found in the OKL records of the *Chef für Ausz. und Dizsiplin Luftwaffe-Personalamt LP(A)V* (available via various online sources)

German loss records can be found in the *Oberfehlsaber der Luftwaffe Genst. Gen. Qu/6 Abteilung/40.g. Kdos.I.C*, records, preserved by the Imperial War Museum

Unpublished Sources

Correspondence, papers and interviews, Dilip Sarkar Archive.

Original and uncensored manuscript of *Spitfire Pilot*, Flight Lieutenant D.M. Crook DFC.

The memories and thoughts of the late Reverend J.H.K. Dagger, Battle of Britain Padre: RAF Exeter 1940-41. (Courtesy of his son Christopher Dagger).

Unpublished memoir of Group Captain R.G. Kellett.

Unpublished memoir of Group Captain T.P. Gleave, and his *Eagles of Nemesis*, the unedited and uncensored manuscript of what became *I Had A Row With A German* (see published sources below).

Unpublished memoir of Flight Mechanic (Airframes) H.T. Mead, *RAF & Ready: Or How Did We Win The War, Dad?*

Unpublished memoirs, Air Commodore J.B. Coward, Mr John Milne, both 19 Squadron

Published Sources

Adams, P., *Hurricane Squadron: 87 Squadron at War 1939-1941*, Air Research Publications, New Malden, 1988

Aders, G. and Held, W., Chronik: Jagdgeschwader 51 'Mölders', Motor Buch Verlag, Stuttgart, 2009

Addison, P., and Crang, J.A. (eds.), *The Burning Blue: A New History of the Battle of Britain*, Pimlico, London, 2000

Addison, P., and Crang, J.A. (eds.), *Listening to Britain: Home Intelligence Reports on Britain's Finest Hour – May to September 1940*, Vintage Books, London, 2011

Alexander, Kristen, *Australia's Few and the Battle of Britain*, Pen & Sword, Barnsley, 2015

Allen, Wing Commander H.R., *Fighter Squadron: A Memoir 1940-42*, Granada, London, 1982

Anon, *The Battle of Britain: August-October 1940*, Ministry of Information on behalf of the Air Ministry, London, 1941

Anon, *The Battle of Britain*, Air Ministry Pamphlet 156, Issued by the Department of the Air Member for Training, August 1943

Anon, *Air/Sea Rescue: The Second World War 1939–1945, Royal Air Force*, Air Publication 3232, Air Ministry (AHB), London, 1952

Anon, *The Rise & Fall of the German Air Force 1939–45*, Air Ministry Pamphlet 248, Public Record Office, London, 2001

Ashworth, C., *RAF Coastal Command: 1936-1969*, PSL, Sparkford, 1992

Bekker, C., *The Luftwaffe War Diaries*, Corgi Books, London, 1972

Bekker, C., *Hitler's Naval War*, Corgi, London, 1976

Bishop, E., *The Battle of Britain*, George Allen & Unwin Ltd, London, 1960

Bowyer, M.J.F., *2 Group RAF: A Complete History, 1936-1945*, Faber & Faber, London, 1974

Calder, A., *The People's War: Britain 1939–45*, Pimlico, London, 2008

Caldwell, D., JG26: *Top Guns of the Luftwaffe*, Orion Books, New York, 1991

Caldwell, D., *The JG26 War Diary: Volume One, 1939–42*, Grub Street, London, 1996

Campion, G., *The Good Fight: Battle of Britain Propaganda and The Few*, Palgrave-Macmillan, London, 2010

Cannandine, D. (ed.), *The Speeches of Winston Churchill*, Penguin, London, 1990

Churchill, W.S., *The Second World War, Vol II, Their Finest Hour*, Cassell & Co, London, 1949

Clapson, M., *Britain in the Twentieth Century*, Routledge, Abingdon, 2009

Clausewitz, Carl von, *Principles of War*, Dover Publications Inc, New York, 2003

Collier, B., *The Defence of the United Kingdom*, HMSO, London, 1957

Cox, S. and Probert, H., (eds.), *The Battle Re-Thought: A Symposium on the Battle of Britain*, Airlife, Shrewsbury, 1991

Cox, S., 'RAF & Luftwaffe Intelligence Compared' in Handel, M.I. (ed.), *Intelligence & Military Operations*, Frank Cass, Abingdon, 1990

Dean, Sir Maurice, *The Royal Air Force in Two World Wars*, Cassell, London, 1979

Deere, Air Commodore A.C., *Nine Lives*, Hodder Paperback Ltd, London, 1959

Deighton, L., *Fighter: The True Story of the Battle of Britain*, Triad/Panther Books, St Albans, 1979

Dierich, W., Kampfgeschwader "Edelweiss": *The History of a German Bomber Unit, 1939–45*, Purnell Book Services Ltd, London, 1975

Dierich, W., Chronik: Kampfgeschwader 55 'Greif', Motorbuch Verlag, Stuttgart, 2012

Deighton, L., *Fighter: The True Story of the Battle of Britain*, Triad/Panther Books Ltd, St Albans, 1979

Donnelly, M., *Britain in the Second World War*, Routledge, London, 1999

Donnelly, L., *The Other Few: The Contribution Made by Bomber and Coastal Aircrew to the Winning of the Battle of Britain*, Red Kite, Walton-on-Thames, 2004

Dowding, ACM *Lord HCT, Dispatch: The Battle of Britain*, London Gazette, London, 1946

Ellan, Squadron Leader B.J., *Spitfire! The Experiences of a Fighter Pilot*, John Murray, London, 1942

Fleming, P., *Invasion 1940*, Rupert Hard-Davis, London, 1957

Foreman, J., *RAF Fighter Command Victory Claims of World War Two, Volume One*, Air Research Publications, Red Kite, Walton-on-Thames, 2003

Forrester, L., *Fly For Your Life: The Story of RR Stanford Tuck DSO, DFC and Two Bars*, The Companion Book Club, London, 1956

Galland, A., *The First and the Last: Germany's Fighter Force* in the Second World War, Fontana, London, 1954

Gleave, Group Captain T.P. (writing as 'RAF Casualty'), *I Had a Row with a German*, MacMillan & Co, London, 1941

Gleed, Wing Commander I.R., *Arise to Conquer*, Victor Gollanz Ltd, London, 1942

Green, W., *Aircraft of the Battle of Britain*, MacDonald & Co. (Publishers) Ltd and Pan Books Ltd, London, 1969

Hallam, I.N., *One of The Few: Ian Lewis McGregor Hallam*, privately published, 2020

Handel, M.I. (ed), *Intelligence and Military Operations*, Frank Cass, Abingdon, 1990

Hough, R. and Richards, D., *The Battle of Britain: The Jubilee History*, Hodder & Stoughton Ltd, London, 1990

Humphreys, R., *Dover at War 1939–1945*, Alan Sutton, Stroud, 1993

James, T.C.G., *The Battle of Britain*, Frank Cass, London, 1990

Johnson, Air Vice-Marshal J.E., *Wing Leader*, Chatto & Windus Ltd, London, 1956

Johnstone, Air Vice-Marshal AVR, *Spitfire into War*, William Kimber & Co Ltd, London, 1986

Jones, Wing Commander I., *Tiger Squadron*, Award Books, New York, 1966

Kesselring, Field-Marshal A., *The Memoirs of Field-Marshal Kesselring*, Greenhill Books, London, 1997

Kershaw, I., *Hitler: 1936-1945, Nemesis*, Penguin, London, 2001

King, R., *303 Squadron: Battle of Britain Diary*, Red Kite, Walton-on-Thames, 2010

Kingcome, Group Captain B.F., *A Willingness to Die: Memories from Fighter Command*, Tempus Publishing, Stroud, 1996

Legg, R., *Battle of Britain Dorset*, Dorset Publishing Company, Wincanton, 1995

Lisiewicz, Squadron Leader M. (ed.), *Destiny Can Wait: The Polish Air Force in the Second World War*, William Heinemann Ltd, London, 1949

MacDonell, Air Commodore ARD (MacDonell L. and MacKay A. (eds.), *From Dogfight to Diplomacy: A Spitfire Pilot's Log 1932-1958*, Pen & Sword, Barnsley, 2005

Mason, F.K., *Battle Over Britain*, Aston Publications, Bourne End, 1990

Middlebrook, M. and Everitt, C., *The Bomber Command War Diaries: An Operational Reference Book 1939–1945*, Midland Counties Publications, Hinckley, 1996

Morgan, E. and Shacklady, E., *Spitfire: The History*, Key Publishing, Stamford, 1987

Muggeridge, M. (ed.), *Ciano's Diary 1939-1943*, William Heinemann Ltd, London, 1947

Orange, V., *Park: The biography of Air Chief Marshal Sir Keith Park*, Grub Street, London, 2001

Orange, V., *Dowding of Fighter Command: Victor of the Battle of Britain*, Grubb Street, London, 2008

Overy, R., *The Air War 1939–1945*, first edition, Europa Publications Ltd, London, 1980

Overy, R., *The Battle of Britain*, Penguin, London, 2004

Overy, R., *Goering: The Iron Man*, Bloomsbury Revelations, London, 2021

Pope, R., *War & Society in Britain 1899-1948*, Longman, Harlow, 1991

Prien, J., *Jagdgeschwader 53: A History of the "Pik As" Geschwader, March 1937-May 1942*, Schiffer Publishing Ltd, Sedona, Arizona, USA, 1997

Priestley, J.B., *Postscripts*, William Heinemann Ltd, London, 1940

Quill, J.K., *Spitfire*, Arrow Books, London, 1985

Ramsay, W. (ed.), *The Battle of Britain: Then & Now, Mk V Edition*, Battle of Britain Prints International Ltd, London, 1986

Ramsay, W (ed), *The Blitz Then & Now, Volume I*, Battle of Britain Prints International Ltd, London, 1989

Rayner, G.H., *One Hurricane: One Raid*, Airlife Publishing Ltd, Shrewsbury, 1990

Richards, D., *RAF Bomber Command in the Second World War: The Hardest Victory*, Penguin, London, 2001

RAFHS, *Air Intelligence: A Symposium*, RAFHS, London, 1997

Rootes, A., *Front Line County: Kent at War, 1939–45*, Robert Hale Ltd, London, 1980

Roskill, Captain S.W., *The War at Sea 1939–45, Volume 1*, HMSO, London, 1954

Rohwer, J. and G. Hunnelchen, *Chronology of the War at Sea*, Ian Allen Ltd, London, 1972

Sarkar, D., *Missing in Action: Resting in Peace?*, Ramrod Publications, Worcester, 1998

Sarkar, D., *The Final Few*, Amberley Publishing, Stroud, 2015

Sarkar, D., *Letters from The Few: Unique Memories From the Battle of Britain*, Pen & Sword Ltd, Barnsley, 2020

Sarkar, D., *Battle of Britain 1940: The Finest Hour's Human Cost*, Pen & Sword Ltd, Barnsley, 2020

Sarkar, D., *Sailor Malan: Freedom Fighter*, Pen & Sword Ltd, Barnsley, 2021

Sarkar, D., *Forgotten Heroes of the Battle of Britain*, Pen & Sword Ltd, Barnsley, 2022

Schenk, P., *Operation Sealion: The Invasion of England*, Greenhill Books, Barnsley, 2019

Shirer, W.L., *The Rise and Fall of the Third Reich*, Simon & Schuster, New York, 1960

Shores, C. and Williams, C., *Aces High: A Tribute to the Most Notable Fighter Pilots of the British & Commonwealth Forces in WWII*, Grub Street, London, 1994

Smith, M., The RAF. In Addison, J. and Crang, J.A. (eds.), *The Burning Blue: A new History of the Battle of Britain*, Pimlico, London, 2000

Spurdle, B., *The Blue Arena*, William Kimber & Co, London, 1986

Steinhilper, U. and Osborne, P., *Spitfire on my Tail: A View From the Other Side*, Independent Books, Bromley, 1989

Townsend, Group Captain P., *Time & Chance: An Autobiography*, Collins, London, 1978

Townsend, Group Captain P., *Duel of Eagles: The Classic Account of the Battle of Britain*, Weidenfeld & Nicolson, London, 1990

Trevor-Roper, H.R. (ed.), *Hitler's War Directives 1939–45*, Pan Books, London, 1966

Vasco, J.J. and Cornwell, PD, Zerstörer: *The* Messerschmitt *110 and its Units in 1940*, JAC Publications, Norwich, 1995

Vasco, J., *Bombsights Over England: The History of* Erprobungsgruppe *210 Luftwaffe Fighter-Bomber Unit in the Battle of Britain*, JAC Publications, Norwich, 1990

Wakefield, K., *The First Pathfinders: The Operational History of* Kampfgruppe *100, 1939-1941*, Crécy Books, Somerton, 1992

Wallington, N., *Firemen at War: The Work of London's Fire-fighters in the Second World War*, David & Charles, London, 1981

Warner, G., *RAF Biggin Hill: The immortal story of one of the Battle of Britain's most famous fighter stations*, Putnam & Co Ltd, London, 1969

Wicks, B., *Waiting For The All Clear: True Stories From Survivors of The Blitz*, Bloombury, London, 1990

Willis, J., *Churchill's Few: The Battle of Britain Remembered*, Guild Publishing, London, 1985

Wheatley, R., *Operation Sealion*, Oxford University Press, Oxford, 1958

Wright, R., *Dowding and the Battle of Britain*, Corgi, London, 1970

Ziegler, F.H., *The Story of 609 Squadron: Under the White Rose*, MacDonald, London, 1971

Websites

The National Archives:	www.nationalarchives.gov.uk
Commonwealth War Graves Commission:	www.cwgc.org
Battle of Britain Memorial Trust:	www.battleofbritainmemorial.org
Battle of Britain: The People's Project:	www.battleofbritainthepeoplesproject.com
Dilip Sarkar:	www.dilipsarkarauthor.com
Digital History Archive:	www.digitalhistoryarchive.com
Kenley Revival Project:	www.kenleyrevival.org
Battle of Britain London Monument:	www.bbm.org.uk

Films

Although produced for either propaganda purposes or popular culture, the following films can provide an idea of the timeframe this book concerns:

The First of the Few, directed by Leslie Howard (British Aviation Pictures, 1942).
Battle of Britain, directed by Guy Hamilton (Spitfire Productions, 1969).

Television

The World at War, directed by David Elstein (ITV, 1973).

Other Books by Dilip Sarkar

Sailor Malan – Freedom Fighter: The Inspirational Story of a Spitfire Ace
Spitfire Ace of Aces – The Album: The Photographs of Johnnie Johnson
The Real Spitfire Pilot, being the previously unpublished original manuscript of *Spitfire Pilot*, by Flight Lieutenant David Crook, with introduction, commentary and photographs by Dilip Sarkar
Bader's Big Wing Controversy: Duxford 1940.
Bader's Spitfire Wing: Tangmere 1941
Spitfire Down: Fighter Boys Who Failed to Return
Forgotten Heroes of The Battle of Britain
Faces of The Few
Spitfire Faces
Arise to Conquer: The Real Hurricane Pilot by Wing Commander Ian Gleed, introduction, commentary and photographs by Dilip Sarkar
Free French Spitfire Hero: The Diaries of and Search for René Mouchotte (with Jan Leeming)
I Had A Row with a German by Group Captain Tom Gleave, introduction by Dilip Sarkar.
Battle of Britain: The Finest Hour in Cinema
Battle of Britain: The Movie (contributor to and publisher of the now late Robert Rudhall's original edition (2000), and editor and substantial contributor to 2022 revised edition)
Faces of HMS Royal Oak: *The 'Mighty Oak' Disaster at Scapa Flow*
Battle of Britain Volume I: The Gathering Storm – Prelude to the Spitfire Summer of 1940
Battle of Britain Volume II: The Breaking Storm – 10 July 1940 – 12 August 1940
Battle of Britain Volume III: Attack of the Eagles – 13 August 1940 – 18 August 1940

Index

Dear Reader,

We hope you have enjoyed this book, but why not share your views on social media? You can also follow our pages to see more about our other products: facebook.com/penandswordbooks or follow us on X @penswordbooks

You can also view our products at www.pen-and-sword.co.uk (UK and ROW) or www.penandswordbooks.com (North America).

To keep up to date with our latest releases and online catalogues, please sign up to our newsletter at: www.pen-and-sword.co.uk/newsletter

If you would like a printed catalogue with our latest books, then please email: enquiries@pen-and-sword.co.uk or telephone: 01226 734555 (UK and ROW) or email: uspen-and-sword@casematepublishers.com or telephone: (610) 853-9131 (North America).

We respect your privacy and we will only use personal information to send you information about our products.

Thank you!